# The Music of Stravinsky

# The Music of

# *Stravinsky*

Stephen Walsh

CLARENDON PRESS · OXFORD

Oxford University Press, Walton Street, Oxford OX2 6DP

Oxford  New York
Athens  Auckland  Bangkok  Bombay
Calcutta  Cape Town  Dar es Salaam  Delhi
Florence  Hong Kong  Istanbul  Karachi
Kuala Lumpur  Madras  Madrid  Melbourne
Mexico City  Nairobi  Paris  Singapore
Taipei  Tokyo  Toronto
and associated companies in
Berlin  Ibadan

Oxford is a trade mark of Oxford University Press

Published in the United States by
Oxford University Press Inc., New York

First published in hardback by Routledge 1988
First published in paperback by Oxford University Press 1993

British Library Cataloguing in Publication Data
Data available

Library of Congress Cataloging in Publication Data
Walsh, Stephen.
The music of Stravinsky.
(Companions to the great composers)
Bibliography: p.
Includes index.
1. Stravinsky, Igor, 1882-1971—Criticism and
interpretation.  I. Title.  II. Series.
ML410.S932W34  1987  780'.92'4  87-12896
ISBN 0-19-816375-4

10 9 8 7 6 5 4 3

Printed by Interprint Ltd, Malta

*To Mary,*
*first in all things*

# Contents

# *Acknowledgements*

Without the co-operation of Stravinsky's main publishers in the UK, who kindly supplied me with scores and, in some cases, unpublished material, this book would have been a great deal harder to write. I should particularly like to thank Malcolm Smith and Janice Susskind of Boosey and Hawkes; Sally Groves and Nicholas Williams of Schott & Co.; Sally Cavender of Faber Music; Sheila McCrindle, Robin Boyle, and James Rushton of J. and W. Chester. I have also been helped by research grants from University College, Cardiff, and, lately, from the British Academy, who gave me money to pursue research intended for a subsequent book some of which has, however, found its way into this one. I should also like to thank the staffs of the Arts and Social Studies and Music Libraries, University College, Cardiff; of the music section of the Bibliothèque Nationale; of the music section of the Library of Congress; of the library of the School of Slavonic and East European Studies, University of London; and above all of the Paul Sacher Stiftung in Basel.

Stephen Walsh

*Welsh Newton, 1987*

# Note to the Paperback Edition

I have taken the opportunity to correct a few factual errors and misprints, and to update the bibliography. But this is not a new edition of the text, which remains otherwise exactly as originally printed. This is not, of course, because I regard the text as beyond improvement or even because my ideas are unchanged. But small modifications lead to larger ones and involve adjustment for inconsistency, and before long one is writing a new book. It seemed better to let the old one stand, warts and all (whatever the composer of *Petrushka* would have said).

S. W.

*Welsh Newton, 1992*

# 1

# *Biographical Introduction*

Igor Fyodorovich Stravinsky was born on 5 June 1882 (OS)* in the seaside town of Oranienbaum (now Lomonosov), close to St. Petersburg, the son of one of Russia's leading operatic basses, Fyodor Stravinsky. The Stravinskys were well-to-do, rather than rich, bourgeois with noble connections. They had a substantial flat in St. Petersburg and spent their summers on country estates owned by close relations, or else at German or Swiss resorts of the kind frequented by the characters in Turgenev (who was a friend of Fyodor's). The family atmosphere was cultivated but severe. Stravinsky had three brothers, his father was a stern, bookish and sometimes choleric paterfamilias, and as for feminine warmth, Igor seems to have preferred his nurse Bertha to his mother. When he married his first cousin, Catherine Nossyenko, in 1906 it may well have been at least half from a need for sisterly companionship. The Stravinsky family endured tragedy and illness to go with the unsmiling image they present in photographs of the time. Igor's eldest brother Roman died in 1897 and his father (of throat cancer) in 1902. His younger brother Gury died of typhus in 1917, and his wife Catherine of tuberculosis – after a quarter-century of suffering – in 1939; Igor himself was consumptive, and his elder daughter, Lyudmila, died of this same disease four months before her mother. Stravinsky the composer now seems curiously remote from this Chekhovian world. But the truth is that its importance to him has not yet been properly understood.

Igor learnt the piano as a child, but was far from a prodigy. By vocation he was intended for the law (like Tchaikovsky) and he in fact studied

*The difference between so-called Old-Style (OS) and New-Style (NS) dates comes from the fact that Russia did not adopt the Gregorian Calendar (used in Western Europe since 1752) until 1917. In the eighteenth century the Gregorian was eleven days ahead of the astronomically less precise Julian, but this went up to twelve in the nineteenth (because 1800 was a leap year in the Julian but not the Gregorian) and, similarly, to thirteen in the twentieth century. Stravinsky was thus born on 17 June (NS). But by the time he left Russia in 1910 his OS birthday coincided with 18 June (NS), and this was the date on which he always subsequently celebrated.

that subject at St. Petersburg University, and used what he learnt in his voluminous business correspondence of later years (of all composers he was perhaps the most litigious). But the stirrings of creativity prompted him, in 1902, to show his work to another friend of his father's, the composer Rimsky-Korsakov, who eventually took him as a pupil. Rimsky's weekly gatherings, with performances of his pupils' work, were a crucial help to Stravinsky at this time, providing him with a context where invention could flourish within a disciplined environment. At the same time he heard new music (not only Russian) and, in the artistically liberal atmosphere of proto-revolutionary Petersburg, made the acquaintance of artists and writers, as well as musicians.

In 1908 Rimsky-Korsakov died, and less than a year later Sergei Diaghilev heard some orchestral music by Stravinsky and commissioned him to write for the Paris seasons of his company, the Ballets Russes. This was effectively the end of Igor's Russian life. In 1910 he went to Paris for the premiere of his first ballet, *The Firebird*, and thereafter returned to St. Petersburg only as a visitor, living in France and Switzerland (mainly in pensions and rented apartments), but retiring to his country house at Ustilug near the Polish border for the summers, until the outbreak of war in 1914 made even that impossible. (Afterwards he returned to Russia only once, for a tour in 1962.)

Before the war, he had already effectively established himself as the most brilliant composer of the new generation, with three successive ballets for Diaghilev culminating in the scandalous première of *The Rite of Spring* in May 1913. It was a reputation he never really lost. During the war years, and for a time thereafter, he lived in Switzerland and experimented with an austere but richly suggestive style derived from Russian materials (*The Wedding*, *Renard*, *The Soldier's Tale*, as well as innumerable songs to folk texts). In 1920 he moved to Paris and after that lived in France until the Second World War, coming increasingly under the influence of French thought and taking what he needed from the hedonistic, pavement-café atmosphere of the Paris of Cocteau and Les Six, of the Ballets Russes and Picasso and Matisse, as well as the more exhausting cerebralism of Valéry and Catholic theoreticians like Maritain. The mixture, unique to Stravinsky, informs the works of what is known as his neo-classical period, and especially masterpieces such as *Oedipus Rex* and *Persephone*.

For a time Stravinsky may have seen himself as French. Ever since *The Firebird* he had been lionised by mondaine Paris (his income during the First World War was appreciably augmented by donations from assorted princesses and countesses). He took French citizenship in 1934, and in 1936 applied unsuccessfully for membership of the Académie des Beaux-Arts. His rejection (or perhaps the humiliation of being exposed in an unsuitable application) cut him to the quick, and thereafter the Gallicism in his work began to fade, to be gradually replaced by American influences. In 1939 he was in the USA lecturing at Harvard (the lectures were published as *The Poetics of Music*), and he settled in that country, re-entering as part of the

Russian quota from Mexico in August 1940. In 1945 he became a US citizen. For nearly thirty years he lived in the same street in Hollywood, the focus of a society made up substantially of émigrés (as had been the society in the Swiss Vaud during the First World War). But he died in New York (1971), whither he had moved in 1969 to be closer to the medical facilities he increasingly depended on.

The superficial account of Stravinsky's life disguises complex undercurrents which it would be misleading to ignore. Both psychologically and in fact he led a divided existence. While French or American, he remained profoundly and consciously Russian. Russian ways of thinking constantly resurface in his music. Russian Orthodoxy is latent in much of his work and some of his prose writing and it governed his life for certain short but crucial periods. His relations with his first wife symbolise this division. Although he was openly unfaithful to her, in particular pursuing a candid affair with another Parisian/Russian émigrée Vera Sudeikina (from 1921), he remained close to her in many ways and seems to have been deeply affected by her death in 1939, soon after that of their eldest daughter, and just before that of his mother. Catherine Stravinsky, quite as much as her mother-in-law, seems to stand during this time for 'loyalty to old Russia'. Vera, whom Stravinsky married in 1940, was closer to the world of the instinctive émigré. Not only their marriage, but also their life in America, was made possible only by the death in rapid succession of so many of Stravinsky's female relatives. It seems certain he would not have left Europe without them otherwise.

The other important current is that of Stravinsky the concert artist. At first as a pianist, then as a conductor, he was continuously engaged for almost half a century in the exhausting life of a touring performer. He endured this at first partly out of a sense of duty to his own music, but mostly because (in his own estimation, at least) he needed the money. Concert-giving often threatened his whole existence as a creative artist. In America especially it provided a painless way for that touching of the hem of the garment so important to a society whose theoretical enthusiasm for culture is sometimes greater than its practical understanding of its needs. The pressure on Stravinsky to conform to this convention was almost irresistible. In the end it was only thanks to the extraordinary vitality and strength of his creative consciousness, and to the tactful guidance of the young Robert Craft (who came into Igor's and Vera's lives in 1948, and remained as a cross between a professional associate and an adoptive son) that he was able to overcome the pressure and continue writing as he needed without abandoning his concert work.

# 2

## A Russian in St Petersburg: The Firebird

To most writers on Stravinsky his works before *The Firebird* have meant less than the early works of almost any other great composer. Even Robert Craft, Stravinsky's candid but sympathetic Boswell, finds them 'surprisingly plodding, evincing little more than an acquisition of competence in other composers' idioms'.[1] Plenty of composers have taken till their late twenties to discover a personal manner. But with Stravinsky the effect is magnified by the meteoric success of *The Firebird* when Diaghilev presented it in Paris in June 1910, a success which Stravinsky himself always felt was out of proportion to the work's merits but came from the fact that the music was brilliant and surprising without being in any way challengingly new. No doubt this is the natural exaggeration of an artist who went on outgrowing his first conquest. After all, the general reaction to *The Firebird* was at least prophetic. But musically it does nevertheless belong with the 'pre-Stravinskian' works, even if the competence it evinces is and was devastating; and once this view is accepted the gradient of the composer's development before *Petrushka* (the real turning point) seems more regular and intelligible.

The difficulty has been to form a complete picture of that development. Until comparatively recently the earliest Stravinsky work known by its music was the Symphony in E flat, which he wrote under his teacher Rimsky-Korsakov's supervision between 1905 and 1907; and, even now that one or two earlier manuscripts have emerged, we still have only a piano sonata, a couple of keyboard miniatures and a song or two to help explain how Stravinsky came to be accepted by so distinguished a master in the first place. In *Memories and Commentaries* Stravinsky stated that 'before [my father's] death I had written nothing'.[2] Fyodor Stravinsky died in late November (OS) 1902. The previous summer, however, Igor had visited Rimsky-Korsakov at Neckargemünd, hoping for approval of his ambition to become a composer, and played for him 'some of my first attempts'.³ Only two pieces have survived which may have been in this portfolio: a short piano Scherzo in G minor and a Pushkin song called *Storm Cloud*, and though the song at least is in some sense accomplished it seems incredible that the notoriously blunt Rimsky-Korsakov can have seen in these unremarkable miniatures by a twenty-year-old any evidence of special ability. Something in Igor's manner may have struck him, coupled perhaps with consideration of the young man's close friendship with his son Vladimir (a fellow law-student of Stravinsky's at St Petersburg University), as well as respect for his father, who was the leading Russian operatic bass of the day. Rimsky surely did not foresee any extraordinary success for Stravinsky, since he does not mention the Heidelberg meeting in his memoirs, nor does any later entry refer by name to the man who was to be his most famous pupil, though the final entry is dated August 1906, almost three years after Stravinsky had begun formal lessons with him.⁴

Stravinsky's close relationship with Rimsky-Korsakov, which lasted five or six years until the latter's death in June 1908, is a richly fascinating aspect of his early career. In later years Stravinsky was apt to be caustic about his first teachers: Mlle Snetkova ('I do not remember having learnt anything about music from her'); the 'blockhead' Kashperova and her idiosyncratic, though evidently influential, embargo on the sustaining pedal; the 'unsympathetic' Akimenko, Stravinsky's first harmony teacher; and the monosyllabic Kalafati, whose reluctance to explain his corrections 'taught me to appeal to my ear as the first and last test'.⁵ Towards Rimsky, however, Stravinsky retained an ambivalence suggestive of a more complex master–pupil relationship. One reason for this may well have been an ambivalence in Rimsky's own nature. As a young member of Balakirev's circle in the 1860s he had adopted the circle's idea that orthodox technique and theory were the enemies of inspiration and progress, and only later, when he was quixotically appointed professor of composition at the St Petersburg Conservatory, had he gradually come to feel the overriding necessity of such disciplines. In the elderly Rimsky-Korsakov one senses the coexistence of an academic/pedantic and an empirical/progressive streak. While doggedly whittling away at his young pupils' sonatas and symphonies (a discipline which oddly recalls Balakirev's setting of such tasks forty years before), he clearly tolerated their taste for novelty and was careful to distance himself from the merely philistine distaste for modernism. Although Stravinsky, in *Memories and Commentaries*, refers to his teacher as a reactionary (in music, that is; politically he was radical), Rimsky's sympathies could still extend without difficulty to the 'Debussyisms' of the *Scherzo fantastique* and perhaps even of *The Nightingale*, whose sketches Stravinsky may have shown him in the spring of 1908.⁶

It seems obvious that Rimsky-Korsakov was a fortunate choice of teacher for Stravinsky. The draconian sonata/symphony discipline of the years 1903–7 no doubt irked him; yet it must have usefully nurtured his ability to compose architecturally, while his empirical skills were being developed by Rimsky's admirable method of tuition in orchestration – he would show Stravinsky recent music of his own in short score, get him to orchestrate it, then compare the young composer's solution with his own. Stravinsky was also lucky in the opportunities Rimsky's weekly class-meetings gave him of hearing his music well played in a sympathetic environment. Moreover Rimsky could and did use his influence to arrange private performances of his pupil's orchestral works. The symphony was done at least in part in this way (in April 1907), and Stravinsky we know revised it extensively before its first public performance the following year. Finally, the direct and personal nature of Stravinsky's contact with Rimsky's own later music, including the operas *Kitezh* and *The Golden Cockerel*, may well have had its effect in bringing out emphases in his own writing which assumed increasing importance after the meeting with Diaghilev. One notes already the rhythmic and harmonic basis of the orchestral scherzos Stravinsky was writing in the year of Rimsky's death, as well as the colouristic use of harmony in the first act of *The Nightingale*. He soon outgrew the actual style of these works, as witness the problems he faced in completing *The Nightingale* a mere five years later. But their technical achievement formed the basis of his development for a good deal longer than that.

It was through Rimsky that Stravinsky gradually assumed the task of carrying forward the Russian tradition of the nineteenth century. This was of course a romantic tradition, and romantic models are paramount for Stravinsky up to *The Firebird*. In the little piano Scherzo of 1902 the exact nature of the influence is still unclear, and we are confronted with a nondescript miniature in G minor, distinguished only by certain peculiarities of rhythm. But *Storm Cloud*, the Pushkin song of that year, owes a specific debt to Tchaikovsky, while in the large-scale Sonata in F sharp minor which Stravinsky began in the summer of 1903 and continued under Rimsky's supervision he unfurls the full panoply of Russian late-romantic pianism, as filtered through the piano works of Rakhmaninov and Glazunov. All these scores were lost, or presumed so, until near the end of Stravinsky's life, and in view of the sonata's romantic bravura it is amusing that the composer himself remembered it for many years as 'an inept imitation of late Beethoven'. Finally Tchaikovsky and Glazunov are the unwed parents of the Symphony in E flat, composed in 1905 and thereafter much revised for its performances in 1907 and 1908.

The direction of these works for the time being evaded the specific issue of Russian music in the late nineteenth century which it was to be one of Stravinsky's eventual achievements to resolve: the struggle, that is, between academicism and the so-called realism of the Balakirev clique. Any student of the period is bound to be struck by the peculiar and apparently shifting relationship between the two sides in this controversy – a controversy which sprang from the much deeper-seated disagreement between Slavophiles and pro-Western modernisers. Even in that crucial argument battle lines were often very unclearly drawn. For its originators, Belinsky and Chernishevsky, literary realism was more a socialist concept than a nationalist one, but in practice it tended to obliterate ideological divisions, finding its way into both the pro-modern, liberal works of Turgenev and Tolstoy and the conservative, anti-Western works of Dostoyevsky. In music, through the influence of the historian Stassov, it was from the start a way of asserting specifically Russian national character as against conservatoire academicism, with its strong German bias. In *Khovanshchina* Mussorgsky suggests, through the character of Galitsin, that westernising liberalism was no more than a façade (like the parlour liberalism of our own day), disguising a barbarism no less repressive than that of 'old Russia'; and in both his major operas he shows that for the mass of the people, weighed down by poverty and superstition, political ideology had in any case little importance. For Mussorgsky realism was pre-eminently a way of asserting the individuality of Russian people, whether they were tyrants like Boris or Khovansky, or poor men like the simpleton in *Boris Godunov*, or rogues like Varlaam. But he was almost alone among Russian composers of his time in making a clear correlation between verism, popularism and the anti-academic stance. In Balakirev, Borodin and Rimsky-Korsakov, Western forms and genres are not so much displaced as infiltrated by a no less artificial orientalism, which in much of their work merely overlays a fundamentally academic approach to musical form. Their symphonies, symphonic poems and even operas stick closely to Western patterns; and when Rimsky took it on himself to revise Mussorgsky, all he did in reality was to regularise, academicise, in fact westernise it.[7]

The results of this effective re-occidentalisation of music in Russia can be seen in the symphonies and ballets of Glazunov, with their brilliantly accomplished but somewhat faceless adoption of standard Western models: German in the case of the symphonic works, French in the case of the ballets. Glazunov was the most gifted of Rimsky-Korsakov's early pupils, and it was probably for that reason that Stravinsky adopted him as his model when he first came to Rimsky for tuition. Glazunov's own piano sonatas, both composed in 1901, are three-movement works. But Stravinsky's four-movement sonata is Glazunovan in spirit; in its painstakingly 'correct' pursuit of formal balance, its dependence on sequence within the four-bar phrase, its rigid containment of the emotion implied by its gestural language. Stravinsky began the sonata under his own steam, while staying on his uncle's estate at Pavlovka in central Russia in the summer of 1903; but, he tells us in his autobiography, he soon ran into trouble with the form, and decided to consult Rimsky (this seems to have led directly to their regular lessons the following autumn).[8] Here, as on other points, the autobiography is a little confused. Rimsky apparently made Stravinsky write part of a sonatina (nothing else is known of this work), and there is no further mention of the sonata. But from a letter of March 1908, quoted by Craft, we learn that this latter work 'incorporated many suggestions by

Rimsky-Korsakov'.[9] What these were we do not know, but we do know
something of the extent of Rimsky's advice where the symphony Stravinsky
wrote next was concerned, because a manuscript four-hand draft of that
work is preserved in the Bibliothèque Nationale in Paris, with Rimsky's
annotations clearly distinguishable.[10] In the sonata even Rimsky seems to
have been unable to solve all the formal problems; the development section
in the first movement, with its wearying build-up of unresolved cadential
preparation, calls to mind the typical nineteenth-century Russian inability
to break away from crude development by harmonic sequence. At one point
(bars 136 *et seq.*) Stravinsky even gets trapped in rising sequences of minor
thirds and whole-tones which seem to anticipate his later enthusiasm for
symmetrically constructed modes like the octatonic and whole-tone scales,
though the sense here is harmonically traditional (Ex.1). Also typical of
Russian academicism is the penchant for exact reprise. It is only fair to
stress, however, that although this sonata has been taken up by several
pianists since its publication in 1974 (and although it was played more than
once by its dedicatee Nicholas Richter at Rimsky's weekly classes), it is
really a student exercise – a study in procedural rectitude rather than the
elaboration of an artistic idea. As such it has real brilliance. But one can
quite see why Stravinsky was inclined later to misremember what it was
like.

The Symphony in E flat is a slightly different case. Here too the primary
consideration must have been to make a successful job of a conventional
form (as witness Rimsky's often quite radical equalisations of rhythm and
phrase structure). So we have an entirely standard symphony in the
Glazunov manner, built of well-shaped two- and four-bar phrases, repeated
with contrasting orchestration, developed by sequence with diminution
and augmentation, balancing themes in orthodox keys, and solid four-
movement form beginning with a grand sonata movement and ending with
a rondo.

But so quickly did Stravinsky learn from strong models that the whole
score feels no more like a student work as such than does the symphony
which the seventeen-year-old Bizet modelled on Gounod. There are fewer
miscalculations than in, say, Borodin's own First Symphony in this key,
and the ideas are not inferior to those in Rimsky's E flat minor, composed
under Balakirev's supervision. In token of this Stravinsky occasionally
conducted the work in later life, made a (none too brilliant) recording of it,
and according to Craft often revised it in one particular or another.

Moreover, certain details intrude into its studied design which cannot
have been part of Rimsky's formula. The influence of Tchaikovsky is here
and there extremely marked. Stravinsky tells us that Rimsky was jealous
of Tchaikovsky and unkind to his admirers, who perhaps by now included
the young Igor. In any case the slow movement of the symphony seems
strongly affected by the Andantino of Tchaikovsky's Fourth, including its
orchestration (the brass scoring at no.6 and the woodwind counter-melodies

*Ex. 1* Piano Sonata in F sharp minor, 1st movement

whole-tone scales

*(a)*                              *(b)*

octatonic scales

*(a)*                              *(b)*

Ex. 2

at the reprise, no.21, are particularly Tchaikovskian details), and in the
finale there is a virtual crib of a passage at the end of Tchaikovsky's Fifth
(at the presto after no.21). In the coda of the Largo third movement one
finds also a not specially covert reference to Wagner, both in the sliding
chromatic chords before no.28 and in the 'Magic Fire Music' drifting triads
which follow. Like the episode in the sonata's first-movement development,
these chord progressions have a schematic appearance which reflects both
the Russian composer's instinctive leaning towards sequence and his
interest in symmetrical divisions of the octave. The chromatic chords are
all based on whole-tone scales, and the triadic sequence rises (below the
descending violin line) by strict minor thirds. Since this music is concerned
with (formal) dissolution, it may even remind us of two famous 'structured'
scales in romantic Russian music: the descending whole-tone passage which
accompanies Chernomor's abduction of Lyudmila in Act I of Glinka's
*Russlan*; and the plummeting octatonic scale which carries Sadko down to
the realm of the Sea King in Rimsky's tone poem (see Ex.2). In Stravinsky's
own work it distinctly anticipates yet another scene of dissolution and
transformation, the collapse of Kashchei's magic palace at the end of *The
Firebird*, which is similarly scored for converging tremolando strings. One
other *Firebird* harbinger is the flickering scherzo, which links Glazunov's
*Seasons* with the 'Dance of the Princesses with the Golden Apples' via
Stravinsky's *Scherzo fantastique*. This type of scherzo ostinato is common
enough in Russian music, symphonic as well as balletic, and the most
remarkable thing about Stravinsky's first essay in the genre is that, having
never previously written for orchestra, he should handle so adroitly a kind
of writing dependent above all on orchestral flair. Both Glazunov and
Rimsky, according to Stravinsky's own reports, considered the scoring too
heavy, but they can hardly have been thinking of the scherzo, since here,
even when the brass is used chorally and fortissimo, it never weighs down
the rhythm. In the outer movements, perhaps, the brass is overused. Even
so, in its orchestral texturing the symphony is a remarkable début and must
have alerted many at the Belyayev concert in January 1908, where it was
first publicly presented, to the emergence of a new specifically colouristic

talent on the Russian musical scene, however unoriginal the music may have seemed in other respects.

The symphony brought to an end Stravinsky's formal pupillage, and with it his direct interest in the Russian academic tradition. In later years he was to remember Glazunov with undisguised contempt and Rimsky himself with condescension, and in return the Rimsky family and Stravinsky's best-known fellow pupil Maximilian Steinberg came to regard him with suspicion growing into hostility. But musically the break was perhaps less complete than Stravinsky liked to believe, and in his neo-classical period he returned to a form of ironic academicism which has certain points in common with the earlier tradition.

Nevertheless, as early as 1906 he was ready for a change from these rigid conventions and the pedantry they attracted. The vocal-orchestral suite, *The Faun and the Shepherdess*, which according to one account he began on his honeymoon at Imatra in February of that year, shows two important influences away from the symphonic world: on the one hand Mussorgsky, and on the other the contemporary French school, in particular Debussy, Ravel, and perhaps Dukas. The French influence can be summed up as a general atmosphere of paganism and *fêtes-galanterie* (though the poems are again by Pushkin), and more especially a preoccupation with the whole-tone scale to give a feeling of misty, faintly disturbing eroticism. But the texture of the music is not really at all French, and owes far more to the Russian verist tradition which, indeed, had itself had a profound effect on Debussy. This is most evident in the sharp picture of the repulsive little faun in the second song; the sketch is like a supplementary portrait for Mussorgsky's *Nursery* and has none of the drowsy sensuality of the faun in Mallarmé/Debussy. There is even something Mussorgskian about the melodic treatment in the last movement. The poem describes the faun's vain but terrifying pursuit of the shepherdess, but Stravinsky's telling of the story – though it builds up a certain formal excitement – has an incantatory quality which recalls Mussorgsky's ruthlessly unsentimental descriptions of children's games. No wonder the conventional cadential gestures which end these two songs sound out of place.

*The Faun and the Shepherdess* is not altogether an accomplished or successful work, but it has symbolic importance. In attempting such Mussorgskian oddities as anecdotal harmony in which dissonance is descriptive rather than grammatical (as, for instance, at the start of no.2), Stravinsky was specifically aligning himself with those aspects of Mussorgsky which were most frowned on by the Russian academics, as Rimsky's corrections to the harmony of *The Nursery* show. Moreover, the strong flavour of Tchaikovsky in the first song, which comes closer to a description of feeling than the other two, is somewhat different from the Tchaikovskyisms in the sonata and symphony. The idea of the pure but passionate young girl apparently prompted thoughts of another Pushkin heroine, Tatyana, as portrayed by Tchaikovsky in scene 2 of *Eugene Onegin*.

But while the orchestral and vocal figuring here is Tatyana-like, Stravinsky plainly went out of his way to avoid the pat four-bar balancing phrases so typical of Tchaikovsky, as it is of his own earlier music. The seemingly arbitrary phrase-counts of this song will surely have irked Rimsky-Korsakov almost as much as the harmony in the other two. Yet oddly enough they do nothing to reduce the schematic effect of rhyming phrase-ends: rather the reverse, since by taking the gestures out of context, Stravinsky draws attention to intrinsic properties which are, so to speak, isolated and structurally unexplained, deprived of their purely conventional function. Thus in its own way *The Faun and the Shepherdess* too anticipates certain traits in neo-classicism, though it could hardly be farther from that movement in outward style.

The natural successor to this Pushkin cycle is the curious pair of songs (op.6) which Stravinsky wrote to poems by the symbolist Sergei Gorodyetsky; the first of them in the spring of 1907, the second probably the following winter. A third song, *Pastorale*, a vocalise with piano accompaniment, also dates from 1907, but the style and technical achievement of this piece are so remarkable as to demand separate consideration. An air of stylistic crisis hangs about the Gorodyetsky songs. They show Stravinsky, working once again on his own, struggling to reimpose form on a succession of wayward pictorial ideas which seem to be his version of the graphic realism of Mussorgsky. The bells which dominate the first song, 'Spring', are distant if emasculated relatives of the great bells in *Boris Godunov*, while the recitative beginning of the 'Song of the Dew', as well as some of the descriptive figuration later on, refers apparently to the manner of *Without Sun*. But Stravinsky was unlucky in his choice of verse. Gorodyetsky's jejune pictures of old Russia – the girl unwillingly taking the veil, the flagellant women invoking the Holy Spirit in the character of bridegroom – have little of the authenticity of the peasant rituals in Rimsky's operas, which may have first attracted Stravinsky to such subjects;[11] and they certainly bear no more than a passing resemblance to his own magnificent handling of such ideas later on, notwithstanding the possibility that *The Rite of Spring* is itself based on an idea taken from Gorodyetsky (see Chapter 3). The songs' main interest lies in the colourful and often quite discordant treatment of the higher dominant (and tonic) dissonances. But there is as yet no specifically Stravinskian flavour, still less structure, about these effects.

With this failure in mind, the achievement of the *Pastorale* seems doubly remarkable, for here, in a wordless song of minimal pretensions and based on the simplest of ideas, Stravinsky suddenly hits on a persona and technique which, with hindsight, we can see to be purely his own. The subsequent history of this piece sheds some light on its unusual character. In 1923 Stravinsky arranged the accompaniment for wind quartet (oboe, cor anglais, clarinet, bassoon), and ten years later he returned to the piece again and made extended versions for violin with piano and violin with

wind respectively. These later arrangements are based directly on the original material with very little change (the longer violin version simply adds
one whole cycle to the ABA form of the vocalise). But a close examination
of the various texts reveals that, while retaining his original bass-line with
only trifling changes, and while deploying no new melodic or harmonic
material, he subtly rearranged the internal sequence of events so as to
provide what he presumably felt to be a better pattern of incident and
ornamentation. A comparison of bars 9–12 in the two wind arrangements
will show the kinds of alteration involved. The reversal of the pitch-level
of the entries in bar 10 seems to be associated with the addition of an F
sharp pedal, in this bar only, below the original C sharp, so that with the
added D sharp melody entry on the cor anglais we get a pile-up of fifths
instead of the simple open fifth of the original (Ex.3). But this fifth-cycle
character is already present elsewhere in the first version (in bar 11, for
example); it would be wrong to see it as a 'more modern' addition by the
mature Stravinsky.

What is the nature of a work which lends itself to adjustments of this
sort? In a conventional piece of romantic music – say a song by Tchaikovsky
– it would be inconceivable to reverse the harmonies in a progression or
bring in a pair of imitative entries in reverse order of pitch; to do so would
nearly always make nonsense of the line of thought, just as much as it
would in this sentence of mine if I had written 'thought of line' instead.
But Stravinsky's brief Mussorgskian phase seems to have given him a
feeling for harmonies which, rather than expressing a 'line of thought', as
in the academic sonata and symphony supervised by Rimsky-Korsakov,
simply describe, or better still apply to, incidents or anecdotes which may
or may not have a logic of their own but which are in any case considered
as existing: things to which music can add a dimension or a degree of
vividness. However, whereas in Mussorgsky this approach is usually
applied to dramatic events or poems rich in factual incident, Stravinsky in
the *Pastorale* removes it into a world of, so to speak, pure being. Here there
are no events, but only states, or rather a single state of calm rural repose.
This Stravinsky takes as a subject for exploration, not, like Keats, by grafting
a legend of unfulfilled longing on to the poised immutability of the classical
tableau, but by studying its components and, so to speak, testing their
immutability. The outcome is a new kind of quasi-sculptural music, something close to the temporal expression of a spatial idea, free from the
tensions of a developing harmony. Of course this is an exaggeration. There
is changing harmony in the *Pastorale*; but the movement is slow and without
rhetoric, its directional force weakened by the treatment of diatonic dissonance as a 'fact' rather than an agent. Debussy had experimented with
something of the sort in his pentatonic piano 'estampe' *Pàgodes*, as well as
in *Pelléas et Mélisande*, and elsewhere. But his most extreme essay in this
genre, the whole-tone *Voiles*, was still unwritten in 1907. In any case
Debussy's pieces are to some extent limited by their purely harmonic terms

*Ex. 3(i) Pastorale* (1923 version)

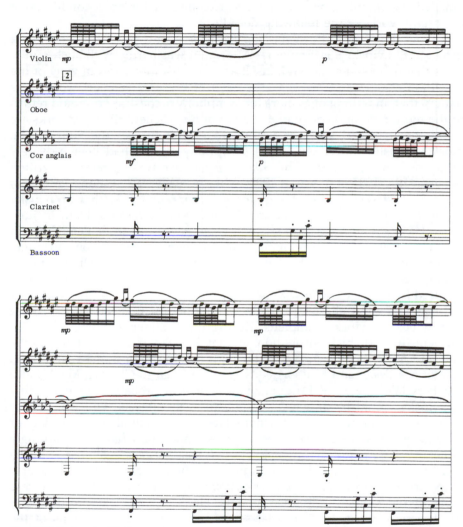

*Ex. 3(ii) Pastorale* (1933 version)

of reference; in *Voiles* the part-writing, such as it is, is chiefly a way of
articulating an inert chord, and tends to lack structural energy of its own.
The essentially thematic, linear facture of *Pastorale* generates a succession
of small formal units, or cells, capable of manipulation and, as we have
seen, rearrangement. This cellular way of writing, once Stravinsky had
grasped its potential, was to have consequences for some of his most
important works of the following decade.

For the time being, however, the *Pastorale* stands apart from the main
thrust of Stravinsky's endeavours. After all it was hardly with such miniatures that he would establish himself as a creative force; and in view of the
uncertain character of his 'realist' essays of the past year or two, it was
natural that, in writing once more for symphony orchestra, he should return
to the more tried and conventional style of his teacher. His next works are
a pair of orchestral scherzos written to exploit further the style of the
most successful movement in his symphony, which had been privately
performed in April 1907. The *Scherzo fantastique* was apparently written
between July 1907 and March 1908, when Rimsky saw it along (perhaps)
with the first sketches for *The Nightingale*; and soon after that Stravinsky
began *Fireworks*, finishing it at about the time of Rimsky's death in June
1908. These are the two works which Diaghilev heard in St Petersburg in
February 1909 and which prompted him to commission first some arrangements and then an original ballet, *The Firebird*, from the virtually unknown
young composer. In turn, *The Firebird* was the logical result of a commission
inspired by two such scores.

Taken as a group these four works – including the first act of *The Nightingale*, which Stravinsky completed during the summer of 1909 – make up
the sum total of his contribution to that Russian tradition of the exotic
and fantastic which reached back through the operas of Rimsky-Korsakov,
Balakirev's *Tamar* and Mussorgsky's *Bare Mountain* to Glinka's *Russlan* and
the fairy-tale operas of Dargomizhsky.[12] It was probably inevitable that
Stravinsky would be drawn for a time to such subjects, which were not
only the basis of most of his teacher's latest works but also, in the sixty or
seventy years since *Russlan*, had inspired much of what was startlingly
novel in Russian music as a whole. The *Scherzo fantastique* is almost painfully
loyal to the tradition, notwithstanding its obvious debt (which it shares
with *Fireworks*) to Dukas's *Sorcerer's Apprentice*, a work which in any case
certainly owes much to Russian models. Here we find, taken to the point
of obsession, the typical artificial scales based on equal divisions of the
octave (the augmented triad, the diminished seventh, the whole-tone and
octatonic scales) which had been the stock-in-trade of Russian musical magic
since Lyudmila's abduction, given harmonic mobility by a superimposed
grid of chromatic scales and a tight four-bar phrase-structure. In the shorter
and more brilliant *Fireworks* this apparatus is more flexibly deployed, though
in essence much the same (and here the debt to Dukas amounts practically
to quotation). Curiously enough neither of these pieces is in fact based on

a magical or fantasy subject. The *Scherzo fantastique* seems to have occurred to Stravinsky in some abstract form before being attached to a detailed programme derived from Maeterlinck's *Life of the Bees*, so the music's quick-silver magicality is meant to conjure up specific images of buzzing insects in the manner of Rimsky's 'Flight' (it will be remembered, however, that the bumble-bee in Rimsky's and Pushkin's *Tsar Saltan* was a transformed prince). Stravinsky later repudiated all these associations, rather disingenuously it seems, but they are proved by a letter to Rimsky of July 1907 in which the composer explains the music's programmatic origins and refers to it as 'the Fantastic Scherzo, "Bees" '.[13] *Fireworks*, on the other hand, seems never to have carried any programme, though its *diablerie* is unmistakably evocative of the stage wizardry of Glinka's Chernomor as well as Dukas's sorcerer, rather than the mechanical pyrotechnics of Debussy's *Feux d'artifice*, not yet written.

The obvious medium for this *diablerie* is the orchestration, which must have been the element in both works which excited Diaghilev, with his love of wit, extravagance and colour. It is true that *Fireworks* is cleverly composed on various levels. Its rhythmic design is much more diverse than the *Scherzo*'s, and delights in the subtlety with which Stravinsky materialises tonal 'objects' like the E major main theme out of the harmonic miasma of the octatonic and whole-tone scales, a technique he was soon to put to good use in *The Firebird*. Nevertheless it is in the orchestra that his mastery is most precocious and individual. Both works call for a large orchestra with multiple wind, a mixed battery of percussion (but without piano) and, in the case of *Fireworks*, a specified (large) number of string players apparently worked out so as to allow complicated *divisi* without loss of body or attack in important touches like the bounced *jeté* bowing at fig.23 (the precursor of a famous effect in the 'Dance of the Firebird') or the swirling offbeat chords in fig.7. Stravinsky's general approach is in the Russian tradition of allowing important melodies to be carried in bold, pure timbre, while harmonic or fragmentary detail is distributed round the rest of the orchestra in a riot of prismatic colour. Broadly this was already Glinka's manner. But Stravinsky certainly takes it to a new stage in his use of elaborately detailed 'soundscapes' to spin out an unchanging background harmony – an energetic version of the Debussy technique described earlier – and above all in that flashing, quasi-pointillist method, with its characteristic soft harmonics and glissandi, its subtle interior rhythms and delicate melodic highlighting. In *The Nightingale* and *The Firebird*, these seem no more than the appropriate means to convey the exotic, sensuous or symbolistic flavour of the action. But when we find extensions of the same technique depicting Petrushka's cell, or the coarse wit of the peasant verses in *Pribaoutki* or the *Cat's Cradle Songs*, or serving a purely formal purpose in the later symphonic or serial scores, we recognise it as an authentic discovery about the possibilities of instrumental sound which opens up completely new concepts of musical movement. No doubt this is the only link between Rimsky-Korsakov's

*Spanish Caprice* and twentieth-century music, but it is at least an interesting one.

The sheer sound of the orchestra is also the most arresting feature of *The Nightingale*, to whose first act (of three) Stravinsky returned after the completion of *Fireworks*, and the composition of the now regrettably lost *Chant funèbre* in memory of Rimsky-Korsakov and the four piano studies, op.7 (July 1908). In this context it is worth mentioning that, when he came to finish this short opera in 1913–14, and probably again before its publication in 1923, Stravinsky made changes to the orchestration of Act I which left a somewhat drier, more sharply etched texture in keeping with that evolution in his style (*Petrushka* and *The Rite of Spring* had intervened) which for a time made him doubt his ability to continue *The Nightingale* at all. The introduction of a piano into the orchestra in the revised score, though it plays for only two bars, is symptomatic of this change. In the original the texture is both more melting, with doublings and smoother spacings which were modified presumably in 1913, and more tinselly, with more music for celesta and more complicated arpeggiation for the strings. Admittedly such alterations were far from drastic, and the essential character of the music was not much changed. The few adjustments of harmony involved cutting out decorative chromatics, and generally emphasising the new simplicity of Stravinsky's post-*Rite* harmony.

In turning Hans Andersen's bizarre tale into an opera text, Stravinsky and Stepan Mitussov fell inevitably under the spell of contemporary Russian verse, with its taste for obscure sensual imagery and its heady air of saturated refinement. When the Nightingale herself, having started as a solo flute (in the 1909 score, piccolo), gives voice in the form of a mysterious reference to 'roses weeping diamond tears', we may reflect that, unlike Wagner's wood-bird, she has nothing of more obvious relevance to the story to sing. And indeed it is a weakness of the story as an opera plot that, taken out of Andersen's witty and magical narrative frame, it has very little action as such, but instead boils down to a succession of atmospheric tableaux. The same is no doubt true of *The Firebird*, but then the terms of ballet are fundamentally different from those of opera. Act I of *The Nightingale* is more or less all atmosphere. It has a scene-setting introduction, very candidly influenced by Debussy; an attractive song for the Fisherman which, as Roman Vlad has pointed out, vaguely resembles the *Pastorale* in its static, cellular design (but this resemblance was increased in the 1913 revision);[14] the Nightingale's ornate song itself, the most romantic number in the act; and the quaint ensemble for the Courtiers at the end of which the Fisherman's song is briefly and exquisitely reprised. The ensemble, with its strange, angular vocal lines often outlining inert harmonies, is obviously the most modern thing in the score of Act I, though it hardly makes us think of anything in later Stravinsky, except perhaps Acts II and III. But what is more striking about these various sections is that they are all, without any help from the lapse of time, in different styles. Stravinsky is said to have recorded at the time the remark, 'Why should I be following Debussy so closely when the real originator of this operatic style was Mussorgsky?' One wonders why he did not add Ravel and Rimsky-Korsakov, not to mention Scriabin, whose languishing middle-period style is an influence here, as in the op.7 piano studies and *The Firebird*.

Yet although *The Nightingale* sets out as a charming period-piece, an opera of porcelain figurines and twinkling Chinese lanterns, something argues it as the work of a distinctive genius – something which is still hard to pin down but can be vaguely described by the convenient word 'texture'. Certainly the rhythm, even in the lively Courtiers' ensemble, is not Stravinskian. But the sound of the score, even in the original version, betrays the master's hand in its meticulous placing of detail, its avoidance of impressionist 'wash', its preference for hard detailing over soft. An example is the quite complicated score at fig.12 in the Fisherman's song, where it can be seen how carefully each string part has been composed to contribute a particular sound and type of movement to the whole. If this were piano music it would have to be played (unlike Debussy) without the sustaining pedal, despite the held horn chord. And indeed in the four excellent, if decidedly Scriabinesque, piano studies Stravinsky wrote at this time, it is striking that, in the printed edition at least, all but the first study lack right-pedal indications throughout, while no.4, though an arpeggio study, is expressly marked 'staccato sempre' in the bass. This, as we now feel, characteristic dryness and clarity of sound are oddly enough less in evidence in *The Firebird*, a work which one has associated with Stravinsky for so long that the question of whether it is truly representative or not is much more difficult to answer.

In his entertaining account of the origins of his first ballet in *Expositions and Developments* (pp. 127–33), Stravinsky remarks that he disliked the subject (which was a firm part of Diaghilev's commission) because 'it demanded descriptive music of a kind I did not want to write'. Since it would be hard to imagine anything more 'descriptive', in its particular way, than *The Nightingale*, his reservations presumably concerned the blow-by-blow nature of the *Firebird* scenario, with its conventional *pas d'action* (Stravinsky complains about the 'dialogue' between Kashchei and Ivan 'where the music is as literal as an opera'). While such things still play a major part in *Petrushka*, a work conceived entirely in Stravinsky's own mind, one could argue that the general direction of his art was away from realism of this picturesque type and towards a more ritual and sculptural form of drama, even if it seems unlikely that he can have realised that at the time. In all the circumstances *The Firebird* was probably the ideal commission for a composer of his age (twenty-seven) and gifts. It gave him the opportunity to shine as a dance composer and orchestrator without taxing his audience with undue modernism. It enabled him to prove himself to himself. It brought him out of the provincial Russian arena. And, by making him famous, it guaranteed him that rare and relatively painless freedom to

*Ex. 4 The Firebird* (from the complete ballet)

innovate which is not accompanied by indigence and self-denial.

In itself *The Firebird* is a work of synthesis rather than innovation. As a fairy-story ballet in which set dances are linked by a quasi-symphonic texture of motives (some of them leitmotivs) it hardly breaks the mould of late Tchaikovsky or Glazunov, whose ballets were in turn an extension of basically French principles. It may be that the sketchy character of the interludes reflects Fokine's interest in a music which would merely support his elaborately detailed choreography. But this no longer strikes us as particularly modern. On the other hand there is little harmonically, rhythmically or in essence orchestrally that cannot already be found in Stravinsky's music of the previous year or two, and most of his effects in these areas are, as we have seen, little more than a continuation of earlier Russian practice, however much Stravinsky may surpass his models in quality and discrimination of technique. The one thing in *The Firebird* which is plainly new to Stravinsky's work is the use of borrowed folk tunes, but there is no sign here of that individual manner of setting which gives such freshness to the folk tunes in *Petrushka*; the arrangement in the Khorovod, attractive as it is, could well be by Borodin, while the final Coronation, inspired perhaps by Mussorgsky's 'Great Gate of Kiev', uses a traditional Glinka-esque changing-background method of variation, admittedly to brilliant theatrical effect. In one other movement, the Lullaby, Stravinsky may have drawn on folk material; a Polish musicologist quoted by Craft[15] found in it a close resemblance to Volhynian folk music, from a region not far from Stravinsky's country home at Ustilug in the Ukraine. But again the treatment is conventional.

Certainly this folk material, introduced for the ostensible purpose of distinguishing the human characters from the supernatural, breathes a kind of freshness into his diablerie which it had lacked before. But it is hardly the best music in *The Firebird*. In the conventional war between good and evil, the normal and the magical, Stravinsky was not alone among late romantic composers in finding the latter component of each pair more stimulating than the former, and the most remarkable numbers in the ballet are generally agreed to be the 'Dance of the Firebird' and the 'Infernal Dance of all Kashchei's Subjects'. As for the 'Dance of the Princesses with the Golden Apples', Stravinsky himself later 'condemned' this as Mendelssohnian/Tchaikovskian (it is surely more like Glazunov). Its smoothness contrasts with the dazzling unpredictability of the Firebird's dance, with its marvellous suggestion of fluttering wings and iridescent colours, achieved not by any marked irregularity of rhythmic design (the phrases, as Eric Walter White points out, are still mainly 4+4, like those in the *Scherzo fantastique*[16]), but by variety of subdivisions of the beat and by textural mobility of the kind already noted in *Fireworks*. A glance at the score will show how many different ways Stravinsky finds of dividing a 6/8 bar, as well as how he generates sudden spurts of movement by catapulting the music from instrument to instrument and register to register, a technique which suggests the Scriabin of the Fourth and Fifth Sonatas for piano and the *Poème de l'extase* (Ex.4). The 'Infernal Dance' relates to a more virile Russian tradition, but again, curiously, if one compares it with say Mussorgsky's original *St John's Night on the Bare Mountain* of 1867, it is the Mussorgsky which emerges as by far the more adventurous in the matter of uneven phrase groupings and colouristic harmony. In the 'Infernal Dance', as before, it is the variety of detail within the bar, and even within the beat, which creates most of the excitement, not only in the famous main theme with its lumbering syncopations, but in the subsidiary theme (at figs. 150, 154, 171), where the copious rhythmic ornamentation sets up an impressionistic swirl round the bewitched dancers and seems to blur a pulse which is, all the same, as firm and regular as ever.

Much of the atmosphere of these magical sections is evoked by a harmonic palette mixed from the artificial scales and chromatics in the *Scherzo fantastique* and *Fireworks*. But their handling is noticeably less stiff than before. An important mechanism here is the leitmotiv, and in particular the characteristic figure for Kashchei, where a tritone (exactly half an octave) is filled in by alternate major and minor thirds with crossing parts. The grimacing effect of this idea is emphasised by biting rhythm and grotesque scoring, especially for low bassoons in the introduction and at the entry of Kashchei. But other ideas derive from it without that sort of emphasis, such as the very opening ostinato theme and the theme of the 'Infernal Dance', which is more galumphing than demonic. This obsession with the tritone as an image of Evil is closely tied up with Stravinsky's Russian past, as can readily be heard in the strange 'Carillon férique' (little known because it appears in none of the *Firebird* suites), where the whole-tone writing again recalls Mussorgsky's *Bare Mountain*, as well as the scene in Chernomor's magic garden in *Russlan*, with its remarkably similar dramatic setting. In the Lullaby these same major and minor thirds are fitted into the compass of a perfect instead of augmented fourth, as it were calming to sleep the diabolism which has possessed Kashchei and his subjects (Ex.5).

Although it marks the start of an international career which was to span a further sixty years, *The Firebird* is still best seen as the brilliant culmination of a specific tradition, perhaps actually the first and last work in that tradition which can be unreservedly praised for its expertise as much as its imagination. After it no serious composer could contemplate a fairy-tale drama without satire, irony or social comment. In orchestration alone Stravinsky had carried the idea of the soundscape to the point where imagery was beginning to break up into a kaleidoscope of rapidly changing colours, just as it was doing, in a more abstract context, in the post-romantic scores of his exact contemporaries in Vienna. This is shown by the extent to which one carries away from the work memories of specific effects, like the miraculous-sounding string harmonic glissandi in the introduction, which Stravinsky claimed to have discovered. Such things, he later admitted, were a conscious attempt to out-Rimsky Rimsky. But he also soon recognised

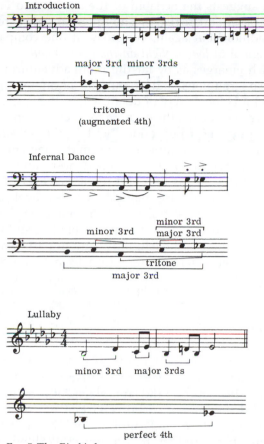

Ex. 5 The Firebird

that the exoticism to which they were attached was a dead letter, an ultimate academicism. Abandoning it, he was able to pick up more useful threads in the fabric of Russian music, which soon brought him back to a part of himself that he seems, for a time, to have suppressed.

# 3

## *A Russian in Paris:* Petrushka *and* The Rite of Spring

My last visit to Petersburg did me much good, and the final scene is shaping up excitingly . . . quick tempos, concertinas, major keys . . . smells of Russian food – shchi [cabbage soup] – and of sweat and glistening leather boots. Oh what excitement.[1]

The emergence of Stravinsky as a modernist, with an individual manner unlike any other, can be dated with some precision to his early work on *Petrushka*. In March 1910, during the later stages of composing *The Firebird*, he had experienced the famous 'fleeting vision' out of which *The Rite of Spring* was to grow. But when Diaghilev and Nijinsky visited him in Lausanne in September 1910 they found him at work on something quite different, a concert piece for piano and orchestra called 'Petrushka's Cry'. Together with a 'Russian Dance' composed soon afterwards, this music was to form the basis of the ballet which Diaghilev instinctively urged him to write instead.

'Petrushka's Cry' became the second tableau of the ballet, where it immediately follows the 'Russian Dance' in which the Charlatan brings his three puppets to life. Both pieces are dominated by the piano. 'I had in my mind,' Stravinsky wrote a quarter of a century later in his autobiography, 'a distinct picture of a puppet, suddenly endowed with life, exasperating the patience of the orchestra with diabolical cascades of arpeggios.'[2] Stravinsky must have written the music at the piano, as was by now his habit, perhaps improvising in response to an imagined scenario. In 'Petrushka's Cry', the piano writing has the feel of the actual physical presence of the keyboard, above all in the numerous passages where the left hand confines itself to the black notes and the right hand to the white, and it was perhaps here for the first time that Stravinsky abandoned a harmony based on rules for a harmony based on touch and instinct. In the famous Petrushka fanfare, which typifies the black note/white note colouring, an irregular pattern of discord is an automatic result of the spacing of the hands, and has nothing to do with dissonance in the old sense of tension and release. On the contrary the harmonic colouring is stable; compare the fanfare at fig.95 (49)[3] with the orchestral cluster made out of the same notes just after, at the passage labelled 'Petrushka's Curses' (Ex.6).[4] In the 'Russian Dance', similarly, the parallel white-note discords are simply a comfortable way of thickening the tune, just as the near-mechanical repetitions (apt as they are to the story) seem to arise from the sheer enjoyment of an elementary tune under the hands.

As a piece of musical architecture 'Petrushka's Cry' is unremarkable. Its dramaturgy of musical and mimetic gesture is within the nineteenth-century tradition of the *pas d'action* – the ballet equivalent of the recitative – which is no doubt why Diaghilev saw its possibilities so quickly. What is remarkable is that, in expanding these two short pieces into a thirty-five-minute ballet, Stravinsky took a completely new direction compared to that of the romantic story-ballet, adding only one more short tableau of 'relevant' action, together with two short sequences towards the end of the first and last tableaux respectively, and for the rest building the work up out of a mass of seemingly disconnected and dramatically quite peripheral genre scenes, as if the standard divertissement of the traditional ballet had risen up and engulfed the supposed plot. There is, no doubt, a particular dramatic point being made by this means. Petrushka, the helpless individual trapped in an insignificant personal tragedy while the world hurries past, survives his own death as the embodiment of a unique creative spark, possessed by nobody else. But this is very much a finished interpretation of the work. At the conceptual stage, Stravinsky could draw on a variety of models for such a dramaturgy, most notably Mussorgsky's *Boris Godunov*, whose loose chronicle form had also placed its nominal hero at a disadvantage in relation to the massed scenes of Russian life. Like Mussorgsky, Stravinsky could see that such an arrangement had a special appeal since it allowed the plight of his central character to gain in point and vividness from the sheer detailed authenticity and precision of atmosphere of the world in which he moved. This world had suddenly become of more than passing interest to Stravinsky, who was all the more consciously of it for being no longer in it. Such is clearly the burden of his letter to Andrei Rimsky-Korsakov, written when the composition of *Petrushka* was at its height. He had returned to St Petersburg for consultations with Benois, the scenarist for the new ballet, in December 1910, and it seems evident from his many later references to this visit (for example in the autobiography and in *Expositions and Developments*) that it made an unusual impression on him. Perhaps more than anything it was that curious mixture of the old and the new, the rustic and the urban, which still distinguished Russian life from the sophisticated milieus of Paris and Monte Carlo. Within days of his return to the South of France, where he lived from October 1910, Stravinsky was writing to

*Ex. 6(i) Petrushka* (1947)

*(ii) Petrushka* (1947)

Andrei, urgently requesting two Petersburg street songs which he could not remember accurately (the tunes are those played by the rival organ-grinders in the first tableau).[5]

It is from the systematic attempt to render this particular flavour of traditional Russian life into music that *Petrushka* derives many of its freshest and most original qualities. More than any other work, Stravinsky based it on borrowed material, and with a true awareness of the melting-pot nature of city life he took his tunes from a wide range of sources. *Petrushka* contains rustic folksongs (both sacred and secular), and popular urban tunes of the kind Stravinsky had requested from Andrei; but it also includes the cries of street merchants. It incorporates a French melody, 'Elle avait une jambe en bois', which Stravinsky picked up in Beaulieu-sur-mer (ill-advisedly, as it turned out to be still in copyright); and it takes over a pair of waltzes by the Viennese composer Josef Lanner, suitably conventional dance material for the ballerina in the third tableau. These tunes are treated in a style far removed from the chocolate-box manner of the folksong arrangements in *The Firebird*. The Lanner waltzes, set with mocking banality for solo cornet and flutes to a childish tonic-dominant accompaniment, already look forward to the oblique classicism of *The Soldier's Tale* and the easy pieces for piano duet.

However it is in the first tableau and its complex recreation of the Shrovetide Fair, that we encounter the liveliest evidence of a new kind of music. The first part of the tableau, up to the so-called 'Tour de passe-passe' where the Charlatan appears with his puppets, might seem a conventional scene-setting, but in fact both its elements and their treatment are novel. Unlike a work such as *Carmen*, with its 'drôles de gens' regimented musically into a tidy sequence of more or less self-contained numbers, *Petrushka* presents its crowd for what it is, an irregular throng of humanity, on whom our attention as observers focuses unpredictably. At the very start the various street cries[6] weave an erratic counterpoint against the undifferentiated murmur of the fairground (clarinets and horns). Each is constructed out of tiny repeating melodic cells in such a way as to cut across the written (if inaudible) barring; equally their relation to each other is variable, as can be seen by comparing the music after fig.1 with the equivalent passage four bars before fig.3 (Ex.7(i)). They do at least, however, use a common pulse. A few bars later, where the *balagani*, or fairground barker, is announced by repeated quaver Gs (flutes, oboes), his call contradicts the underlying pulse so irrationally that Stravinsky seems, not for the last time, to have had difficulty notating the music as precisely as he must have imagined it (the changed notation of the revised 1947 version highlights the problem but hardly solves it: Ex.7(ii,iii)). The murmur of the crowd rises to a hubbub in preparation for the rise of the curtain a page or so later. Here to some extent the interior ostinatos of harp, keyboards, clarinets, horns and strings serve to animate an essentially immobile harmony, in a way that still owes something to Debussy. But the vigorously independent elements of the

*Ex. 7(i) Petrushka* (1947)

barker's cry and the lumbering Easter Song (bassoons, cellos, double-basses), which are in fact the same tune played at different speeds and in contradictory time systems, lend the music a contrapuntal energy which is new and highly personal.

This sense of a crowd as an undifferentiated mass from which individuals stand out haphazardly is commonplace enough in itself. To give it artistic form, Stravinsky adopted a technique which was to become normal in modern art but which was still in its infancy in 1911: that of montage. Using his music like a cine-camera, he turns his lens now on this group, now on that, sometimes standing back for a general shot, sometimes moving in for a close-up. For the finished work a sequence of shots is assembled to form a particular impression of the much larger scene.[7] Admittedly the first tableau of *Petrushka* is a more formal affair than this analogy suggests, and still obeys the convention that to be coherent music must have repetition. However, the many brief recurrences of the opening music and the barker's cry are less like formal reprises than accidental intrusions of events going on elsewhere in the fairground. The one rather artificial reprise accompanies the 're-passing' of the Volochebniki, or Easter singers (fig.20). Artificial in a slightly more stagey sense is the central episode of the rival organ-grinders, where the two tunes are made to 'fit' in the same sort of way as Mozart's three dances in *Don Giovanni*. Charming as it is, this episode differs from its surroundings in that it draws attention to the musical trick it embodies.

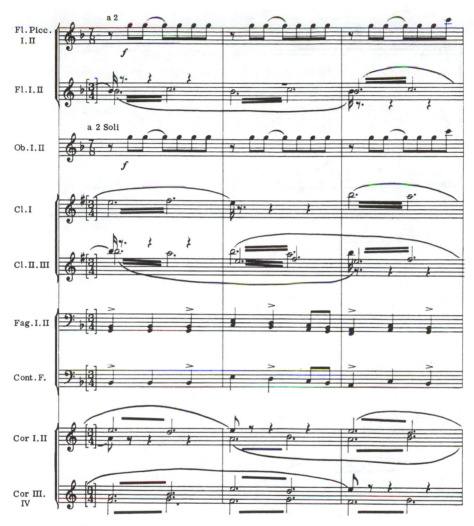

*(ii) Petrushka* (1911) (wind parts only)

Looked at in general terms, this opening sequence of *Petrushka* is a proto-type of later Stravinskian form. Its underlying rhythmic design may not be complex in the same way as that of *The Rite of Spring* or the later Russian works, but its intricacy of rhythmic detailing and its mixture of a highly fluid pattern of melodic stress with an inert background harmony laid the groundwork for a technique which, through many changes of superficial style, was to serve him for the rest of his life. The transitional nature of the

technique can be judged by a comparison with the final tableau of *Petrushka*. Here the much broader sweep of the ballet is formed out of a sequence of fully-fledged dances for a whole series of local Petersburg types, like the wet-nurses in their special hats, the peasant with his tame bear, the two young gypsy girls with the drunken merchant playing his *garmoshka* (squeeze-box). The music consists mostly of popular tunes, laid out unevenly against various kinds of ostinato pattern; and though Stravinsky's writing has astonishing vitality, and unprecedented vigour of sonority and gesture, and though it would be hard to imagine anything more colourful

*(iii) Petrushka* (1947) (wind parts only)

or stimulating or amusing than this typology of Russian popular culture, nevertheless the style owes much to an existing Russian tradition of setting folk tunes against a background in which colour and movement are more important than harmony in the usual sense. Perhaps its limitations are suggested in the fact that Stravinsky never again resorted so completely to unmediated folksong.

In one other respect the style of these outer tableaux is transitional. Though the harmonies are technically dissonant – a rich background texture formed by ostinatos which keep many notes in play – the clashes are seldom harsh, because the notes usually belong to the same scale. For example, the first part of the final tableau (before the appearance of the wet-nurses) is entirely in D major with no foreign notes at all except in the three bars before fig.167 (88). In *The Rite of Spring* this style is superseded by a more chromatic system of interfering scales, and thereafter Stravinsky usually applied the harmonic-field ideas of *Petrushka* to chords of a more complex or ambiguous structure. But there is chromaticism in *Petrushka* as well. We have seen how the hero's own motive is made up of black and white note triads in combination. More generally these central tableaux – which contain practically the whole of the 'plot' from Petrushka's impotent cursing in his cell to his fight with the Moor over the Ballerina – use a harsher harmonic colouring to catch the mood of oppression and conflict, in sharp contrast with the brightness and pageantry of the fairground outside. And at two points this mood spills out momentarily into the brightness: in the 'Tour de passe-passe', the conjuring trick by which the Charlatan brings the puppets to life; and at the very end, when the Moor chases Petrushka out into the fairground and kills him in full view of the people. There is an air of mystery about each of these passages. The Charlatan with his flute animates the puppets in the manner of a snake-charmer, and when they dance it is in the brilliant and showy style that a fairground crowd expects of its entertainers. Yet something of what the man breathes into them is absent from the dance, some darker dimension which we only begin to perceive later in the expression of Petrushka's torment. This conjuring-trick episode fascinated contemporary musicians such as Debussy, to whom it emanated 'a kind of sonorous magic, a mysterious transformation of mechanical souls which become human by a spell of which, until now, you [Stravinsky] seem to be the unique inventor'.[8] Debussy was particularly intrigued by the orchestration, with its prismatic arpeggios for harp, celesta and strings playing on the point of the bow, picked out later by woodwind – a kind of sound Stravinsky was to explore further in the *Three Japanese Lyrics*. But he must also have been impressed by Stravinsky's economical assemblage of tiny self-contained cells, and the way of achieving a refined and subtle effect by the meticulous placement of every note rather than by thematic development or complicated harmonic syntax. Such refinement had for a long time been part of Debussy's own art (which is doubtless why he was able to use the lesson of *Petrushka* in his own Diaghilev ballet *Jeux* without any loss of individuality). But in Stravinsky we find an electric charge, a kind of expressive friction, that is more Russian than French. When, at the end of the ballet, Petrushka's ghost appears on top of the booth and frightens even the Charlatan away, we recognise the dark spirit of the 'Tour de passe-passe', released at last from its bondage to the commonplace.

Thus in the end *Petrushka* maintains a double aspect. The figure of the puppet himself is above all a late nineteenth-century creation, the misfit of romantic artistic mythology, less sentimentalised, certainly, than the pierrots of *Pagliacci* or *The Yeoman of the Guard*, but perpetuating the same essential conflict between the inward and the outward life. But Stravinsky identifies just as much with the world under which his hero suffers. The detachment of *Petrushka* is its most modern feature, and there is no bitterness against this world of teeming, colourful insouciance, any more than in *The Rite of Spring* we shall be invited to take up arms against the barbarity of human sacrifice. Certainly *Petrushka* typifies the new artistic creed of Diaghilev, a creed of movement, colour and illusion. But beyond that it exemplifies a new mood in the arts generally, in which the self-absorption and anguish of romanticism and expressionism begin to be opposed by an outward-looking objectivity eager to participate in the joy of existence. This is the force of the pageantry in *Petrushka*, and if it ultimately places the puppet's own misery in an equivocal light, it is fitting that his final gesture should be, not an apotheosis nor a transfiguration, but a rude nose-thumbing gesture at his tormentors.

*Petrushka* was performed by the Ballets Russes in Paris in June 1911, just under a year after the triumph of *The Firebird*, and within two months Stravinsky, now back at Ustilug, was starting to compose *The Rite of Spring*. 'The success of *Petrushka*', he wrote many years later, 'was good for me in that it gave me the absolute conviction of my ear just as I was about to begin *Le Sacre du printemps*.'[9] All the same, and despite technical and stylistic similarities, most musicians would argue that *The Rite* was, in sonority as much as anything, an even bolder step than *Petrushka*. Stravinsky himself wrote to Andrei Rimsky-Korsakov in March 1912 that 'it is as if twenty and not two years had passed since *The Firebird* was composed.'[10] Though many sketches for *The Rite of Spring* have survived, it seems impossible to retrace this immense journey through documentary material. And, what is perhaps still more disconcerting, the few other compositions of these years hardly tell us more, though they display experimental features and some revealing similarities with the ballet. There are four of them: the pair of Verlaine songs, composed in Brittany immediately after the première of *The Firebird*, in July 1910; the two Balmont settings, composed similarly just after *Petrushka*, at Ustilug in July or August 1911; the choral/orchestral *Zvezdoliki*, also written at Ustilug in July 1911; and the *Three Japanese Lyrics*, composed late in 1912 when the substantial work on *The Rite of Spring* was complete but before its final touching up and, above all, before it had been played by an orchestra.[11]

The Verlaine songs are of slight interest and seem to belong, in their lack of Stravinskian profile, to a period earlier than their date of composition. Like parts of *The Faun and the Shepherdess* they aspire to a French tone of utterance which is naturally outside the composer's range. 'La lune blanche' is unimaginably far from Fauré's rapturous setting in *La bonne chanson* (which Stravinsky presumably knew), and indeed hardly ventures far in texture or tonality from the frank despair of the other song, 'Un grand sommeil noir'; both are in B flat minor and a slow crotchet tempo. But these clearly deliberate similarities may mean that Stravinsky was consciously experimenting with the possibilities of subtle variation within a single range of mood and gesture – consciously, that is, approaching feeling from the direction of interior detail rather than exterior emotion. The Russian symbolist works of the following summer (*Zvezdoliki* is also a setting of a text by Balmont) are more arresting, not least because of the symbolist allusions pointed out by Lawrence Morton in the scenario of *The Rite of Spring*. Morton, a close friend of Stravinsky's in the USA, believes that at the time that the composer selected his two Gorodyetsky poems for his settings of 1907 he must also have read a poem in the same collection called 'Yarila', which describes a fertility sacrifice similar in outline to the one in *The Rite*. Later the idea will have surfaced from Stravinsky's subconscious, at a time when he was becoming interested in Slavic ethnography (a photograph taken probably in 1910 shows him at Ustilug noting down a folksong at the dictation of a blind peasant).[12]

The connection between ethnography and symbolism is not quite as tenuous as it might at first seem, especially in the context of Russian art in the early twentieth century. For seventy years the Slavophile movement had identified the study of indigenous Russian culture with an abstract idea of Russian spiritual revival which would herald the dawn of a new age. The atmosphere surrounding this movement became increasingly mystical and at the same time anarchistic as the Russian state machine grew more and more oppressive, and by Gorodyetsky's time it had acquired revolutionary overtones. Gorodyetsky himself seems to have been a conscious myth-maker, but Yarila was nevertheless a known fertility god of Slavonic mythology; the poem thus characteristically mixes up genuine ethnology with a priestly, quasi-religious symbolism and a flavour of demagoguery into the bargain; and this is also very much the tone of Balmont's *Zvezdoliki* ('Star-face'), for all its apparently perverse obscurity of meaning.[13] Stravinsky claimed much later that he set this poem for its verbal sonority: 'Its words were good, and words were what I needed, not meanings.'[14] However, it is not hard to glimpse through Balmont's astrophysical metaphors a neo-primitive fertility thaumaturge comparable to Yarila but without his ethnographic credentials, and if this is accepted it is reasonable to see *Zvezdoliki* as an overflow from the mood of *The Rite of Spring*, as well as a deliberate preparation for it.

Disappointingly, the connection seems not to be supported by the music. In *Zvezdoliki* Balmont's words are set for male-voice chorus and large orchestra, and both the scale and the character of these forces imply a direct response to the poet's graphic but somewhat heightened imagery which turns out to be damaging to Stravinsky's sense of movement and structure. The whole piece, which lasts six or seven minutes, feels like an introduction to something much grander, perhaps in the manner of Scriabin's *Divine Poem* (Stravinsky is known to have been playing Scriabin during the summer of 1911[15]). Though the music is dominated by a melodic and chordal motto, which stands at the head of the score as a setting of its title (and which Stravinsky includes in his recorded performance), it lacks the rigidly patterned figuration which articulates the cell-structures of *Petrushka* and, above all, *The Rite of Spring*. In this respect the music remains slave to its text, in a way that the Balmont songs do not and that Stravinsky systematically abandoned in his next choral work, *The Wedding*. As Robert Craft has observed, *Zvezdoliki* lacks extensive musical repetition, an extraordinarily untypical feature of a Stravinsky score at this or almost any other time.[16]

But naturally the music is not wholly without characteristic details. In the chording, which has a decidedly exploratory character while retaining underlying tonal structures, Stravinsky tries out a number of 'mixtures', such as the major-minor triad and various complications of the minor ninth chord, which were to assume greater importance in *The Rite of Spring*. Here and there we find an octatonic flavour. But the sound of the score is essentially unlike that of *The Rite*, and indeed the most Stravinskian passage is the chorale-like music (derived from the motto) to which 'Star-face' pronounces his law, a phrase whose emblematic solemnity and wind scoring remotely anticipate the closing music of the *Symphonies of Wind Instruments*, composed nine crowded years later. If this is a coincidence, it is a strange one, since both works happen to be dedicated to Debussy, whose influence Craft detects in the closing pages of *Zvezdoliki*. Not surprisingly, though, Debussy was baffled by this mysterious music. 'It is probably Plato's "harmony of the eternal spheres",' he wrote to Stravinsky on receiving the dedication, 'and, except on Sirius or Aldebaran, I do not foresee performances of this "cantata for planets".' Glossing this letter in *Conversations*, the composer suggests that the work 'remains in one sense my most "radical" and difficult composition'. But 'radical' must have a limited meaning here, since this particular new root seems to have put out few if any shoots.[17]

By contrast the tiny Balmont songs, 'The Forget-me-not' and 'The Dove', are plainly studies for *The Rite of Spring*, though their decorative lyricism is far removed from the earthy aggressiveness of the ballet. The exquisite vocal melodies, based on a folksong style but with chromatic embellishment of a kind foreign to *Petrushka* but fundamental to *The Rite*, are extended by a variable-cell technique closely akin to the overriding principle of the later work, as can be seen by a comparison of the central section of 'The Forget-me-not' with the passage from fig.91 of the 'Mysterious circles of the young girls'. The obvious difference here is that in the song Stravinsky accommodates the melodic embellishments within a regular metre, whereas in the ballet the metre is governed by the embellishments, a small but crucial change of chemistry whereby hangs, needless to say, an explosive difference of effect, not just in rhythm but also in texture and harmony, since the irregularity produces a variable relationship between the melody and its ostinato accompaniment, which in the song is fixed (Ex.8). The point of 'The Forget-me-not' in this respect seems to have been its readiness to seek

*Ex. 8(i)* Two Poems of Konstantin Balmont (1912 version)

beauty in simplicity and in the superficially monotonous repetition of tiny self-contained units. In practice nothing could be less monotonous. The refined economy of these songs is far more affecting than the complicated interestingness of *Zvezdoliki*. Notice, for instance, how subtly Stravinsky uses chromatic inflexion in the framing melody of 'The Forget-me-not' and throughout 'The Dove' to add a tonal dimension to the modal line. The equivocation between B sharp and B natural in bar 2 of 'The Forget-me-not' is both an expressive vocal detail (balanced by the move from D sharp to E) and a veil thrown over the modality of G sharp (major or minor), while the G natural in the next bar is an even more piquant touch, drooping melodically against the trilling G sharp while introducing a disruptive element in tonality, an effect of displaced, or mistuned, octaves such as will play a still bigger role in the harmonic language of *The Rite*. Here the effect is not harsh but poignant. But it is worth noting that when Stravinsky later arranged the accompaniment for the *Japanese Lyrics* ensemble, he chose to bring out semitone clashes of this kind where in the original they are only latent. The very first chord of 'The Forget-me-not', an open G sharp/ D sharp trill in the 1912 piano version, is now coloured by a high cello ostinato on A and E *spiccato* harmonics, turning what was originally a

*(ii) The Rite of Spring, 'Mysterious Circles'*

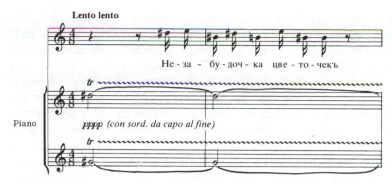

*Ex. 9(i)* Two Poems of Konstantin Balmont (1912 version)

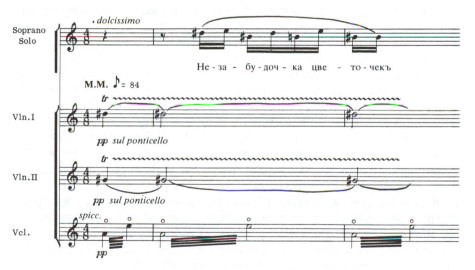

*(ii)* Two Poems of Konstantin Balmont (1955 version)

succession of notes into a simultaneity (Ex.9: note also the rebarring). It goes without saying that Stravinsky's abiding interest in rearranging his early works often arose (as in the case of the *Pastorale*) from a feeling for what they offered his later ones. And in this sense the Balmont songs are more, not less, radical than *Zvezdoliki*.

The *Three Japanese Lyrics*, composed some fifteen to eighteen months later when *The Rite* was more or less complete, nevertheless refer back to the Balmont songs. Again structures made up of small repeating melodic cells are varied by embellishment. In the first song, 'Akahito', a six-note ostinato in slow ornamented quavers runs through the entire setting, varied only by changes in scoring and by octave displacement, while in no.3, 'Tsaraiuki', there is a foretaste of the mechanical ostinato schemes in the Three Pieces for string quartet in the way tiny refrain figures are allocated to specific instruments. But all the time the most intriguing use of cells is in the voice part. Here we find a mobile arrangement of (typically) two-note cells, often placed obliquely to the more mechanical instrumental patterns. For instance, if the first vocal figure in 'Tsaraiuki' is analysed into four pairs of quavers labelled A,B,C,D, then the second figure is B,C,D, followed by A,B,C,D, picking up off the beat so that what was previously stressed is now unstressed and vice versa. When these songs were first performed in Paris and Moscow in 1914, listeners (especially Russians) commented on the prevailing ambiguity of vocal accent. The observation was that the vocal part had been, as it were, shifted sideways by (usually) one quaver. Stravinsky explained in a letter to the editor of the Moscow journal *Muzika* that his object was to emulate in Russian the accentless character of the Japanese originals.[18]

According to Stravinsky in his autobiography, these metrical experiments were intended as in some way a musical equivalent to what he called 'the graphic solution of problems of perspective and space' in Japanese engravings and in the Japanese poems from which he took his three lyrics.[19] Did he mean that, in a flat, two-dimensional art, movement is dependent on subtle distortions of line and proportion? Certainly 'Akahito' is a 'flat' setting animated by slight irregularities in the way the equally plain voice part lies across the accompaniment. But it is hard to see how this analogy applies to the poems, which, in translation at least, are delicate but flaccid. In any case there is nothing very Japanese about the music. With hindsight we may imagine in the swirling scales of 'Mazatsumi' something of the linear sweep which Art Nouveau took from the Japanese engravings so fashionable at the turn of the century. But the outer songs are pure embodiments of the melodic spirit of *The Rite of Spring*, with its decorative treatment of folksong, while the chief influence on the texture, at any rate, of 'Mazatsumi' is apparently Schoenberg's *Pierrot lunaire*, which Stravinsky heard in Berlin in December 1912.

This influence has been disputed, but on questionable grounds. Stravinsky was struck at the time by *Pierrot lunaire* and argued its merits on his French composer friends, including Ravel and Debussy. The exact choice of instruments for the *Japanese Lyrics* (two flutes, two clarinets, piano quintet – Ravel used precisely the same ensemble in his *Trois poèmes de Mallarmé*, which were first performed in the same concert) was probably influenced by Schoenberg's highly original band of flute, clarinet, violin, cello and piano; and this is supported by the fact that, though 'Akahito' was composed with piano (and sketched for piano quintet, piccolo, flute and a second viola) in October, it was not finally scored with clarinets until mid-December, after the Berlin concert, whereupon Stravinsky quickly added the other two songs. Even so the Schoenberg influence is mainly limited to questions of colouring: compare 'Mazatsumi' with 'Der Mondfleck'. While Stravinsky's harmonic palette had certainly grown harsher and more complex since *Petrushka*, with free chromaticism and dissonance and an oblique tonality, it is not atonal either in *The Rite of Spring* or in the *Japanese Lyrics* (or, one could add, anywhere else before Movements for piano and orchestra nearly half a century on). Nor does it depend much on linear chromaticism except in carefully regulated contexts such as were discussed in connection with the Balmont songs. It was the flickering light of Schoenberg's music which attracted the sharp-eared Stravinsky, and there is no evidence that anything in its syntax passed into his own language until many years later, despite Debussy's well-known Germanophobe remark to Godet, made in 1915, that 'Stravinsky . . . is leaning dangerously in the direction of Schoenberg.' A more revealing, though possibly untrue, observation about what Stravinsky found in *Pierrot* was made by the Russian composer himself in his autobiography, written at a time when he was most anxious to deprecate any possible link with the Viennese school: 'I did not feel the slightest enthusiasm about the aesthetics of the work which appeared to me a retrogression to the out-of-date Beardsley cult.'[20]

One further link between the *Japanese Lyrics* and *The Rite of Spring* should be mentioned. Both have as their subject the coming of spring. Admittedly the treatment could hardly be more different. In the lyrics our attention is drawn to the decorative aspects of the season, symbolised by the colour white – patterns of white flowers against fresh snow. In *The Rite of Spring* it is the violence and elemental force associated with the death of winter which dominate both the scenario and the music. Such violence is not merely a pagan archaism, but belongs inalienably to the idea of spring in cold countries. In one of the most famous passages of *Memories and Commentaries*, in reply to Craft's question 'What did you love most in Russia?', Stravinsky recalled 'the violent Russian spring that seemed to begin in an hour and was like the whole earth cracking'.[21] It is an image as far as possible from the Arcadian idea of spring more familiar in the art of western and southern Europe and enshrined in works as far apart as *The Winter's Tale* and *Parsifal*. But Stravinsky's picture coincides with the ethnographic sources of his ballet, of which he was evidently well aware from the start, since his initial vision of 'wise elders, seated in a circle, watching a young girl dance herself to death . . . to propitiate the god of spring'[22] prompted him almost at once to approach a recognised authority on Slavonic folk customs, the painter Nicolas Roerich, to collaborate with him on a scenario. Whether or not Stravinsky's first unconscious inspiration came from Gorodyetsky, it seems probable that we owe to Roerich that authenticity of detail, from the 'Divination with twigs' in the 'Augurs of·

Spring' to the games of abduction and choosing, the propitiation of ancestors and the so-called 'ritual action of the ancestors', which places *The Rite
of Spring* in the same category as *Petrushka* as a document of Slavic culture.
But Stravinsky was well-equipped to respond in kind to such ideas. As a
pupil of Rimsky-Korsakov he obviously knew all about the older composer's
obsession with Russian peasant customs, which are frequently mentioned
in Rimsky's memoirs and also acted out in his operas, often with music
carefully based on folk tunes appropriate to the ritual in question. Rimsky
had published a collection of Russian folksongs, and although his arrangements do not generally exhibit the freedom from academic convention
which was to typify the collections of a generation or so later, his use of
these tunes in his stage works is sometimes novel and coloured by a feeling
for the elemental nature of the ritual. For years the similar tendency in
Stravinsky's music after 1910 was played down, not least by the composer
himself who, during his years of exile in France and America, tried hard to
detach himself from his provincial background. It was typical of all this
that, despite the obvious folk character of the melodies in *The Rite of Spring*,
it was widely thought that the score contained only a single genuine folksong, the Lithuanian tune played by the bassoon at the start, until the
publication in 1969 of a volume of Stravinsky's sketches, which contain
other neatly written-out tunes from published collections, provided material
evidence that much of the music of *The Rite* is based on real folk tunes.[23]
Since then Richard Taruskin has even shown that Stravinsky was as careful
as his teacher to use the right tune for the right ritual, while skilfully
disguising his borrowings and absorbing them into his style.[24]

The work's performance history contributed to the vagueness
surrounding its musical dramaturgy. After the famous early stage
productions, it lived on above all as a concert work, which it was possible
to hear as a self-sufficient 'symphonic' structure with no more than superficial help from the sacrificial-dance idea that had been Stravinsky's own
first image of the ballet. Unlike *Petrushka*, *The Rite of Spring* is anyway
hardly a 'story' ballet with characters. It does away with even the vestigial
sentimental tragedy of the earlier work, and in taking the public framework
as its sole dramatic mechanism, it strips away the generalised, haphazard
character of the Shrovetide events in the earlier ballet and replaces them
with a strict 'liturgical' sequence, a sequence which, we understand, will
always happen this way, with different participants but the same meaning.
This ritual approach to drama, which Stravinsky was to return to again and
again in subsequent works, is the main source of the work's symphonic
power. As the composer wrote to N. F. Findeizen, 'I give not one measure
for pantomime.'[25] The absence of digression, the avoidance of genre and
the restriction of decorative colour to such as is absolutely implied by the
action, are the negative condition for a music whose positive force is based
on a rigorous control of movement and the most stringent economy in the
use of melodic and harmonic ideas.

Nevertheless the dramatic details remain a vital key to the music's nature. After all. the work had its beginnings in a vision, and it preserves this visual association in its subtitle, 'Pictures from Pagan Russia'. Each of the thirteen sections in the score (apart from the introductions to the two parts, which are played with the curtain down) presents a single intensely imagined tableau in the complete ritual, somewhat along the lines of the stations of the cross. Moreover, if we leaf through the published sketchbook we become conscious of an almost eidetic quality in the actual musical invention. We notice how, time and again, the essential idea for a scene flashes on to the page out of next to nothing: the merest hint of a preliminary sketch, some keyboard experiments no doubt (Stravinsky invariably found his ideas at the piano), and suddenly the music is there fully formed, needing nothing but extending and some attention to detail. This is naturally not always the case, but often it is. It is as if we are actually witnessing a series of visions, like the first one but experienced now as music (perhaps the first one was too, but if so Stravinsky kept the fact to himself). The most violent scenes are invariably the most powerfully glimpsed in this way. The 'Dance of the Earth' and the 'Sacrificial Dance', which Stravinsky later claimed gave him notational problems, crystallise as if they were clichés that might come into a composer's head at any time; yet these are the most daring passages in the whole score, whereas, as Craft notes in his commentary to the sketches, the more conventional slower episodes gave Stravinsky trouble and took much longer to find their eventual form. We may suppose that this is because the violent dances coincided with the original vision, while the slower music was rather a necessary recourse, in the interests of contrast and linkage. The fact that it was the introduction to Part 2 that caused the most trouble of all tends to support this view, since it apparently had no visual correlative. By contrast, Stravinsky's physical involvement in music like the 'Honouring of the Chosen One', which is obvious from the sheer flamboyance of the pen-strokes in the sketchbook, is tantamount to a choreographic act in itself, an almost personal participation in the ritual.

We have already noticed a tendency in *Petrushka* for the music to be formulated in ways that suggest cinematic montage, and one could similarly think of *The Rite of Spring* as a sequence of cinematic stills. The difference is that, whereas in *Petrushka* the 'camera' had many simultaneous actions to dwell on, and a varied repertoire of 'shots' to make into its picture of the fairground, in *The Rite* the unity of the action insists that we attend to one image at a time, and since at the same time the musical images occurred to Stravinsky in even more concentrated form than the scraps of borrowed material he had used in the first tableau of *Petrushka*, the question arises. how can the music be given duration – how can musical ideas that are apparently complete and instantaneous, like plastic objects, be made to take up temporal space appropriate to their weight and energy?

Here we are posing the question whose solution – which obviously came

to Stravinsky almost at once and probably never even struck him as problematical – made *The Rite of Spring* into a revolutionary work, a classic of
modernism, and one of the greatest moulders of new sensibilities in the
history of Western music. Other composers had written music that was
very discordant, in which dissonant sound was part and parcel of the basic
idea. Nor was there anything devastatingly new about music based on
fundamentally static musical images; to take a single example, Debussy's
piano piece 'Et la lune descend sur le temple qui fût', written in 1907, is
both dissonant and essentially immobile, a dream-like association of images.
What nobody seems to have done before *The Rite of Spring* was to take
dissonant, irregularly formed musical 'objects' of very brief extent and
release their latent energy by firing them off at one another like so many
particles in an atomic accelerator. In dissonant works of the nineteenth
century, from Liszt's *Prometheus* to Schoenberg's *Verklärte Nacht*, discord
always implies concord, however long it may be in coming, and when
Schoenberg abandoned this specific function of dissonance he at once ran
into problems of musical motion. For Debussy, on the other hand, dissonance was essentially a colouristic matter to do with more or less complex
detailing, and without necessary structural implications. Stravinsky took
from Debussy the idea of the dissonant musical cell (he may also have been
influenced in this, as Debussy certainly was, by earlier Russian experimenta-
lists such as Mussorgsky and Borodin). But he infused the cell with an
explosive energy which could never be contained within the sensuous,
veiled patterns juxtaposition favoured by the Impressionists. It is important
not to confuse this energy with the dramaturgical violence of the works in
which it first occurs: in the strife-ridden central tableaux of *Petrushka* and
throughout *The Rite of Spring*. In later works like *The Wedding* or the
*Symphonies of Wind Instruments*, to name only scores from the so-called
Russian period, the principle operates if anything still more boldly without
the impetus of explicitly violent subject-matter. It might be more sensible
to argue that Stravinsky fastened initially on violent subjects because they
seemed to offer a natural outlet for his new manner; and this would account
well for the excitement which brims over on page after page of the sketches,
as the technique responds to the image.

The most discussed vehicle for this new sensibility is rhythm. Stravinsky
was widely credited with rediscovering the 'ancient' idea of rhythm as a
bearer of structure, though since musical structure is inevitably borne on
rhythm it would perhaps have been more helpful to say that he reintro-
duced the old idea of rhythm as material. Many of the primary ideas in *The
Rite* seem to have come into being as rhythmic essences, which are retained
in final versions remarkably close to the ones in which they originated. This
is the case with the principal cells of the three great climactic dances, the
'Dance of the Earth', the 'Honouring of the Chosen One', and the 'Sacrificial
Dance'. In each of these the unstable rhythmic patterning is in the nature
of the idea, while the grouping of ideas may be a later consideration, as

with the 'Honouring of the Chosen One', where Stravinsky took time to decide on the immediate repeat of the five-quaver nucleus. In other movements the rhythm is not strikingly present in the idea, but is a vehicle for its reiteration, as in the 'Augurs of Spring', where the rhythmic basis of the tiny cells in which the music first appears is conventional, while the famous thrown stresses of the dance emerge only at the next stage, where the ideas are being assembled into a composition draft. Possibly the 'Dance of the Earth' is an intermediate stage between these two types. Like the 'Augurs of Spring', it is laid over an absolutely regular and unbroken ostinato (in what Taruskin memorably called the 'dance-until-you-drop' vein), but seems nevertheless to enjoy independence as a rhythmic idea. In the other two dances the utter irregularity of the cells is not modulated by an underlying pattern but determines the rhythmic structure as it goes along.

Since these and many of the other dances of *The Rite of Spring* are above all thrilling as movement, like the scenario they dramatise, it is tempting to see these new rhythms as primarily a matter of violent gesture. But if that were the whole story, Stravinsky's technique would hardly have survived his interest in barbaric subjects, whereas, as we shall see in later chapters, it in fact adapted itself equally well to intimate and light-hearted subject-matter, to non-theatrical works in a wide variety of moods, and later even to the monumental scores of the neo-classical period. It is true that all these works, without significant exception, are rhythmically rich and vital. A renewed vigour of movement was perhaps Stravinsky's greatest gift to an art labouring under a century of heavy emotional torment, and he certainly came to music as a dancer rather than as a singer. But he was nevertheless in part a singer too, and in the broader view it is not possible to understand his rhythmic language properly without taking into account his unusual and hardly less revolutionary attitude to melody.

Like *Petrushka*, *The Rite of Spring* is based on folksong. Some of its themes were adapted from published collections, others were either collected by Stravinsky himself or cleverly fabricated by him in the image of Russian folk music. But *The Rite of Spring* lacks that broad treatment of melody which helped make *Petrushka* popular from the start. Rather, it uses its source melodies as raw material, plundering them for minute figures to use as patterns or ostinatos and even treating them in a purely parasitic way as a habitat for rhythmic motives, as in the 'Dance of the Earth', whose fierce characteristic rhythm encases a basic melody in a way that could scarcely have been perceived without the sketchbook's drawing our attention to the source.

One of the most fascinating things about the melodic technique in *The Rite* is that the method itself, like the material, comes from folk music. The type of song favoured by Stravinsky is limited to only a handful of different notes (typically four) arranged often as a miniature system of related cells with a few ornamental notes but the stress falling at different times on different notes in the cell; such a tune, taken from Rimsky's collection, was

*Ex. 10 The Rite of Spring* sketchbook

entered by Stravinsky on page 8 of the sketchbook (Ex.10). The opening
tune of *The Rite*, a Lithuanian song from a collection by Juszkiewicz, is
treated in precisely this fashion, though its fluidity of rhythm, which might
suggest the improvisatory style of an actual folk singer, is untypical of the
work as a whole. Stravinsky's real interest in these tunes lay in reducing
them to simple essences which could then be used as motives for rhythmic
and ostinato treatment. Often he will extract such an essence from a much
more elaborate tune. The 'Augurs of Spring' presents a string of these
ideas, combined with amazing resource considering the rather stiff rhythmic
context, itself untypical. But the technique only fully takes wing where
Stravinsky, perhaps following the instinctive practice of the peasant singer,
lets the barline fall, not according to a rhythmic schema, but as dictated by
added or subtracted melodic values. The best-known example of this, which
was analysed in detail by Pierre Boulez,[26] is the *khorovod* (round-dance)
tune of the 'Mysterious Circles', which has an irregular barring pattern
determined by the varying phrase-lengths of a strictly cellular tune (see
Ex.8 above). But there are other clear and beautiful examples in the 'Spring
Rounds' and the 'Game of Abduction', and an intriguing, ambiguous one
in the 'Evocation of Ancestors', where a two-note melody and irrational
barring counterpoint one another in such a way that it is hard to decide
which is the governing factor.

Stravinsky did not invent the concept of the added value (once again it
is found in Debussy), but it is in his ballets that it first assumed overriding
architectural importance. As an aspect of melody it breaks new ground
quite gently. But where its effects begin to be felt in music that is pre-
eminently rhythmic, the result is often drastically new and unexpected.
Such a passage occurs in the 'Game of Abduction', at fig.43, an isolated
appearance in this section of what will later be the main theme of the 'Game
of Rival Tribes'. The first two bars of the theme are melodically identical,
while the third bar, starting with the same six quavers, adds a seventh as
a kind of trigger to the continuation of the theme. It is hard to be sure
whether this added F sharp is essentially melodic or rhythmic in origin, but
there are strong contextual arguments in favour of rhythm. While the first
bar after 43 is superficially a simple bar of 6/8, the same as the preceding
music, it has an ambiguity in that the first four quavers tend to make two
identical pairs, and this veiled suggestion of 3/4 time is unveiled in the next

bar where the strings accent forcibly the start of each pair. In the sketch of
this passage the first figure is not repeated, but gives at once on to what
became bar 4 of the whole theme, unambiguously in 3/4; but in the light
of the final version the contrast here seems bland and even conventional.
By first moving towards a 2+2+2 and then interpolating a 7/8 bar in which
the added value shifts the crotchet pulse from the first four notes to the
last four, leaving the first three quavers so to speak stranded in their original
grouping, Stravinsky secured a much more dynamic pulsation, an effect
like a coiled spring which is then smoothly rolled out in the unambiguous
triple-time bar which ends the phrase (Ex.11). One should add to this

*Ex. 11 The Rite of Spring,* 'Game of Abduction'

analysis the observation that Stravinsky seems to have composed this
passage (along with the whole 'Game of Abduction') after the 'Game of
Rival Tribes'. There (fig.57+2) the music of bars 3 and 4 after fig.43 is
written as a 4/4 bar followed by a 3/4. with the first beat of the longer bar
a full crotchet. So the 7/8 bar at fig.43 must have emerged in Stravinsky's
mind as a discovery about a relation between the material in the 'Game of
Abduction' and a theme he had already composed, and the added value
was a step towards crystallising the connection, though whether or not we
hear it in that way with the music in its eventual order is a question of
psychology rather than analysis.

   In any case this concept of the variable-length cell underlies much of the
rhythmic innovation in *The Rite*. We can see from the sketches that Stravinsky thought of these cells as flexible musical objects which could take a
number of related forms, just as his melodic figures lent themselves to the
added or subtracted value. In the most famous of the dances in irregular
metre, the 'Honouring of the Chosen One' and the 'Sacrificial Dance', one
can tell at a glance how variations in the length of a motivic group – one
bar in the former, initially five bars in the latter – supply the desirable
instability of structure to match the instability in the groups themselves.
The cell technique is thus hierarchical; it works at all levels of structure.
Units of form can themselves be made out of a variable number of variable
cells. This temporal aspect of form is ofen very easy to 'read' on the printed
page, thanks to the changing density of notes. But there is equally a 'spatial'
aspect which is also very clear from the strip-like appearance of many
pages in the score, though it is not always so easy to hear. It comes from

Stravinsky's love of piling up his cellular motives into those great towers of strident sound which, together with the pounding rhythms, were the most provocative feature of *The Rite* to its early audiences. These sections, as is again evident from the sketches, were composed along empirical lines. Throughout the work, starting with the introduction, Stravinsky combined his ostinatos and motivic cells in mobile patterns whose changes were in principle determined by the different lengths of the cells, although as these lengths mostly seem to vary empirically the statistical character of the patterns, for instance in the 'Procession of the Oldest and Wisest', is no doubt an illusion. Clearly in such music he relied on his ear (as he later insisted, 'I had only my ear to guide me'). This is even more abundantly evident in the arrangement of formal elements. On the whole ideas seem to have come to him in isolation and without built-in implications about context or sequence. They have a jewel-like self-sufficiency. In working out the order of events, Stravinsky seems to have experimented with different possibilities, and sometimes actually composed the music in reverse. Nothing illustrates better the essential difference between this music and music of the classical symphonic type, in which so much hinges on sequence, contrast, and a logic of growth and resolution.

But if *The Rite of Spring* draws its energy from the repetition and collision of simple rhythmic and melodic cells, one might well ask what role is left for harmony, that traditional vehicle for musical argument. The answer must be, a much more restricted one, though perhaps not so restricted as in certain of Schoenberg's or Webern's atonal works of this period. Unlike Schoenberg, Stravinsky still favours the basic chord types of tonal music, above all the primary triad and the dominant and diminished sevenths. But he ignores their traditional functions, and he combines them in jarring complexes which in no sense figure in the vocabulary of tonal harmony. Allen Forte has shown, in a book devoted exclusively to this recondite subject, that *The Rite of Spring* is composed against the background of four related eight-note chords, and it is from them that it derives its unmistakable unity of harmonic colour (one of the chords is made up of the notes of Stravinsky's beloved octatonic scale, from which can be drawn four different dominant seventh chords on roots which between them produce a chord of the diminished seventh).[27] In other words harmony is a unifying or motivic element rather than a syntactic one, like the colour in a figurative painting. Even so it is misleading to deny *The Rite* all tonal functions. Schoenberg, after all, refrained consciously from the use of commonplace tonal chords precisely because he wanted to avoid their familiar implications. It is just as clear that in retaining these shapes Stravinsky accepted their inherited burden of meaning as part of their symbolism. Had he not done so, he would hardly have adhered to a kind of orchestral layering which not merely retains the chord shapes as they must have emerged under his hands as he felt for them at the piano, but actually in many cases emphasises them; an obvious example is the start of the 'Game of Abduction' (Ex.12).

A better explanation of Stravinsky's harmony perhaps lies in Pieter van den Toorn's concept of interference.[28] In this view, simple patterns on the surface of the music, such as for example the plain modal formulae which return again and again in the melodies, are complicated by the intrusion of background chromatic notes which belong not to the context of the simple pattern but to an enriched context which suggests the simultaneous operation of two or more such patterns. Van den Toorn cites the example of the Dorian mode (D to D on the white notes of the piano), which shares a scale of four notes with the octatonic scale, so that a fruitful ambiguity is available in Dorian music based mainly on those four notes (as folk tunes often are), as to whether the harmonies will be Dorian or octatonic. In the famous opening of the 'Augurs of Spring', the earliest part of the work to be sketched, the Dorian motive played by the violins pizzicato becomes a chord enriched chiefly by two notes which belong to the octatonic downward continuation of that scale: G (which turns the motive into a dominant seventh on E flat) and E (written F flat), which turns it theoretically into a dominant minor ninth on E flat in fourth inversion, a familiar rogue chord (it was officially disapproved of) in late romantic music. Stravinsky then interferes with this chord in turn by adding to the E the notes of its own simple primary triad, so that we end up with an unclassifiable chord with, nevertheless, a rich fabric of tonal and modal implications (Ex.13). This chord is a recurrent one in *The Rite*; its importance is proved by the fact that it is the 'base' chord of the 'Sacrificial Dance'. It is perfectly obvious, in fact, that Stravinsky found it by moving his hands, comfortably held, round the keyboard – found it, that is, and fell for it. In this sense it is a 'gem', like the other motivic cells in the score. But its biting ferocity comes as much from its tonal load of meaning as from its discordancy. We cannot argue, in the presence of so beautifully constructed a dissonance, that any old crash would have done just as well.

Throughout his career Stravinsky's judgement in such matters remained acute. Since dissonance in his music, unlike in Schoenberg's, is only incidentally a result of part-movement (counterpoint) but comes from decisions taken primarily on grounds of sonority, it often seems that success or failure with a work can depend for him on finding dissonant chord structures with the right profile and moreover on finding exactly the right instrumental colour, even though the chords will usually have been found at the piano. Precision of timbre is intimately bound up with precision of spacing. *The Rite of Spring*, with its quadruple woodwind, eight horns, five trumpets, and large battery of percussion and strings, was Stravinsky's last score for many years (apart from the completion of *The Nightingale*) for the expanded symphony orchestra that had become standard in the late romantic period, and in his next ballet the selection of instruments was to precipitate a crisis which would delay performance for eight years. Nevertheless, although the orchestration and chord-layering of *The Rite* have a certain deliberate

*Ex. 12 The Rite of Spring, 'Game of Abduction'*

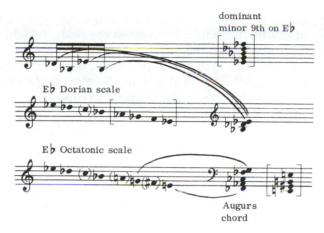

*Ex. 13 The Rite of Spring, 'Augurs of Spring'*

heaviness (there is no piano to provide the mordant athleticism of *Petrushka*), much of the elaborate internal detailing shows Stravinsky's characteristic concern for rightness of colour. This historically Russian trait, inherited from Glinka, comes out for example in the refined string divisi in the introduction to Part 2, the frequent use of multiple string harmonics to lend radiance to potentially turgid chord aggregates, and the care evidenced by the sketches for accurate choice of wind timbre. The solo wind writing, including for such at that time unusual instruments as alto flute or, most famously, high bassoon, is one of the most particular qualities of *The Rite*. But an even more distinctive aspect of this concern comes out in Stravinsky's extension of solo wind sound into the idea of group sonority, an application of Glinka's principle of unmixed colours to a music of dense polychords. There are lucid examples in the close-position trumpet duet in the introduction to Part 2 (which was first scored for clarinets), and the passage actually for clarinets in parallel major sevenths in the 'Mysterious Circles'. But much of the tutti writing is also characteristically built up out of family groupings, which help give the score its curiously layered appearance. Such groupings may be internally polyphonic: that is, they may consist of a number of independent lines forming a complex in a single timbre; or they may be homophonic, with new complex sonorities growing out of the familiar simple ones. In any case Stravinsky's frequent association of thematic complexes with discrete timbre groupings may well reflect the birth of his ideas under his hands at the keyboard. The remarkable thing is that music so intimately connected in origin with one instrument should eventually live so vividly in terms of others. A more startling contrast with the blended abstract sounds of classical music would be hard to imagine.

Not surprisingly instrumental sonority, the search for the right sound, played an increasing part in Stravinsky's music of the next few years. These works would inherit the energy and vitality, but not the violence or barbarism of *The Rite of Spring*. They would separate its radical elements of sound, form and rhythm from its expressionist elements, which, for all the shock waves they sent through the Théâtre des Champs Élysées on 29 May 1913, now seem comparable in their late-romantic extravagance to anything in Mahler or Strauss. Looked at in this way, *The Rite of Spring* seems like the collision of two epochs. When the smoke and dust cleared, very little was left of the older one.

# 4

## *Willing Exile:* The Wedding

The successful completion of *The Rite of Spring* presented Stravinsky with the first serious psychological challenge of his career. This work, and to some extent *Petrushka*, established a manner so powerful and distinctive, and so apparently rich in possibilities, that one could imagine it providing the impetus for a whole series of further works, as it in fact did in the music of other composers. But Stravinsky seems to have had an immediate intuition that *The Rite* was an end rather than a beginning. Certainly he would hardly wish to abandon the startling technical discoveries he had made in relating the raw materials of this piece to its finished architecture. But the surface extravagance of the music, its heavily matted textures, its sense of inhabiting only the strangest and most remote regions of experience – these were crypto-romantic elements which had little or no part to play in the music that was already germinating in Stravinsky's mind. So it is not surprising that the one score he worked on after *The Rite* in which these elements do to some extent survive gave him difficulty and in the end came out as something of a hybrid.

As we saw in Chapter 2, Stravinsky had completed the first act of *The Nightingale* in 1909 before starting work on *The Firebird*. But the opera had then been shelved during nearly four years of dizzying change in the composer's style and artistic horizons. It does appear that, immediately after the first performance of *Petrushka* in June 1911, Stravinsky conceived a plan for finishing the opera with the help of Benois, the scenarist and designer of *Petrushka*.[1] But this seems to have come to nothing for another two years, presumably because he became intensely preoccupied with *The Rite of Spring*, to the exclusion of all other projects. Thus when Alexander Sanine wrote to him in February 1913 announcing the formation of the Moscow Free Theatre and commissioning a three-act work from him on the theatre's behalf, Stravinsky offered him *The Nightingale* in its short one-act form, without even mentioning that it was incomplete. After more correspondence he agreed to write the further scenes obviously required by Andersen's tale, in return for what he later called an 'unrefusable fee' of 10,000 roubles.[2]

Bearing in mind that the first act belonged to Stravinsky's saturated pre-*Firebird* period, one can well imagine that the prospect of returning to it from the acerbities of *The Rite* inspired in him mixed feelings. Moreover, there was the problem of writing 'descriptive music', to which Stravinsky had supposedly objected at the time of *The Firebird*. With the ritual austerities of *The Wedding* taking shape in his mind, it must have been hard to address himself to the elements of simple melodrama in *The Nightingale*, such as the chorus of spectres in Act III or the dialogue between Death and the Nightingale, while the more decorative parts of the scenario – the Emperor's porcelain palace with its festoons of chinese lanterns, the mechanical nightingale. the funeral cortège for the supposedly dead Emperor, the general air of glittering chinoiserie – have next to nothing in common with the single-minded plainness and directness of the settings in *The Rite of Spring* and *The Wedding*.

Stravinsky approached the problem by way of a fairly detailed revision of the first act, a revision designed as far as possible to paper over the inevitable differences in harmonic and orchestral texture between the old music and the new. For instance, in the Fisherman's Song he thinned the harmony and converted it by subtle changes of detail into a colouristic added-note texture instead of one governed by chromatic part-movement – a significant change because this song is the only music which returns substantially in the later acts (the Nightingale, by contrast, having quite a new repertory for her appearance at court and her contest with Death). At the same time he modified the scoring towards a more precise, needlepoint articulation. But none of these adjustments seriously disguise the change in style that anyone will notice at the start of the second act, the so-called 'Draughts' entr'acte ('Courants d'air'), with its abrasive octatonic harmony, its strident scoring with piano (an instrument only added to the score for the first time in 1913), and its agitated ostinato rhythms – a kind of chinoiserie transcription of the background rhythm in the 'Augurs of Spring'. This movement sets the tone for the more astringent music of the rest of the opera. Yet curiously enough the later acts of *The Nightingale* are not harsh in the integrated manner of the other works of this period. The modernisms of harmony have a picturesque quality, and never quite escape the confusion between the exotic, the barbaric and the merely whimsical. For instance, the 'Chinese March', to which the Emperor is carried in on a palanquin, builds up a densely-layered texture that plainly descends from similar pile-ups in *The Rite of Spring*; however, its elements are not themselves 'raw', but belong to a familiar world of artificial chinoiserie, to which the *meccanico* treatment that is part and parcel of Stravinsky's technique adds a faint flavour of mockery. In the same way the sliding chromatics of the Nightingale's song to the Emperor carry a label of 'true sentiment' that is neither more nor less impressive than the label of 'false sentiment' borne by the Japanese toy nightingale, with its up-and-down pentatonic scales, in the manner of Ravel's 'Laideronette'. In all this music Stravinsky seems to have been drawing with conscious artifice on materials to hand, and the music shows little trace of creative impetus, even in the 'death' scene of the last act, which Stravinsky himself considered to contain the best music in the opera. On another occasion. however, Stravinsky implied a preference for the first act, 'which is at least operatic, whereas the later acts are a kind of opera-pageant ballet'.[3] When in 1917 Diaghilev asked Stravinsky to extract a ballet from the opera score, the composer duly concentrated almost exclusively on the music of the later acts, with their predominance of orchestral music which, however, he considerably rescored.

*The Nightingale* remains something of an oddity in the Stravinsky canon, and although it had distinguished admirers (among them Bartók and Ravel) this perhaps reflects the decorative charm of the whole conception, including no doubt Benois's designs for the original Paris production with their rich colour symbolism, as much as any very forceful originality in the music. Certainly the work has little to do with Stravinsky's creative direction after *The Rite of Spring*. Even in its 'modernised' form, the exoticism and sumptuous play of musical colouring belonged precisely to that world out of which the Diaghilev ballets grew, and which Stravinsky's next works showed him anxious to put behind him. Already the works he wrote in 1914 display a studious dryness and severity which irritated many of those who prided themselves on having absorbed the modernism of *The Rite of Spring*. It seemed at the time (and for long afterwards) that Stravinsky could not be wholly acquitted of wanting to *épater le bourgeois*, and this became the convenient explanation for the many seeming changes of direction with which he continued to annoy historians of the modern movement. However, a careful examination of the history of the key work of this period, the ballet *The Wedding*, shows that Stravinsky was responding, at first uncertainly, to a specific creative need. It took him ten years to discover the final form of this work, of which four were spent (intermittently) on composition and the remaining six on finding the right instrumental sound. In other words the essential austerity of the music was a quality that even Stravinsky himself did not at first grasp, though there are regular intimations of it in the much smaller pieces to which he kept returning, and which gave him his experimental basis.

These small works are a distinctive feature of what came to be known as Stravinsky's Russian period. In the years just before, such miniatures as he had written had been a side issue – a relaxation from the major work of the day. But from 1913 until the completion of *The Wedding* in 1923 the small pieces are central; they contain many vital innovations, and are of the highest quality as art. It is easy enough to see the reason for this shift in emphasis. Most of the technical innovations in *The Rite of Spring* had to do with detailing and the way in which fragments of musical language are put together into sentences and paragraphs. So it was natural that, in discarding the expressionist apparatus of *The Rite,* Stravinsky should be left juggling with the bits and pieces of a still partially decomposed syntax. His recourse to miniaturistic writing under these circumstances recalls the experience of other composers at about the same time – for example Webern, and also Schoenberg whose *Pierrot lunaire* may have encouraged Stravinsky in this type of work. But for Stravinsky the miniature was not so much an admission of inarticulateness as a direct reflection of his artistic interests at the time. In July 1914 he made what was to be his last trip to Russia for almost half a century, visiting his summer home in Ustilug and the city of Kiev, where according to Craft he bought some books of Russian folk poetry, including a volume of wedding songs recently published as a supplement to the nineteenth-century collection of Kireyevsky.[4] From Ustilug he doubtless collected his own copies of Kireyevsky and the tales of Afanassyev; returning to Switzerland by train, he re-read the satirical nonsense poems of *Kozma Prutkov,* with such enthusiasm that he at once suggested to Benois a new collaboration based on a part of the collection (Benois reacted coolly).

This sudden and intensive interest in folk poetry, genuine and fake, looks like the final crystallisation of a tendency which had been at work in Stravinsky since his studies with Rimsky-Korsakov. Many of these stories and poems he knew already. The early song, *How the Mushrooms prepared for War* (1904), contains lines from Kireyevsky,[5] and we have Stravinsky's testimony that at that time he had also made settings from *Koz'ma Prutkov.* Somewhat later he dabbled in the pseudo-ethnic symbolism of Gorod-yetsky. But the re-readings of 1914, together with the music which came out of them, suggest a much more thoroughgoing idea of what folk subjects might offer to a regenerate art. Not only was this material fresh, lively and authentic – a distinctive Slav voice speaking to the half-unwilling Russian exile – it was specifically anti-intellectual and irrational, and hence answered Stravinsky's own reaction against the rational syntactic values of the European musical mainstream. Its emotional world, in which personal feeling is distanced into a general or ritualised expression, must also have been deeply sympathetic for a composer in open rebellion against the extravagances of romantic music. Finally, the rigidly patterned verse-refrain forms and incantatory repetitions common to all genuinely ancient folk poetry will have suggested formal procedures remarkably close to those Stravinsky had already begun to evolve in his recent music. The fact that most of the poems he set at this period have some nonsense element should not blind us to Stravinsky's overriding need for an architectural framework for his ideas.

The new direction is apparent in two short works composed in the spring and summer of 1914: the Three Pieces for string quartet and the *Pribaoutki* for voice and eight instruments. The first substantial work on *The Wedding* also dates from this time. Stravinsky maintained that the project had been in his mind for more than two years, awaiting only the right text and the physical opportunity for work on it to begin in earnest.[6] But after the first performance of *The Rite* he was laid up for several weeks with typhoid (like many people who live a very long time, Stravinsky was repeatedly ill as a young man), and was then for some months engaged in the difficult task of completing *The Nightingale*. During the autumn of 1913 he wrote the charming cycle of Three Little Songs with piano now usually known by their subtitle 'Souvenirs de mon enfance', whose pithy style and acid harmonies already look forward to, without yet wholly adopting, the fragmented 'pribaoutki' manner. But even these are arrangements of songs written some years before. Stravinsky remembered playing them to Rimsky-Korsakov, and the tune of the final song is prominent in the finale of the Symphony in E flat. As for definite new projects, 1913 was fallow.

The next year soon made up for that. In the first of the quartet pieces Stravinsky launches into an experiment which shows that he was completely aware of the implications of his recent music. Here a rigid pattern of (3+2+2/4) bars is laid over a strictly recurring twenty-three-beat tune (the bars being marked by a cello ostinato), so that their changing relationship is governed primarily by the pre-compositional scheme. The only subsequent decision is when to stop, which Stravinsky does apparently arbitrarily after six beats of the fifth statement of the tune. Apart from the viola's ostinato Ds, the only other element is the second violin's four-note descending quaver scale, which also seems to cut in arbitrarily in a changing but this time irregular relationship with the fixed elements. Stravinsky seems to use this figure as a marker for the duration of the piece. Its occurrences, though not mathematically regular, drift back according to a noticeable pattern towards the beginning of the main tune, and when the two coincide Stravinsky takes it as a cue to stop.

Such a description naturally sounds unpromising, and Eric Walter White tried to defend the music against traditionalist criticism by suggesting that the point only became clear when Stravinsky published arrangements for orchestra and gave titles to the pieces, thus making their graphic intentions plain.[7] But this seems far-fetched. The musical point of the first piece could hardly be clearer anyway. Two or three related ideas, all based on three- or four-note modal scales but in different keys, are thrown into collision in such a way that any audibly regular relationship between them is avoided. Stravinsky called the piece a dance (it was known as such by his friends even before it was played), but if a graphic image is wanted, a good one might be that of a permanently revolving target (the main tune) at which the second violin hurls missiles, always hitting it at a different point until it eventually stops it by hitting it on the head. This kind of mechanical game-playing suggests Satie. But where Satie's anti-structural music (at least before 1917, when he wrote *Parade*) usually has a satirical tendency, Stravinsky's is much more in the nature of an independent 'act'. Everything about the first quartet piece is sure and self-contained. Stravinsky chose the simplest possible ideas, or cells, simply repeating them with unpredictable accents and articulations and so placing them that sparks will fly when they bang into each other. This idea of friction also underlies the other two pieces. In no.2 Stravinsky relies just as heavily on boldly delineated profiles (the piece is variously said to have been inspired by a clown called Little Tich and by a female dancer on horseback; in the Four Studies it is christened 'Excentrique'). The first profile is based on the grinding mechanical repetition of two chords, which are indeed the same chord in two different inversions, with two semitone clashes built in; and much of the subsequent figuration, including the little 'sur la touche' tune, and the characteristic grace-notes and ostinatos, persists with the idea of semitonal displacement. The abrupt alternation of material is also, naturally, an aspect of the music's friction, though it will be noticed that the many different barrings and 'movements' are linked, in theory at least, by a single unit pulse. The extraordinary final piece, an antiphon-like chant which later became 'Cantique', goes to an extreme in its dependence on the composer's feel for the spacing of discords. Each chord in this entirely homophonic piece contains a semitone clash displaced by an octave, but the chords, though all closely related, go through a series of minutely subtle alterations, like perspective changes in a slowly rotating sculpture. Stravinsky remained intensely proud of this piece, and understandably so since it shows, as much as anything he ever wrote, how a creative presence can be established in a single sonority, once the ear no longer expects the sounds to behave according to any conventional syntax. There are isolated examples of this in his earlier work: for instance, the famous 'kiss of the earth' string harmonic chord in *The Rite of Spring* and certain chords in *Zvezdoliki*. But this 'Cantique' is the first piece to chance everything on that sense of discovery-in-sound which was to be so crucial for his later music.

The same quality is important in the *Pribaoutki* though slightly less weight is placed on it. The compound semitone, which clashes with the octave of the note rather than with the note itself, is again the vital sonority in all four songs, and it is the very first sound we hear, just as it is the first sound in the quartet pieces, and later will be the first sound in *The Wedding*. Since Stravinsky is now writing accompaniments to a vocal line, he avails himself of rather more variety of colour (flute, oboe, clarinet, bassoon, string trio and double-bass), and – a characteristic and brilliant discovery – he extends the idea of the clashing 'octave' into a polyphonic effect in which the voice is doubled at the seventh or ninth instead of at the octave or unison. For instance, in bar 3 of the first song 'Kornilo' the viola doubles the voice's G-E flat-F with F-D-E. Asafyev called this kind of doubling a chroma and related it to the traditional peasant technique of heterophony in which everyone sang slightly different versions of the same tune, starting and finishing on the same note but with individual variants in between. Using the term fairly loosely Stravinsky's Russian-period vocal settings are heterophonic in this sense. The secondary lines 'colour' the tune, and are not necessarily to be understood as independent counterpoints.[8]

Stravinsky composed these tiny masterpieces in August and September 1914, and they were thus the first direct musical outcome of his visit to Russia in July and of his re-reading of Kireyevsky and Afanassyev. Their generic title, *pribaoutki*, describes a type of verse which crops up a good deal in Stravinsky's songs of this period, and even provides a framework for the stage entertainment, *Renard*. A *pribaoutka* is a saying, but more specifically a popular rhyme; Stravinsky compared it to the limerick, but a much closer parallel would seem to be with the rhyming games that are found in all languages ('There was an old woman who swallowed a fly/I don't know why she swallowed a fly/I think she'll die' etc.). Such games above all embody the sheer pleasure, enjoyed by adults as well as children, in making language dance to one's tune. Sometimes the result is nonsense, but of a just meaningful kind: 'There was an old woman who swallowed a horse/She's dead of course'. The third poem in Stravinsky's *Pribaoutki* is like this; the poem is an alliterative joke (every word begins with 'p'), and to keep up the alliteration the quail is subjected to an improbable series of accidents, ending with its falling through the ice and being caught by a priest called Pyotr Pyetrovich. In Russian, one further aspect of word-play, peculiar to that language, is involved in such verse: the practice of ignoring natural word-stress, which is extremely emphatic in normal speech, in favour of internal rhymes or other verbal jokes. In *Expositions and Developments* (p.121) Stravinsky wrote that 'the recognition of the musical possibilities inherent in this fact was one of the most rejoicing discoveries of my life; I was like a man who suddenly finds that his finger can be bent from the second joint as well as from the first.' He does not tell us when he made the discovery, but it was in any case implicit in much of the music he had composed before 1914. The thrown accents in *The Rite of Spring* show an intuitive fascination for the idea of playing on the listener's sense of regular rhythmic pattern, while the asymmetrical relation between melody and barring in the first of the Three Pieces for string quartet leads to an exactly similar punning on melodic stress, if with a less clear distinction between the right stress and the wrong. It is the matching of this general procedure to the more precise either-or effect of variable word-stress that leads through *Pribaoutki* to the splendid word-music of *The Wedding*.

The *Pribaoutki* themselves are tiny pieces, and their content is humorous, but they are not for that reason trivial. The distinction between the earnest and the frivolous was a typical romantic prejudice which has persisted to some extent into our own day but has little basis in common experience. Stravinsky practically never made it. He shared, it seems, the feeling that we love those with whom we laugh, that laughter is a faculty which takes us close to the profoundest springs of our common humanity. One has only to compare the vividly humorous solemnity of *The Wedding* with the embarassed politeness of the average modern middle-class wedding to see what this means. The *Pribaoutki* too have their solemnity. They are, in feel, not folksong settings at all, but acts of identification with the spirit out of

which the poems grew, and from this they derive that sense of ritual re-
enactment which gives them their artistic intensity. An essential basis of
this feeling is a certain formality in the treatment. Each song apart from the
third (whose alliterations demand a unified form) is in two contrasted parts,
each part brief, concentrated and with a studiedly precise arrangement of
its components. In the first song, part 1 depicts Uncle Kornilo's journey to
the pub: we hear the jingle of the harness and the churning of the wheels;
while part 2 takes us into the pub, where uncle is already putting it away
with a steadiness that is evidently habitual.[9] But this simple portraiture is
expressed in musical terms of an almost constructivist precision. The vocal
line of part 1 is a fourteen-beat melody on a five-note diatonic scale, rising
and falling to a cadence on the pivot-note E flat every seventh beat – the
whole melody then repeated once. As in the first quartet piece, the barring
is strictly arranged on a 3+2+2 grid; but to evade the regularity this might
impose, Stravinsky shifts the whole melody sideways by two beats (to the
right), so that what ought to be the last two crotchets of the whole tune
come at the start and the tune is left hanging at the end, ready for part 2
(Ex.14). But the melody can be further broken down into one-bar cells, each
with a return to E flat, arranged in the sequence ABCDBCABCDBC, each
cell having its own proper accompaniment which always goes with it (so
the barlines express the cellular structure). In part 2 there is again a diatonic
melody, more regular in design but with an irregular repeat, cadencing
now on D, which becomes a rather slurred D flat and then C in the bibulous
coda. The whole song lasts about forty-five seconds. Moreover the sense
of single revolving images is so strong, and the ease with which Stravinsky
could have extended his design so obvious, that his refusal to do so itself
seems like an aspect of the music's wit.

In the other two-part songs, the second parts are essentially illogical in
their relation to the first. In 'Natashka' the sudden talk about farmyard
animals seems studiously irrelevant to the seemingly imminent seduction
of the eponymous heroine, as if her mother had come unexpectedly into

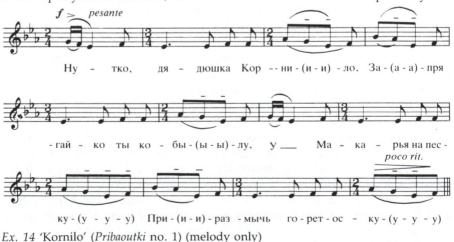

*Ex. 14 'Kornilo' (*Pribaoutki* no. 1) (melody only)*

the room. In 'The Old Man and the Hare' the man simply gibbers at the hare's request for gruel, the poem having presumably become too absurd for any imaginable 'sensible' completion. Stravinsky again takes the poems entirely on their own terms, with true Russian respect for apparent lunacy. When the ducks and cranes appear in the poem of 'Natashka' they do so in the music too. The ducks play *dudki* (bagpipes) like the old men in *The Rite*, presumably because 'utki v'dudki' rhymes nicely, and the wind scoring here is as colourful as any even in that work. Similarly the old man's ravings are supported by a deadly serious ostinato for pizzicato strings, and oracular flourishes on the bassoon. The two parts of this song provide the clearest possible illustration of Stravinsky's new formal economy. In the first part, which sets the scene, the singer 'improvises' in peasant fashion on a four-note scale (tetrachord) of the Aeolian mode on A, while the violin interferes with this scale with its G sharp in a way that suggests instead the octatonic scale on A – the bassoon's low F belongs to either scale (Ex.15). Once established, these tonal materials remain constant until the second part; they are both the 'idea' of the first part and its colour, a sort of prismatic modern reflection on a timeless scene. In part 2 there is an abrupt shift in the voice to the Aeolian scale on D, again interfered with by the notes of the octatonic scale on the same root, while the A, carried over from the first part but belonging neither to the Aeolian tetrachord nor the octatonic scale on D, lends a more decisive tonal impetus which is matched by the sudden ostinato movement. The A descends each time to the D, like a dominant to its tonic, and the sense of closure, or finality, this gives might reinforce the sagacity of the old man's teaching if it were anything but pure nonsense. Instead the song returns poker-faced to its opening music for a coda, fracturing the solemnity of the scene only with its very last gesture where the note F sharp, heard literally for the first time in the song, intrudes a harsh cackle – the one self-conscious moment, perhaps, in the whole cycle.

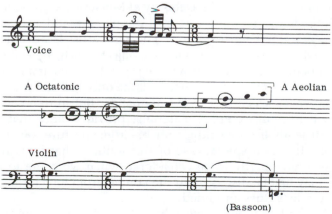

*Ex. 15* 'The Old Man and the Hare' (*Pribaoutki*, no. 4)

A crucial point about these songs is that the constructivist principles they embody are not purely and simply a function of their ethnic subject-matter, but are a stylistic or expressive aspect of the composer's response to it, just as the cubism in Picasso's *Demoiselles d'Avignon* is brought by the painter to the subject (however wary we may be about the chronology of the relation between style and content in such cases). Although Stravinsky worked these ideas out for the most part in works on Russian peasant subjects, at least until the completion of *The Wedding*, he was already in late 1914 applying them to material of a completely different kind, having in common with the Russian pieces only a derivation from popular or demotic genres. In November he composed the Polka which appeared as the last of the Three Easy Pieces for piano duet, and which he himself later claimed as marking the birth of neo-classicism.[10] It was quickly followed by the March and Waltz; and if a line can be traced from the *Pribaoutki* through *Renard* and *The Wedding*, so there is a line joining the Three Easy Pieces to *The Soldier's Tale* and the Octet.

All these works invite our appreciation in the light of some associated style or genre with which we are presumed familiar. The Polka, for instance, with its absolutely unvarying oomchah bass (the easy 'left-hand' of the subtitle) would be incomprehensible unless we understood implicitly its irony at the expense of an idiom whose banality was all the more for its modest pretensions to a subtlety Stravinsky studiously avoids. In this sense the easy pieces, as well as the dances in *The Soldier's Tale*, derive not so much from any inchoate neo-classical principle, such as came to be associated after the war with the return to ordered formal techniques, as from the obsession with popular styles which runs through the music of the early 1900s, from the Chat Noir pieces of Debussy and Satie to the German *Überbrettl*, not to mention the somewhat different associationism of Ives and Mahler. In general this popularism sprang doubtless from some feeling that art in the romantic era had become too detached from common life, too idiosyncratic and too esoteric. But pieces like Debussy's 'Minstrels' suggest also a fascination with the immediacy and colour of popular art, and a weariness with cerebral processes and introspection. The new artist is an onlooker who transfigures what he sees into a symbolic object which, by some alchemy, avoids the ephemerality of what it symbolises. If he turns first to the popular or commonplace, it may be because it is at once the simplest and least personal matter on which he can lay his hands. But in due course he can apply himself to more complex materials, provided only that they have acquired sufficiently fixed meanings for his ironic posture towards them to be noticeable. It is as a special case of this attitude that Stravinsky's neo-classicism will have partly to be considered when we come to it. But the easy pieces may first be discussed in the context from which they emerged, that of Stravinsky's Russian period.

Technically the two types of work have a good deal in common. All the keyboard pieces, including the slightly earlier *Valse des fleurs* (September

1914), the *Valse pour les enfants* (1916) and the Five Easy Pieces (1917, for duet with 'easy right-hand') use mechanical ostinato accompaniments often surprisingly like the ones in the Russian songs, as can be seen by comparing the March in the Three Easy Pieces with the second part of 'The Old Man and the Hare' (Ex.16), or the Andante in the Five Easy Pieces with 'Kornilo'. Some of the pieces, like the Waltz and the Polka (which the composer said was inspired by the idea of Diaghilev as a circus ringmaster), are jokes at the expense of the kind of mechanical writing Stravinsky himself had experimented with in the Three pieces for string quartet, or a *reductio ad absurdum* of the cell technique in *The Rite* or *Pribaoutki*. Stravinsky wrote out his *Valse pour les enfants* using an alphabetical short-hand for the fixed elements, and he might have done the same in the first part of 'Kornilo' (as Boulez in fact later did in his cellular analysis of *The Rite of Spring*).[11] But some of the pieces are more serious stylisations. The March, for instance, seems to attempt a fresh imaginative perception of the nature of march music, and though it is very witty it also satisfies the conditions of a rather weighty account of modernism, such as Herbert Read's characterisation of the two tendencies in Cubism, 'one proceeding towards a fragmentation of perception and a reconstruction of form according to laws of the imagination; the other towards a "realisation" of the *motif*'.[12] The breaks in duple time in the March are not a satire against its marchness so much as imaginative intensifications of it; the displaced accents are comparable to the varied syllable stresses in the Russian works. Moreover it is no accident that this is harmonically the most complex of the Three Easy Pieces. The ostinato chords interfere with the tonal fanfares in the melody, just as in 'The Old Man and the Hare' they interfere with the Aeolian tune; and incidentally there are numerous Russianisms in the march tune, like the descending modal cadence from A to D, which echoes the one in the *Pribaoutki* song.

We should not conclude from this that Stravinsky's Russian songs are in any sense neo-classical prototypes. The referential, ironic posture of the easy pieces, the ragtimes, and the various phases of the neo-classical period, typifies the composer-as-exile and is lacking in the Russian pieces which, though written in exile, draw profoundly on native experience. This ironic character is typical of Parisian music of the time. It figures constantly in the piano pieces of Satie, to whom, significantly, Stravinsky dedicated his Waltz. 'Satie teaches our epoch the boldest thing of all,' Cocteau later wrote, 'how to be simple. . . . It is the poetry of childhood reblended by a technician.'[13] But in truth the description fits Stravinsky better. It is in his pieces that we find that sharpness of image refracted on to oblique planes that so pungently expresses the anti-sentimental feeling that Cocteau saw as the spirit of the age. In the Waltz and Polka the routine accompaniment and the conventional tune we are initially led to expect provide an unambiguous background against which the unexpected angles of the melody make their point. In the Five Easy Pieces, where the untutored player has the melody line, the tunes are mostly diatonic and the refraction, which varies in degree from piece to piece, is in the accompaniment – which again suggests the procedure of the *Pribaoutki*. As it happens the Five Easy Pieces are themselves national, rather than salon, stereotypes. The 'Española' is a most subtle parody of complex Spanish rhythms, which carries syncopation and hemiola to the point where the underlying pulse is sometimes completely obscured. In this it looks forward to the *Piano Rag Music*, where in much the same way rhythmic ambiguities are exaggerated to the point where they obscure their original context. The simpler pieces in this set seem to enshrine some mysterious principle of Stravinsky's art. The 'Balalaika', with its multiple repetitions of a plain C major melody, looks quite uninteresting on paper but fascinates in performance, perhaps through its constantly varied phrase lengths. Still more intriguing is the Andante which opens the set. An air of the surreal hangs round its derisory folk melody, with its suggestion of some unrevealed action 'beyond the scene', in Edith Sitwell's phrase. Later in 1917 Satie's ballet *Parade* was staged by Diaghilev in Paris, in which the action presented on-stage is finally revealed as a mere trailer for an unseen show of . . . what? The same air of enigma invades the simple repeated patterns of both Satie and Stravinsky, as if the emotion and meaning so studiously excluded by 'the spirit of the age' were still hovering just out of sight, waiting for the opportunity to get back into the act.

In 1917, too, Stravinsky completed what we know as the first version of *The Wedding*. He had written the libretto and some of the music three full years earlier in July 1914, a month before starting the *Pribaoutki*, and there is every reason to suppose that he could have gone on to compose the rest of the music, without much delay, had circumstances been propitious. The technical means in the songs, despite the small canvas on which they are deployed, ought to have made them an adequate study for the ballet, though it remains possible that Stravinsky was still uncertain how such methods would work in a twenty or thirty minute score. In any case much of the first tableau was drafted by November 1914,[14] parts of the score were played to Diaghilev in February and April 1915, and work continued on it throughout the rest of that year, alongside a handful of further settings in the manner of the *Pribaoutki*: the brilliantly concentrated *Cat's Cradle Songs*, with their ornate vocal figuration so close in manner to parts of *The Wedding*, and the female partsongs 'The Pike' and 'Puzyshche' or 'Mr Paunch' (eventually nos. 3 and 4 of Four Russian Peasant Songs), whose vigorous rhythmic chanting suggests that they may indeed be based on material discarded from the ballet.

But the continuing war, which had effectively trapped Stravinsky in western Europe (he spent most of it in neutral Switzerland), was already beginning to threaten his livelihood, and now forced him to shelve *The Wedding* in favour of more immediately lucrative work. In January 1916 he started work on *Renard*, to a commission by Princess Edmond de Polignac,

*Ex. 16(i)* March (Three Easy Pieces, arranged as no. 1 of Suite No. 2 for small orchestra)

*Ex. 16(ii)* 'The Old Man and the Hare' (*Pribaoutki*, no. 4)

and when this was finished, in September, he at once accepted Diaghilev's commission for *The Song of the Nightingale*. Not until the spring of 1917 was he able to return to *The Wedding* and complete (in October) the first version of the score. None of these works, incidentally, were performed until the war was over: *The Song of the Nightingale* in 1919, *Renard* in 1922, *The Wedding* in 1923. And this accident of history certainly influenced the way their music was heard in the early 1920s, by which time Stavinsky's direction had radically changed. Asafyev's study, published in Russian in 1929 but soon suppressed and not translated until after the composer's death,[15] was unusual for its time in recognising the major significance of these wartime theatre pieces and their exact place in Stravinsky's development. The tendency in Stravinsky's own aesthetics of the 1920s was so much away from the particularity of the Russian works and towards a kind of abstract universalism, perhaps influenced by contemporary French thought, that it is hardly surprising if his Western admirers gave less attention to the comparatively little performed works of the period just before that transition.

  *Renard* is nevertheless the climax of that phase in which Stravinsky effectively remade his musical language along radical lines that broke with all recent musical tradition while establishing the mature details of Stravinskian style. From a technical point of view it no doubt simply transfers the various melodic, rhythmic and colouristic processes of the songs on to a larger canvas. But for Stravinsky the architect and dramatist this was a major step. From the point of view of modernism, *Renard* was crucial because it showed that the new music need not be inhibited in scale or scope by its rejection of all the well-tried mechanisms for writing music of 'stature'.

The original Polignac commission, as early as 1912, had referred to a short instrumental work for some thirty players (Stravinsky agreed to write 'a fifteen-minute concerto'[16]). What emerged was something very different: a play with music, 'histoire burlesque chantée et jouée', for four male singers and fifteen instrumentalists. Once again Stravinsky found his material in Afanassyev (not of course in Aesop or Lafontaine). But as with the tale of Petrushka, he chose to distance the story somewhat by presenting it in a frame. In his version, the tale of the Fox, the Cock, the Cat and the Ram is imagined as being acted by a troupe of travelling minstrel-buffoons (*skomorokhi*) in a 'pre-Petrine village'.[17] And it is the presentation of this show, in this context, which, as in *Petrushka* but more completely, is the work's real subject-matter.

Why was Stravinsky so preoccupied, in these Russian works, as well as in later dramas like *Oedipus rex* and *Persephone*, with 'frames'? It is possible to blame the growth of a new kind of sterile scholarly culture in which the artist and his audience, having lost their own potent feeling for art, are reduced to a voyeuristic ogling at the performing rituals of earlier times. However, we should perhaps first recognise this trait of Stravinskian theatre as another sign of his debt to the Russian symbolist movement, and especially to the post-symbolist theatre of Vsevolod Meyerhold. Too little has been written about this connection,[18] and at no point in his reminiscences of his early life in Russia does Stravinsky mention that he met Meyerhold or was familiar with or influenced by his work. Nevertheless, since Meyerhold's early career reached its height in St Petersburg in 1906–7, and since the great director worked closely with such leaders of the symbolist movement as Blok and Bryussov at a time when Stravinsky was also living in St Petersburg and friendly with Gorodyetsky, it seems likely that he was aware of the new temper Meyerhold was bringing to the Russian theatre of the day. Under the influence of the symbolists Maeterlinck and Fuchs, Meyerhold rejected the current conventions of stage realism and envisaged a production style in which the sole aim would be to realise the hidden or inward sense of the action. At first (and later, in the post-revolutionary Soviet theatre) he experimented with severely restricted gesture, a reduced stage and highly abstract design and lighting.[19] In due course he incorporated certain artifices from ancient popular theatre, including the use of masks to signify 'the emotional self-control and physical dexterity that enable the actor to assume the various aspects of his part, "to manipulate his masks", and at the same time to comment – both implicitly and explicitly – on the actions of himself and his fellow-characters, thereby affording the spectator a montage of images, a multi-faceted portrait of every role.'[20] 'The new *theatre of masks*', Meyerhold himself wrote, 'will learn from the Spaniards and Italians of the seventeenth century and build its repertoire according to the laws of the fairground booth, where entertainment always precedes instruction and where movement is prized more highly than words.'[21] Meyerhold used music to impose a rhythm on his productions, and he seems to have approved Fuchs's contention that acting originates in dance. The influence of these ideas can already be traced in *Petrushka* and in *The Nightingale*, of which indeed Meyerhold was responsible for the first Russian production (after the failure of the Moscow Free Theatre), in St Petersburg in 1918. But it comes out most markedly in the dramaturgy of *Renard* and *The Wedding*, with their repertory of stylised techniques, including dance, mime, a fluid relation between the singers, the dancers and the action, an atmosphere of what Fuchs called 'festive ritual' and (in *Renard* at least) the 'abrupt changes of mood, the sudden switches of personality, the deliberate disruption of illusion, the asides to the audience.'[22]

The frame is thus part of the ritual character of the action and at the same time a way of evading the facile naturalism of the conventional stage. Although the story of the cock being enticed down from his perch by flattery is universally familiar, Stravinsky does his best to obscure any simple meanings which might reside in the general outlines of the fable. On the one hand he pointedly renounces any conventional one-for-one relation between the actors (or dancers) and the singers, who are conceived as part of the orchestra. On the other hand he endows the story with purely local and remote symbolisms which are most unlikely to be directly apprehended by a modern Western listener. Thanks to the work of Russianists like Karlinsky and Russell Zguta[23] we now know something of what these are. We understand that the *skomorokhi* were originally pagan priests who, in Christian times, adopted the subterfuge of teaching through entertainment, as a result of which they were persecuted by both the church and the state until, in the mid-seventeenth century, they were finally outlawed altogether. So *Renard* as acted by these mendicants becomes an anti-clerical skit in which the peasantry are literally preyed on by a vulpine nun (because in Russian 'fox' is feminine), a version of the story recorded by Afanassyev as 'The Fox Confessor'. But while Stravinsky was obviously fascinated by such details, it does not seem that he regarded them as essential to a grasp of the work since he did nothing to explain them at the time, so far as we know, and then later half-forgot them, if Karlinsky is to be believed when he points out the ways in which the conversations with Craft falsify the ethnic background to the Russian works. What seems to have counted most with Stravinsky was the spirit of a completely authentic world given him by Afanassyev's tales, working in conjunction with his own childhood memories of what old rural Russia was like. It must suddenly have struck him that all the sentimental, patronising, theorising, self-centred falsehood of romantic folk-revivalism had been swept aside by a vision with a more

powerful inner truth. But *a fortiori* he must not muddle himself up with
that truth and become a kind of modern Childe Harold wandering disconso-
lately in the Abruzzi of Russian history. Instead he would clinch his detachment from his subject-matter by placing it in a frame which explicitly
excluded both the artist and his audience from any facile self-identification,
while re-involving them through the deeper symbolism of the total work.
In this sense the work becomes a ritual act, but one that is continually
revitalised by the creative energy of the composer's vision.

Although the writing itself is graphic and tightly linked to the stage
action, a certain formality of design is evident from the start. Points of
similarity to Aristophanic comedy are worth noticing, especially bearing in
mind the supposed origin of Greek comedy in a semi-ritualistic masquerade
known as *komos*, which itself had a popular history not unlike that of the
theatre with which Meyerhold associates himself. *Renard* has both a parodos
and an exodos (entry and exit of the chorus), an agon, or dispute between
the protagonist and antagonist, and even a hint of parabasis, in which the
chorus draws the audience's attention to the meaning of the story. The
agon, the cock's seduction from his perch by the fox, is in fact presented
twice, the second time with a more catastrophic ending, and the parabasis
such as it is follows each time. Stravinsky, with his acute intuition for
form, singled these sections out but called them *pribaoutki*, and indeed any
moralising tendency they may show soon dissolves into nonsense. Leaving
aside the question of form it is very obvious that the singers' role is to some
extent like that of the Greek chorus, in that they sometimes participate in
the action but at other times step outside it. Moreover the vital dance
element, and the way this is linked to verbal rhythm, reproduces a central
feature of Greek comedy. The essentially coarse nature of the action and
the satirical use of animal masks as a thin disguise for topical reference
are also Aristophanic traits, even if they came to Stravinsky by way of
Meyerhold.

According to the composer, 'as I started to compose the music [of *Renard*]
I discovered that my text was too short. I then conceived the idea of
repeating the "salto mortale" episode . . . this repetition was a most
successful accident, for the reprise of the form is a chief element in the
fun.'[24] The symmetries, that is, do not work against the spontaneous vitality
of the action, but actually enhance it, just as the repetitive, alliterative and
in other ways patterned elements in the tiny *Pribaoutki* are a basic part of
their comedy. The first part of *Renard* to be composed was in fact the closing
vocal section, which Stravinsky labelled 'Pribaoutka Gospodi Pomilui' ('God
have mercy'), and which builds up a brilliant climax on the basis of ostinato
and repetition, on a scale similar to that of the *Pribaoutki* themselves. By
placing the second agon, or 'action', with its slightly less frenetic music, in
front of this Stravinsky produced a larger form along the basic two-part
lines of 'Kornilo' or 'The Old Man and the Hare', a form which he then
doubled in size by the procedure already noted. Finally he added the

opening and closing march as processional music for the actors. Described in these terms, *Renard* emerges as the prototype for a number of procedures which later became clichés of the genre known as music-theatre; one notes, for instance, the importance of Greek dramatic form in the somewhat Stravinskian theatre music of Birtwistle, and of the processional idea in Britten's church parables. Its formal and statuesque elements are likewise revealing in view of the overt preoccupation with such things in Stravinsky's own neo-classical works.

However the music of *Renard*, which still strikes one after seventy years as unbelievably fresh and original, is as far as can be imagined from neo-classicism, at least in outward effect. It has an abrasive, flamboyant vitality which can only be related to its ethnic subject-matter as refracted through the idiosyncratic style of the *Pribaoutki*. Here, as there, the core of the music is the melody made up of short, irregular cells shuffled into apparently random sequences and laid over barrings whose own sequence, though often regular in itself, contradicts the melodic stress. Such passages are interspersed with another type of music, no less rhythmic, where strict, regular repetitions are insisted on with the swirling flourish of acrobats and jugglers. The entrance march, with its ABA form, presents us with both types. The introductory 'choral' section, which I have compared with the Greek parodos, favours the underlying regular quaver ostinato (after a curious initial hiccough which Stravinsky corrects with a 5/8 bar), given variety by a changing texture of ostinato patterns in the upper instruments and by vivid contrasts of colour. The ensuing 'agon', with its mock-plainsong for the fox disguised as a nun (and singing in whole tones) is a good deal more fluid, until the first *pribaoutki* section, after the fox has been chased away by the cat and the ram, when the strict but unevenly barred chattering quavers of the introduction are resumed. This contrast of movement is intensified the second time round. The fox, having abandoned his disguise, no longer sings in plainchant, but instead has a wheedling song in falsetto in which he tries to tempt the cock down by offering him food (the implication is still that it is heavenly indulgence which is on offer, and the music does not quite lose its ecclesiastical tone). The attempt is repeated, and there are two verses to the song. The vocal refrain, though based on a single figure and always coming to the same strongly emphasised cadence, changes in length and also in its relation to the viola's demisemiquaver ostinato, so that what feels at first like a mechanical scheme of repetitions is in fact considerably varied, while its most decisive gesture, the melodic and rhythmic cadence, is both comically monotonous and at the same time irregular in spacing. After the second *salto mortale*, the cock struggles to the same music as before (this is the most extended recapitulation in the work); but there then follows an inserted episode, in which the cat and the ram sing a 'nice little song' to the accompaniment of a gusli (or Russian psaltery) to entice the fox out of hiding, before the final *pribaoutka*, more vigorous than the first and to new material.

The rhythmic language of *Renard* is essentially that of the smaller songs, but the treatment is very much bolder, more daring, and quite simply more extreme. The essence of the work is movement of the most boisterous kind; but it sustains interest not so much through the physical excitement of repetition (though there is plenty of that) as through a consistent teasing of the listener's expectations of crude regularity, a process in which the various passages of regular motion play their part of course. Asafyev (p.116) gives a valuable example of this, which also illustrates how Stravinsky's rhythmic practice reflects (or else prompts) his interest in variable word-stress. At the start of each of the two 'actions' the cock sings the same melody to the same words, with a fairly even stress (though related to the half-bar rather than the bar). But in the second action, when the fox tries to tempt him down with peas, he sings the same tune a tone higher and with the pulse distorted by the additional syllables of a new text (Ex.17).

Ex. 17 *Renard*                                         (stress shown by acute accents)

However, Stravinsky in this new phrase does not observe the natural stress of the words so much as impose an artificial stress of his own choice; so it seems that to a Russian listener the previously regular figure is doubly refracted. This kind of distortion is continuously noticeable in *Renard*, with or without knowledge of the language.

Throughout, Stravinsky uses instrumental colour to underline his rhythmic effects, and it is this usage, rather than harmonic or contrapuntal thinking, which makes *Renard* such a complicated score. Indeed the music is practically devoid of harmony in the conventional sense. Even where there is something like block harmony, as at bar 21 in the entrance march, the supporting notes are heard as harmonics, or in Asafyev's phrase 'chromas', of the melody, giving the sound something of the quality of an organ mixture – an effect Stravinsky used again, in a more thoroughgoing way, in the *Symphonies of Wind Instruments*. Many of the vocal sections can be reduced to melody-plus-ostinato, or even just plain melody, as in the passage between bars 55 and 62, where the ostinato notes all double the vocal melody, in various octaves. Even quite complex-looking and sounding passages can be reduced in this sort of way. *Renard* has its own technique of *Klangfarbenmelodie*, or tone-colour melody, with melody notes doubled in different octaves and on different instruments, so that the line takes on a prismatic quality, but not quite as in Schoenberg or Webern since Stravinsky usually maintains the binding stepwise motion of folksong in at least the vocal part. In any case the concept of melody plus rhythmic accompaniment, so basic to folk music, remains paramount as it does also in *The Wedding*.

In instrumentation alone *Renard* is one of the most inventive of scores, its bizarre repertoire of sounds standing in sharp contrast with the hieratic austerity of the final version of *The Wedding*, if not with the original 1917 version. Stravinsky must have drawn his inspiration for this from many sources, some of which are documented. In January 1915 he heard, by chance, the cimbalom player, Aladar Racz, performing in a Geneva restaurant, and he was so taken with the instrument that he got hold of one, taught himself to play it and even, he tells us, composed *Renard* 'at' the cimbalom just as he usually composed 'at' the piano.[25] There is a cimbalom also in the first version of *The Wedding*, no less than two cimbaloms in its second version (1919), a cimbalom in *Ragtime* (1919), as well as much evidence of the influence of the instrument, which is played with two sticks, in Stravinsky's piano accompaniments of this time, especially in the Four Russian Songs with piano (1918–19), the last of which also survives in a version with cimbalom. In *Renard* the cimbalom is used to suggest the gusli, not only in the passage where the ram plays that instrument, but throughout the score, its plangent tone contributing much to the music's village-band flavour. Indeed the *Renard* orchestra has a good deal of the 'band with the curious tone' about it. The brass writing is overtly rustic; Stravinsky excludes the trombone but manages to imitate it when necessary by doubling horn and low trumpet. And the strings almost never play lyrically but instead contribute a variety of wheezing harmonics, dry, whirring ostinatos, and articulative pizzicati. The cimbalom is also used for punctuation. Its flourishes introduce each of the 'actions', just as the side-drum prepares the cock, circus-fashion, for his *salto mortale* – a reminiscence of the fairground drum in *Petrushka*. Perhaps the circus-band itself was in the composer's mind, for instance in the march, with its thumps on the cymbal and bass drum.

As a conception in sound, *Renard* is an intermediate stage in Stravinsky's development of that hard, diamantine sonority which became so characteristic of his music in the post-war years. The 'objectivity' he was to aim at in the *Symphonies*, the *Octet* and the *Piano Concerto* is still tempered by the decorative exuberance which is found also in the contemporary songs, and which expresses the music's closeness to its peasant roots. The exact significance of this can perhaps be better grasped through a comparison with the first sketch-draft of *The Wedding*, which Stravinsky completed about a year after *Renard*. Here a comparatively large orchestra, but still with solo strings and a prominent cimbalom part, gives graphic, painstaking expression to the rustic ceremony and the verbal-rhythmic detailing of the voices. That Stravinsky never fully realised or authenticated this draft is a great shame, since it surpasses the final version in sheer beauty and refinement of sound. But his search for a drier, more austere concretisation of the music seems to have been connected with his wish to move away from the particular connotations of peasant culture towards a more lofty, universal embodiment of the ideas that that culture had triggered in his mind. It is surely no accident that the four-piano version of *The Wedding* only emerged at a time when Stravinsky was formulating his early neo-classical works, with their architectural approach to orchestration, their 'play of movements and volumes'[126] and their open hostility to nuance and 'expressiveness'.

None of this is yet apparent in the remaining Russian songs and choruses composed during and just after work on *Renard* and *The Wedding*. Certainly they continue the reductive tendency of the *Pribaoutki*, but in the manner of studies or sketches, with an essentially specialised aim. For example, the four tiny *Cat's Cradle Songs*, written in 1915 during work on *The Wedding*, are wonderfully intimate studies in melodic ornamentation, in the folksong manner, with an accompaniment for three clarinets which essays a stylised form of heterophony. The choice of clarinets was perhaps determined by the idea of making the instruments sound like extensions of the voice (which would therefore be, for preference, a mezzo-soprano). The Four Russian Peasant Songs for unaccompanied female chorus, on the other hand, are exercises in vocal dance music with a shifting pulse based on the same principle of a movable word-stress that we have already seen in *Renard*, and that plays such a vital part in *The Wedding*. A good example, obvious even to non-Russian speakers, is the changing emphasis on the title word of the second chorus 'Ovsen', which looks forward to Stravinsky's well-known equivocation on 'Oedipus' in *Oedipus rex*. The Russian subtitle of these choruses, *Podblyudnye*, was incidentally translated by Stravinsky as 'Saucers', but Karlinsky corrects this to 'dish-divining songs'. In his account of the original custom:[27] 'a large dish filled with water was put on the table and each participant would place her ring, comb or some other small trinket in it, after which the dish was covered with a towel. Next came the singing of the *Podblyudnye* (lit., 'in the presence of the dish') songs, whose texts dealt with allegorical descriptions of agricultural activities, gigantic symbolic animals, and possession of gold, jewels and other treasures. Most of these songs featured the obligatory refrain of 'slava!' or 'slavna!' ('glory!' or 'glorious!'). During the singing, the trinkets were extracted one by one from under the towel over the dish and the fortunes of their owners were predicted in accordance with the imagery of the line that was sung while it was withdrawn.' A glance at Stravinsky's choruses will show how closely they fit this description, and it is a distance not much greater to the more elaborate and formal superstitions of *The Wedding*. One could well imagine Nastasya Timofeyevna, the bride in that work, deciding whom she should marry by just this method, if we did not know that her marriage was arranged by the 'cruel, heartless matchmaker'.

A number of songs with piano also date from the time when Stravinsky was again preoccupied with *The Wedding*, and it is fascinating to observe in these, alongside the cimbalom influence already mentioned, many indications which with hindsight we can see pointing towards the final keyboard version of the ballet. The tremolo accompaniment to the second of the *Three Tales for Children* is so close in texture to several passages in *The Wedding* that one can hardly believe it took Stravinsky another five years to settle on this colouring for a score which, in 1917, still had only a minor part for piano. There are further indications to the same effect in the first of the Four Russian Songs, another nonsense-song about ducks, and in the counting-game of the second song. Here there seems no doubt that the unbarred tremolo and glissando writing comes from Stravinsky's improvisations on the cimbalom; and whereas the *Three Tales* are to some extent retreading old ground, musically the Four Russian Songs, written in 1918–19 after *The Soldier's Tale*, seem like an attempt to guide the Russian idiom into new and more complex territory. The rhythmic experiments now have an almost recondite appearance, of which the frequent abandonment of barring is perhaps a symptom, and there is a new asperity in the modal clashes between voice and accompaniment, as well as untypical clutter in the instrumental sound. It may be said that Stravinsky, though he composed *at* the piano, was not always at home composing *for* it. In the curious 'Sectarian Song' which ends the cycle, he several times breaks away from the keyboard in flourishes which seem additional to the basic accompaniment, and indeed an autograph fair copy of this song exists with an obbligato part for flute. Craft, quoting the many pages of sketches Stravinsky made for the piece, suggests that its music derives from a thirteen-note palindrome, which might account for the rather crabbed quality of the music's *facture*.[28]

Throughout this time the problem of *The Wedding* continued to preoccupy him. Although it seems as if it was above all a problem of sonority, what was really at issue, as I have already suggested, was the exact aesthetic focus of the music. This will become clear if we briefly examine the history of its composition. According to Craft, the earliest sketches date from 1913.[29] But the bulk of the early composition was carried out in 1914, at which time Stravinsky envisaged the ballet as 'Songs and dances on Russian folk themes, for voices, woodwinds, brass, percussion, plucked and bowed instruments'. Craft further tells us that 'the plucked instruments were to have included balalaikas, guzlas [*sic*], and guitars' and that the ballet was conceived on realistic lines, as an authentic rendering of a peasant wedding, complete with individualised portraits of the bride and groom, the best man, the minstrels (*skomorokhi*), and a great deal of detailed action.[30] The later history of *The Wedding* is the history of the gradual abandonment of this graphic scenario in favour of an increasing stylisation. As early as November 1914, when he drafted much of the first tableau, Stravinsky may have realised the need for a more formalised approach, and he must have done so by 1915, when most of the score was written in its first version; it seems likely that the dissociation of the singers from individual roles in *Renard* was merely the continuation of a practice evolved for *The Wedding*, while the statuesque nature of *Renard* almost certainly reflects a stage in the evolution of the ballet.

But Stravinsky took much longer to adjust his conception of the sound-picture of *The Wedding*, and it is not hard to imagine why. It seems certain that strong impulses towards new works were nearly always accompanied for him by specific images of sonority;[31] in the case of *The Wedding* we know that he was partly inspired by the sound of the bells of St Paul's Cathedral in London, but it is also fairly clear from the original constitution of the orchestra as well as from the use of the chorus that particular wedding noises were in his mind from the start: the plangent, mistuned twanging of the peasant orchestra, the chanting of the priest. It was his search for a modern orchestral equivalent of this tintinnabulation that for years stood between him and a realisation in sound of the ritual elements towards which his scenario had moved and which were finally clinched by his own changing aesthetic posture after the war. Hence his original idea of bala-laikas and guslis, and the prominence given to cimbalom, harpsichord and pizzicato strings in the first nearly complete draft of 1917. In 1919 he experimented with the improbable combination of pianola, harmonium, two cimbaloms and percussion, an ensemble which reflects his growing interest in mechanical, non-gesticulatory performance while still capturing (or endeavouring to capture) the jangle of the peasant orchestra. He scored two of the four tableaux for this band, and also, if his recollections in *Expositions and Developments* (p. 118) are to be trusted, tried 'to combine pianolas with bands of instruments that included saxhorns and flügelhorns'. As late as March 1921, having realised the difficulty of finding one, let alone two, good cimbalom players, he seems to have contemplated substituting no fewer than four pianolas, with harmonium and percussion, but soon gave this up as uncoordinatable. He then reverted briefly to a version with wind instruments before hitting, probably early in 1922, on the idea of using four pianos and percussion but without the dulling effect of the harmonium. In an interview with *Musical America* published in January 1925 he made the significant comment that 'I did not want anything so human as violins', and in *Expositions* (p. 118) we find him apostrophising his *Wedding* orchestra as 'perfectly homogeneous, perfectly impersonal, and perfectly mechanical'. The peasant band has now, it may be thought, made way for a typical neo-classical abstraction.

But as so often with Stravinsky's pronouncements on music, his terms are misleading. The final orchestra is not un-human, but it avoids the sentimental associations of strings. At the same time, by abstracting from the specific sound of the peasant band which may first have inspired the music, it opens the way for a transfiguring of this highly particular and esoteric ceremony into a universally moving work of art. The vital catalyst is the sound of bells, one of the work's earliest inspirations and, in the final version, a pervasive symbol of the lofty character of the proceedings, however ribaldly they may be expressed. With all their beauties, neither of the surviving earlier versions begins to capture this image, which is such a feature of the final score.

*The Wedding* took longer than any other work by Stravinsky to reach a final form, so it is perhaps not surprising that it is something of a hybrid, inhabiting many genres at once and resonating on many planes and in many different ways. Stravinsky called it, in the end, 'Russian Choreographic Scenes' and it was staged by Diaghilev in 1923 as a ballet, with the voices in the pit (as in *Renard*) but the pianos on-stage in the manner of an alienating or illusion-breaking device, in the Meyerhold tradition. As a choral work, it naturally has features of a cantata. But as Asafyev rightly insisted, the spirit of movement and gesture is so vital to it that the cantata as such is incomplete (the same can be said, of course, of Stravinsky's other theatre works). The point about this, however, is not that the scenario is simply built round a sequence of wedding dances like the Act III finale of *The Marriage of Figaro* (it is not), but that the dance flows inexhaustibly out of the ritual action itself, expressing its excitement and joy. So the choreography, and *a fortiori* the music, are noticeably detached from the action implied by the words – the ethnic detailing and general ribaldry – and instead represent the hidden meaning of what is being enacted. It is this absence of any purely superficial relationship between the wedding conventions and the music which describes them that accounts for the work's extraordinary complexity and richness of feeling, despite its apparently simple materials.

Stravinsky adapted his text from Kireyevsky (with its supplement), taking, according to Karlinsky, 'not a set of songs to be set to music, but a complete script of a ritual that was actually a folk play'.[32] In other words the action of *The Wedding* is not a unique drama, but a prescribed ceremony as carefully laid down as any Western church service. What we are witnessing, so to speak, is *the* Russian peasant wedding (though this is an exaggeration, as there were obviously variant ceremonies) but presented to us as a unique occasion, since the bride and grooms are named. The ceremony is thus a 'frame' in the same sense as the *skomorokhi* performance in *Renard*. This wedding is a nominally Christian affair: saints are invoked, and the Virgin Mary summoned to the aid of both bride and groom. However, we do not witness the wedding itself, which takes place in church, but only the preliminaries in the bride's and groom's houses, and the marriage feast culminating in the ritual bedding of the newly-weds. Nearly all the action is pagan and ritualistic, in the sense that, while it obviously carries weight for those taking part, it may be that they could not explain if asked why these things have to happen as they do: why the bride must have her hair plaited before her wedding, why the groom's hair must be curled, why the mothers have to lament that their children 'have forgotten the golden keys', why the parents must sit on guard outside the bed-chamber. Stravinsky himself was impatient of explanations: 'the bride weeps in the first scene not necessarily because of real sorrow at her prospective loss of virginity, but because, ritualistically, she *must* weep',[33] though indeed even Western brides habitually cry, and usually at moments in the proceedings which suggest that in any case Stravinsky's rejected explanation is the wrong one. Loss of virginity is, after all, merely a symbol of the whole 'catastrophe' of marriage (or at least it used to be). *The Wedding* derives its solemnity exactly from this sense of crisis formalised through the participation of the whole community, while the ritual character of the drama emphasises the cyclic nature of these events. Confronted with Asafyev's interpretation of *The Wedding* as a death-and-rebirth fertility rite, Stravinsky apparently gave vent to a flurry of abusive marginalia.[34] Yet the reading seems obvious enough and perfectly satisfying.

It reminds us moreover that *The Wedding* was conceptually Stravinsky's next large work after *The Rite of Spring*, whose fertility symbolism is explicit. Despite the evident differences between the two masterpieces, a preliminary comparison between them is well worth making. Both are ritual dramas about the preparation of a young girl, in the presence of her elders, for a 'sacrifice' in the interests of fertility; in Gorodyetsky's 'Yarila' the chosen ones are actually seen as brides of the tree on which they are to be killed. Choreographically both ballets are designed as sequences of ritual 'acts', each with its own interior mobility but, seen as a whole, statuesque and self-contained like stations of the cross.[35] Within these acts, the music is a tightly organised network of repeating melodic and rhythmic cells, again often violently energetic but rendered formally statuesque through repetition offset by almost instantaneous shifts of 'position' – a tendency more marked, however, in *The Wedding*, where there is practically no conventional sense of climax, notwithstanding the orgiastic spirit of the final tableau. Both are, of course, folksong works, and in so far as they are motivic this can be traced as much to their characteristic reliance on the modal tetrachord (or four-note scale) as to traditional thematic workmanship, though at the same time both scores use cyclic elements: that is, the return of notable themes in different parts of the work. Finally both ballets are non-harmonic, in the old sense of harmony. There is no harmonic syntax, but instead a series of planes or fields of activity which serve partly to define structure, though apparently not to promote it in any organic sense. Harmony, in Stravinsky's hands, assumes a powerful symbolic role, and in these Russian works especially, whole sections may be underpinned by no more than one or two distinctly profiled chords. In *The Wedding* he achieves an 'emancipation of the dissonance' more thoroughgoing than Schoenberg's, since with Stravinsky individual chords, whether consonant or dissonant, are endowed with an autonomy quite independent of contrapuntal or motivic considerations.

Taken as a musical entity, *The Wedding* belongs clearly, with the *Pribaoutki*, the Three Pieces for string quartet and the other small works of 1914 and 1915, to Stravinsky's post-*Rite* austerity drive. Even in its more fully scored first draft, it has none of the cumulative weight and density of the earlier ballet, none of its conscious barbarism or exotic cultivation of the violent and strange. In place of these qualities, it offers a certain controlled intimacy, a sense of bawdy humour, and an almost homely ordinariness, elevated into ritual. The more one tries to describe the sheer plainness of *The Wedding* in words, the duller it is likely to seem. Yet it would be hard to find a work of art less dull or commonplace. In reducing the elements of his style to the barest minimum, Stravinsky placed nearly total reliance on the two parameters for which he possessed a unique instinct: colour (both of timbre and chording) and rhythm. But where *The Rite of Spring* had laid stress on rhythm as something extraordinary and sensational, *The Wedding* asserts the normality of rhythm as a medium for musical expression and structure. It says, in effect, that since music is before anything else movement, movement on its own can be used to convey the subtlest inflexions of which music is capable. This may seem a routine observation, but it is one which even twentieth-century music, with its frequent concentration on rhythmic constructs, has often failed to understand. So much of the music of our own day, including pop and jazz, has seen rhythm as an emphasis on the purely animal (or, alternatively, as a medium for *denying* contrast or change), that it is still something of a shock to experience music which treats rhythm as a vehicle for refined, intellectual and subtly emotional utterance.

One other factor contributes to the purity of effect which *The Wedding* shares with the songs, and perhaps not with *The Rite of Spring*: its unusual conciseness of form. Everything here is on the most economical scale. Repetition, which had been used in *The Rite* for, among other things, sheer barbaric emphasis, now serves mainly to establish the basis for variations of internal detailing; the cumulative power of the repetitions in the earlier ballet gives way to a terraced arrangement of short, incisive musical gestures depending mostly on contrast, and with only a discreet intensification towards the end of the work. In this, the text is obviously crucial, since its layout determines the changes of movement and focus in the music. As in *Renard* there is something of the architectural planning of Greek drama, with its formal contrasts between dialogue and choral narration or invocation. But a comparison nearer home might be with the ritual dialogue which we associate with church services. Both the music and the ceremony of the Orthodox Church were a significant influence on *The Wedding*, and though not much of it sounds like what most of us would call 'church music', the form of the work is highly suggestive of a religious ceremony in which dialogue and drama have simply been stereotyped into a series of fixed exchanges.

This is very striking in the first tableau. After the Bride's opening invocation to her tresses, she engages in a verse-antiphon sequence with the female chorus, in which her role is to lament the tying of her hair while theirs is to enact it. The sequence is twice interrupted by repeats of the invocation, always sung by the bride – Stravinsky indicates this in the score, except at the very start before curtain-up, which of course suggests that the stage directions may be meant to refer only to the visible action. The solemnity of the dialogue is greatly intensified by the obvious derivation of the music from liturgical chant. Until fig. 9, where the first structural change takes place, the vocal lines consist of inflected monotones, and the only fundamental difference between them and liturgical intonations lies in the regulated pulse of Stravinsky's music, written for dancing. But at least one Soviet scholar has pointed out the similarity of Stravinsky's irregular groupings of twos and threes to the natural rhythmic stress of plainsong, with its tendency to stylise verbal accents into patterns of alternating duple and triple rhythm.[26] Curiously Kholopova cites the 'Evocation of ancestors' section of *The Rite of Spring* as an instance of this in Stravinsky, though she might well have preferred the opening of *The Wedding*, which not only demonstrates such patterns arising out of actual word-groupings, but at the same time shows him typically playing on the natural stresses by moving the barline in unexpected ways. The choral section at fig.2 is one of the best examples in all Stravinsky of this kind of rhythmic punning. The passage is dominated by the word 'pochessu' ('I will comb'), and especially by its second and third syllables, which, with the occurrences of the related word 'chessu' ('I comb'), occur altogether five times in the musical sentence (up to fig.3). The text itself meanwhile falls into three phrases of, respectively, eleven, twelve and thirteen syllables. As the basis for his setting, Stravinsky observes both the syllabic scheme, with exactly one quaver per syllable, and a regular stress on the key word, which he invariably accents aberrantly on the 'che' (note the percussive underlay on the first two occasions, and the rise in pitch on the third). But the barring contradicts these groupings by preferring a scheme of 6+6+6+5+6+6+1 quavers, which amounts to an established 6/8 pattern with one shortened bar, and the final quaver serving as downbeat for the next bar (not included). The rhythmic consequences of this apparently trivial change are momentous. Since the first two lines of text are 11+12 but Stravinsky's barring suggests 12+11, the first 'che' of the second line of text – which was previously a downbeat – becomes a musical upbeat (the last quaver on the second 6/8 bar), still accented, however, by its higher pitch, by an actual stress-mark, and above all by the chordal attack on the four pianos (Ex.18). The same sideways shift of the barline, a device we have already encountered in several Stravinsky works, produces a similar ambiguity on the second syllable of 'pochessu' in bar 3 of this section. Metrically it is now on a weak beat but still stressed by the scoring. The regular verbal stress is thus only one of several rhythmic patterns which Stravinsky keeps in play simultaneously. Each pattern has its own rationale, and it is the variety of agreement or disagreement between them which gives the music such extraordinary elasticity.

Although not every section of *The Wedding* rests on ambiguities of this kind, they typify its spring-heeled vitality as a whole. The shortened-bar principle operates at the start of the second tableau as well. In the third bar one of the quaver Ds is simply discarded to fit the verbal metre, and the accent over the second D shows that Stravinsky considers that the missing quaver would have been the second in the bar, a fact to which, however, the ear is unable to adjust as fast as the music, so that a momentary uncertainty arises which is only resolved by the strong downbeat of the next bar. Here the bar-lengths are straightforwardly set by the shapes of the vocal figures. At other times the composer had changes of mind on how best to bar the music. The new theme at fig.41 in the second tableau was quite differently barred in 1917 (the final version appears in the 1919 draft), and it is hard to see at first glance why one barring should be preferred to the other (Ex.19). Originally Stravinsky barred at the top of each melodic phrase, while in the end he settled for a grouping which recognises the strength of the crotchet notes. But neither barring is really consistent, and one is tempted to conclude that the latent ambiguities of such a passage are so numerous that any barring would vulgarise it. A notation based on some sliding scale of stress values would come closer to the musical reality. But of course the best answer of all is musicianly performers.

The insistent quaver articulation of these rhythmic episodes, with their predominantly syllabic word-setting, is typical of *The Wedding* as a whole, as it is of the quicker passages in *Renard* and the Russian songs. It establishes a norm for much of Stravinsky's later music, and is the basis of the so-called 'motor' rhythms of his neo-classical works, though its use is too subtle in the Russian period for any such term to be appropriate. Here instead the persistent quaver unit lends itself to the idea of the added or subtracted values by which Stravinsky varies the length of his rhythmic/melodic cells. The fact that it also suggests the normal syllabic practice of ecclesiastical chanting, as well as the pounding steps of peasant dance, merely goes to emphasise the multiplicity of levels on which this music works. Against such episodes Stravinsky deploys his slow music with typical economy but to overwhelming effect. The abrupt cut-offs in the second tableau to allow the bridegroom to implore his parents' blessing in the manner of a priestly organum addressed to the throne of God (unaccompanied in the true Orthodox style); or the short coda to the third tableau where the two mothers lament the loss of their children, rocking between A and B flat as if in a trance; or the invocatory coda to the last tableau, in which to the chiming of bells Fetis Pamfilyevich exorts his new wife to live with him in happiness 'so that all men may envy us' – these are among the profoundly solemn moments of twentieth-century music. Perhaps significantly, it was these two last codas whose timing gave Stravinsky the most

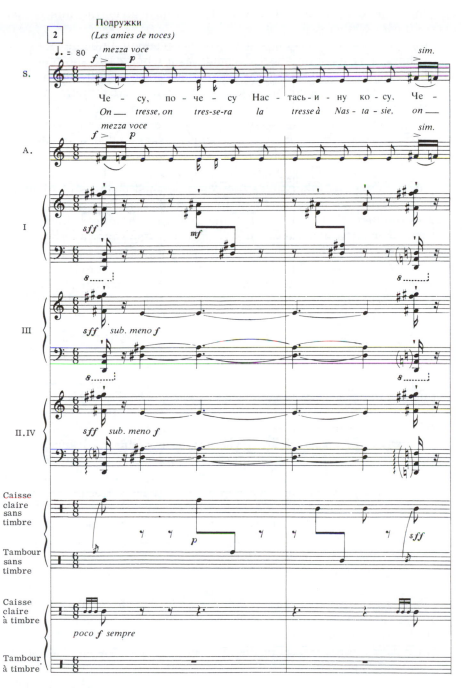

*Ex. 18 The Wedding*

1917 draft

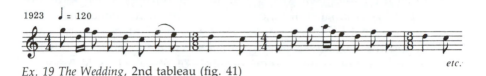

*etc.*

1923 ♩ = 120

*etc.*

Ex. 19 *The Wedding*, 2nd tableau (fig. 41)

trouble, and both were lengthened between 1917 and the final version (they do not figure in the partial 1919 draft): in the first case by delaying the start of the coda, and in the second by physically extending it. As Asafyev rightly pointed out, this closing 'prayer' is above all a signal of the creative act, which all await in stillness and a spirit of awe. The emblematic pealing of bells echoes Nastasia's first lament for her tresses. More generally, the bells are a summons, a call to participation, much as bells have always been in religious ceremonial. They denote the beginning of the ceremonial act and its consummation.

This brings us back to the whole question of Stravinsky's instrumentation, and the nature of his accompanying of the voices. *The Wedding* is best described as an interplay of words, melody and rhythm. Possibly it was the first accompanied vocal work on any scale since Bach's motets in which there is no music for instruments alone (overlooking, for the purposes of this generalisation, the last twenty-one bars of the whole score, and a few downbeat strokes here and there earlier on). In the final version the accompanying harmony, which displays much of the characteristic compound-semitone dissonance we have noticed in other Stravinsky works of the period, feels like timbre-colouring, in much the same way that the many internal harmonics of large bells serve chiefly to colour their sound. And it may well be that Stravinsky's final decision to use pianos and percussion was influenced by the variety of bell-like tones that such an ensemble can produce. Yet oddly enough the harmony in the first orchestral draft is essentially the same as in the final version. It consists almost entirely of rhythmic ostinatos of varying complexity, together with instrumental lines radiating out from the vocal melody, either by way of direct doubling, or in parallel chords, or contrary motion, as at the start of the second tableau. This is closer to Asafyev's idea of 'chroma'. A few arpeggio figures which look purely pianistic in the final version turn out to have 'originated' on quite other instruments: for instance, the accompaniment at fig.103 in the last tableau was scored in the first draft for bass clarinet. On such occasions we are far from any bell or indeed any other percussive sonority. Bells are suggested at certain points by cimbalom or bright metal percussion such as triangle or cymbal. But there are many fewer such instruments in the 1917 band (no crotales, no tubular bells); there is no xylophone, the single piano doubles harmonium, with its tendency to muddy the texture, and the more plangent harpsichord is prominent.

The obvious reason for all this is that Stravinsky as usual composed the score at the piano, instinctively orchestrated it in his mind, and only later realised that the piano itself was best at those colourings which were most important in his original conception, even if it could not equal the variety or subtlety of the 1917 orchestra. So the hard, brilliant bell sounds were restored, and the harmony made again subservient to colour. In this final version, the harmony is an extreme example of Stravinsky's technique of interference, combined with simple or complex parallelisms. The opening invocation is an elaborate exercise in instrumental doubling, but with a D sharp (at the octave) added to the first melody E and subsequent melody Ds. At fig.1 the lower pianos add an ostinato vibration, not at the fifth above or below the tune, but at the tritone which divides those two intervals; at fig.2 the loud D major 'marker' chords are complicated by added G sharps and F natural, while the held chords are D sharp/A sharp against the chanter E. None of these effects are harsh in the manner of the similar spacings in *The Rite of Spring*, perhaps because the voices mask the clashes, or perhaps because of some tendency in the piano's resonance to soak up its own dissonance. The effect is rather of a prismatic harmony similar to that which we noted in the *Pribaoutki*: a flat modal colour split on to two divergent planes. The two planes can still be seen as those of the pianist's two hands placed, so to speak, out of alignment, as in *Petrushka*'s fanfare motive. Here, however, the whole work is based on such divergences, which range widely in type and richness, though always remaining subservient to the vocal melody, with its clear-cut modalities and strong pivotal notes. To some extent Stravinsky can avail himself of the eight independent hands of his four pianists. But in fact the pianos mostly double one another in pairs, adding weight and resonance to each other's effects but seldom enriching the harmony beyond what the ear can reasonably perceive. The percussion, on the other hand, is of the dry, clear, articulative type, with only the xylophone, sparingly used, timpani and the single tubular bell giving pitched notes – usually doublings.

Although others among Stravinsky's theatre works have enjoyed greater prestige – *Petrushka*, *The Rite of Spring*, *The Soldier's Tale*, *Oedipus rex*, *The Rake's Progress* – *The Wedding* is in many respects the most radical, the most original, and conceivably the greatest of them all. Musically it comes at the start of his headlong break with romanticism; it fulfils all the architectural, rhythmic and harmonic implications of *The Rite of Spring*, with much greater economy than that work and in terms of a subject-matter that is, when all is said and done, more genuine and more subtly moving. Admittedly its Russianism, allied to an autochthonous text which, Stravinsky always insisted, must remain in its original language (though his own recorded performance is alas in English), introduces an esoteric element which is present in *The Rite* as well but inessential to its enjoyment. Aspects of *The*

*Wedding* will perhaps always escape the Western listener, even if we ever mature to performances in English or French which translate the full audacity of the bawdy humour in its final tableau. In this respect it forms a group with the other Russian-text pieces of the immediately post-*Rite* years, including *Renard*. But most art, and perhaps all theatre, has its esoteric side; what Englishman can fully understand Ibsen? And music transcends such barriers in any case, as recent performances of *Renard*, *Mavra* and the songs have shown.

In the case of *The Wedding* special pleading is unnecessary, since Stravinsky himself sought to universalise the work both by the treatment of the subject and through the music. As drama, *The Wedding* perfects the idea of ritualised action, so that while we shall not ourselves ever be married in the fashion it depicts, we enter readily into the archetypal spirit of this stage wedding – more readily, no doubt, than into that of many real-life weddings, let alone the paste-board ceremonies of nineteenth-century opera.

As for the music, *The Wedding* was the culmination of Stravinsky's evolution of a new language stripped of the sensationalism to which music had recently been prone, and stripped also of the soft underbelly of that quality: the sentiment and self-obsession. Its cool brilliance and subtle rhythmic vitality are all the more striking for being allied to a subject that artists had had difficulty handling without sarcasm, representing as it did the intrusion of bourgeois values into the bohemian world of art. Stravinsky's music implies no 'angle' on marriage, no hint of disapproval or regret (such as that experienced by the hero of Schumann's *Dichterliebe*). Its aim is to observe and, through the spirit of music and dance, empathise with the life force embodied in its subject. In this it anticipates many of the attitudes of neo-classicism, just as, in its ethnic detail – its modal tunes, its rhythms and cell structures, its fascination with sheer colour – it still belongs recognisably to the Russian tradition of Glinka and his successors, though it may shed their exoticism. It is indeed one of the great transitional works. After it Stravinsky, constitutionally unable to repeat himself, would have to look elsewhere than Russia for his material. When he (quite soon) returned consciously to his origins, in *Mavra*, Russianism had become as much a style towards which it was necessary to take up a posture as classicism or the music of Bach.

# 5

## *Enforced Exile:* The Soldier's Tale

If *The Wedding* was, in its universalisation of a timeless act, the least contemporary of works, *The Soldier's Tale* is openly a parable both of the times in which it was written and of Stravinsky's predicament as a prisoner of those times. Marching home on leave, the Soldier is suddenly and forcibly removed from the normal passage of time, so that when he eventually reaches his native village his friends and loved ones, having supposed him dead, refuse to accept him back.[1] Forced to live in a strange country, he makes money and marries well but cannot find happiness or peace of mind. So he again crosses the border into his own land, but is seized by the Devil and carried off to hell. The resonances of this tale, adapted by Stravinsky and C. F. Ramuz from various stories in Afanassyev, are rich and far-reaching. In 1918 the symbolism of the exile, and of the frontier beyond which lurk menace, deprivation and destruction, must have seemed painfully real to those many, artists and others, whom the war had cut off from their homes. In Stravinsky's case, the way home was doubly barred. The Bolsheviks, in power in Russia since October 1917, signed an independent peace treaty with Germany at Brest-Litovsk in March 1918 – a treaty which was widely regarded as humiliating to Russia but which left Lenin free to wage social and economic war at home. It is not hard to imagine the uncertainty, amounting perhaps to dread, with which Stravinsky will have viewed the possibility of life in Russia at that moment.

The uncertainty is reflected in the music he composed to go with the tale. Rejected by his village and everyone he loves, the Soldier sinks down in despair, while the 'Music to Scene 2' ('Pastorale') instils into the pure Russian idiom of *The Rite of Spring* and the *Cat's Cradle Songs* a feeling of loss that is completely new to that style. Later on, when the Soldier has found his way to 'un autre pays', the music takes on a generally alien colour; the Royal March, or palace music, has elements of the *paso doble*, and even the music which the Soldier himself plays on his newly retrieved violin to bring the Princess back to life is a suite of 'foreign' dances: a tango, a waltz and a ragtime. Although Stravinsky had written characteristic pieces in these and other Western dance styles before, in his easy keyboard pieces and even as an ironic device in a stage work (*Petrushka*), the sudden intrusion of a cosmopolitan temper in *The Soldier's Tale* is especially significant because it marks in the story exactly the same crisis as confronted Stravinsky in his own life. Severed as he was from his cultural and spiritual roots, like his Soldier, he too might well be reduced to fiddling foreign airs to preserve his soul. The moment is as symbolic as Schoenberg's writing his first atonal music to the words 'I feel the breath of other planets', since it denotes the first appearance in a major work of that stylistic acquisitiveness which led to neo-classicism, while at the same time dramatising its necessity.

In fact the break with the immediate past is nothing like as clear-cut in Stravinsky's work as in the events which may broadly be said to have caused it. The music he composed between the completion (in draft) of *The Wedding* in October 1917 and the first unequivocally neo-classical score, the Octet written mainly in 1922, presents a somewhat confused picture in which the new referential approach mingles unpredictably with a vestigial Russianism until the two finally become indistinguishable in the brilliantly synthetic *Mavra*. Admittedly this picture now seems less baffling than it did before it emerged, from Stravinsky's sketch-books, that he did not write the *Symphonies of Wind Instruments* and the Concertino for string quartet from scratch in 1920 after the completion of *Pulcinella*, but sketched both works quite extensively (along with music that eventually went into the Octet) in the spring and summer of 1919, before there was any mention of the Pergolesi transcriptions.[2] What we may glimpse in the undercurrent of all these works is the gradual and perfectly consistent evolution of Stravinsky's personal manner from one phase to another while, on the surface, specific projects are drawn into the current according to their individual character and momentum. This is obviously the sense of Stravinsky's assertion 'that I created the possibility of the [Pergolesi] commission as much as it created me, and that *Pulcinella*, though it may seem to have been an arbitrary step at the time, was an entirely logical step for me'.[3]

*The Soldier's Tale* is another such work, and the more evidently so when it is seen in the context of Stravinsky's other projects of 1918. We again owe to Craft the information that the short chamber piece *Ragtime* was largely composed before, not after, *The Soldier's Tale*, and that the *Piano Rag Music* was in part sketched at the same time, in the early spring of that year.[4] Thus one of the main musical innovations of the tale, its infusion of ragtime and modern dance music into Stravinsky's established Russian manner, was something more than a bit of casual pastiche worked in to fit the story; it was part of the direction of Stravinsky's work in early 1918. Similarly the Spanish or Latin dances in *The Soldier's Tale* carry on where the Study for pianola, which later took the name 'Madrid' in the Four Studies for orchestra, left off the previous November. The impression is that Stravinsky, having used up his Russian ideas in *The Wedding* and its satellite pieces, is casting around for fresh models to use as 'subjects' or stylistic material. But some of these models had already served him in his smaller keyboard pieces, which were themselves, as we saw in the last chapter, second cousins to the contemporary Russian songs. The easy keyboard March of December 1914, with its hidden kinship to the *Pribaoutki*, leads ahead to the opening march in *The Soldier's Tale*, via the one in *Renard*, just as the 'Española' of 1917 anticipates the pianola study and the *paso doble* in *The Soldier's Tale*. There is, on the other hand, no apparent precedent for the ragtime pieces of 1918, which is perhaps surprising since Stravinsky seems to have been familiar with the genre from gramophone records as early as 1914. It looks as if the 'completion' of *The Wedding* opened a gap in his creative consciousness, into which these various external idioms were ready to pour.

The ragtime pieces, which are conveniently examined as a group, show much the same preoccupations as the works – Russian or genre-portrait – which preceded them. They are studies in rhythm, internal movement and sonority. *Ragtime* itself is the closest of them to what Stravinsky called 'a composite portrait of this new [*sic*] dance music'.[5] Like a true written piano rag, which perhaps it originally was, it sticks strictly to the rapid *tempo di marcia* characteristic of ragtime, while rhythmic interest is confined to inequalities in the distribution of internal syncopations, and unexpected elongations of repeated figures, as in the fourth bar after fig.5 (where, however, the added crotchet most untypically fails to produce an extended bar but is brusquely squeezed into the four-beat pattern), or the following phrase, after fig.6, where a delay of half a bar does actually lead to a momentary disintegration of the regular structure, though not of the bar-unit. On the whole the effect of these disruptions within a nominally regular metrical scheme is to interfere with the smooth swing of the 'rag' syncopations without adding much by way of metric variety or subtleties of stress. What is intriguing about this five-minute study, apart from the dry instrumental colour and the matter-of-fact bordello-piano twang of the cimbalom, is the emergence of certain fingerprints of Stravinsky's high neo-classical style. We shall meet the jogging quaver groups, with their somewhat mechanical feel (so apparently remote from the volatile and unpredictable ostinatos of the Russian ballets) again and again in works of the 1930s and 1940s, often enlivened by syncopation, as in the finales of the *Symphony of Psalms* and the *Symphony in Three Movements*; likewise the two-in-a-bar swinging ostinato bass. Although *Ragtime* is not, so to speak, a candidly tonal work, its criteria of vertical combination are much more nearly those of tonal music than, say, *Renard*'s, a fact which goes a long way towards accounting for the very different flavour of two works written within two years of each other and for ensembles that have a good deal in common. Throughout *Ragtime* Stravinsky makes the most of the tonic-dominant clichés of the style he is satirising, as he was later to do in his 'classical' pieces. Not only do the chords push relentlessly (if unsuccessfully) towards tonic resolution, but the phrasing hints at the idea of a four-square harmonic rhythm with a strong downbeat cadence – which, needless to say, never happens. There is something of all this in the earlier keyboard pieces, but *Ragtime* is the first work of Stravinsky's maturity not for keyboard to introduce stock tonal devices as part of its stylistic symbolism.

The *Piano Rag Music*, written for Artur Rubinstein (who, however, loathed it and rarely if ever played it in public), has the same general repertory of rhythmic and harmonic gestures, but deployed with much greater freedom as befits a virtuoso piece. Even certain motives are common to both pieces. But the quasi-dominant chording is much richer and more adventurous in the piano work while the metre, though in essence two-four or four-four, has many irrationalities and on a number of occasions actually dissolves into long unbarred cadenzas (apparently meant, however, to be played evenly; there is not a single *rubato* indication). The *Piano Rag Music* is more of a fantasy than *Ragtime*, and makes more of the idea of detaching clichés from their usual context, combining them obliquely, in the manner of a cubist painting, while at the same time deriving from them new meanings which may pointedly contradict the old ones. For example, in the unbarred episodes (and this is incidentally a reason for leaving out the barlines) Stravinsky twists the syncopations so that a crotchet which results from the tying of a weak quaver to the next strong one is treated, in reverse, as a downbeat crotchet (i.e. a strong quaver tied to a weak one) (Ex.20). He encourages, that is, an ambiguity as to where the true accent lies, a procedure obviously comparable to the treatment of verbal accent in the Russian-language vocal works, but a most peculiar concept in ragtime or jazz. Details of this kind make the *Piano Rag Music* a more interesting work than *Ragtime*, and perhaps even a more Stravinskian one, though it may be less compact and, taken as a whole, less coherent – to say nothing of its technical awkwardness.

But for all the surface novelty of these pieces, they have more in common with the Russian works than one might suppose, and not only in the matter of accent. Asafyev regarded *Ragtime* as 'a wholly linear composition',[6] but he omitted to observe that it is a *free* linear composition, in which the fitting of the tune into the regular metre often looks merely like the most expedient of several possible choices. The melody is in fact composed by the association of variable cells, as so often in the Russian pieces, but laid over an inflexible four-beat bass unit. In the ensemble score this is most easily seen

*Ex. 20 Piano Rag Music*

in individual parts, like the cimbalom from bar 5, which, taken out of its rhythmic context, has the appearance of a little ornamented two- or three-note melody like the one which opens *The Wedding* or the second theme in *The Rite of Spring*. Such metric hints as it contains are ambiguous. Stravinsky's own piano reduction, with the famous single-line Picasso drawing on the cover (which perhaps gave Asafyev the idea about the linearity of the music), is more revealing of such interior structures. Is it only by accident, one may wonder, that the first nine notes of the vamped bass starting in bar 5 are a palindrome? On page 7 of this reduction, third system, the main theme in the right hand is clearly a string of variations on the initial cell, rather arbitrarily blocked out to fit the four-beat scheme, where in the Russian works one would expect the bar lengths to vary with the melodic units. No doubt it was to avoid this difficulty that Stravinsky abandoned barlines for much of the *Piano Rag Music*, where he allows the melody to form its own lengths, as in the past, within the general rhythmic idiom of ragtime – with the ambiguous consequences already noted. This is also precisely the technique of the marching and dancing movements in *The Soldier's Tale*, though for reasons of co-ordination Stravinsky is forced there to bring back the barline.

We do not find in these rag pieces tunes of evident folksong pedigree like the ones in *Renard*, *The Wedding* or the smaller Russian pieces, and yet the melodic lines are curiously similar. They nearly all have the feature that they oscillate, typically by step, round a focal note, like the chant of the fox disguised as a nun, or the lament of the mothers in *The Wedding*. Now however the modal idioms characteristic of folk music are replaced by chromatic ones, so that the step is normally a semitone instead of a tone. In *The Soldier's Tale* one finds both types of melody: the 'open', or modal type in the fiddle tune ('Music to Scene 1'), the 'closed', or chromatic, type at fig.10 of the Soldier's march. This passage in fact comes, very little changed, in the first unbarred section of the *Piano Rag Music* (Ex.21). But it is an intriguing comment on Stravinsky's technique of stylisation that in its march context the music sounds march-like, whereas in its rag context it sounds rag-like.

The 'Ragtime' in *The Soldier's Tale*, which is the last and liveliest of the three dances for the convalescent Princess, emerges by an exactly similar process. Its main theme, hinted at in the closing stages of the waltz, is a rag version of the theme of the first dance, a sultry tango for solo violin

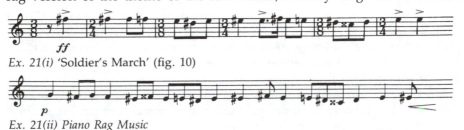

*Ex. 21(i) 'Soldier's March' (fig. 10)*

*Ex. 21(ii) Piano Rag Music*

and percussion. According to Craft, these movements were all among the later parts of the score to be completed, possibly in July and August.[7] Yet they too preserve an intimate connection with *Ragtime* and the *Piano Rag Music*. The theme of the tango is simply the theme of *Ragtime* transmogrified and transposed. The accompaniment here is for unpitched percussion. But Stravinsky must have retained the original harmonic image in his mind since his arrangement of this music for piano, in the trio suite from *The Soldier's Tale* made soon after the première, forms the same initial six-four chord as in *Ragtime*, slightly blurred by the added lower minor ninth which is meant to suggest the drums of the original (Ex.22). These and other parallels between the three works show not only how integrated was Stravinsky's thinking even while the surface of his music changed drastically, but how easy he found it to impose a variety of symbolic forms on any given material or process. This is apparently because his creative images were so definite as to impose themselves on whatever material was to hand. Even in the ragtime in *The Soldier's Tale* Stravinsky had not done with some of this material, which crops up yet again in the third of the Three Pieces for clarinet, written in October or November for Werner Reinhart. These two ragtime 'portraits' are marked by an extreme simplicity of line and a motivic coherence less evident in the two earlier ones, while metrically they compare with the *Piano Rag Music* for ambiguity and subtlety. Though barred (for ease of co-ordination), the passage from fig.27 in the Princess's 'Ragtime' is equivalent to the unbarred 'break' sections of the *Piano Rag Music*, but it is more sharply drawn thanks to the cadences which define the phrase-ends and to the meticulous scheme of stresses which indicate how the accents relate to the pulse; there is no better example of Stravinsky's use of added or subtracted values to set up rhythmic tension that uncoils like a spring at the cadence. He must have concluded that the barline was too valuable an aid in such cases to be abandoned simply because it could not always define metre unequivocally. The solo clarinet ragtime retains barlines in just this spirit, while the brilliant second piece in the set shows that Stravinsky was still quite ready to do without them where matters of accent were secondary to the idea of free improvisation.

The economy of *The Soldier's Tale* is one of the most famous things about it. For both Stravinsky and his Swiss collaborator Ramuz (already the translator of *Renard* and many of the songs) royalties were virtually non-existent in the latter part of the war, and the tale grew out of the need for a work which could be frequently performed, if necessary under adverse circumstances, with minimal scenery and few players. It is the prototype of the farm-wagon school of music-theatre, though it was premiered in a theatre in Lausanne and would have been played in other Swiss theatres but for the Spanish flu epidemic. But in fact the resources of *The Soldier's Tale* are not exceptionally small by Stravinsky's standards of the time, and Ramuz had hoped they would be smaller. Stravinsky had preferred small mixed ensembles since *The Rite of Spring*, and he continued to do so until

*Ex. 22(i) Ragtime* (piano version)

*Ex. 22(ii) The Soldier's Tale,* tango (original score and trio version respectively)

the mid-1920s, finding in them the clarity and accuracy of balance which suited his mordant sound imagery. But the particular economy of *The Soldier's Tale* comes out less in its physical apparatus than in its musical composition. Of all Stravinsky's works for mixed ensemble, this is the one which depends most on solo playing, and perhaps of all his works none is more daringly – which is to say unsensationally – repetitive of tiny motifs and simple textural ideas. Again the music shows him to have been ready for the particular circumstances which brought it into being.

No doubt the peculiar form of the work was more directly conditioned by these circumstances. A highly integrated piece of continuous music drama like *Renard* is undoubtedly harder to put together for *ad hoc* perform-ance than a work in which different pieces and 'acts' can be worked up independently and assembled on the day, even if continuity and pacing are an important part of the end product. So, in *The Soldier's Tale*, we have the story linked for the first time by a narrator out of costume (at the first performance he wore evening dress); we have a dancer for the Princess and actors for the Devil and the Soldier, and no singing of any kind; we have a series of short self-contained musical numbers separated by speech, though as in all the best Singspiels the music tends to take over the more the action intensifies. But yet again the tendency in these various devices is by no means new to Stravinsky. The dissociation of narrative and action is simply a down-to-earth version of the separation of singing and dancing in *Renard* and *The Wedding*, and the narrator's occasional interventions in the play, combined with those passages where, for no particular reason, the dialogue is spoken by the characters themselves rather than vicariously by him, recall the distinction in those earlier works between passages where the singers do and do not stand for specific dramatis personae. Thus, while the device of the go-between narrator may well have come from Pirandello, as Stravinsky suggests in *Expositions and Developments* (p.91), it is an idea perfectly consistent with the Meyerholdian leanings of his theatre since *The Nightingale*. These leanings, it will be remembered, have to do with the composer's interest in a theatre of artifice and ritual, as opposed to the 'realistic' drama of romantic opera and ballet, and they associate a rejection of romantic fantasy and self-importance with a rejection of its sumptuous-ness and grandiosity. But now the narrator calls in question the wholeness and self-adequacy of the stage world at the very moment that he breaks into its musical fabric. The idea is a modification of the 'frame' motif we observed in *Renard*, since the frame itself, as defined by the alienating presence of the narrator, turns out to be a less inhibiting structure than before. We can, in the person of the narrator, walk into it, influence what happens inside it, converse with the people there. In fact it is a world we may already feel we understand quite well. We, after all, surely know more about telephones, newspapers, stock-market reports, not to mention tangos and ragtimes, than do people in fairy-tales who get mixed up with the Devil, marry princesses and ride in carriages drawn by flying horses. This deliberate break in the frame round *The Soldier's Tale* looks like a further reflection of Stravinsky's loss of his roots. There are no telephones in *Renard* or *The Wedding* and the particularity of either work would be ruined if there were. Real or unreal, their world is integratedly separate from us, and we have to accept it as it is. But when it comes to the fairy-tale of the Soldier and the Devil, we find ourselves dealing no longer with peasants from a far country or actors dressed as animals, but with the archetypal figures of our time, the bringers of war who destroy our lives, the customs men, the purveyors of material welfare. This is surely the meaning of the breaks in idiom in the dramaturgy of *The Soldier's Tale*, the technical device of alienation, and the abrupt intrusion into an ethnic style of tawdry modern popular dances. It is a mixture that has often been imitated, but never remotely equalled, so brilliantly do the ingredients fuse. The work has remained *sui generis*, and even (perhaps especially) Stravinsky knew better than to attempt it again.

Its characteristic sounds converge from two directions: from the story, in the shape of the fiddle which is the best of the Soldier's possessions but which he foolishly sells to the sinister lepidopterist; and from the idea of a miniature orchestra, a circus or ragtime band, small but representative, with high and low members of each main instrumental family. But Stravinsky rarely seeks a blend from this ensemble, preferring as in the past to emphasise pure timbres and let them collide in much the same way that he opposes regions of harmony. The effect here, however, is particularly stark, both because the texture is studiedly thin and because the music constantly refers to tonal procedures, so that one is more instantly aware of oblique planes in the harmony than in the modal world of *Renard*. There are early examples of this in the mock cadence which ends the opening brass flourish, and in the ironic mixture of a plain tonic-dominant bass in G with melodies and fanfares predominantly in A in the march which follows. But Stravinsky does not simply purvey wrong-note harmony to annoy his customers. The mixture of roots a major ninth apart is thematic and is already expressed in the double-bass ostinato, with its dominant made up of D and E combined. Moreover the oblique harmony is echoed by the rhythm, in which the double-bass stolidly persists in its one-two-one-two accompaniment regardless of the shifting pulse of the march tune. The Soldier may march, as he has been trained to, but the spirit of *congé* and freedom is not to be tied down by dull routine. It asserts itself again in the famous fiddle tune of the 'Music to Scene 1', where both the pizzicato bass and the double-stopped violin equivocate between cadences on G and A, though here the effect is harmonically smooth because the music is modal and the mode can accommodate both levels. Whether or not the Soldier's soul is Russian, as hinted by the second theme, after fig.10, which Craft tells us is a Russian street song,[8] it does not contain in itself the conflicts imposed by the world it will soon enter.

Not the least fascination of this haunting piece is its simplicity, lit by wonderful internal subtleties of metre and timbre certainly, but so far from traditional ideas of what makes music interesting. For many bars the violin and bass wind along, in or out of phase, like two people who have met casually in the road and are going the same way. Bassoon then clarinet play a wistful countermelody in the Russian manner of the *Cat's Cradle Songs*, in the middle of which the Devil appears unnoticed by the music (or the Soldier) sinisterly holding a butterfly net. The effect is distinctly that of some serene golden age which cannot endure; its epitaph is sung by the little 'Pastorale', also in the Russian manner, which follows the soldier's rejection by his family and friends. Much of what immediately ensues is narrated without music, a procedure which may simply reflect the absence of any direct occasion for it, apart from the reprises of the march which twice, ironically, take the Soldier back to his starting-point, and of the fiddle tune which, by mocking at the Soldier's inability to play his violin when he gets it back (or is it the wrong violin?), draw attention to the 'soulless' lack of any other music at this point in the story. In any case it is worth noticing just how little music has served Stravinsky for the entire first part of the tale: a march of about 100 bars, an air of roughly the same length, and a pastorale of some 50 bars. Nothing could be more sparing or more to the point. In the second part, however, the musicians have to work much harder.

The atmosphere of this part of the tale is no longer either wistful or poetic, but on the one hand a reflection of the vulgar and empty outside world, and on the other an image of the demonic struggle for possession of the Soldier's soul, a struggle in which, of course, the violin plays the major part. Thus in the 'Little Concert' over the insensible body of the Devil (who has appeared this time disguised as a travelling fiddle virtuoso) the violin almost bubbles over in triumph at being restored to its rightful owner – though there remains a flavour of the diabolic in this obsessive piece, just as an air of menace hangs over the suite of dances in which the Soldier fiddles the Princess back to health. The violin, traditionally the instrument played by the Devil, is clearly still possessed, which goes with the fact that getting it back does not save the Soldier from his fate. Though the final dance, the Devil's 'Triumphal March', leaves us with the idea of the percussion as the dry, rattling bones of Satan, the earlier part of the march is again dominated by the violin, at its most pyrotechnical, played once more by the Devil.[9]

If *The Soldier's Tale* is in a category of its own as a dramatic work, it is also hard to place in Stravinsky's work at the period when it was written. As a morality it harks back to *The Firebird* and *Petrushka* rather than to the more recent Russian dramas, with their detached, almost ethnographic attitude to ritual. But while this certainly is a reflection of Stravinsky's enforced re-assimilation into the multi-faceted world of Western European culture, it brings with it some of the work's most modern features, for example its stylistic plurality, its readiness to absorb all kinds of idioms and types. In 1917 it would still have been possible to look at Stravinsky's work and grade it as, on the one hand, the 'real' Stravinsky of the *Pribaoutki* and the Russian ballets, and on the other the casual, derivative Stravinsky of the easy pieces. In 1918 it no longer makes sense to separate these styles; they have all become part of the essential artist, the mixing up of tonal and modal allusions every bit as much as the jostling of popular modern dances, archetypal marches and folk ditties, not to mention the Lutheran chorale which Stravinsky guys in a manner distinct from the hieratic Orthodoxy of the 'Cantique' in the Three Pieces for string quartet or the as yet unwritten chorale in the *Symphonies of Wind Instruments*; and, finally, the fusion of accentual irregularities from the Russian settings with the highly predictable rhythmic schemes of marches, waltzes and tangos. The ironic effect of these colliding planes, so different from the calm objectivity of *The Wedding*, is directly associated with the work's moralising tendency. As we listen to the 'Chorale' in *The Soldier's Tale*, it is hard to resist that sense of superior knowledge carefully avoided in *The Wedding*, which comes from the parodying of a solemn observance. In this sense only, the characters in the tale are puppets, like those in *Petrushka*, and this may be why the marionettes that Stravinsky so much loved have always been especially successful in these two works.

The years after the Russian Revolution, when Stravinsky was facing the certainty of permanent exile, must have been particularly unsettling for him, and the disruption shows in his music. In 1919 and 1920 he wrote the Concertino for string quartet and the *Symphonies of Wind Instruments*, as well as the reduced orchestral suite from *The Firebird* – works which proceed directly from the premises of the Russian style. But between sketching and completing these scores he wrote, for Diaghilev, the ballet *Pulcinella*, in which, as it seemed to contemporary audiences and critics, the great radical of the day sold out to the current vogue for pastiche: the vogue of Tommasini's *Good-humoured Ladies* and Respighi's *Boutique fantasque* as well as Ravel's *Tombeau de Couperin*, Strauss's *Ariadne* and Busoni's *Arlecchino*. In view of Stravinsky's subsequent direction, *Pulcinella* is a work of symbolic as much as actual importance, though unsurpassed in its own genre. The works to which it seemed in due course to lead, the Octet and Piano Concerto with their overt 'classical' posturing, have at bottom just as much in common with the Concertino or even the *Symphonies*, the sketches for which include preliminary ideas for the Octet.[10] But *Pulcinella* in a sense expresses the possibilities of Stravinsky's art at this period. Having already incorporated borrowed idioms, at first in pieces of no great substance, then in a major work of music-theatre, he could logically proceed to an extensive ballet score based entirely on found material: and not just logically, one could add, but necessarily, since as a profoundly autochthonous artist cut off from his native soil he must have felt the need for an alternative source of nourishment. That he should have found this in the *galanteries* of Pergolesi allied to a scenario wholly dependent on the artifices of mask and disguise seems equally in keeping with the objective, ritualistic tendencies in his earlier ballets, and their use of framing techniques and the devices of alienation.[11]

But Pergolesi (or 'Pergolesi') was not the only source of *Pulcinella*. The idea for the work came from Diaghilev; it was his first fruitful suggestion to Stravinsky since *The Firebird*. And he presented it to the composer as a kind of package, complete with copies of the original manuscripts, the scenario, and a plan for a collaboration with Picasso and Massine. Stravinsky had met Picasso in 1917,[12] and there is something so Picassoesque about *Pulcinella*, with its reversion to a simple linear classicism distorted in certain ways which seem trivial but change the whole emphasis of the music, that it is hard to believe that the idea of working with his Spanish contemporary did not to some extent influence Stravinsky's attitude to the project. He must certainly have known Picasso's early Harlequin paintings (if not his designs for Satie's *Parade*, whose Paris production in 1917 Stravinsky did not attend[13]). Much of the spirit in which Picasso himself approached the new ballet is conveyed by a drawing of two *commedia* figures which he inscribed to Stravinsky in September 1919, the month in which composition began in earnest.

Stravinsky's own approach can best be described by distinguishing between those aspects of the original material which he left unchanged and the particular types of gloss which he placed on it. Pergolesi's tunes, which are not unlike an Italian equivalent of the melodies in the contemporary *Beggar's Opera* (more elegantly turned, certainly, and with a rococo artificiality more suitable to the world of Neapolitan masquerade), he retained virtually intact apart from certain distortions of their even phrase structure and regular metres. Moreover he made comparatively few changes to the bass lines of these tunes. His marks on the Diaghilev copies are confined mainly to added inner parts and harmonies, minor cuts, a few new links, and indications of scoring, dynamics and key. In a few cases he hardly marked his copies at all; but where he did mark, his changes usually look like additions rather than modifications.

Here we come to the peculiar character of his additions to Pergolesi's harmonies. Most eighteenth-century pastiches of the time take it as read that classical or rococo harmony is too dull and predictable to be worth transcribing (or imitating) without subtle enrichments which intensify its flavour while keeping the pretence of a classical purity and elegance. Indeed this is the only sense in which Strauss's Lully arrangements in *Le bourgeois gentilhomme* or Ravel's Couperin pastiches or Prokofiev's *Classical Symphony* remain stylistically 'correct' for more than a few bars at a time. However their impurities are typically kept within the tradition of good voice-leading and so-called vagrant harmony, which can introduce richness and even ambiguity but in a strictly controlled sense whose rules can be traced back to the style being parodied, and beyond. Such arrangements gaze back at their models down centuries of stylistic evolution as one might gaze at a faded portrait of one's great-grandfather, his known features but unknown personality encrusted with years of accumulated anecdote and speculation. Stravinsky adopted a different procedure. Instead of modifying the given text in this evolutionary way, he chose to accept it as it stood but add to it irrational colourings which obeyed no rules other than those of his own sensibility, developed through an alien school. Thus Pergolesi's harmonies are always present in *Pulcinella*; they are the entire basis of the harmonies we hear, but in the sense that the printed drawing is the basis of what one sees looking through a fairly but not painstakingly accurate tracing of it. In this way Stravinsky's harmonies are simply superimpositions on Pergolesi's. Their gently piquant diatonic clashes (a kind of tonal version of the pan-diatonicism in *Petrushka*) have the effect of inhibiting, but not obscuring, the conventional tonic-dominant formulae and simple harmonic sequences which are the bread and butter of the early classical style. Especially in those sections where Stravinsky's favourite device of the ostinato is held against the simple directionality of the written harmony (for instance, at fig.27 in the 'Scherzino', where the violas and cellos play only open-string harmonics, or throughout the 'Serenata'), the idea of a static, block structure, in his Russian manner, is opposed to the conventional syntactic harmony with brilliantly invigorating effect. Most of the time, the harmonic grammar of Pergolesi has enough energy to sustain the classical kind of phrase structure proper to the original material. But just occasionally Stravinsky's way of neutralising the harmony tends to isolate the phrases to the point where they can be freely reconstructed in ways that much more closely resemble the cellular montages of the Russian works. The most striking examples of this are in the finale, where the simple cadential figure of the theme, with its characteristic four-semiquaver upbeat, is manipulated like the cells in, say, the 'Dance of the Earth', with its mobile accentual patterns but rigid triple metre. Here Stravinsky sticks to duple time, but moves the internal accents around exactly as if they were the verbal accents in a piece of Russian folk poetry. The result is a significant and amusing, if not yet substantial, premonition of his handling of tonal structures in the neo-classical works: seldom as an organic syntax, more often as a source of materials which can be subjected to procedural rules independent of their own native grammar (Ex.23).

In 1919–20 Stravinsky was not yet at the stage of manifesto classicism. All the same its tenets shed some light on the success of *Pulcinella*: for example his remark of 1930, 'For me, constructive form is predominant, and all of my music, even of the early years, is constructive. It seems to me that the tendency of all art today is constructivist.'[14] *Pulcinella* does at times have such a feel to it, perhaps precisely because of the essential blandness of the style from which it derives. Its vitality is architectural, a skilful balance of movement and proportion, just as in a cubist painting almost everything hangs on the harmony of intersecting planes and almost nothing on the intrinsic harmony of the subject. In this respect *Pulcinella* is

*Ex. 23(i)* 'Pergolesi': Trio Sonata no. XII

much more like Stravinsky's other main works of these years, the Concertino and the *Symphonies*, than is likely to strike one if one attends only to
its superficial 'style'.

As we saw, the Concertino and *Symphonies* were sketched at the same
time, apparently at first as self-motivated projects though Stravinsky was
later able to fit them, at least partly, to commissions received, the former
from the Flonzaley Quartet, who asked him for a successor to the Three
Pieces in the summer of 1919, the latter from the *Revue musicale*, who were
publishing a supplement of piano pieces in memory of Debussy (December

*Ex. 23(ii)* Stravinsky: *Pulcinella*

1920). As a pair they seem to reflect some need to establish a structural basis for abstract instrumental works that were neither suites from stage works nor stylistic portraits, such as the recent ragtime pieces. Stravinsky had written nothing of the sort since the Three Pieces, and nothing of any formal complexity since before *The Firebird*. So it is perhaps not far-fetched to see in these later works a definite classicising tendency, not yet converted into a doctrinaire or referential classicism.

Few pairs of works by Stravinsky offer such an intriguing comparison, in which material of obvious similarity has been put to such radically different uses. Both scores derive their impulse from the confrontation between a very mobile kind of idea articulated in sudden bursts of quavers, and an arresting or punctuating gesture of abrupt, imperative chords. Related types in both categories can be found in the two scores. The sudden flurry of quavers in the trumpets in the bar before fig.11 of the *Symphonies*, which seems to exteriorise an energy already latent in the preceding chords, resembles the more prevalent quaver patterns in the Concertino. On the other hand the chordal basis of the flute passage at fig.6 of the *Symphonies* clearly implies some common origin with the *sur la touche* interpolation just before fig.10 of the Concertino, though oddly enough this is much less noticeable in the 1920 scores of the *Symphonies* than in the revised version of 1947 (Ex.24(i)). Most blatantly the actual melody of the first flute in this section of the *Symphonies* is a compressed version of the almost Bartókian dance tune at fig.22 of the Concertino, the rhythms of the two being

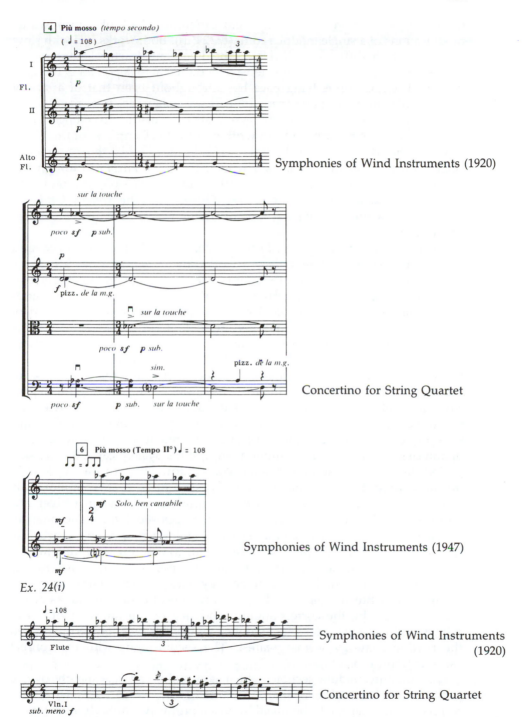

Symphonies of Wind Instruments (1920)

Concertino for String Quartet

Symphonies of Wind Instruments (1947)

*Ex. 24(i)*

Symphonies of Wind Instruments (1920)

Concertino for String Quartet

*Ex. 24(ii)*

the same to the point where the slight differences look like unconscious modifications of a single modular form (Ex.24(ii)). Both works end with slow chorales, whose different scale reflects the divergent structural emphases in the two scores: the grand and extensive coda to the *Symphonies* is the goal of a work whose underlying pace has throughout been that of a stately ritual, while the more parenthetic (not to say enigmatic) final page of the Concertino seems to question the essential drive of the preceding music. But both sections must have been written with the 'Cantique' of the Three Pieces in the back of Stravinsky's mind. And indeed to list the examples of such apotheosis in his music as a whole, from *The Firebird*, through the Three Pieces, *The Wedding*, the two works under discussion, and on to the *Symphony of Psalms*, the Symphony in C, *Orpheus* and the *Requiem Canticles*, is to show how fundamental this kind of ending was to Stravinsky's conception of form.

While the *Symphonies of Wind Instruments* is no doubt the finer score, and one of the greatest of all Stravinsky's works, the delightful Concertino was to prove the more productive for later music. This is apparently because of the sheer variety of device it employs, within its single-movement, six-and-a-half minute span, to generate formal energy. Here we find in a sort of fusion the powerful ostinato rhythms and violent offbeat chords of *The Rite of Spring*, the winding violinistic figuration of *The Soldier's Tale*, the mechanical repetitiousness of *The Wedding*, and – on the other hand – the suggestions of tonic-dominant formulae together with the rhetorical use of cadence, a tendency towards thematic integration, and a liking for motor-rhythm, all of which anticipate recurrent features of neo-classical style. The mixture is held in a kind of tension, brilliantly sustained. The C major scale played first by violin and cello at once hints at the 'plain' white-note diatonicism of *Apollo* or the Symphony in C, but stays typical of the Russian period through the use of a 'chroma', or shadow line, such as we saw in 'Kornilo', played by the viola in the form of a Dorian C sharp minor scale against the C major. This is thus not so much a tonal as an emblematic gesture: a mobile object which is instantly opposed by a static one, an arrangement of open-fifth chords spaced similarly a semitone apart. The rest of the first part (the piece is in A-B-A form) amounts to an attempt to reconcile these conflicting elements. On the face of it the music moves forward with irresistible brio, helped by jazzy syncopations from the ragtime style. But it is held up by the intrusion of static chords, as at the start, and also by the corresponding tendency of the quaver motives to orbit round particular notes – a tendency which acts most powerfully when the rhythmic energy seems greatest. The section ends with the conflict essentially unresolved.

The Andante middle section, which is a violin cadenza mainly over a pedal-point chord of E-G sharp, ruminates on the same material and resolves it in what might be called an unhelpful way, through moments of uncharacteristic harmonic repose. So we have contrast without resolution, and the stage is set for a return to the original argument but with a subtle change of emphasis. In the finale the Allegro material begins to escape from its previous orbit; there is an attempt at imitative counterpoint, and even a hint of canon by augmentation (fig.16) amusingly prophetic of the Symphony in C. Moreover the music twice rises progressively towards what is practically a dominant pedal (at figs. 20 and 29), in further anticipation of the symphonic neo-classical works. And yet all in all the balance has not yet tipped towards the pseudo-dialectical structures of the later works. The emphasis remains on powerful empirical chord inventions allied to ostinato rhythms enlivened by accentual surprises, and the Concertino is not yet sufficiently tonal for the mosaic form of the Russian period to have been countermanded by harmonic implication, as it sometimes is in the high neo-classical style. Oddly enough the nearest Stravinsky came to writing this kind of music later in life was in the transitional phase *out of* neo-classicism: in the first movement of the Septet (1953) and the not-yet-serial parts of *Agon*.[15]

By comparison, the *Symphonies of Wind Instruments* is a pure product of Stravinsky's Russian phase, and hardly suggests the imminent neo-classical idioms at all. The one exception to this – the suspicion of a V-I cadence at the very close, which might seem to echo the dominant suggestions in the Concertino – is only heard in this way retrospectively, as Pieter van den Toorn has pointed out.[16] That is, the dominant is not felt as such until it has 'resolved' – a sure sign that the cadential feeling is not intrinsic. What the *Symphonies* signally lacks is any attempt at organic thematic working. Its multiple sections are intercut but hardly at all integrated. Instead Stravinsky achieves coherence through a purely architectonic scheme of movement relations, formally expressed in the score by the three precisely related metronome marks which govern the whole work. Stravinsky described it as 'litanies in close tempo relations succeeding one another'.[17] The score simply regularises this in terms of the medieval proportional relation of the sesquialtera, the proportion of three to two. The tempos are crotchet (or minim) = 72 and crotchet = 108. Strictly observed, this scheme provides a structural correlative of a rhythmic and phrasing pattern which can be noticed throughout Stravinsky's Russian works, and underpins the *Symphonies* from the outset. Here we see a phrase-grouping based on the alternation of twos and threes, in which the bar-lengths observe the same ratio as the metronomic values. Thus the whole motion of the work is governed by a pattern of common relationships in terms of pulse and phrase-length, and no doubt it is from this that it derives its unusual feeling of calm order and architectural repose. The first part, up to the first tempo change at fig.6, already presents a variety of sesquialtera relations within the single tempo of crotchet = 72, some of which overlap, like the wood-wind and trumpet phrases in the very opening theme (2+2+3 against 2+3+2; the octave figure for the third clarinet, which further complicates this scheme, appears only in the 1947 revision). All these initial relationships

are smooth, because of the underlying unity of pulse, but at fig.6 a quali-
tative change takes place since, although the basic proportion is three-to-
two Stravinsky makes no attempt to engineer a transition between the two
tempos, as he might have done, for instance, by introducing triplet quavers
in the passage before the change.[18] By contrast the change back to Tempo
I at fig.9 *is* preceded by a link, though Stravinsky conceals this, wryly,
behind an untypically regular barring. The bassoon theme at fig.8 is barred
as 2/4, but grouped exclusively by twos and threes, with the threes
becoming dominant; and since three quavers in crotchet = 108 are equal to
two quavers in crotchet = 72, a common value is set up between the two
sections. Almost at once the music goes back to crotchet = 108 (at fig.11)
but expressed in terms of the dotted crotchet, which has the same value as
the previous crotchet (72). So here there is no obvious change until the new
quaver value (216 instead of 144) is asserted three bars later, and not for
another seven bars is this quaver used in a duple-time bar, at which point
we find ourselves unexpectedly back in Tempo II, crotchet = 108 (Ex.25).
The extraordinary sense of tranquillity at the end of the work, with its
broad incantatory chorale, must be due in part to the return to the initial
tempo of crotchet = 72, but without the internal subdivisions. There are
no quavers after fig.65, and therefore (presumably) no possibility of a tempo
modulation based on the regrouping of smaller values, as earlier in the
score.

This whole approach is remarkably suggestive of contemporary constructivist painting, like the work of the Russian Suprematists with its constel-
lations of coloured squares and rectangles. Stravinsky, too, used colour, in
the form of sharply distinguished sonorities, to make his shapes stand out
clearly from one another and to accentuate perspective, just as, one might
suggest, Malevich used colour to give his paintings depth as well as
variety. This quality is admittedly enhanced in the 1947 revision, which is
to this day the only published version of the full score. But the original
1920 score, with its bold emblematic combinations of timbre, is already
evidence of the importance of colour as a structuring medium within the
basic conception of the music. It can easily be seen how the different
sections, and sections-within-sections, are defined by internally stable
instrumental combinations and textures. Some three years after the
completion of this work, Stravinsky wrote an article about his Octet in
which he stated that 'wind instruments seem to me more apt to render a
certain rigidity of the form I had in mind than other instruments . . . the
difference of the volume of these instruments renders more evident the
musical architecture. And this is the most important question in all my most
recent musical compositions.'[19] Such distinctions, expressed substantially or
entirely through the medium of wind instruments, are a constant factor in
his music, as he says, from as long ago as the *Cat's Cradle Songs*, through
*The Soldier's Tale*, the *Symphonies*, *Mavra* and the Octet, up to the Piano
Concerto of 1924.[20] But in the *Symphonies*, which does not share the neo-

tonal orientation of the other main works in this list, the chording is a crucial additional aspect of the music's sonority: timbre and harmony are hard to separate. Take the organ-mixture colouring of flutes and clarinets with trumpet at the start: is it pure sonority or is there a harmonic effect? Or take the pivotal chord of the chorale, first heard at fig.1 and increasingly important until the last two or three pages. This is traditionally speaking a dominant minor ninth chord in second inversion, but by spacing it 'awkwardly' (with the dissonant ninth near the bottom of the chord) and by harping on it as a sound in its own right, Stravinsky strips it of its harmonic value and instead invites our enjoyment of it as a pure, as it happens octatonic, sonority. In fact the whole chorale consists harmonically of nothing more than an arrangement of such sonorities: almost weightless harmonic objects which arrive gradually at a mutual balance so perfect that we hardly expect the work to end at all, and so beautiful that we almost wish it would not.

Any discussion of the harmony in this work must also take account of the substantial differences between the 1920 and 1947 versions of the score.[21] For instance, the rewriting of the chords after fig.1 (and later repeats) tells us more about Stravinsky's harmonic thinking than any analysis unaided by such a comparison could ever do. In the 1920 score Stravinsky typically keeps the clashing B natural and B flat far apart in register, with the B natural near the bottom of the chord; but when he revised the passage he added another B flat an octave *below* the B natural, a change which seems designed primarily to improve the resonance of the upper B flat, rather than to intensify the dissonance with the B natural (Ex.26(i)). Voicing changes of this type abound in the 1947 score. Sometimes they improve the articulation of successive chords, as at fig.45, where the new layout avoids the muddying pedal effect of the upper F in the 1920 score (Ex.26(ii)).[22] Sometimes, however, they have the opposite effect of stabilising a chordal image that is more shifting in the original. The comparatively immobile flute accompaniment at fig.6 in the revision makes a telling contrast with the rather slippery crotchet counterpoints in the original. It is striking how the 1947 version insists on the 'chroma' dissonances which are so characteristic of early Stravinsky but which are oddly weakened in the 1920 score by the occasional rather glaring octaves formed by the moving parts.

These textural changes are the essence of the 1947 revision. As regards instrumentation, Stravinsky did no more than substitute a conventional flute and clarinet for the alto flute and basset-horn of the original. But he greatly revised the actual scoring for the whole ensemble. On the whole the 1947 score has a reedier and more mordant sound than the 1920: oboes and cor anglais are more prominent, clarinets less so; the double bassoon has more to do, the horns less. And the articulative point of these changes is often brought out by moving inner parts, or by contrasts of register. The question of resonance seems to have been more thoroughly examined. But while the revision is beyond any question an improvement on the original

*Ex. 25* Symphonies of Wind Instruments (1947)

*Ex. 26(i)* Symphonies of Wind Instruments (fig. 1, 1st chord)

it would be a gross over-simplification to say that it altogether fulfils or crystallises the work's original intentions. Why, if that were the case, should the composer suddenly in 1947 discover the high bassoon timbre for the solo at fig.8 (originally scored for alto flute), when high bassoon was already in 1920 an established Stravinskian colour? It is hard not to feel that in such cases the revision took a new view of an old problem, rather than simply solving it in the old terms. This is, incidentally, exactly the case with other major revisions of the 1940s and early 1950s, most notably that of *Petrushka*, whose tendency is extremely close to that of the *Symphonies*.

In whichever version, the work is the culminating moment of Stravinsky's Russian period. It represents a kind of high classicism in the manipulation of rhythmic cells, accentual subtleties and modal-harmonic fields. Unlike contemporary works such as *The Soldier's Tale* or the Concertino it has no

*Ex. 26(ii)* Symphonies of Wind Instruments (1947)

*Ex. 26(iii)* Symphonies of Wind Instruments (1920)

traffic with tonality; its world is modal. Its melodies wind through their chosen repertoire of pitches with few deviations, just as did the melodies in *The Rite of Spring* and *The Wedding*. And such chromaticism as it admits works either on the principle of interference, like the displaced octaves in *The Rite*, or as 'chroma', or it has a constructivist origin, like the trumpet B flat in bar 3, which comes from opposing the melodic descent of a minor third from D to B in the clarinets with a melodic rise from G in the trumpet. Admittedly the chord structures are probably at bottom empirical, worked out at the keyboard, and tonal thinking cannot be wholly excluded from the thinking behind that empiricism, any more than it can from the chord structures of *The Rite*. But only rarely does such feeling resurface as a functional issue in the *Symphonies*, and it never does so unmistakably.

In one other important respect it echoes the world of the Russian works up to *The Wedding*, which was still, it should be emphasised, work-in-progress in 1919–20. Like that ballet, the *Symphonies of Wind Instruments* has the character of a ritual, but one which has been abstracted from any specific context. We seem to be observing some austere procession, curiously like the one Stravinsky described in his autobiography as the idea behind the lost *Chant funèbre* which he composed in 1908 in memory of Rimsky-Korsakov (this was also, apparently, a wind piece). And of course the *Symphonies*, too, is a memorial offering, dedicated 'To the memory of Claude Achille Debussy' and originally published as a chorale for solo piano in a memorial anthology for that master. Although the work betrays no sign of Debussy's influence, it seems highly significant that Stravinsky should take the opportunity provided by his death to compose what amounts to a summatory masterpiece bringing to an end an epoch in his own music.

# 6

# *Synthesis:* Mavra *and the New Classicism*

However one defines neo-classicism – whether one regards it as a classicising tendency coming from romanticism, or on the contrary as a symbol of dissociation from the immediate past, whether one concentrates on the idea of borrowed styles or on the question of form or technique, whether one sees it as a move towards abstraction or as a reassertion of the objective usefulness or functionalism of music – it is hard to attribute its invention to Stravinsky. Instead he seems to provide a focus for these various ideas. At the time of *Pulcinella* (1919) there was nothing at all new about basing a work on historical pastiche. It had been done recently by Tommasini in *The Good-Humoured Ladies*, and was a commonplace in French music since Massenet, Delibes and Chabrier, and had even been imitated – in the character of a specifically French trait – by Strauss in his music to *Le bourgeois gentilhomme* and by Puccini in *Manon Lescaut*. In its origins it is a nineteenth- rather than twentieth-century phenomenon, and comes from the growing obsession with history and historicism. Its role in French music is an inextricable complex of action and reaction; it shares both in the fantasy world of late-romantic archaicism (the dream world of Verlaine's *Fêtes galantes*) and in the reaction against late-romantic emotionalism, particularly the heavy German variety. The former case may be purely decorative, but the latter holds a distinct foretaste of modernism which comes out in a variety of ways in, for instance, the songs and piano pieces of Debussy, with their clear, sharp impressions of life outside the artist's passions. Debussy's images are partly antique, partly exotic, partly vulgarian and low-life, but they seldom wholly abandon the self-consciousness of the romantic composer. We are usually aware, if only through subtle and isolated rhetorical gestures, of an ironic relationship between him and his subject. The music of Debussy's contemporary, Satie, on the other hand, is devoid of such rhetoric. Through imagery comparable to Debussy's, Satie detaches himself (perhaps a shade ostentatiously) from the elaborate histrionics of late romanticism and constructs an art of studied inconsequentiality, taking as his raw material precisely those trivial dance formulae which the romantics were fond of viewing in a sardonic relation to their own emotional and spiritual earnestness. Stravinsky's dedication to Satie of the little mechanical waltz in his *Three Easy Pieces* (1915) seems to acknowledge that there was meaning for him in the desiccated waltzes, quadrilles, polkas in Satie's *Le piège de Méduse* and *Cinq grimaces pour 'Le songe d'une nuit d'été'*. That meaning seems to reside in the possibility of treating emblematically a style that is specifically not in itself expressive of the artist's personality.

Between 1915 and 1921 Stravinsky experimented often with this way of writing, basing himself impartially, as we saw in Chapter 3, on classical and music-hall dance styles, on national types (including the Russian) and on ragtime. But there is no suggestion at this stage of any neo-classical manifesto, in the spirit of Cocteau's *Le coq et l'arlequin*, published in 1918. It was only gradually after the war that Stravinsky, no doubt under the influence of the French taste for artistic theorising – including the contemporary writings of Paul Valéry against the idea of poetry as a direct expression of the writer's experience, and of the philosopher Jacques Maritain on art as 'a virtue of the practical intellect' – began to formulate his stylistic tendencies into a doctrine supposedly governing everything he wrote, and even, by implication, everything he had written before.[1] The first clear signs of this tendency accompanied the composition and performance of *Mavra* between August 1921 and June 1922, and the preparation of Diaghilev's production of Tchaikovsky's *Sleeping Beauty* in London in November 1921, for which Stravinsky made some new orchestrations. Later, after the performance of his Octet in October 1923, he published a substantial article on the ideas behind this work.[2] In Stravinsky's attitude to these scores there is an obvious echo of the common desire for the reimposition of order and system on art after the chaos of romanticism, which was inevitably connected in artists' minds with the social disorder of the time. Maritain's 'la contemplation artistique touche le coeur d'une joie *avant tout intellectuelle*', and Valéry's 'le calcul logique, le dessin, la versification régulière, sont des exercices de tout premier ordre pour l'esprit', are characteristic statements of this mood. But there is no unequivocal suggestion in any of these writers that the new orderedness could or should be achieved through a repertoire of borrowed styles or forms. As Alan Lessem has pointed out, Valéry was mainly concerned with that classicising tendency which follows any romantic period of exploration and which sets out to codify its discoveries.[3] But in Stravinsky the urge to classicise, which is the apparent subject of writings like 'Some Ideas about my Octuor', goes in his music with mannerisms that come at first from an earlier classicising period, rather than the romantic period just past. As it happens a more organic classicism, one which derives its forms and gestures from Stravinsky's immediate tradition (including his own earlier work), exists in certain scores of the period after *The Rite of Spring* and before the Octet: scores such as *The Wedding* and the *Symphonies of Wind Instruments*, with their distillation of ideas traceable through the early Diaghilev ballets back to Russian romanticism. At that time the occasional parodies or borrowings stand apart from the main current of his style; they are geographically rather than temporally separate, like things heard (as they were) far from home. Stravinsky's initial response to these found objects is one of amused gratification, a sympathetic echo of their studied naughtiness and ostentatious triviality. However their simplicity, itself a kind of distillation from the more arch postures of the *nostalgie de la boue* and the whole café obsession of turn-of-the-century Parisian art, turns out to appeal to the developing classicist in him. Like the classical artist engaged in perfecting an organic and self-contained language from the random speculations of his predecessors, he sees in these apparently casual fragments of romantic popularism the materials for a concentrated and systematic idiom, responsive to techniques of his own. Typically he bases many pieces on the same parody – several waltzes, several ragtimes, several marches – reducing the flabby conventionality of the popular models to a series of abstractions which he treats *all'ostinato*, in the manner of his contemporary Russian works, and with similar rhythmic and harmonic obliquities.

The problem with these pieces is that, for all their gem-like precision and wit, they are irretrievably small-scale; they may be perfect miniatures, but they are miniatures. Even in a substantial work like *The Soldier's Tale* the role they play is miniaturistic; the princess may be a more vivid figure than the ballerina in *Petrushka*, but when she dances she is hardly any less of a doll. In this respect the so-called 'easy pieces' reflect a particular phase in Stravinsky's work. The component parts of the *Symphonies of Wind Instruments* are, in a comparable way, fragmentary, and the work's undeniable continuity is hard to account for. It seems absurd to say (what is nevertheless often said) that further progress in that direction would have been impossible. But one can reasonably suggest that Stravinsky was himself conscious of some difficulty in this regard. There is evidence in the fact that the two most striking features of the three large-scale works which took him into a completely new stage of his career – *Pulcinella*, *Mavra* and the Octet – are both elements, absent from the *Symphonies of Wind Instruments*, which were traditionally associated with formal architecture: regular periodic rhythm and tonal harmony. When we find alongside this unexpected trend a sudden burst of theorising about the importance of form (and the unimportance of expressive gesture), and the superiority of classical or quasi-classical models over the supposedly formless tracts of Wagnerian drama and the supposedly brainless intuitions of the Russian Nationalists, we may feel justified in concluding that questions of continuity and architecture were occupying his creative thoughts at the time.

*Pulcinella* may well have been one stimulus in that direction; certainly its conventional tonal and rhythmic traits seem to liberate a new formal exuberance which is purely Stravinsky's contribution. But another, and no less important, was Stravinsky's work on the score of *The Sleeping Beauty* in 1921. This, and the composition of *Mavra* which grew out of it, provoked his first serious essays in aesthetic propaganda. In October 1921, a fortnight before the London première of the revival of *The Sleeping Beauty*, *The Times* published an open letter from Stravinsky to Diaghilev praising his initiative in staging this ballet at a time when Tchaikovsky was considered not quite artistically respectable. After the première the same paper carried an interview in which Stravinsky reaffirmed his admiration for Tchaikovsky. And seven months later, just before *Mavra* had its first performance in Paris, *Le Figaro* published a further letter from him, in which he pointedly sets Tchaikovsky with Glinka over against the other main Russian nineteenth-century composers. *Mavra*, a short *opera buffa* based on a story by Pushkin, is dedicated 'à la mémoire de Pouchkine, Glinka et Tschaïkovsky', and it is the first major work by Stravinsky apparently inspired by, and openly adopting, a posture towards musical and artistic tradition that is other than spontaneous or completely innocent.[4]

In writing the first of these letters, Stravinsky must certainly have known that such an attitude to Tchaikovsky on the part of a leading modernist would be regarded as perverse, and no doubt he was happy to be able to reconcile what was undoubtedly a genuine, rediscovered love with a conveniently novel artistic doctrine. Just when Cocteau and his clique were calling loudly for 'une musique sur la terre, *une musique de tous les jours . . . une musique où j'habite comme dans une maison*', Stravinsky alone could afford to praise Tchaikovsky's emotional directness at the expense of those 'who are neither simple, nor naive, nor spontaneous, [but who] seek in their art simplicity, "poverty", and spontaneity'.[5] Taken as a whole, the main tendency of these articles is to place Stravinsky himself fairly exactly in relation to certain aesthetic ideologies which he seems to have decided it was time to abandon. He rejects the neo-frivolity and studied commonplaces of the Paris intellectuals; but he also rejects the Russian Nationalists, with their 'boyars' costumes . . . out of date in the period in which they lived.'[6] Clearly under the influence of Tchaikovsky's magnificent late music, with its brilliant integration of Russian fantasy and splendour and the symphonic values of Western music, he looks for a new synthesis which will justify him in aligning himself with a tradition that is itself at once Russian and synthetic; and this tradition he finds musically (as do most Russians) coming from Glinka, and poetically from Pushkin. And finally with a side-step so deft that it leaves most of his admirers, not to mention critics, rooted to the spot, he collects up the various stylistic souvenirs of his Swiss/Parisian decade and brings them back in homage to that great Russian century whose main issue was precisely the war between isolationism and cosmopolitanism.

For all its eccentricities, *Mavra* is therefore a work of crucial importance: nothing less than Stravinsky's first authentically neo-classical score, though

since its references are not exactly classical, it would never have conjured
up that term on its own account. What aligns it forcibly with the later
works, despite its Russian subject, is its conscious sense of opposing one
tradition to another: and specifically of identifying itself polemically with
an intellectually unfashionable art against a fashionable one. By contrast,
the earlier ballets and theatre pieces, though Stravinsky certainly thought
hard about the tradition to which they subscribe, lack this polemical slant.
Their fusion of artistic and ethnic strains, of ideas and techniques and
mythologies, is nothing if not natural. But *Mavra* is an essentially artificial
product, almost a statement *about* art, but carried through with such wit
and invention, such variety of colour and liveliness of tone, that it at once
establishes itself as a new kind of art in its own right. Its Paris première in
June 1922, in a Diaghilev double-bill with *Renard* (itself first staged some
two weeks before), was a flop. But it may not have been well done, and
certainly it is not a work that readily survives inadequate performance.
Stravinsky's own recording is a travesty. But he never forgave its early
failure; he wrote frequent propaganda on its behalf (it is the only work of
his that is discussed in any detail in the *Poetics*), and his faith in it has been
vindicated in recent years by performances whose polish has at last released
the music's charm and urbanity.

The synthetic qualities in *Mavra* start with its text. Asafyev described
Pushkin's verse story, *The Little House at Kolomna*, on which Boris Kochno
based his own verse libretto, as a piece of 'stylistic declination'; it imitates,
he says, the popular vaudevilles of Pushkin's day, adopting the sentimental
tone appropriate to the petit-bourgeois world whose manners it satirises.[7]
The story has none of the peasant dignity of *The Soldier's Tale* or the ritualistic
absurdity of *Renard*. Instead it makes fun of the deracinated shallowness of
life in a small town whose modern equivalent, leaving aside the servant
problem, might be a suburban housing estate (Pushkin's tale is set at the
time of the Thirty Years' War, but there is no trace of this in Kochno's stage
directions). Not only is the story trivial: Parasha, the daughter of the 'little
house', smuggles in her hussar lover disguised as the new cook Mavra,
whose cover is however quickly blown when Parasha's mother comes home
to find the girl shaving. But the detailing is also obsessively inconsequential.
The mother and neighbour chatter only about the shallow preoccupations
of the home-owning middle classes: the cost of living, the weather, the
washing-up. Stravinsky attached to this nonsense a music which he
described as 'Tchaikovskian in period and style.'[8] In fact Tchaikovsky's own
best-known Pushkin subjects are the romantic/ironic *Onegin* and the fantasy/
ironic *Queen of Spades* (in each case treated without the irony). However,
what Stravinsky really meant was that *Mavra* studiously avoided the epic
Pushkinism of *Boris* and the 'tourist-office orientalism of the *maguchia
kuchka*'.[9] For this purpose he discovered a masterfully apt musical blend as
deracinated in its way as the subject-matter of the opera.

Musically the most important source of *Mavra* is Glinka's Pushkin opera

*Russlan and Lyudmila* and, to some extent, *A Life for the Tsar*. Parasha, though not quite of Lyudmila's social pedigree, is her direct descendant musically. Parasha's song is, one assumes, the last of the line of Russian maiden's laments which Glinka established with Antonida's Cavatina and Romance and Lyudmila's Act 4 aria. This style contains elements of folk singing, but they are frequently submerged in conventions which Glinka took back to Russia from his travels in Western Europe: rhythmic and harmonic commonplaces of early romantic German and Italian opera, an expressive coloratura lifted from Bellini. The result is a curious hybrid of peasant modalism and stereotyped cadential formulae; of decorative exuberance and chugging one-two rhythms. In Glinka it can seem unsatisfactory, for all the astonishing inventions in his operas. But Stravinsky, who specifically needed a hybrid style, managed to make a virtue of the mixture. Parasha is rightly a conventional town girl enlivened precisely by that capriciousness (which in her becomes coquetry) that trivialises the aristocratic Lyudmila; and the work's varied lamentations, from the Mother's complaints about servants to the Hussar's 'loneliness' aria, are parodied by a musical expression which associates them with the conventions of romantic melo-drama. Parodied rather than ridiculed. The absurdity of the situation is certainly built into this oblique relationship between music and subject, but once the convention is accepted (and after all most operatic lamentations are ludicrous if it is not) the musical treatment is essentially direct. Asafyev pointed out that the Hussar's 'Alone, I wait alone', with its tone of a Pushkin elegy in the manner of 'Never sing to me the songs of sad Georgia', belonged to the classic Russian tradition of ardent, 'virile' melody (Ex.27). The best-known examples are in Tchaikovsky, but it was an idiom which he had perfected rather than invented. In the same way the gossiping duet of the Mother and the Neighbour merely transfers to a *petit-bourgeois* context a standard type of romantic 'genre' dialogue; Madame Laryna and Filip-yevna chatter in much the same way in *Onegin*, and there are also strong reminiscences of that opera in the Mother's music (for instance, in her lament for the death of her cook Fiocla, after fig.34). But the breathlessness of the ensembles in *Mavra* goes back to Glinka once again, who in turn borrowed the idea, perhaps, from the comic finales of Italian opera, including Mozart.

Stravinsky, as we have seen, readopted these various idioms self-consciously and with a partly polemical object. In 1922, as he himself later remarked, they seemed *démodés* to the audiences who took an interest in the Ballets Russes.[10] Unlike his recent mixed-media stage works, with their fusion of peasant ritual and stylised modern theatrical techniques in the manner of Meyerhold, *Mavra* was a 'number' opera of apparently traditional format with a pseudo-realistic setting. Even more disturbing, its music was tonal, with old-fashioned cadences and vamped accompaniments, and a style of vocal coloratura that reminded one of the sort of romantic opera which pretended to be serious and truthful when it was actually being silly

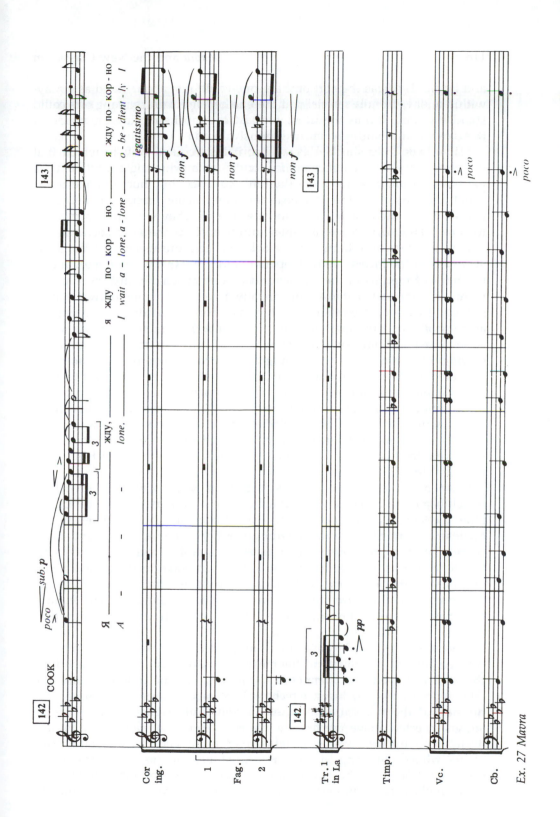

Ex. 27 Mavra

and artificial. It was the sort of thing one could just about stand as a play-within-a-play, like the *commedia* at the end of *Pagliacci* (assuming one could stand *Pagliacci*). But as the latest work by the most shocking modernist of the day it could hardly be taken seriously.

*Mavra* thus duly shocked Paris, but it did so in a way to which that neophiliac city was not accustomed; it did so by ducking expectations of yet more dissonance, yet more rhythmic violence, yet more strange Slavic ritual, and instead offering a neat and affectionate parody of just those genres which the artistically up-to-date thought they were now supposed to reject. They may have cast their minds back to the easy pieces or the parody marches and dances in *The Soldier's Tale*, and recognised the same approach in the lovers' waltz duet (just before 'Mavra' is left alone), and in the hints of ragtime in the quartet and closing ensemble. But those pieces were the merest bagatelles, and in any case their intention was surely satirical. However, the intention of the easy pieces was not so much satirical as symbolic, and the main difficulty in transferring their technique to the scale of a half-hour comic opera was structural. Stravinsky went about solving this problem by applying his 'parody' approach to formally extended models, and the result brilliantly met his need for a synthetic art based on synthetic archetypes. *Mavra* thus opened the door to what is so misleadingly (in this book and elsewhere) called neo-classicism, but might more usefully be termed Stravinsky's 'synthetic' period, which was to last thirty years or more. Many details of style which appear here for the first time were to become the hallmarks, even in some cases the clichés, of his middle years.

In a sense *Mavra* is a work of reconstitution, starting with the orchestra, which begins to reinstate the traditional layout Stravinsky had abandoned after the abortive first version of *The Wedding* (at the latest: even that orchestra is, by intention, highly idiosyncratic). *Mavra* is still a wind-based score, like the *Symphonies of Wind Instruments* and as the Octet and Piano Concerto were to be. But in place of the chorus-like mixtures and heter-ophonies of the *Symphonies of Wind Instruments*, we find something closer to the traditional theatre-orchestra with strings (though only one of each) designed to supply textural and rhythmic support and the occasional melodic solo. Admittedly Stravinsky makes brass instruments do much of the work strings would have done in the past; the horns especially are worked hard as a family, and the most expressive instrumental melody in the work is played by a trumpet in A. He was influenced here, on his own admission, by the jazz band, which probably also determined that peculiar division of the full score into melody and rhythm-bass with the upper strings inserted above the brass while cello and bass, mostly playing the 'beat', prop up the score as usual. *Mavra* is the first of many Stravinsky works whose chugging marcato rhythms seem to fuse the idea of the classical ostinato and the modern popular-song accompaniment. But though these rhythms constantly imply the regular periodic design of their models, they do so only in the very process of fragmenting its regularity. Parasha's song is a much-anthologised example of a tendency which had already been vigorously deployed in *The Soldier's Tale*, for instance in the violin tune with its *meccanico* double-bass accompaniment, where, however, the individuated texture still belongs to Stravinsky's authentic 'pribaoutki' style. Parasha's song, which sets off in a text-book B flat minor and with a standard four-in-a-bar tonic-dominant bass, soon starts to dislocate the smoothly integrated planes of traditional melody, harmony and rhythm, in a manner that again irresistibly suggests early Cubist portraiture. Throughout the first section of the song, the bass maintains a steady four-beat pattern, but the tonic-dominant off-beat chord sequence in the horns, conventional in itself, follows an independent pattern – basically of six beats: ABBABA – which leads to systematic confusion between the functions of rhythm and harmony. Meanwhile Parasha, singing quietly to herself as she embroiders, floats a metrically free folk tune across both accompanying schemes – a tune which might well have featured, with a rather different accompaniment but otherwise unaltered, in Rimsky-Korsakov's collection, from which Stravinsky had borrowed freely for his early ballets. All these three 'planes' Stravinsky averages out into a regular alternation (from the point of the vocal entry) of 3/4 and 5/8 bars, which fits none of them and so implicitly introduces a fourth (Ex.28).

Such devices, in a multitude of variants, were to serve Stravinsky throughout his neo-classical period. They have the effect of changing tonality, with its associated phenomena of rhythm, phrasing and harmony, from a process into a system of gestures which constantly alludes to, but does not pursue, the logic which the listener expects of them. Picasso referred to his Cubist style as 'reasonable'; but in Stravinsky's case, at least, the dislocation is specifically against the implicit rationale of the material. In this respect he was not a process composer at all,[11] and it was typical of him that he should reduce processes to non-contingent 'events' in a way that oddly suggests an Einsteinian description of matter. The synthesis in *Mavra* involves the translation of tonal materials (among other things) into mobile cellular organisms very much cognate with, if stylistically and gesturally unlike, the melodies, chords and rhythmic ostinatos of the Russian works. And this is the kind of description we shall encounter over and again in the music of the next thirty years.

The Octet, Stravinsky's next work, is more often given than *Mavra* as the first fully-fledged score in the new tendency. After its performance in October 1923 he associated with it a manifesto which seemed to set the seal on the highly self-conscious ideas we connect with neo-classicism. In 'Some Ideas about my Octuor' he discusses the piece in ruthlessly constructivist terms. He calls it 'a musical object' and 'a musical composition based on objective elements'; he refers to its 'rigidity of form' and its 'play of movements [tempos] and volumes that puts into action the musical text [and] constitutes the compelling force of the composition and determines its

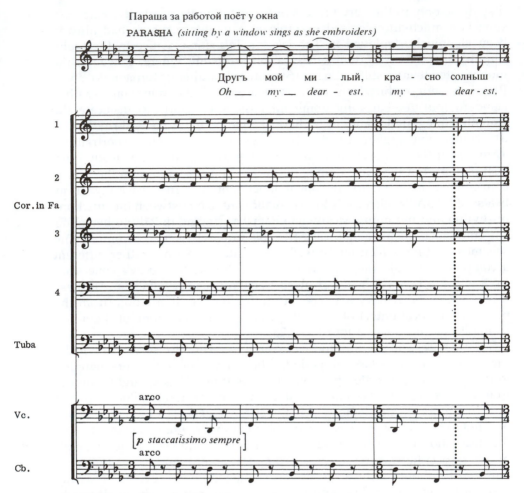

Ex. 28 *Mavra*, 'Parasha's Song'

form.' He denies any role for expressive nuance in its performance, but claims that its 'emotion' resides in its form: 'to interpret a piece is to realise its portrait, and what I demand is the realisation of the piece itself and not of its portrait . . . I consider that music is only able to solve musical problems; and nothing else, neither the literary nor the picturesque, can be in music of any real interest. The play of the musical elements is the thing.' However, so far as they can be understood at all, these remarks all apply to Stravinsky's post-war instrumental works as a whole: certainly to the Concertino and the *Symphonies* at least as much as the Octet. Only in one remark does Stravinsky betray any overtly classicising intention. 'Form, in my music', he says, 'derives from counterpoint. I consider counterpoint as the only means through which the attention of the composer is concentrated on purely musical questions. Its elements also lend themselves perfectly to

шко мо - ё, ——————— Со - колъ я - сный, си - зо -
dear - est one, ——————— You my dar - ling. —— my love.

an architectural construction.' Listening to the Octet, it seems obvious that Stravinsky is thinking here of Bach. Yet functional counterpoint in Bach's sense is hardly more in evidence in the Octet than it was in *The Rite of Spring*, and the idea that the work's form derives from counterpoint, whatever that may mean, is extremely hard to take seriously.

What exactly is Stravinsky getting at in this strange and apparently muddled article? Obviously it is polemic more than analysis, and it probably has to be understood as yet another piece of agile footwork in what was to be a lifelong fencing-match with aesthetic fashion. Constructivism as such had been a feature of his music for nearly a decade – since, at the latest, the Three Pieces for string quartet. But after the war his physical and psychological alienation from Russia seems to have induced some unease at the picturesque folkloristic basis of most of his work up to that time.

*Mavra*, with its new Russo-European synthesis, was a direct response to that problem. But it is also, in some respects, a sign of anxiety, just as his remark about *The Rite*, made at the time of its revival by Diaghilev in 1920, that it was a 'pure musical construction' seems to show an excessive urge to reshape the past in the image of the present.[12] The fact is that, around 1920, Stravinsky was in the throes of the first of two major stylistic crises of his career.[13] Evidence of this abounds, for example, in the preliminary sketches of the *Symphonies*, the Concertino, the Octet, and an abandoned work called *Five Monometric Pieces*, whose initial ideas are all jumbled up in a way that, as Craft has pointed out, is unusual in Stravinsky. Early ideas for the Octet emerge in a context that makes it clear that their eventual stylistic setting cannot have been predicted, whereas Stravinsky usually seems to have sketched specific works from distinct creative images. Moreover the *Symphonies*, when completed in 1920, was (perhaps) withheld from publication and, to some extent, from performance too. In these circumstances Stravinsky's polemics suggest a desire to justify creative steps which, with his obsessive need to be thought up-to-date, he was afraid might be construed as compromises. We saw how deftly he achieved this with *Mavra*, turning an apparent stylistic recidivism into a new kind of synthetic modernism. With the Octet, which goes farther than *Mavra* in restoring cadential tonality, periodic rhythm and traditional forms, it was doubly important to interpret these old friends in terms of the modern doctrine of abstract order and logic, which may be why Stravinsky nowhere mentions the term 'classicism' as such and always detested the concept of 'neo-classicism' ('a much abused expression meaning absolutely nothing'[14]). This is not to say that the article is based on a falsehood. On the contrary Stravinsky was almost certainly right to draw attention to the consciously formal basis of the Octet, even if his way of doing so was not all that coherent. Instead of claiming a purely abstract language for this music, he would have done better to admit its synthetic, referential character; and instead of pretending that organic counterpoint was the driving force of the whole work, he could have noted that the idea of counterpoint was merely one musical object among several. As with *Mavra*, the listener's response to conventions which he can recognise is a primary part of his understanding of the music, even while those conventions are being manoeuvred into shapes and continuities which, if he were to stop and think about them, consistently violate his sense of their innate logic. In other words the Octet, and the works which follow, are a direct expression of stylistic dislocation and a loss of the automatic, or natural, character of style: above all Stravinsky's own, but also, by implication, that of the world in which he now willy-nilly found himself.

These works are four in number: the Octet, the Concerto for piano and wind, and two works for solo piano, the Sonata and Serenade. Several general points can be made about them, as a group and in their relation to the music which immediately precedes them. First, they are all purely instrumental concert works, and in that respect they sum up a tendency which we have noticed in Stravinsky's music since before *Pulcinella*. Secondly, they use only the dry, bright sounds of the piano and of wind instruments with strong emphasis on the brass, the sole exception being the Concerto, where double-basses and timpani are used for rhythmic support. This tendency also antedates *Pulcinella*, but its aim is less clear than Stravinsky and his 1920s associate, Arthur Lourié, imply in their contemporary writings.[15] *The Wedding* seems to have heralded a period of uncharacteristic indecisiveness about sonority on Stravinsky's part. The *Symphonies of Wind Instruments* includes strings in its earliest drafts, and the Octet had a concertante piano part plus, at one stage, timpani, a combination that of course suggests the Piano Concerto (which however, Stravinsky later wrote, was not itself first thought of as a piano work at all).[16] There is in any case no doubt that he was obsessed with the piano at this period. Its 'neat, clear sonority and polyphonic resources suited the dryness and neatness I was seeking in the structure of the music I had composed', which recalls his earlier theories about the function of wind instruments, which were 'more apt to render a certain rigidity of form I had in mind than other instruments' and whose differences of volume 'render more evident the musical architecture' ('Some Ideas about my Octuor'). These somewhat abstract considerations found practical embodiment in Stravinsky's genuine and for a time consuming passion for the pianola, which had featured in an intermediate version of *The Wedding*, and for which he composed his Study and arranged many of his other works, including *The Rite of Spring* and *Petrushka*.[17] The pianola attracted him, it appears, for its polyphonic richness – its ability to play any number of notes at once – and for its mechanical, or nearly mechanical, precision of performance. In general, dryness, hardness, a certain metallic brilliance, a repressive distaste for any hint of sentiment or gush, are the governing aesthetic of the time. Asafyev, viewing these works with the socio-critical eye of a still-progressive commissariat, admired in them 'the synthetic instrumental style of contemporary urbanism', though he was shrewd enough also to see that the style was self-conscious and would probably turn out to be transitional.[18]

A third point about the four works which distinguishes them from their predecessors and aligns them instead with *Mavra* is their outward approach to form. Here for the first time we find that conscious mimicry of academic convention which is a hallmark of Stravinsky's neo-classicism. The Octet, Piano Concerto and Sonata are all in three balanced movements, fast-slow-fast (with, in the first two cases, a slow introduction), the sort of form which instantly suggests classical models even though it may be hard to think of precedents that exactly explain Stravinsky's use of it. The Serenade, with its odd slow fourth movement ('Cadenza-Finale'), was probably planned as a suite in six movements, and left in its final more arbitrary form for lack of any opportunity to carry the scheme through.[19] But the

Serenade is the last of these four works and shows in several ways a relaxation from the severe posture of the others.

In all Stravinsky's early neo-classical works the use of classical form is referential rather than organic, and is best interpreted, like his other 'classical' devices, as symbolic. The Octet is a brilliant example of this, not least because it is the most entertaining of these early neo-classical instrumental scores, whose doctrinaire dryness can so easily sound like aridity. Even on close acquaintance, the sonata-like first movement with its introduction has an unmistakably 'correct' feel compared with the uncompromisingly radical *Symphonies of Wind Instruments* or the Concertino. But once one examines the reasons for this, they begin to look disconcertingly inadequate to the difference one experiences. Stravinsky calls the movement by the baroque title 'Sinfonia', which was applied (among other ways) to the introductory movements of instrumental suites and to short, peremptory operatic overtures, before it became the standard term for an orchestral work in several movements. But Stravinsky's Sinfonia itself has an introduction whose upbeat character is essentially that of the classical slow introduction. The movement is in E flat; the introduction starts with a trumpet B flat (dominant of E flat) and ends with an applied B flat seventh chord which resolves conventionally on to the E flat first subject of the Allegro. This E flat itself is diatonic, that is pure (as it might be in Mozart), and the metre is basically that of a march. There is a cantabile second subject and a rather more unstable middle section after which the movement is clinched by returns of the second and first subjects in reverse order, a device found in Haydn, who also sometimes wrote development sections like Stravinsky's which use new material. At the end E flat is triumphantly reasserted in the manner of a structural tonal conclusion.

Yet despite this orthodox-looking set of procedures, the movement has only an oblique connection with organic classicism. The introduction achieves the necessary length not by systematic tonal tension but by an elaboration of cellular motives not unlike that in the introduction to *The Rite of Spring* except that it alludes constantly to tonal, rather than modal, phraseology. Nevertheless by archly side-slipping on to the traditional dominant seventh at the end, Stravinsky tricks us into hearing the whole introduction as classical. In the Allegro, similarly, all the tonal areas are applied, not one is 'logically' argued (the need for so many quotation marks in discussing this whole subject gives some indication of its symbolic complexity). Why do we believe that they are? First, because Stravinsky makes subtle use of the classical distinction between tonally stable and unstable areas. Secondly, because many of his melodic lines, if not always the crucial ones, move by step or sequence: that is, in a clearly hierarchical way, which apes the grammar of tonality. These points may be worth looking at more closely. In the first subject of this *Allegro moderato* (from figs. 6 to 10) there are three obvious sections; the first, up to fig.7, is diatonically in E flat, the second repeats the theme in close imitation, still

*Ex. 29* Octet, transition to second subject

in E flat but with A flat underpinning which very mildly destabilises the tonality; the third treats the theme in a more elaborately imitative way and is both rhythmically and tonally definitely unstable. The second subject, when it comes (fig.10), is more or less in G major, but the section which 'prepares' it does not move the tonality towards G, as a transitional section would do in a classical movement. It dissolves the preceding E flat, while presenting the image of transitional, that is unstable, music with no clear tonal aim at all (Ex.29). The trumpet in A, which carries the theme at fig.8, has a descending sequence in which the tune comes a whole tone lower each time, while the accompanying trombones actually rise a semitone at each statement. Moreover the trumpet sequence contains tonal 'mistakes' (wrong accidentals) which keep twisting the modulations in the opposite direction to what one expects, while it is the rising bassoon line which in the end establishes the trumpet D of the new theme at fig.10. The whole passage is a brilliant parody of a contrapuntal transition ('its elements lend themselves perfectly to an architectural construction'). It does enough to imply one, and yet it is not one.

In this way the whole Octet divides up into symbolic functional blocks, mobilised by incisive rhythms and irregularly dovetailed melodic scales and sequences. Stravinsky's use of scales, in particular, is an often unremarked aspect of the music's wit. He must have observed how, in the most routine eighteenth-century music (and, let it be said, not only the most routine) mechanical formulae play a big part in keeping things going. In his classical music, similarly, the scales chug along, often irrelevantly, providing movement and a spurious sense of direction. The finale of the Octet starts in the manner of a Bach three-part invention, but the lowest part, played by the second bassoon, consists simply of a scale of C major (extended up to E) plied up and down without regard to the phrase structure or the melodic lie of the upper voices. The joke is on the listener as much as on Stravinsky's supposed models (surely not Bach himself). We accept this as good counterpoint, whereas it is really no more nor less than the translation into a different convention of an ostinato technique harking back to the Russian ballets.

The music's polyphonic wit is matched by its comedy of rhythm. Again the march element in the first movement is a referential background for a display of typical Stravinsky virtuosity in the handling of multiple layers of accent and phrase length. This is essentially the rhythmic technique of the Russian-period Stravinsky, but with one major new element – the cadential feeling of tonal harmony. In tonal music the cadence is typically an upbeat-downbeat gesture, and Stravinsky, in restoring partial tonality, also generally respects this crucial aspect of the architectural relation between rhythm and harmony. But just as his tonal references are, on examination, superimposed, so his cadences work referentially within a phraseology which consistently distorts the patterns to which it alludes. The first subject of the Octet begins like a straightforward eight-bar march tune,[20] but soon dissolves in a 5/8 bar. The next statement overrides the classical formula still further by inserting a 3/4 and a 3/8 plus a concluding 3/8 up to the cadence; and the 'transitional' section (fig.8) adds to these complications an off-beat canon, syncopated against the three-bar phrases of the *dux* (leading voice), though itself internally irregular. As in all his music, Stravinsky works with a complex polyphony of accents. In the foreground are the natural accents of the various lines, in the middle-ground the mediating effect of the barlines, in the background (and this is more evident in the neo-classical music than before) the style formulae. The barring, being the same in all parts, is a compromise (as in Parasha's song) but one which, however uncertainly, influences the surface accents. In the little fugato in the first movement recapitulation (fig.19), the opening bassoon figure looks as if it ought to be barred with the first low C as a downbeat, making a 4/8 bar instead of upbeat plus 3/8; and Stravinsky may have been influenced by a desire to end the fugue subject with the natural stress of a 3/8 bar to the cadence, which in turn necessitates an upbeat-plus-3/8 pattern for the same opening figure on the trumpet, where the two parts overlap (Ex.30). In any case, the 'wrong' barring is bound to influence the bassoon's phrasing, however slightly, giving it a faint kick on the weak quaver. At the very end of the movement (fig.23, a near repeat of fig.7) the answering voice on flute and trumpet in A could easily have been barred as 4/8 right up to the end. But Stravinsky preferred to fit it to the natural barring of the leading voice (trumpet in C) which itself cuts across the regular duple time that the whole passage implies. We know that he regarded the different voices in such cases as independent, as they are in sixteenth-century polyphony, and the barring often gave him trouble. In the Octet he occasionally draws a quaver or semiquaver beam across the barline to indicate a counter-accent, and when he revised the work in 1952 he made some changes to the barring. But he must have enjoyed the multiple implications of these rhythms. Clearly they suggested jazz syncopations, and the Octet actually ends with a jazzy 3+3+2=8 swung coda, which has some affinity with the closing pages of *Mavra*. However the whole point of this coda is that it is a very simple version of the sorts of pattern with which the music has been concerned, and it therefore unwinds them in the same way that the thumping tonic-dominant ending of a Beethoven symphony unwinds its tonal conflicts. To say that Stravinsky's rhythms were inspired by jazz would be to put the cart before the horse.

The slow movement stands slightly apart from the two quick movements, and its style owes rather more to earlier works. It contains those parts of the score which Stravinsky sketched first, at a time when he was probably uncertain of the use to which he would put them: the waltz variation[21] and the fugal Variation E (fig.51), which emerges as keyboard music from the aborted sketches for the *Five Monometric Pieces*. The theme is a broad melody completely in the octatonic scale on A (semitone first, or what van den Toorn calls Model A), and Stravinsky follows it with five variations of which the first acts as a ritornello, returning after each of the others except the last. But the octatonic flavour is not pure. In the theme it is obscured by attempts at D minor in the accompanying chords (D is not one of the notes in the scale itself), and in the recurring Variation A, by D minor scales, while the freer 'character' variations, whose spirit recalls that of the easy pieces, lose it almost completely. This particular octatonic model is one which, as van den Toorn has shown, Stravinsky later used to provide the tonal references of his neo-classical music, since it contains the major third and fifth (or dominant) of the scale, which the alternative model does not, and also offers the leading notes to those notes. But in the Octet this use of the scale seems not to have struck the composer, and instead he exploits its modal and chromatic qualities in opposition to tonal references brought in from outside. The result is a harmonic tension much greater than anything in the outer movements: a tension which, as Stravinsky observed in *Dialogues* (p.40), reaches its climax in the fugue and is then dissolved in the bright C major of the finale, with its *meccanico* scales and rhythms.

The Octet, completed in May 1923 and first performed, with Stravinsky himself conducting, at the Opéra in Paris in October of that year, seems at first to have posed more problems for him than it solved. The idea of a symbolic re-creation of historical styles and gestures looked promising, not least because the Octet, for all its obvious nods towards classical formulae and its half-humorous Bach parodies cleverly integrated with jazz and vulgarisms of the easy-piece variety, remained an utterly modern and personal work with the by-now familiar pungencies of harmony and rhythm

*Ex. 30* Octet, 1st movement

simply shown up in a new light. Above all the piece had wit, and it had precision; there is no better account of a Stravinsky performance than Cocteau's of the Octet première. 'S'il dirige l'*Octuor*,' he wrote in a 1924 appendix to *Le coq et l'arlequin* (pp. 110–11), 'il nous oppose un dos d'astronome pour résoudre ce magnifique calcul instrumental aux chiffres d'argent.' But the dangers of academicism were soon to become obvious, none the less for being aspects of a style which itself fed on academicisms. Moreover there were dangers of sterility, too, in such doctrinaire impassiveness. When Prokofiev writes to Myaskovsky in August 1925 that 'Stravinsky has written a dreadful sonata . . . the music is Bach but with pockmarks', we may feel a twinge of sympathy, even while we enjoy the irony that Prokofiev had only just unveiled in Paris his deliberately unpleasant Second

Symphony – 'this highly organised "fierceness"', as Claude Samuel calls it
– partly modelled on Beethoven's C minor Sonata, op.111.[22] The fact is that
Stravinsky, writing now piano works for his own concert tours (a necessity
imposed on him by exile, as it was on Prokofiev, Rakhmaninov and, for
different reasons, Bartók in the same years), could churn out harsh
keyboard style parodies with alarming fluency and justify their rebarbative-
ness on purely theoretical grounds. Indeed Lourié's articles about Stravinsky read very much like the music they are describing. As a summing
up of the Piano Concerto and Sonata, not to mention the more relaxed
Serenade, this may be unjust, but it contains a grain of truth.

The Piano Concerto, completed in April 1924 only two years before
Bartók's forbidding first concerto and a year or so before Berg's thickly
composed and somewhat schematic Chamber Concerto, is one of Stravinsky's least felicitous works. This is not to deny it a certain memorable
vigour, nor some striking ideas. But its heavy brilliance, which seems to
come from a miscalculation of spacing and resonance, is untypical of Stravinsky, and the music is more than any other of this period clogged up
by mechanical figuration of the type that in due course spawned that
uncomplimentary epithet, 'motor rhythm'. Stravinsky's practice of
requesting pianos with a light touch when he played the concerto (which
he did more than forty times up to 1929) may reflect some anxiety on his
own part about the instrumental balance. But the real problem may be one
of sound spectra. The piano writing itself is percussive in a way that often
recalls the brittle piano style of *Petrushka*; but the shimmer of that score,
with its prismatic effects of diatonic harmony scattered across the whole
range of the instrument, is replaced here by a more middle-of-the-register
continuity, governed largely by the contrapuntal considerations expounded
in 'Some Ideas about my Octuor', which was perhaps written while Stravinsky was at work on the concerto. Less easy to explain away is his muddy
scoring for horns. In the slightly pompous Handelian introduction the four
of them struggle to articulate their polyphony like a choir of contraltos and
basses battling their way through an arrangement of 'Surely he hath borne
our griefs'. And in the slow movement they serve often to thicken piano
chords which already seem sufficiently opaque.

The three-movement work has all the same a number of significant and
striking features. The sheer vitality of the first movement is hard to resist,
and though it has more unbroken duple-time writing than the Octet it also
introduces more extravagant rhythmic hiccoughs. But these are mainly in
the passages for solo piano, which thus have something of the character of
solo breaks in a piece of jazz. White also drew attention to the unusual
amount of literal repetition in this movement;[23] a large chunk of the exposition is recapitulated intact, and the slow introduction also returns in
modified form to close the movement (as well as, again, near the end of
the finale). These procedures have respectable precedents; Schubert often
recapitulated without change, and the baroque overture sometimes repeats

its *grave* opening after the Allegro. But they do, in Stravinsky, tend to reinforce the sense of mechanical process. Moreover the symbolic force of the references in this concerto is weakened by the fact that in its hardness and heaviness the writing seems to musunderstand the essential character of its presumed models, a point that is not unsettling in the Octet, lightened as it is by parody. The earnestness of the concerto works against it. The slow movement, in an airless diatonic C major, is not obviously purer in sentiment than any number of romantic concertos which Stravinsky would certainly have placed beyond the pale at that time.[24] At such times one is almost tempted to forget that Stravinsky is a respectable modern composer writing according to stringent aesthetic precepts, and place him instead in the well-populated ranks of post-Lisztian Russian concerto writers.

The Piano Sonata, composed in the late summer of 1924 immediately after the concerto, shares with it certain features. It has the same arrangement of movements, though no slow introduction, and it has cyclic elements (much less obtrusive), of which the most notable is a brusque reprise of the first movement's unison opening and close just before the end of the finale, with changed rhythm. It is also hardly less fraught with *meccanico* figuration. But it lacks, of course, the problems of texture and balance that plague the concerto, and above all its lyricism is better integrated with the factors of energy and movement. This is nowhere clearer than in the true first subject of the opening movement (bar 13), which combines expressive grace with flowing movement in much the same way as its ancestor, the 'Quoniam' in Bach's B minor Mass (Ex.31). Prokofiev was right to hear Bach, pock-marked or otherwise, as the parent of this music, even though Stravinsky, who understandably disliked being pigeon-holed, called the slow move-ment 'Beethoven *frisé*' – in fact, the slow, endlessly spun and curlicued melody of this movement is one of the work's most Bachian features. But on the level of style such features are more or less ubiquitous, from the unison opening with its direct reference to Bach's C minor fantasy style, to the sparkling two-part invention of the finale, with its subtly disguised canons by augmentation. Traces of Beethoven, whose music Stravinsky had been rediscovering only two years after telling Proust that he detested it,[25] are confined to a few details of form, including the immediate reprise of the first subject a tone up. And indeed the remarkable thing about the Sonata, assuming that Stravinsky had recently been playing the Viennese master's keyboard music, is that so little classical piano style seems to have filtered into his own. One is more inclined to detect the influence of Wanda Landowska's harpsichord revival in the Sonata's light, dry, brilliantly mobile lines and textures.

The Piano Sonata is certainly the purest example of Stravinskian synthe-tism, in its suppression of personal elements and its economy of sources – at times it comes close to actual pastiche, though its harmonic astringency in the end saves it from that fate. Both here and in the Piano Concerto

Ex. 31(i) Bach B Minor mass, 'Quoniam'

(ii) Sonata for piano (1924), first movement

Stravinsky's handling of tonality shows an extraordinary consistency with the chordal practices of his earlier works. For example, his fondness for the octave-displaced semitone (that is, for intervals such as the minor ninth, minor sixteenth, and, less obviously, the major seventh and fourteenth), which underpins the complex harmony of *The Rite of Spring* and persists through the Russian period, now comes out in conflicts between major and minor chords and in composite harmonies which contain the leading note (B in the key of C) and keynote at the same time. A good and simple example of this in the Sonata can be seen in the second bar of the first subject (bar 14 of the first movement: see previous example), where the real melody note in the trill is the B, though the rest of the chord is C major (Bach has a trill here as well, but with altered harmony). As in the Octet, Stravinsky adopts a fake linear counterpoint to link his chords, but in essence the effect is governed by a succession of vertical combinations – the very opposite of Bach, whose chords are the result of the integration of nominally free lines which obey laws designed to keep the harmony coherent. The impression of Bach made by the Sonata is due to texture and rhythm rather than organic counterpoint.

Nevertheless this style might suggest its own academicism, and it is typical of Stravinsky that, just when he might have seemed trapped in a cul-de-sac of ever-narrowing imitations, he should have produced a work like the Serenade, which is quite different in style and feeling and actually contains, despite its modest title, important anticipations of the next major phase of his work. The piece is longer than the Sonata, but it manages entirely without the pseudo-baroque note-spinning of that work. Reminiscences of Bach are confined to the more lyrical 'Romanza', modelled on the flowing style of the master's violin slow movements and framed by miniature cadenzas in the free-recitative manner of the organ toccatas. For the rest the music shows signs of that much wider frame of reference we shall begin to take for granted in works like *Apollo* and *Oedipus rex*. The harmony is often curiously romantic, and not only at the very start, with its much-remarked similarity to Chopin's F major Ballade. The wholly delightful 'Rondoletto' might be an eccentric cousin of one of Beethoven's bagatelles or one of Schubert's lesser sonata finales, though even here Stravinsky's love of false-relation and his lack of concern about harmonic progression soon intrude to lend an air of what Kandinsky called 'constructive dispersal' around the very simple background style. As for the so-called 'Cadenza-Finale', a slow piece written throughout in smooth, flowing quavers, for the first time since the *Symphonies* Stravinsky's music seems not to invite historical comparison, but inhabits a proto-classical world of its own distillation, suddenly close to the self-consciously purified texture of *Apollo* or *Persephone*. Although the top line of this piece is in fact Bach-like in the same way as the lines in the sonata, the texture of smooth parallel and contrary-motion chords has no obvious antecedents. This is perhaps a true neo-classicism, in that it foretells an Apollonian world of the composer's own creation.

Stravinsky called the work 'Serenade in A', and underlined the point by having each movement start ostentatiously with either the note A or its chord, and end on a unison A. These cadences are interesting, by the way, in that they arrive at their tonal closure not by a traditional process of resolution but by a kind of textural dissolution in which the conflicting notes simply evaporate leaving nothing but a resonance reinforced by Schoenberg's technique of silent depression of a bass key to encourage the sound to ring (Ex.32). But though parts of the Serenade do seem to be in A, in something like the classical sense, it certainly is not so as a whole – not just because the very first chord is F major, but because of Stravinsky's persistent avoidance of perfect cadences, and also because of peculiarities of chord spacing which already appear in *Mavra* and the Octet and remain a feature of his tonal writing up to *The Rake's Progress*. Broadly this can be described as an avoidance of root-position triads, or chords of the key in question with the keynote at the bottom. In the Serenade this colour emerges as an aspect of the 'idea' of the music, but it does not yet acquire the architectural importance it later has in the Symphony in C, where the E at the bottom of the first-inversion C major chords both gives them a particular profile and tries to assert the opposing key of E minor. In the piano work, the third (or its inversion, the sixth) which separates the upper and lower notes of so many of the chords is more in the nature of a textural motif. Parallel thirds and sixths are ubiquitous, and they seem to be as much a part of the sound image as the opposed C/F sharp triads in *Petrushka* or the motto chord of the Violin Concerto. The fact that they come more directly from traditional chords is strictly beside the point, since those chords are not used with their traditional value, though obviously Stravinsky is well aware of that value and has it in mind as a reference. A concomitant of this slightly evasive use of the tonal third is his general avoidance of the more decisive fifth, both as a melodic and as a chordal interval: 'tonality without fifths,' this has been called.[26] But the phrase contains an irony, since it is precisely in the avoidance of fifths that the music misses being tonal in the organic sense that, according to theory, demands the tonic-dominant relation. Or, to put it more bluntly, it is a contradiction in terms. What we encounter in the Serenade is, once again, the symbolic use of a certain interval, carefully divorced from its context, but not so far as to lose all touch with it, as perhaps Schoenberg's 'Mondestrunken' in *Pierrot Lunaire* does. And the work's full title is allusive to just the same extent.

\* Depress without striking

*Ex. 32* Serenade, 'Romanza'

The smooth, somewhat timeless effect of this piece is already worlds away from the spirited neo-tonality of the Octet, which counts the perfect cadence among its repertoire of symbols. It shows that in late 1925, when the Serenade was completed, Stravinsky was ready for a move away from the doctrinaire severity of a music that owed allegiance only to the didactic manifestos of the early 1920s. The change opened the way once more for music on the loftiest spiritual plane, and it is not surprising to find that it was accompanied by important changes in Stravinsky's life.

# The Christian Rites of Spring:
# Oedipus *and* Persephone

According to Stravinsky's *Dialogues* (p.26), *Oedipus rex* was 'composed during my strictest and most earnest period of Christian Orthodoxy'. Both there and in his autobiography he records Joergenson's *Life of St Francis*, which he picked up on a bookstall in Genoa in September 1925, as a crucial inspiration for the new work. In April 1926 he returned to the Orthodox Church as a regular communicant 'because of an extreme spiritual need'.[1] At this time he was under the influence of Father Nicolai Podossenov, his confessor, who 'was practically a member of our household' for some five years after the Stravinskys' move to Nice in 1925.[2] 'Intellectual and priestly influences', Stravinsky goes on, 'were not of primary importance to me.' But 'Jacques Maritain may have exercised an influence on me at this time.' In fact echoes of Maritain's *Art et scolastique*, first published in 1920, can be detected in Stravinsky's prose writings, and by implication in his music, from the time of the Octet until *The Poetics of Music* (1939–40). Maritain had derived from St Thomas Aquinas a theory of art which combined the honesty and humility of the work of the artisan (*homo faber*) with the idea of art as an intellectual virtue or 'habit'; and just as neo-Thomism, like other conservative movements in Catholicism around the turn of the century, was in part an assertion of order and authority against the diversity and heterodoxy of nineteenth-century religious tendencies, so *Art et scolastique* is an attempt 'de sortir de l'immense désarroi intellectuel hérité du XIXe siècle, et de retrouver les conditions spirituelles d'un labeur honnête.'[3] As a religious aesthetician, Maritain was probably anxious to make room within the Faith for current artistic attitudes which may, in their secular expression, have seemed dangerously rootless and materialistic. But it is easy to see the religious-minded Stravinsky of *The Wedding* responding at once to so purely and morally focused a view of art. His remarks on form in 'Some Ideas about my Octuor' seem a direct reflection of the Thomist idea quoted by Maritain that 'la beauté est le resplendissement de la forme sur les parties proportionnées de la matière' (p.39). By that time he had struck up an association with another expatriate Russian composer, Arthur Lourié, who according to Craft was a disciple of Maritain, and whose articles on Stravinsky's new works from the Piano Sonata to *Apollo* are distinctly Thomist in spirit, with their insistence of 'l'unité du principe moral et esthetique'.[4]

Craft has suggested that Stravinsky's 'new religiosity' was 'one of the many consequences of [his] personal situation during the 1920s and 1930s' (that is, of his unconcealed affair with Vera Sudeikina at a time when his wife Catherine was slowly dying of tuberculosis).[5] But it may be that a full study of his intellectual life in the 1920s will show it as the natural consequence of the permeation of his essentially devout nature by the atmosphere of intellectual and spiritual renewal which was gaining intensity in France at that time. Though he never turned to Catholicism as such, his rediscovered Orthodoxy sufficiently fits the picture of growing Gallicisation that led in due course to his taking French citizenship in 1934, to his disastrous candidacy for the Académie des Beaux-Arts in 1936, and finally to the intensely French tone of the *Poetics*, which marks the climax of his anti-Russianism at the very moment when he was leaving France for good.[6] A similar tendency is apparent in his music. The extraordinary spiritual grandeur of *Oedipus rex* somehow emerges from the rather condescendingly intellectual classicism of Cocteau's text and from the whole curious idea of a language 'impersonnel et effacé',[7] in which there surely lingers some trace of Valéry's 'poésie pure'. *Apollo*, (or, to give it is original title, *Apollon musagète*) is openly French in musical inspiration, while *Persephone*, Stravinsky's first significant setting of a text in French, epitomises the Gallic virtues of purity and grace combined with intellectual rigour. Together with the *Symphony of Psalms*, these works bear a spiritual witness that can only be explained as the result of a sudden fusion of ideas, over and above the mere fusion of styles we have already examined in the works of the early 1920s.

The revived sense of awe in these works of 1926–35 is perhaps their most striking common feature. Leaving aside the openly religious *Symphony of Psalms*, and the three little unaccompanied sacred choruses (*Pater noster*, 1926; *Credo*, 1932; *Ave Maria*, 1934), there remains a profound spirit of Delphic mystery about the other works of this time, including even the easily-disregarded *Fairy's Kiss*, – an atavistic blend of monumental classicism and Christian allegory which harks back to the ritual purity concealing powerful psychological undercurrents in *The Rite of Spring* and *The Wedding*. It hardly comes as a surprise to read, in every account of the origins of *Oedipus rex*, that at the end of 1925 Stravinsky 'had been aware of the need to compose a large-scale dramatic work' for at least five years.[8] During those years he had written nothing for the stage, apart from the brilliant but featherweight *Mavra* and the final instrumentation of *The Wedding*, nor anything to equal the *Symphonies of Wind Instruments* (1920) in sacramental presence. The opening bars of *Oedipus* might almost be a graphic expression of an emotion imprisoned by half a decade of abstraction and detachment cemented by aesthetic theory.

It is in this light that the 'opera-oratorio' should be discussed. In October 1925 Stravinsky wrote to Cocteau, whom he had already invited by word of mouth to collaborate on the new work: 'For some time now I have been pursued by the idea of composing an opera in Latin on the subject of a tragedy of the ancient world, with which everyone would be familiar.'[9] The idea, evidently, was for a work purely in Latin in the manner of the Catholic Mass. Somewhere in the back of his mind may have been Verdi's *Requiem*, which balances theatrical and ecclesiastical modes of utterance in a rather similar way; the influence of Verdi on *Oedipus rex* is obvious in any case, and has been documented by Craft with reference to Stravinsky's known enthusiasm for Verdi's operas during the 1920s.[10] On the other hand the idea of a spoken narration in the vernacular came from Cocteau. It looks like a straightforward explanatory device; but oddly enough Cocteau's narration is sketchy and often confusingly obscure. Whereas in Sophocles's play, which is the basis of the libretto, every detail of the situation is made gradually clear, and indeed has to be made clear if the dramatic irony of Oedipus's moral blindness is to make its effect, Cocteau does not even explain properly such crucial facts as that Oedipus is the adoptive son of King Polybus of Corinth (until the announcement comes of Polybus's death), or that, when he killed Laius, Oedipus was on his way from Delphi, where the oracle had foretold that he would kill his father and marry his mother, whom he still believes to be Polybus and his wife, even while realising that the man he killed was the King of Thebes.

The fact is that the narration is a device of alienation similar to the one Stravinsky had already used in *The Soldier's Tale*. And although Stravinsky blamed Cocteau for the idea that the narrator should wear evening dress, that is exactly what Ramuz's narrator had worn in Lausanne.[11] There seem grounds for supposing that Stravinsky was later anxious to discredit Cocteau's contribution to the success of *Oedipus*, just as he played down Gide's to that of *Persephone*, precisely because he knew that a crucial part of the musical perspective was provided by their texts. In *Oedipus* the narrator supplies two important components of the architecture, which between them replace the Sophoclean irony. In the first place he draws attention, by his urbane omniscience, to the ritualistic or ceremonial nature of the drama we are witnessing and the fated character of the action. For this role he should be in modern, and best of all evening, dress to satirise our remoteness from such a ritual by honouring it with the sort of dress we reserve for smart recreation and specifically not for religious observance. In this sense the narrator is a theatrical representative of that archetypal modern master, the professor of comparative religion, who knows everything and believes nothing. As we shall see, this provides for a violent 'break' with the subject-matter of the drama itself, which combines what many classical scholars regard as one of the most perfectly formed Greek tragedies with a considerable latent Christian symbolism. In the second place the narrator brings into play successive shifts in time sequence which reintroduce irony as a function of the music. By the end of each of his short speeches he has carried the story forward to its next crisis, but the music which follows must revert every time to the situation as at the start of the speech. This turns out to be a much more powerful effect than might seem likely from its bare description; and there is little doubt that Stravinsky recognised the fact since he made musical capital out of it. For instance, one might conjecture that his hidden reason for preferring playing the 'Gloria' reprise at the start of part 2 after the narrator's speech rather than before was the superb irony of following the narrator's 'il a peur' with a brilliant chorus in C major – though he could not give this as a reason, because in the very next paragraph of *Dialogues* (pp. 29–30) he attacks the whole device of the speaker, 'that disturbing series of interruptions'. Even finer is the rhythmic link to the words 'roi est un roi' in Tiresias's revelation of the identity of Laius's murderer. Here the revelation, which is yet to come in the actual music-drama, provides *ante hoc* the rhythm of the chorus's anxious anticipation of Tiresias's arrival (Ex.33). Stravinsky had used this same device in *The Soldier's Tale* (more extensively indeed) to convey the narration into the musical action, but without any equivalent cargo of irony.

For the musical parts of *Oedipus rex*, Stravinsky envisaged a series of monumental tableaux in which the classical idea of verbal elucidation without overt action would be carried to an extreme. Not only were the actors to be masked, as on the Greek stage, but with the exception of Tiresias, the Shepherd and the Messenger, the oracular characters who bring the information that changes the complexion of the story, they were also to be deprived of motion apart from their heads and arms. Cocteau's note printed in the score suggests: 'they should give the impression of living statues'. Theodore Strawinsky's set design, which is also reproduced in the score but was apparently never used for a stage production, adds to this the further restriction of an essentially two-dimensional concept with the singers in the same vertical plane but at different heights. The idea was that the characters would be fixed in their original positions, helpless in the face of destiny, and able to express their despair only by gestures as futile as those of a drowning man. The entire conception, which must have come *en bloc* from Stravinsky's original discussions with Cocteau, is like a visual realisation of those theories of pure expressive form and self-terracing dynamics which had accompanied his recent instrumental works. In neither what we see nor what we hear is anything to distract us from the drastic architectural and functional unity of the work taken as a whole in all its various elements. Or, as Maritain's follower Lourié explains it, the composer 'renonce complètement à la tentation esthétique. . . . La signification d'*Oedipe* consiste dans l'expression nue de la vérité et de la pureté, et tout est sacrifié à cette expression.'[12]

*Ex. 33 Oedipus Rex*

It might seem that in all this Stravinsky is expressing some latent hostility to the stage presentation of *Oedipus Rex*, perhaps in the way that the devout might object to the staging of Handel's *Messiah* or Bach's *St Matthew Passion*. It certainly is true that the monumental, tableau construction of the work is akin to that of the baroque oratorio, and that the grandeur of the music often seems Handelian. It is also true that the first performance, arranged with great difficulty by the authors as a present to Diaghilev for his twentieth year of Paris seasons, was given in concert form. But this was only because the cost of stage production could not be guaranteed in time for it to be put into rehearsal.[13] One can in fact hardly doubt that Stravinsky saw his apparently rigid and self-limiting stage concept as a crucial part of the work, and that the hybrid subtitle is meant to indicate, not that *Oedipus* is an opera *or* an oratorio at the convenience of its interpreters, but that it is an opera on which certain aspects of the concert oratorio have exerted an influence. These include: the statuesque dramaturgy; the pivotal structural role played by the chorus; the strict sectionalisation imposed by the narrator, who in this respect resembles the Evangelist of the baroque Passion; the closed forms and rhetorical manner of the music, in which the ceremonial, the ornate, the pastoral, the pathetic and so on are treated as distinct 'characters' or 'modes'. Lourié, perhaps echoing the master himself, saw the forthright rhythmic style and comparatively plain harmonies as direct allusions to Handel, 'ce général allemand . . . [qui] composait à Londres une musique impersonelle, aussi formelle et conventionelle que le langage juridique.'[14]

Yet the neo-baroque character of *Oedipus rex* is much less absolute than Lourié and others have made out. In the Serenade we have already seen Stravinsky mixing baroque and classical ingredients with reminiscences of the early nineteenth century. In *Oedipus* the specific model is Verdi; and more generally, Italian romantic opera up to and including Puccini's *Turandot*, which Stravinsky presumably saw in Milan in May 1926 during its first run of performances.[15] Some of the allusions to these composers are so direct that one is tempted to believe they may have been unconscious by-products of a current enthusiasm, rather than items in an aesthetic manifesto, like the Tchaikovsky-isms in *Mavra*. For instance, the Messenger's 'Divae Jocastae caput mortuum', which Stravinsky later irreverently described as a four-word singing telegram, is like an echo of the riddle theme in Act 2 of *Turandot*, and especially of Calaf's answers; in each case the emblematic motif is repeated several times in ritual fashion.[16] The Verdian character of Jocasta's aria is obvious, including the scoring for clarinets in sixths. But throughout the work the 'routine' accompaniments are closer to Italian opera than to baroque or classical music. Their hallmark is repeated chords on the weak quavers as opposed to the running passage-work which typifies the Octet. And gesturally, even to the shock-horror use of the diminished-seventh chord, the work is consistently Verdian. The entire structure of the opening scene, from the violent chorus imploring deliverance from the plague to Oedipus's confident reassurances, suggests that of *Otello* – a significant parallel, since Otello's fall is by far the most classical in Verdi's tragedies.

Referring later to the diverse musical sources of *Oedipus*, Stravinsky applied to it Schwitters's term, *Merzbild* – that is, a picture made from rubbish. But the expression is inapt, for the good reason that neither his intention nor his achievement was Dadaistic. What we have instead is a synthetic style, as in *Mavra*, adapted to a particular purpose. While the references to the baroque oratorio, together with the monumental (or, as Stravinsky called it, 'still life') character of the stage picture, gave a desired quality of ritual to the dramatic form, the no less necessary immediacy and violence of passion could only come – in Stravinsky – through a musical language still associated with such things: a melodramatic language that had not yet dated. Italian opera could supply this (Wagnerian opera could have done so too, of course, but here Stravinsky was naturally influenced by his own taste). Thus the coldness or remoteness of the total formula is balanced by the emotional thrust without which even the drama of Sophocles would have been mere empty rhetoric. Or, in the Nietzschean terms adopted by Stravinsky in the *Poetics*, Apollo is balanced by Dionysus and vice versa.

All the same, the purely musical means through which Stravinsky re-creates the classical tragedy are not derived but personal. Like all his music since 1920, *Oedipus Rex* is built round tonal centres, and indeed these are now altogether clearer and more unambiguous even than in the Octet or Serenade. In a famous article on this work, Wilfrid Mellers argued that its dramatic form was defined by tonal symbolism, in which the classical relation of dominant and tonic has a literal meaning: for instance 'Man', represented by E flat, is dominated by 'Destiny', represented by B flat major/minor. Like so many writers who pursue the idea of musical symbolism, Mellers made elementary mistakes of analysis. He said, for example, that the middle section of Jocasta's aria is in F major, though it is in fact in D minor leading to F minor. But his general idea is convincing. It hinges on the fact that Stravinsky still treats keys, as he treated modes in his Russian works, as static entities, rather than organic elements of grammar. Each of these tonalities – the B flat minor of the opening chorus, the C major of Creon's aria, the G minor of Jocasta's – has a certain weight and a dramatic location comparable to the fixed position of each of the dramatis personae on the stage. Stravinsky seems deliberately to exaggerate this weight. *Oedipus* contains the most purely triadic music he has written since *Petrushka*, outside miniature forms. And it anchors its triads by a more rigid system of metre, and by ostinato patterns which, by Stravinsky's standards, are unusually regular and predictable. This too lends itself to a dramatic symbolism. In the early part of the work there is a stark contrast between the choral writing (always for male voices), heavy and demoralised by sickness, and Oedipus's self-confident, high-lying, free-flowing color-atura. But Oedipus's music becomes plainer as understanding blunts his pride. His last aria, 'Nonne monstrum', in which he unconvincingly accuses Jocasta of deserting him out of shame at the discovery of his 'lowly' birth, is both hesitant and, apart from a few short-winded flourishes, devoid of bravura, while his last utterance of all, in which he calmly states the true facts of his situation, is both movingly simple and, above all, without prevarication. The harmony here is as plain (or nearly as plain) as the vocal line, but it shows the subtlety and individuality of Stravinsky's handling of supposedly conventional formulae. The melody looks as if it is in B minor (including the final arpeggio on'Lux facta est'), but Stravinsky harmonises it with alternate chords of D minor and D major, apparently representing darkness and light, since the minor is always below the voice, the major always above. The D major, however, is and remains ambiguous, even on the very last chord (which provides Mellers with his text for interpreting D as the key of Light), because Stravinsky always leaves out the A, or dominant, of the triad, as he had so often done in the Serenade. But a D major chord without its fifth may also be heard as the third and fifth of B minor, the melody key here. The final chord only does not have this option, because at last the note D is at the bottom and below the voice (Ex. 34).

Behind such writing lies the idea of tonality as the opposition of colours, rather than a system of relationships. But it also has to do with the importance Stravinsky attached to 'the musical interval'. Describing his compositional method in *Conversations*, he told Craft that 'long before ideas are born I begin work by relating intervals rhythmically' (p.15), and 'when I compose an interval I am aware of it as an object' (p.17). In *Oedipus Rex* the controlling interval is the minor third; it not only dominates the ostinati, especially in the opening and closing choruses, but it influences the

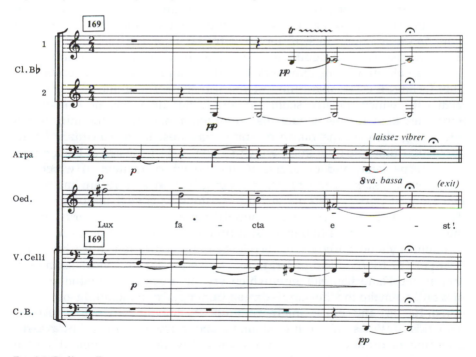

*Ex. 34 Oedipus Rex*

harmony to the extent that the music has a persistent tendency towards the minor mode, while major modes are quickly tinged by the clash of major and minor thirds, as happens early on, for instance, in Creon's C major aria. One could possibly see such an interval as carrying some dramatic symbolism: perhaps 'fate' or 'menace' (Stravinsky himself suggested that the regular metres, which are linked to the minor third from the start, created tension). But its real point is more fundamental; it seems close to the germinal musical idea of the whole work, and as such has more to do with its sound than with its symbolism.[17]

*Oedipus Rex* was composed in 1926 and early 1927, and first performed in Paris in May of the latter year. After a period of stylistic retrenchment and rather modish lightness and dryness in the works of the early 1920s, it marks a new maturity of style in Stravinsky's music, comparable to that which had produced the first great outburst of *The Rite of Spring* and *The Wedding*. Moreover it has significant links with those works of the Russian period. Like them it is a ritual enactment with connotations of fertility, in that the survival of the people depends on the sacrifice of an individual. Like the later Russian theatre pieces it is a play presented in a frame which has the effect of distancing and hence supposedly universalising the action. However, unlike them it is also a work which dramatises the individual's predicament. The king who must 'die' is not simply the latest incumbent of the priesthood, like Frazer's king of the wood at Nemi, but a particular king, Oedipus, a person with recognisable faults and virtues. If his expulsion is necessary for the good of the people, then his sacrifice, to the extent that it is voluntary, is in some way Christ-like and suggests an atonement. This feeling is especially strong at the moment of illumination, the 'Lux facta est', which already seems to anticipate the sense of benediction Sophocles kept for his sequel play, *Oedipus at Colonus*. This minute but interesting slant on the play's meaning prepares the more drastic Christianisation Gide and Stravinsky were to give the Homeric tale of Persephone seven years later, and of course it fits the whole context of which the *Symphony of Psalms* is the focus, including Stravinsky's recent interest in neo-Thomist poetics descending from Aristotle. It is very tempting to feel that the unusual richness of this new phase in his work is partly due to the re-invasion of his ritual style by a note of personal compassion.

Stravinsky's own account of the change was somewhat different: 'What is important for the lucid ordering of the work – for its crystallisation – is that all the Dionysian elements which set the imagination of the artist in motion and make the life-sap rise must be properly subjugated before they intoxicate us, and must finally be made to submit to the law: Apollo demands it.'[18] As in all his writings about neo-classicism, Stravinsky preferred to draw attention to the civilising work of the intellect, rather than to the quality of the feeling that is civilised. But in his next work after *Oedipus Rex*, the actual ballet *Apollo*, the 'lucid ordering' is less striking than the tone of the music itself – that famous calm serenity which seems (yet again) to have puzzled its first audiences, in Washington and Paris in the spring of 1928. There is in fact nothing particularly cerebral about *Apollo*, but it *is* a work of spiritual discipline and grace. De Schloezer, reviewing it in the *Nouvelle revue française*, saw in it Stravinsky's 'soif de renoncement' and predicted that his next work would be a Mass, 'so convinced was he that the moral fibre of the man and the artistic fibre of the artist had now inextricably fused together. . . . Stravinsky had emerged with a work whose "serenity" and "purity" could find a parallel only in religious experience.'[19]

Admittedly it is hard to carry this argument much beyond the mere impression that it is true, because Apollo is the first of Stravinsky's story-less ballets, and though it has a nominal action in which the god is born and apotheosised, the 'events' which link these terminal points are simply classical dances: variations for the three muses whom Stravinsky allows to stand for the nine (Calliope, Polyhymnia, Terpsichore), framed by variations for Apollo and ending with a *pas de deux*. The music certainly derives solemnity from its suggestions of stately baroque dances, for instance in the *ouverture*-like 'Birth of Apollo' or in Apollo's second variation, which is a kind of cross between a slow minuet and a pavan. But the simple grace of French nineteenth-century ballet is just as much in evidence, not to mention reminiscences of Tchaikovsky. And neither the harmony nor the timbre is as austere as it is pure: that is, the water of Stravinsky's Parnassus may be clean but it is hardly cold. What does appear on closer acquaintance with the music is a rhythmic subtlety greater perhaps than in any ballet by this master rhythmicist. Of all his works, it is *Apollo* that could take as its motto the passage, 'Grace danceth. . . . The Whole on high hath part in our dancing. . . . Whoso danceth not, knoweth not what cometh to pass.'[20] The purpose of the extremely diatonic harmonies and of the meticulously balanced and uniform string textures seems therefore to be to supply a medium through which this movement can, so to speak, pass without effort: a kind of musical ether.

Stravinsky himself tells us that 'the real subject of *Apollo* . . . is versi-fication.'[21] Each dance is a variation on the basic pattern of the iamb, and at the head of the Variation of Calliope, the Muse of Poetry, he prints an alexandrine couplet by Boileau which supplies the principal metre as well as the phraseological idea for the main Allegretto theme of the variation. Behind this idea of a *vers donné* – a metre which gives the controlling shape to a whole work – one detects again the influence of Valéry, who tells us, for instance, that 'Le cimetière marin' originated in just such a rhythmic idea, an iambic pentameter. This procedure of identifying the idea of a work with its technique of realisation may seem a typically French bit of academicism, or it may suggest Maritain's *homo faber*, or perhaps both. But in any case Stravinsky's manipulation of it seems more flexible than Valéry's. Where Valéry bases his entire poem on the one metre, so that the balance of the work is maintained by minute variations within a regular flowing pattern, Stravinsky makes his 'versification' by endless small variations of the pattern itself. These variations have much the same character as the changing patterns we have found throughout his music. They consist essentially of three-beat bars inserted into two-beat schemes or vice versa, or of simple lengthenings and shortenings of a given pattern, such as the two-element theme of the Allegro in the overture (fig.7), in which the number of units in each element (the rising arpeggio in trochees, or reversed iambs; and the answering downward scale) is always different. But Stravinsky also makes full use of that possibility, which music has more than poetry, of rhythmic counterpoint. At the end of this same Allegro a rhythmic climax is suggested by a series of quite heavily stressed fives against the implied four, an effect which, in this graceful context, has almost the violence of the accented cross-rhythms in *The Rite of Spring*. This remains admittedly a technique of word-versification. In poetry, word-stress can also bounce off a strict but unheard background metre. But Stravinsky goes well beyond such possibilities in passages like the middle section of the 'Pas d'action', which is a canon by augmentation and diminution in four real parts: that is, there is a central canon in which the two parts move at the same speed, but also a canonic voice in the second cellos which goes twice as fast, and one in the first violins which goes twice as slow (Ex.35). In this harmonically very controlled music the passage is extraordinarily brilliant, not least for a composer who had never been noted as a contrapuntist, despite his experiments in phasing in the Three Pieces for string quartet. It moreover epitomises a work in which the sense of flow and counterflow is profoundly linked to the more general sense of balletic movement which is of course the main point of the music.

These rhythmic touches are invariably discreet. They nudge against the simple patterns in much the same way that the dissonances in the harmony nudge against the consonant patterns which mostly prevail. The world of *Apollo* is one where effects that were formerly made by insistence are now made by hints. At the same time Stravinsky steers towards a melodic style which seems to court the sentimental effect of the chromatic appoggiatura – the note which 'leans' on its note of resolution – and the chromatic passing-note – the note which fills in the step – that music lovers associate with the somewhat frail idiom of certain minor French ballet composers of the romantic era, from Adam downwards. But here such touches are no more than the turn of a hand on a classical statue. They are no more saccharine than the poised fragments of 'commonplace tunes' could possibly be found vulgar by anyone who listened to their place in the texture as a whole. This is presumably because, as with all his previous appropriations, Stravinsky is careful to break into their continuity so that they are never able to establish a facile context like the one from which they are taken. The chromatic notes only seem to lead in the expected direction; as in the Octet, harmonic transition is not in fact governed by such devices, which are used figuratively. And the tunes never fulfil their four-square

*Ex. 35 Apollo, 'Pas d'action'*

destiny but remain mere suggestions – glimpses of solid rock through the mists of Parnassus.

After these two great works on classical subjects, Stravinsky abandoned his overt theatre of classicism until returning to it five years later in *Persephone*. But the intervening works are much more an integral part of that development than may appear at first sight. It is easy enough to regard *The Fairy's Kiss* as an opportunistic pastiche in the tradition of *Pulcinella*. The idea of basing it on Tchaikovsky, and even some of the suggestions as to which pieces, came from Benois, just as the idea and material for *Pulcinella* had come from Diaghilev.[22] And one can scratch one's head in bafflement at the sudden appearance of a sacred masterpiece like the *Symphony of Psalms* amid all this sacrificing to Apollo, as White called it. But then White, along with many Stravinsky critics of his generation, failed to see the religious strain in all the major works of this period, and in any case was perturbed by that part of it which he did see. His approving quotation of Ansermet's incredibly obtuse idea that the symphony 'expresses the religiosity of others' shows how hard it remains for the positivist mind to accept that direct religious feeling might still co-exist with a rigorous intellect, not to mention a rigorous art.

*The Fairy's Kiss* and the Capriccio for piano and orchestra which immediately followed it are both obliquely connected with *Apollo*, in that the suavities of harmonic and melodic language in the earlier ballet provide their more evanescent charms with a kind of handhold within Stravinsky's style. Indeed it is not too far-fetched to see *The Fairy's Kiss*, composed in the latter half of 1928, as an extreme experiment in the kind of synthetic method which had occupied Stravinsky throughout the 1920s. Though directly based on pieces by Tchaikovsky (mainly piano works and songs), it in fact contains a lot of fabrication, and is far from the kind of straight transcription with added notes that we find in *Pulcinella*. Stravinsky not only took the borrowed music to pieces, reassembling it in a kind of collage which amusingly if affectionately mocks Tchaikovsky's own habit of putting his music together in sections. But he also invented phrases that might very well be by Tchaikovsky, and he orchestrated the whole concoction in a way that just, but deliberately only just, avoids the sumptuousness of its model (just as his other Tchaikovsky orchestrations, the 1921 arrangements for Diaghilev's *Sleeping Beauty* and the later chamber-orchestral version of the 'Bluebird' *pas de deux* from that ballet – both of which were intended as good approximations made from piano reduction – are restrained, classicised versions which nevertheless do not evade the emotional thrust of the music). One senses Stravinsky venturing as near to the precipice as he dares while keeping his synthetic stance. The balancing act is brilliant but precarious; or at least the composer teases us into thinking so.

*The Fairy's Kiss* is modelled indirectly on *The Sleeping Beauty*. As Lawrence Morton has pointed out in the most exhaustive study of the work's sources,[23] it copies Tchaikovsky's ballet musically here and there (for instance in the second scene, where the young man is enticed by the sinister fairy, a passage which hints at the fairy Carabosse's music in *The Sleeping Beauty*). But more especially, Stravinsky seems to have hunted for a story which would resemble Tchaikovsky's while enabling him to concentrate on the magical or sinister elements at the expense of the emotional ones, and to avoid a sentimental or facile happy ending. This he found in Hans Andersen's tale *The Ice Maiden*, in which the curse at birth takes the form of a kiss on the child's mouth by the queen of the glacier, who then years later claims the young man's life (by another kiss, on his foot) on the eve of his wedding. The tale ends, in Stravinsky's version, with a glacial apotheosis in the Eternal Dwellings, for which he finds a slow, menacing lullaby that cannot but suggest the one near the end of his earlier fairy-tale ballet, *The Firebird*. So at this point the synthetist comes full circle, recalling no doubt that his own first visit to the theatre, as a child, had been precisely to see *The Sleeping Beauty*, when that work was still new.

But the romantic ingredients of *The Fairy's Kiss*, like the pure harmony and texture of *Apollo*, are only the medium for certain underlying ideas which belong essentially to the period of *Oedipus Rex* and the *Symphony of Psalms*. The familiar style of the ingredients draws attention to the disjointed and even surrealistic treatment they get, and it is through this treatment that Stravinsky suggests the idea of a tragedy that is not sentimental (in the manner of *Swan Lake*) but allegorical. The unnamed young man stood in the composer's mind for Tchaikovsky himself, or so he tells us in a somewhat obscure dedication in the score. But he might as well have compared him with Apollo of the Muses, the spirit of ordered creativity raised aloft from the futile and repetitive ceremonies of daily life; or even with Oedipus at Colonus, whom 'something invisible and strange caught up . . . into a space unseen' (1681–3). Equally present is the idea of beatification which will reach its finest expression in the closing pages of the *Symphony of Psalms*. There is an obvious musical parallel between the final lullaby 'of the Eternal Dwellings' in the ballet and the sublime incantation of the 'Laudate eum' in the symphony. It goes without saying that these are similarities which reflect a possible intention more than an achievement. In *Apollo* the combination of the 'sense of sublime serenity' and the 'sense of tragic fatality'[24] is so completely realised that it is impossible to distinguish the two characteristics; they are simply descriptions of the same thing from opposite directions. Their meeting-point is the spirit of renunciation which gave de Schloezer his intimation of the religious character of *Apollo*, and which informs every detail of the *Symphony of Psalms*. But in *The Fairy's Kiss* the two elements seem often at war with one another, so that in the end it is hard to be sure that the serenity of the closing lullaby is not in reality a mere chill, a freezing over of the waters of feeling: that its renunciation is not simply a deprivation. No doubt this ambivalence reflects the incongruity of the attempt at genre ballet by a composer whose genius was for ritualised dance, and the logic of whose development was increasingly towards abstract ballet. In a sense Stravinsky's embroidery of the various motives in *The Fairy's Kiss* has precisely the effect of abstracting them from their context. But it is a process which leaves us conscious of the violence done to its materials, even while we admire its subtle inventive wit.

By comparison the *Symphony of Psalms* is perhaps the most completely integrated of all Stravinsky's major works and the one which best defines his sense of the spiritual discipline ('habit') and personal effacement of creative work. The score is for the first time inscribed 'À la gloire de Dieu', and the Latin text from the Vulgate Psalms 38, 39 and 150 (Authorised Version, 39, 40 and 150) does not suggest any tension between a suppressed violent drama and a ritual act, as in *Oedipus*, but is simply the most natural language for an act of prayer in the spirit of the Church Fathers.[25] Stravinsky tells us in *Dialogues* (p.45) that he actually started composing to a text in Slavonic, the church language of the Russian Orthodox; and this is not the only evidence that this seemingly impersonal masterpiece comes closer to the soul of Stravinsky's art than any work of his since the *Symphonies of Wind Instruments*. The documentation surrounds the music with a whole devotional apparatus. The third movement, which Stravinsky wrote first, is dated 27 April 1930 and inscribed, according to Craft, 'a week after Ascension,'[26] while the first movement, with that instinct for timing which we noted in connection with *Ragtime*, was finished on 15 August, 'Assumption Day in the Roman Church' (the second movement was completed on 17 July). Stravinsky pasted 'a drawing of the Crucifixion' into his sketch-book, and wrote on it the words 'Adveniat regnum tuum'; and in May 1930 he gave an interview in which he asserted that 'the more one separates oneself from the canons of the Christian Church, the further one distances oneself from the truth', but also 'the overflowing of the framework in art testifies to a lack of internal discipline, which weakens the work'.[27]

What is most fascinating about these remarks is the way they contradict Stravinsky's earlier views (and to some extent, it must be said, his later ones) on the relation between art and feeling. So far as the work of art is concerned, he still insists on the autonomy of form; yet it is obvious that the *Symphony of Psalms* directly articulates a personal faith, and that its power comes from the composer's recognition that this act of faith was absolutely compatible with his aesthetic theory. He would surely have endorsed Maritain's 'toute forme . . . est "une certaine irradiation provenant de la clarté première, une participation de la divine clarté'.'[28] But as we saw earlier, Stravinsky's theory, as expressed in the Octet article, though it may already show the influence of non-musical French thinkers, was implicit in works conceived before he is likely to have come under that influence: for example in *The Wedding* and the *Symphonies of Wind Instruments*. These works, with their ironic terseness and their austerity of method and expression, undoubtedly represent a stage in the classicisation of the typical materials and procedures of his early style. Whether they are actually religious works or, as Ansermet might have said, merely 'about religion' and indebted to certain liturgical turns of speech, is a question that has little meaning in terms of an aesthetic practice as integrated as Stravinsky's. What seems obvious is that, in applying himself for the first time to the setting of an extended sacred text, Stravinsky reverted instinctively to those earlier modes of utterance. In the *Symphony of Psalms* we again find those brief chant-like melodic figures articulating form through a litany of repetitions punctuated by silences or breaks which appear to symbolise the ritualistic, 'frozen' character of the musical action. The E minor chord which marks out the units of form in the first movement, and the Alleluia interjections, for chorus or wind, in the finale, typify this hieratic approach. It is as if the 'meaning' of the work has been caught in a single gesture, like the one which opens the *Symphonies* or the solemn first intonation of its chorale theme. Moreover the instrumental texture of these different ideas is related. In the *Symphony of Psalms*, too, wind instruments predominate, supported only by lower strings, but additionally voiced, in the first-movement chords, by two pianos and harp, while in the finale the wind instruments on their own cast a radiance such as is associated, throughout Stravinsky, with contemplation and prayer.[29] Finally in some important respects of harmony the *Symphony of Psalms* refers back to the works of the Russian period. This is especially so in the first movement, which makes substantial use of octatonic harmony in combination with plain modal writing for the voices, though the preferred mode here is the Phrygian, with its morose descent of a semitone from F to E dominating the penitential vocal chant, in place of the brighter Dorian mode of many of the Russian works. Even so, a passage like the first vocal phrase, 'Exaudi orationem meam', with its rising and falling bassoon arpeggios and oboe minor thirds, so resembles the linking episodes early in the 'Dance of the Young Girls' in *The Rite* that one instinctively feels some atavistic backward reference to the pre-synthetic style, as if by going to church he had wiped out the intervening years of exile and gone directly back to his roots. Mikhail Druskin refers in his book on Stravinsky to the 'Scythian' elements in the *Symphony of Psalms* (he is thinking particularly of the finale Allegro music).[30] And it is true that this is a rare example in the neo-classical period – others are in the Symphony in Three Movements and *Orpheus* – of the Dionysian character welling up and temporarily evading the calming influence of Apollo.

Nevertheless it would be a mistake to see this symphony as in any sense denying the most recent tendencies in Stravinsky's work. On the contrary it fits in with the ethical and proto-religious leanings of all the theatre works which immediately precede and follow it, including *Persephone*. The ideas of prayer, release and transfiguration come through strongly, though with varying degrees of emphasis, in *Oedipus, Apollo, The Fairy's Kiss* and *Persephone*. In the *Symphony of Psalms* they are directly embodied in Stravinsky's choice of texts. Here we proceed from prayer and desolation (Psalm 39, AV), through patience and release (Psalm 40), to praise and transcendence (Psalm 159). And there is another interesting similarity. Just as in *Oedipus* the drama was articulated partly through tonal structure and symbolism, so in the symphony Stravinsky uses key progression to signify, but also to motivate, the gradual transfiguration. The short first movement is essentially static, anchored by the symmetrical octatonic scale and the downward-tending Phrygian mode (E to E on the white notes). Though rhythmically active it is pinned down by pedal notes and motives and by the rigid E minor punctuating chord. Its counterpoint turns inwards, with textures built up from ostinato figures heard in simultaneous augmentation and diminution, and the prevailing motion is a descent (Ex.36). But on the last page there is a sudden change: a lift in the harmony to a closing chord of G major, whose organic role in this first movement seems to lie in the prominence of the note G in the middle of the unvarying E minor chord, but which soon assumes a quite new role as dominant of C minor, the key of the second movement.[31] A similar lift takes place at the end of the second movement, where the quarrel between C minor and E flat major is apparently resolved in favour of E flat, which at once takes on a plagal[32] colouring in the opening phrase of the finale, with its implied cadence on B flat. Here, however, there persists an ambiguity, in that B flat is never once treated as a final goal, since it continually fails to escape the influence of that key of which E flat is the mediant, C minor. This is reflected in the first choral 'Alleluia', which reinstates the motivic rise from C to E flat (the minor third which runs through the work). And it is from the relation between these two notes and B flat that Stravinsky derives the unforgettable radiance of his C major cadence on the word 'Dominum'. Not only does the major chord contradict C minor in the traditional manner of the *tierce de Picardie*, with which all minor-key music up to the time of Bach habitually ended; but it also seems physically to rise up from the note B flat, by simple stepwise melodic ascent (Ex.37).

This feeling for cadence is one of the hallmarks of the neo-classical score, however strictly unclassical its actual treatment of cadences may be. Another sign is the vocal and instrumental part-writing, with its highly self-conscious use of fugal and imitative counterpoint. Fugue had first entered Stravinsky's language eight years earlier, in the final variation of the slow movement of the Octet, where it was one of a network of symbolic allusions to traditional formal practice. But as fugue – that is as an organic piece of structured counterpoint – this little piece scarcely gets off the ground, and in fact soon dissolves into a transition to the finale. By contrast, the second movement of the *Symphony of Psalms* is an authentic fugue; and not merely a single fugue, but a double one, with a distinct and fully worked set of entries for the instruments, based on subject A, and another for the voices, based on subject B. With the possible exception of the fugue at the end of the Concerto for two pianos, this movement is the least obviously synthetic of any of Stravinsky's classical academicisms. The counterpoint is genuine; that is, the parts are truly independent and not merely fractured harmony; and it is masterly. And the movement's symbolism, which perhaps comes

*Ex. 36* Symphony of Psalms, 1st movement

*Ex. 37* Symphony of Psalms, third movement

from the phrase 'direxit gressus meos' ('ordered my goings', or literally 'directed my steps') is in the Bach tradition of esoteric musical word-play. Even the main subject seems derived from one of the most famous fugue subjects in all music, the theme supposedly written by Frederick the Great and used by Bach as the basis of *The Musical Offering*, likewise in C minor.

Against this ancestry one can set certain details which still suggest a synthetic or referential approach to the idea of fugue. Counterpoint is not a prominent feature of the outer movements of the symphony, yet here we are suddenly confronted with a movement which is totally and absolutely fugal, with its entries picked out from the start, in typical Stravinsky fashion, by high solo woodwind instruments whose tone is, of any in the orchestra, the least likely to blend. True, the four-note subject itself is not new but derives from the motive of linked minor thirds which has figured prominently in the first movement. But once stated, these four notes do not proceed organically towards an answer in the dominant, as Bach's theme does, but instead become embroiled in a famous and much-analysed pattern of repetitions of the same four-note cell, one of those rotating schemes, with changing accents, which had typified Stravinsky's music since at least *Petrushka*. Eventually the theme unwinds into a chromatic rise-and-fall which leads correctly enough into the dominant answer. But there is still something wayward about this progression, and when it comes to the end of the answer and the re-entry of the subject in the tonic (second flute) the waywardness is confirmed by the fact that at this point the chromatic tendency is away from the tonic, where a classical fugue would modify the answer to allow a smooth return to the home key. Stravinsky actually plays on this tonal vagrancy by extending the answer for two bars, and still not troubling to contrive a 'correct' modulation back. So we are left with one of those parody transitions which we noticed earlier as a feature of the first movement of the Octet: transitions which pointedly do *not* argue the elements of a superficially academic scheme.

The difference between the two cases is that, while this symphony fugue may not be tonal in the classical fugal sense, it certainly is a tonal fugue in a sense that is valid and, in its context, functional. The gradual increase in polyphonic tension is matched by the conflicting pull of opposed tonal regions: the C minor of the instrumental exposition, the E flat minor of the choral one. And these tensions are not in fact resolved at the end of the fugue, but left open to be sorted out, in the manner already discussed, in the finale. The last chord of the second movement can be heard either as E flat (with added notes) or as C minor, in a typical Stravinskian first inversion with E flat at the bottom; and the music passes without break to the C *major* resolution in the finale, in a passage which also clears away the matted lines of the fugue, leaving luminous block chords and the virile cellular rhythmic ostinato of 'Laudate Eum in virtutibus'.

In all this we can certainly see a change of emphasis. In the Octet and piano works of the early 1920s Stravinsky's native modes of expression and the styles he is synthesising come into collision in a way that calls in question the meaning of the borrowed conventions. In the *Symphony of Psalms* they come to an accommodation which amounts to a genuine synthesis, so that we are not so much aware of a collision as of the music working on a number of different levels. To call this process 'unsymphonic' is senseless. Motivically and tonally the music is both integrated and organic. Moreover, a lot of its expressive power comes precisely from its contrasts of idiom. The finale, reverting to the ostinato design of the first movement, does so in a harmonic context which greatly enhances its conclusiveness. The limpid setting of 'Laudate Eum in cymbalis', with its almost mystical ecstasy, gets its richness every bit as much from the balancing of tension between E flat and C as from the hypnotic blend of threes and fours in the rhythmic ostinato. Generally the symphony gains grandeur from its organisation of harmonic levels; and to that extent at least, Stravinsky's middle-period synthesis begins to offer artistic possibilities that would not have been available to the composer of *The Rite of Spring*.

In the ensuing years Stravinsky was to explore these possibilities in a series of purely instrumental works, which will be discussed in the next chapter. Before passing to those, however, there remains one major work to consider from this central period of vocal-dramatic works, of which the *Symphony of Psalms* is the climax. This work is the so-called 'mélodrame' *Persephone*, Stravinsky's longest single composition before *The Rake's Progress*, and of all his major scores still to this day the most neglected and least appreciated.

After the *Symphony of Psalms* Stravinsky had written two works for violin, the concerto and the *Duo concertant*, and the first movement of a large work for two pianos, when he received a commission from Ida Rubinstein (the originator, also, of *The Fairy's Kiss*) for a sung ballet based on Gide's early poem *Perséphone*. The Protestant Gide had christianised the so-called Homeric Hymn to Demeter, by making Persephone's sacrifice voluntary. Gazing into the chalice of the narcissus, she sees a vision of the souls in Hades: 'tout un peuple sans espérance,/ Triste, inquiet, décoloré'. And, knowing that to pick the narcissus is to consign herself to an eternity in the underworld, Persephone picks it willingly and descends in pity to bring the light of the sky to those condemned to an existence in which 'Rien ne s'achève [et] chacun poursuit sans trêve tout ce qui fuit', a Dante-esque image to place against the Homeric tale of Persephone's forcible abduction.

In Greek legend the story of Persephone and of her mother Demeter's vengeful laying waste of the crops and trees is a cyclic fertility myth as potent as, and of course in many ways richer than, the bloodthirsty rites of the ancient Slavic tribes or even the bucolic wedding ceremonials of Kireyevsky's peasants. Elliott Carter, indeed, described Stravinsky's setting as 'the humanistic rite of spring'.[33] But even this is to miss something of its point. The ideas of compassion and atonement introduced by Gide must have been a prime element in the subject's attraction for the composer of

*Oedipus Rex* and the *Symphony of Psalms*, and it seems obvious that the outstanding richness of the music which resulted was as much as anything a response to the sheer pregnancy of this vision of Christian love among the flowering meadows and hills of Attic Greece.[34] But unfortunately the collaboration with Gide was not happy. Gide, who had pretensions as a musician, tried to influence Stravinsky's setting and took exception to his idiosyncratic approach to French prosody. Stravinsky later, waspishly, made fun of Gide's verse and suggested that it might be replaced by a completely new text by Auden.[35] But the main trouble with the text of *Persephone* is not the poetry itself but the reconstruction of the legend whereby Demeter's wanderings in search of her daughter are observed by Persephone through the same narcissus, which she has carried with her to Hades, and whereby Persephone herself is rescued from perpetual life in the underworld by the sudden *deus ex machina* of Demophoön/Triptolemus.[36] Here the motivation is obscure and the dramaturgy badly proportioned. Perhaps the most serious difficulty is the sheer extent of the speaking role of Persephone. Stravinsky made no attempt to synchronise this part with the music, as he had done in those sections of *The Soldier's Tale* and *Oedipus Rex* where music and speech came together, and as he was later to do, at least passingly, in *A Sermon, a Narrative and a Prayer* and *The Flood*. This long and musically shapeless role tends to overlay the score with a coating of French rhetoric, and it was no doubt Stravinsky's later reaction against the most intensely Gallic aspects of his middle period that led him to reject this use of recitation ('sins cannot be undone, only forgiven') along with Gide's 'leaden-eared' rhymes.[37]

But with all these faults *Persephone* is a hybrid theatre work in the central Stravinskian tradition, and a worthy companion-piece to *Oedipus Rex*. As in all Stravinsky's mixed-media works, the fusion of speech, dance and music (with or without singing) enriches the drama's significance as myth, though it does not, in this case, introduce any element of irony or alienation, which may be one reason why, in the end, we are not completely convinced of the necessity of the narration device (why should Persephone not be a singer?). The choral singing, detached from the choreography, generalises the action in a ritualistic way akin to what happens in *The Wedding* and *Renard*. But *Persephone* differs from all its predecessors, with the partial exception of *Apollo*, in its almost unbroken lyricism, a lyricism that is so all-pervading that even the darker elements of Hades, including Pluto (Hades) himself, are treated episodically and in a mildly grotesque character, without real menace. The influence of eighteenth-century French opera can be detected here, and perhaps especially that of Gluck, whose Elysian mood seems to be evoked in the remarkably diatonic harmony, the overriding femininity of tone,[38] and the transparent scoring, with flutes, harps, piano and strings playing the most prominent roles.

Though *Apollo* has sometimes been given credit for the revolutionary stance implied by its studied absence of rebarbative modernisms, *Persephone* has for some reason never been granted the same importance. This may be because, though a work of astonishing inventive richness allied to a profound unity of musical thought, it places too great a strain on the listener's tolerance of the mixture of incoherent technical ingredients on the one hand and a certain monotony of pace on the other. The music certainly does at times meander, like Persephone herself among the wild flowers of Attica. Unlike *Apollo*, which absorbs a remarkable variety of tempo and texture into its apparently uniform colouring, *Persephone* really is, in some respects, rather unvarying. Its prevailing moderato tempi and diatonic – sometimes pentatonic – harmony induce an effect of languour. Of all Stravinsky's Apollonian scores it is this one, rather than *Apollo* itself, which stands out most integratedly against the 'Dionysian' ebullience that is the common idea of Stravinsky's music.

This monotony is, however, purely superficial. *Persephone* is not only as a whole one of Stravinsky's most imaginative works, but it genuinely sums up the tendencies and preoccupations of what it is by no means unreasonable to regard as his most fertile creative period. The stimulus he drew from the radiant idea of redeemed nature is apparent on every page. It is easy enough to deplore the simple melodies and pure white harmonies of passages like the first female chorus, 'Reste avec nous, princesse', or the B flat chorus, 'L'ombre encore t'environne', or the 'unsuitably' jazzy rhythms of 'Ivresse matinale' (with its 'blue' A sharp), or 'Perséphone confuse' whose breathless phraseology Stravinsky later embarrassedly defended by joking that he wrote it 'on a train near Marseilles whose rhythm was anapaestic'. But the naivety of these inventions is their whole point. Persephone, herself a Parsifalian innocent, emerges from a timeless, childlike world symbolised by the phrase 'C'est le premier matin du monde', and the redemption she brings is not the redemption from sin but 'deliverance from a Schopenhauerian-Buddhist cycle of suffering into mortality'.[39] Stravinsky's handling of these episodes typically purges them of any trace of mawkishness or the commonplace. On a very few occasions the chording may seem to risk blandness: for instance, in the prevailing parallel thirds of the choral writing. But it turns out that under the particular conditions of Stravinskian syntax and texture the harmony retains its poise. Though the chord-structures sound as if they belong to a world of simple-minded harmony, they deny it by denying its most basic premise – the idea of the cadence. Like all Stravinsky's neo-classical tonal works *Persephone* derives a particular character from the *possibility* of cadencing, whereas, as we saw, in the *Symphonies of Wind Instruments* there is no such possibility and so no recognition of cadence when, out of the blue, one occurs. Now he teases the ear with a static diatony which could cadence but rarely does. In 'Reste avec nous', a chorus which sets the tone of a childish desire that the world will never change, he writes in a pure G major with added notes and the merest trace of an alien colour provided by chromatic clashes specially chosen for their effect of *not* leading to an adjacent tonal area. He avoids root-position chords on strong beats, and instead pins the texture by an inner pedal provided by the motivic violin oscillation between B and D. In the extraordinary little lullaby 'Sur ce lit elle repose', which sets off in a placid D major so close in mood to Berlioz's 'Songe de Faust' that it is hard to believe that the comparable context has not sounded some resonance in Stravinsky's mind, sentimentality is excluded by the persistent D sharps of the phrase-ends, by the apparently eccentric prosody which carries mute syllables across the barlines, and by a piquant use of string harmonics which Berlioz himself might have envied. Most remarkable of all are those brief passages where the music seems to evoke the crystalline tintinnabulation of Sanctus bells. In the curious dance where the shades protest their innocence of unhappiness

> Sans haine et sans amour,
> Sans peine et sans envie,
> Elles n'ont pas d'autre destin
> Que de recommencer sans fin
> Le geste inachevé de la vie

Stravinsky has the choir pluck its notes out of the E major scale like a team of handbell-ringers, an effect that is emphasised by the accompaniment for horns, muted piano and harp harmonics.

Such writing is bound to suggest the animated modalism of Russian-period works like *Petrushka* or *The Wedding*. Indeed there is a major item of evidence that the whole subject of the *mélodrame* aroused Stravinsky's atavistic feelings as strongly as the *Symphony of Psalms* had done. At the climax of the work, where Persephone is greeted back on earth with a processional offering of spring flowers, the chorus breaks into a Russian *khorovod*, the more beautiful perhaps for its profound unexpectedness (Stravinsky called this episode his 'Russian Easter Music'). But the Russianness is more often repressed. *Persephone* as a whole is a tonal work in the line of *Oedipus Rex* and *Apollo* which, like them, concentrates on the expressive possibilities of a pure diatony in which the paramount relation is not between the home key and its dominant but between the home key and the keys at an interval of a third. In *Persephone* this type of thinking takes on a form so pure that it looks at times as if a cycle of thirds has completely replaced the cycle of fifths as basis of the harmony. When the note E begins regularly to supply the root of the G major triad, or when C sharp assumes the role of dominant in the key of E (in 'Les ombres ne sont pas malheureuses'), or when the upper seventh F sharp begins to push out the keynote G to bring into prominence the triad on the mediant (B), we may detect the culmination of a tendency in all Stravinsky's neo-classical works – one which no doubt partly reflects the habit of working out chords at the piano. The third-cycle is not only the main technical idea of *Persephone*, but it also gives it motivic coherence, and above all it seems to give it its uniquely placid, lyrical atmosphere. I say 'seems to' because one can attach too much importance to one parameter of a work so coherently imagined. One has only to compare the opening chorus of *Oedipus Rex* with 'Reste avec nous', both of which have a regular ostinato built on the minor third, to see how in practice the one idea can yield quite different characters, even when the underlying conceptual thought ('the people implore the prince') is the same.

It may be that for some listeners, even those who love Stravinsky's music in general, the *Merzbild* aspects of *Persephone*, even more than those of *Oedipus*, will always bar it from full acceptance. When the young goddess's playmates portray their 'morning intoxication' in a vaguely sleazy foxtrot, complete with piano;[40] or when Persephone emerges from Hades to a Lisztian epic theme that would not be out of place in a B-feature movie thriller, the synthetic approach may seem to be in danger of toppling the music's fragile stylistic balance. Part of the intention of the synthetist is indeed to live dangerously by playing on our responses on many levels and thereby bringing to bear every aspect of our conscious and unconscious awareness of the 'meaning' of what he hopes to tell us, including those regions of superficial response which we normally label vulgar or trivial. This is the essence of the technique of symbolism. But the justification of such things in *Persephone* is that the breaks in style serve rather to highlight than to rupture the limpid mood which spreads over the whole work; they give depth to the picture without threatening its coherence. Like a cloth woven from multi-coloured strands of wool, the *mélodrame* presents a calm but lively surface that beautifully projects the simple yet profound idea beneath.

# 8

# A Citizen of France: Concerto and Symphony

Between finishing *Persephone* in January 1934 and composing *Babel* in 1944, Stravinsky wrote nothing for voice except the unaccompanied *Ave Maria* (April 1934); the even more exiguous *Petit Ramusianum harmonique*, in which lines by Charles-Albert Cingria for Ramuz's sixtieth birthday (1938) alternate with simple cantilenas for a solo singer; and the song version of the *Tango* (1940). Since most of the music he did write was commissioned, one might argue that he was merely responding to demand. But a great composer creates the terms on which he works much more than may appear, and there is plenty of evidence that the flow of instrumental works was the expression of a creative need. For one thing there is a consistent preoccupation, from the Concerto for two pianos to the Symphony in Three Movements, with specifically instrumental forms, especially fugue and variation. For another thing, the theatre works of the time have the same tendency towards the abstract. Though they may not count among Stravinsky's best scores, *Jeu de cartes*, *Danses concertantes* and *Scénes de ballet* obviously suggest a definite intention to develop the formulae of classical ballet as symphonic entities, and indeed *Danses concertantes* is strictly not a theatre piece at all but a concert work which, like most of Stravinsky's other concert works, was later turned into a ballet. This process follows on logically enough from *Apollo*, where narrative is little more than an irradiation of formal ceremony. And one could quite sensibly argue that a move towards abstract form was an essential consequence of the 1920s obsession with classical principles, just as Stravinsky had said it was: a move merely delayed by the linking of those principles with ethical drama.

We have already seen how the character of Stravinsky's work was crucially affected by his changing relations with his native land. *Mavra* and what followed are a direct response to exile. *Oedipus rex* and *Apollo* suggest the Orthodox mind reinvigorated by Catholic renewal. By the same token, the works after *Persephone* are the classic utterances of the *déraciné*. In June 1934 Stravinsky took French citizenship, and in newspaper interviews of the time he refers to Paris as 'my intellectual climate' and states that 'ever since I became conscious of the spiritual life, I have been able to breathe only in France'.[1] But from this date the French influence on his music actually seems to decline, or else to become absorbed beyond separation. The climax of his love-affair with France was his application for membership of the Académie des Beaux-Arts in January 1936, whose humiliating outcome may well have prompted a certain disillusion with French cultural life. He increasingly complained that his music was not played or appreciated in Paris. Commissions now came predominantly from the USA, where Stravinsky toured annually as a duo with the violinist Samuel Dushkin, and where, after delivering the Norton lectures at Harvard in winter 1939–40, he finally took up residence and applied for naturalisation. His last years in Europe had been clouded by bereavement. Within seven months in 1938 and 1939 his daughter Mika, his wife and his mother had died. He arrived in America in a state of disorientation. According to his publisher Païchadze, 'he could neither eat nor sleep, he could not work . . . he got angry, nervous and irritable. All he wanted was to get out as quickly as possible, out of Paris, out of Europe, into America where life was still orderly'.[2] In 1945, the year in which Stravinsky became an American citizen, his music was once again the object of hostile and scandalous demonstrations at concerts in Paris.

One would not expect these changing moods to be reflected as such in the work of an artist of Stravinsky's quality, but their trace can be detected in the symptoms of style and artistic concentration. Broadly speaking, his music of the 1930s is the most Europeanised he ever wrote. Its apparent detachment from literary, theatrical, polemical or ethnographic ideas seems to mirror the final breach with Russia, while technically, as we shall see, its concerns are largely those of European classical music: the concern, for instance, with tonal and contrapuntal architecture which reaches its height in the Concerto for two pianos, regarded by Craft as 'Stravinsky's most powerful creation of the 1930s'.[3] At the time of his emigration to the USA, however, the classical intellectual detachment of these works disintegrates. Deracinated for the second time (he continued to regard Paris as his artistic home), he is confronted with a new cultural atmosphere which for a short while threatens him with artistic annihilation. One does not need to denounce such works of 1942 as the *Circus Polka*, the *Four Norwegian Moods*, or the *Danses concertantes* (as René Leibowitz and his students did in Paris three years later) to say that they hardly amount to a characteristic year's work by the author of *The Wedding* or the *Symphony of Psalms*. But in that same year Stravinsky wrote the first movement of his Symphony in Three Movements; in 1943 he wrote its second movement, together with the intimate *Ode* in memory of Natalie Koussevitzky and much of the Sonata for two pianos; and in 1944 he finished the Sonata and wrote *Babel* and the

Kyrie and Gloria of a Mass. In these works it is as if the springs of his music have at last broken again. Artistically they are a mixed bag, no doubt. But their feeling of renewal is unmistakable, and comes out in the abrupt reappearance of Russian materials. Between 1943 and 1946 he revised, in whole or part, all of his first three Diaghilev ballets. On the other hand the Mass, though not completed until 1948, was eventually to prove seminal for a complete new phase of his work – a phase superficially as little connected with neo-classicism as neo-classicism had superficially been with Russianism.

Taken as a whole, the 1930s have generally been regarded as Stravinsky's least adventurous period, and with good reason, since there is very little in this music of that radical spirit which had been associated with him for two decades and which had struck home yet again as recently as *Apollo*. For most of us, radicalism is a feature of language and context. *The Rite of Spring* was radical because of its harshness, *Apollo* because of its tranquillity. The *Symphonies of Wind Instruments* seemed new because apparently formless; the Octet because, though linguistically modern, it re-assumed precisely those forms Stravinsky was supposed to have abandoned. Musicians retrieve radicalism from the ruins of their expectations. By contrast the Capriccio for piano and orchestra, Stravinsky's only instrumental concert work between the Serenade and the Violin Concerto, is radical only in that it contains nothing particularly surprising. It is a work of consolidation, and it sets the tone for the instrumental works of the next decade. The violin pieces written for Dushkin (especially the Concerto), the Concerto for two pianos, *Jeu de cartes*, the 'Dumbarton Oaks' concerto grosso, and the Symphony in C: these are scores in which, for a change, language as such stops being an issue – where, more or less, we can predict the vocabulary and grammar, if not the content. They are in fact the first sequence of works in which Stravinsky, working like his predecessors with an established language and technique, formulated a *modus operandi* which amounted to a craft, and later something like a routine.

One common feature of these works, nevertheless, is that they were written for performance in circumstances whose conditions they faithfully observe. Stravinsky had always been a deeply practical composer, and his music had been promptly and frequently performed. But it had usually involved re-thinking of the genres to which it supposedly adhered. In the 1930s (*Persephone* apart) this is no longer the case. The chamber works meet the particular needs of Stravinsky's own concerts; the orchestral works use a standard Beethoven orchestra, perhaps with some extra percussion and a tuba. The Capriccio and Violin Concerto have triple woodwind. 'Dumbarton Oaks' uses an unorthodox Bach ensemble including a clarinet. But in the main the instrumental complement in these scores is such as enables them to slip discreetly into a standard symphony concert, of the sort which, since the late 1920s, Stravinsky had himself begun to conduct with some frequency.

This is not to say that he is unimaginative in his use of the instruments, or that sonority is no longer part of the formulation of his ideas. The harmonically motionless first page of 'Dumbarton Oaks', for example, brilliantly translates the embroidered pedal harmonies of the Third and Sixth Brandenburg Concertos into a Stravinskian language of colliding wind and string timbres. In many detailed ways his writing for the classical orchestra is unorthodox. In the Violin Concerto the somewhat minor role played by the orchestral strings (especially violins and violas, which had been omitted completely from Stravinsky's previous work, the *Symphony of Psalms*) seems connected with the abrasive character of the solo violin's three-note motto chord, which the composer himself called his 'passport' to the whole concerto, and which always seems to imply wind sonority. But with all due qualification made, the instrumental treatment in these works is more conventional than in any score of Stravinsky's since *The Firebird*.

One thus comes back to the fact that, as an ageing and respectable – almost establishment – figure (he was fifty in 1932), Stravinsky was beginning to receive commissions from conventional institutions, particularly in the artistically conservative USA. The *Symphony of Psalms*, *Jeu de cartes*, 'Dumbarton Oaks' and the Symphony in C were all commissioned by Americans. But Stravinsky was not the only *enfant terrible* of the First World War years for whom the 1930s were a time of consolidation. Hindemith became a theorist and an academic, writing tonal music; Schoenberg accommodated his twelve-note method to classical forms; the composers of Les Six, having long ago abandoned their polemical confraternity, now wrote oratorios and grand operas. Bartók's music of the 1930s is altogether less stridently modern than the violin sonatas or the third quartet. In Russia modernism (or 'formalism', to give it its Soviet name) was categorically outlawed, but not before Shostakovich had already evinced a tendency away from the brittle satire of *The Nose* and the textural experiments of the Third Symphony towards the unstable neo-romanticism of *Lady Macbeth* and the Fourth Symphony. The bourgeoisification of modern music in the 1930s was a general trend which has yet to be convincingly explained as a whole rather than piecemeal, but must partly have socio-cultural origins: the naughty twenties making way for the austere and worried thirties, the prelude to Auden's 'Age of Anxiety', the age of the *déraciné*.

In Stravinsky, it goes beyond the mere choice of orchestra or instrumental ensemble, and invades his entire musical architecture. What is striking about these concert works is not that they adopt this or that form (the idea of revived classicism as such being old hat by 1930), but that they do so repeatedly and in a normalising spirit. From the Capriccio onwards Stravinsky pursues certain lines, instead of, as in the past, ducking and weaving in order to shake off his fashionable pursuers. Sonata and variation forms, of a kind, are standard in these works, and fugue is now cultivated as an organic process rather than purely, as in the Octet, a symbolic form. As already in *Oedipus rex*, the language is tonal and it is nearly always possible to describe sections or movements as being in this or that key without running into insoluble difficulties of nomenclature, though such descriptions always leave something to be said, and it has to be understood that Stravinsky remains uninterested in tonal transition in the usual sense. The forms are symphonic. We get properly behaved first and second subjects, development sections, movement contrasts, and – more vaguely – a harnessing of the conventional principle of growth through rise and fall of tension and traditional ideas of phrase structure and closure. It may be worth repeating that these features are new not so much in themselves (they appear in the Octet, where, as we saw in Chapter 6, they stand out polemically against such works as the *Symphonies of Wind Instruments*, which largely ignore them), as in their standardisation.

The urge to stick to clear-cut conventions probably expresses a desire for stability as much as it reflects the stereotyped conditions of performance for which the music was written. Stravinsky needed the Capriccio for his own use, and the Violin Concerto (1931) was suggested to him by his publisher Willi Strecker. But there are many signs that Stravinsky himself was taking an interest in the conventions of the concert repertoire and examining them as the basis for a stable idiom rather than simply as material for collage or parody or symbolism. We know, for instance, that when planning the Violin Concerto he studied all the well-known violin concertos in the repertory. Moreover, the concertante idea, where a solo player or group is set off against the main orchestra, figures in nearly all his works of the 1920s: in *Apollo*, where a solo violin stands for the young god, or in *The Fairy's Kiss*, with its Tchaikovskian solo cello for the *pas de deux* and its general liking for instrumental solos. Stravinsky went on exploring the possibilities of concertante writing throughout the 1930s, for the obvious reason that the abrupt formal oppositions it throws up suggested analogies with the block structures he had worked with during his Russian period. It also suited his taste for scoring by instrumental family groups, which goes back through *The Rite of Spring* to the Glinka/Tchaikovsky tradition of unmixed orchestral colours. The rather similar themes of the Capriccio second movement and the Violin Concerto first movement (parallel thirds on oboes and trumpets respectively) are both presented initially in this way. In both the Symphony in C and the Symphony in Three Movements concerto elements are at least as important architecturally as the traditional symphonic processes of thematic and tonal growth, though these are also present. A detailed study of the period can do very much worse than start by looking at the ways in which Stravinsky adapts this hallowed principle to his own ends.

The Capriccio, which he composed in 1929 to replace the much dog-eared Piano Concerto, is a model three-movement *Konzertstuck* in the line that stretches from the concertos of Field and Hummel through Chopin and the *concertos symphoniques* of Litolff. The piano maintains an almost unbroken running commentary of cascading scales and arpeggios or, when movement is needed without change of note, a kind of xylophone repeated-note *trillo* – a memory perhaps of Stravinsky's work with the cimbalom, and an effect which pleased him so much that he used it again in the *Duo concertant* and, much more powerfully and substantially, in the Concerto for two pianos. This glittering thread of keyboard virtuosity, often very delicately voiced, binds together a succession of thematic and decorative fragments played by the orchestra, nearly always on solo instruments or clearly demarcated groups; and it also supplies the sense of bustling movement that, in many a romantic concerto, does duty for organic development of themes. At times, in Stravinsky, this movement is openly spurious. For example, in the *più mosso* central section of the ternary slow movement (fig. 41+2) the piano accompanies a jaunty right-hand melody with a repetitive left-hand ostinato on three notes of the F major scale organised as an irregular pattern of two-note cells without any conceivable reference to even the very straightforward harmonic rhythm implied by the tune (Ex.38). Later this same scheme moves on to other degrees of the scale, but seems to avoid any definite sense of modulation. But when we look at the tune itself, we find that here too the movement is deceptive. For four bars the triplet demisemiquavers do no more than adorn an F major triad with melodic auxiliary and chromatic passing notes, a standard early romantic keyboard technique for flavouring a simple harmonic language with a not too pungent expressive spice. The auxiliary note treated as an appoggiatura typifies the melodic/harmonic style of the Capriccio throughout. In the finale, which Stravinsky wrote first and which gave him the idea for the title, the device

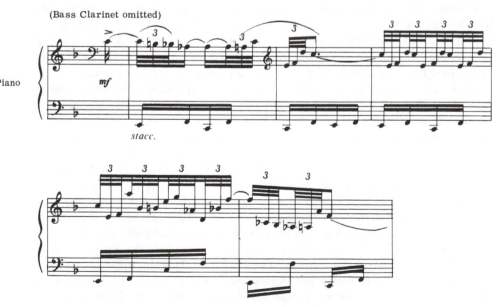

*Ex. 38* Capriccio for piano and orchestra

often takes an extravagant form, as in the first theme at fig.56, where the left hand plays nothing but G major arpeggios while the right explores the many possibilities of the chromatic appoggiatura, resolved or otherwise.

It is typical of Stravinsky that, in modelling himself on such a fragile tradition, he should have produced a work that is light and graceful, certainly, but not in any sense pallid or effete, as we now tend to regard all but the very best of its models. The Violin Concerto, in a similar way, has some qualities of the empty virtuoso concerto, but yet manages to avoid being empty.

Here too the soloist is kept busy in all but a very few bars of all four movements, while the almost incessant motion (including once again decorative filigree) tends to disguise sectional divisions which are remarkably like those we found typical of Stravinsky's pre-*Mavra* style. If one were to take the song 'Kornilo' which opens the *Pribaoutki*, rewrite it as a diatonic D major piece, slightly regularise the barring and add a virtuoso violin part, one could come within spitting distance of the first movement of the concerto. In the ostinato underpinning of this later music there is more than a suggestion of those Bachian Brandenburg textures which were to provide a more striking starting-point for the 'Dumbarton Oaks' Concerto six years later. The concertante idea expresses itself in contrasted blocks of music that are internally homogeneous, both instrumentally and (often even in Bach, who had studied Vivaldi) harmonically. Classical chord progressions act mainly as markers for these blocks, while the texture is based on a mixture of instrumental dialogues – like the trumpet and oboe duets on the first page – and soloistic bravura unashamedly based on traditional formulae, of which the multiple-stopped chord is most in evidence. In the concerto repertory, multiple-stopping is usually a rhetorical device, and Stravinsky makes the most of that quality, as is already apparent in the first two bars. But instead of using the fiddle chord just for emphasis, he reverses the process and uses a source harmony derived from the sound and technique of the violin to trigger off and eventually unify a stream of musical events. The 'passport' chord which starts each movement is simply the top three open notes of the instrument (D-A-E) with the middle note transposed up two octaves, a change which not only makes it harder to play without using harmonics, but also emphasises the dissonant role of the E by sinking the A into the harmonic spectrum of the D, while making the dissonance 'cleaner' since it has only a single element. This idea of the single added-note dissonance, usually diatonic, is fundamental to the sound of the Violin Concerto and is naturally often expressed directly through double-stops using the open strings, though it also colours the orchestral harmony, especially in the outer movements, the 'Toccata' and 'Capriccio'. Thus a commonplace device becomes a part of the music's substance and loses that gratuitous character which can make naked bravura seem so vacuous. It is easy to see why the composer was disappointed when Dushkin at first insisted that the chord could not be played.[4]

*Ex. 39(i)* 'Dumbarton Oaks', opening

Both the Capriccio and the Violin Concerto are like superior *divertisse-ments*. They express the typical buoyancy and verve of Stravinsky in largely extrovert terms, despite the more reflective tone of the 'Aria' movements in the concerto. By contrast 'Dumbarton Oaks' (Concerto in E flat for chamber orchestra), which it is convenient to discuss at this point though it was not written until 1937–8, sets out in what sounds like a diversionary spirit with a kind of portmanteau quotation from the third and sixth Brandenburgs, but soon wanders off into strange territory, where one glimpses only stray fragments of baroque phraseology: a cadence perhaps, or a fugato subject (emerging in the finale at fig.61 in the form of a near-quotation from the finale of Brandenburg no.2). The bell-like opening of the first movement, one of the notable moments of pure sonority in Stravinsky, is based on the same idea as the Violin Concerto of adding dissonant diatonic notes (especially in the horn part) to a harmonically simple figuration which keeps suggesting the basic chord progressions of classical music but in fact never abandons its tonic root. But here we are more conscious of the music's linearity – as one would hope in a homage to Bach – and though it may not be good counterpoint in any sense that a textbook would recognise, it is essentially music of 'line', which debouches naturally into the fugato leading quickly to the close of the movement (or, to be exact, its slow link with the next movement) (Ex. 39(i)).

The concertante lay-out of this first movement suggests a concerto grosso, where, however, the nine real parts (fifteen instruments) are all called on from time to time to fulfil a concertino or solo role. Various individual groupings are set against passages for the tutti. As in the earlier concertos, there is a feeling that we are on familiar ground. But soon we become aware of the emblematic quality in the ideas. Not the 'busy' Bachian motive itself, but only the terminal figure played by the flute, is picked up and toyed with in the characteristic Stravinskian way (Ex.39(ii)). And as the lines thus get curtailed, so the metre fragments to a degree not heard in his music since the *Symphonies of Wind Instruments*; bars of 3/16 and 5/16, in a basic measure of four crotchets, form the dividers between blocks, and throw

*(ii) 'Dumbarton Oaks'*

them into an oblique relationship that once again suggests an analogy with cubism. Hereafter the Brandenburg allusion is largely abandoned, and if the skeletal second movement suggests anything by Bach, it might be one of his solo string pieces, or the start of some keyboard fugue where we wait in vain for the answer and countersubject. The still less baroque-sounding finale starts by making obsessive patterns out of what later emerges as a terminal figure in the fugato theme at fig.61 mentioned above. The music's referential character is by now distinctly surreal. It may seem to hark back to the allusive world of the easy keyboard pieces, especially as refracted through the arrangements Stravinsky had made of them for small orchestra in 1925; the bass ostinato has the same relentlessness as the bass in 'Balalaika', the last of the pieces in the Suite no.1 (no.3 of the original Five Easy Pieces). Or it may look forward to the American commercial parodies, like the Tango. For some it may pre-figure the kinds of serial manipulation we find in Stravinsky's 1950s music, before he went over to the spiky atonality of the works after *Threni*. But such anticipations can be found almost anywhere in his earlier music, because of the self-limiting and rotative character of the cell technique. 'Dumbarton Oaks' is certainly in some respects an inchoate piece, a study in part for the Symphony in C (compare the central sections of their respective slow movements), and a score which begins to show the limitations of a synthetic style. The graceful Mozartian C minor music which provides a central episode in the finale has an ironic flavour, more poised and ambiguous, certainly, than the self-satirical gavotte in the finale of Bartók's Fifth Quartet (1934), but still self-referential in a way unusual for Stravinsky.

If 'Dumbarton Oaks' thus casts doubt on the durability of neo-classicism, and perhaps even heralds its end, the true aesthetic focus of the period should perhaps be sought earlier, rather than later, as is tempting in view of the big works still to come. For a time in the early 1930s, Stravinsky did indeed move so close to a straight-faced modern classicism – in the sense of Schoenberg's Variations for Orchestra or Bartók's (later) Music for Strings, Percussion and Celesta – as to suggest some mid-life crisis of individuality, backed up by a technical review not uncommon in composers of his stature (Haydn, Mozart, Beethoven and Schubert all consolidated in this way). The period is confused, in Stravinsky's case, by the highly synthetic theatre pieces of which *Persephone* partly post-dates the main instrumental work which all but abandons synthetism, the Concerto for two solo pianos. But Craft's correction of the relative dating of these two works helps clarify the issue.[5] Stravinsky started composing the first movement of the Concerto in late 1932, but laid it aside because of concert dates and was then prevented from returning to it by the *Persephone* commission. He eventually finished it in 1935, composing the variation movement last, after the fugue, which, however, in orthodox classical fashion, it precedes in the published score. The Concerto, written for his own performance with his son Soulima, shows his inner creative direction, while *Persephone*, whose conditions were to some extent 'given' by the terms of the commission, hangs over from the earlier direction which probably helped formulate those terms – something similar was to happen later, at the time of the Máss. It says a lot for Stravinsky's essentially theatrical genius that of the two works it is *Persephone* that strikes the more personal note, though the Concerto is the better integrated and in many technical respects the more impressive.

When he embarked on the two-piano work, Stravinsky had just written the *Duo concertant* for violin and piano, his second work for Dushkin. In his autobiography, which was written only a year or two later, he tells us that he had disliked the blend of piano and stringed instruments, but was reconciled to it by a remark of Cingria (in his *Pétrarque*) to the effect that lyricism needs formal rules if it is to generate art. The *Duo concertant*, according to Stravinsky, is a kind of demonstration of this thesis (it would have been contrary to his heuristic nature in the early 1930s to give as a main motive for such a work the need for recital repertoire). One could interpret him as saying that the *Duo* embodies and directs the lyrical impulse, which is certainly present in its untypically rhapsodic odd-numbered movements. But what the *Duo* shows more clearly is that Stravinsky was in a state of anxiety over matters of style, for the work is in this respect incoherent, whatever he may himself have said about a 'theme . . . developed through all the five movements of the piece which forms an integral whole'.[6] Russian dance music rubs shoulders with a Rossinian tarantella – a curiously long-winded piece, as White points out – and a series of improvisatory melodic pieces constantly inhibited by gauche dissonant harmonies that rarely bear the Stravinskian stamp. It was just after writing this *Duo* that he sketched the *Dialogue between Joy and Reason* (also inspired by Cingria), some of whose music went into *Persephone*, though much seems to have been abandoned.[7]

The Concerto for two pianos thus came at a critical moment. As Stravinsky's most ambitious and serious-minded concert instrumental piece since (at least) the Piano Concerto, it must have embodied a need to write a weighty abstract score that would effect a new classicism without overt reference to borrowed styles. In the instrumental works of the early 1920s, there is more than a hint of apology about such references. But in the Concerto for two pianos only the more general considerations of classicism come into play: a balanced and lucid form, the integration of contrasted elements, and the avoidance of colouristic distractions. The severity of intention recalls the ethical tone of the dramatic and choral works of the late 1920s much more than the divertimento spirit of the Capriccio or the violin works. As in the *Symphony of Psalms* the attempt at fusion is uninhibited by stylistic or polemical factors.

All the same, the Concerto is fairly typical of Stravinsky's classicism as a whole in the oblique relation between its ideas and its supposed form as expressed in terms of conventional schemes. It would be obvious that the work was braced by a study of Beethoven even if the composer had not told us that 'I had steeped myself in the variations of Beethoven and Brahms while composing the Concerto, and in Beethoven's fugues.'[8] The fugal finale, with its inverted final entry and preceding set of variations, is a portmanteau version of Beethoven's procedures in his late B flat, A flat and C minor sonatas, but without overt parody of style. In the same degree, the quasi sonata-form first movement suggests a number of models in Beethoven, with its bold arpeggio theme and contrasting bravura figuration. Here as elsewhere Stravinsky adopts the classical idea of reprise, but with a strictness foreign to the Beethoven principle of contextual change and growth. The long reprise of the 'first subject' (bars 170–206, cf. bars 5–41) on the one hand is literal, and on the other leads to different elaborations in each case, while the only secondary material that undergoes reprise (bars

92 onwards, cf. bars 154 onwards) does so almost at once. This ordered but somewhat monumental plan gives the movement an architectural feeling rather different from the discursive character of the late classical sonata. On the other hand the flow of the rhythms and the phrase structure refer constantly to classical types, in a way that an architectural work like the *Symphonies of Wind Instruments* does not. Behind everything is the regular two-bar phrase and the cadential downbeat. Not that there is anything new about such referents, which are basic to all Stravinsky's neo-classical music. What *is* new in the Concerto is the extent to which it does away with the allusive, or synthetic, note sounded in every work of the 1920s, from *Mavra* to *Apollo* and the Capriccio. Instead of constantly surprising and amusing us by the way in which commonplace turns of phrase are placed in irregular or unpredictable contexts, which is crudely speaking what happens in the Octet, it seems to offer an integrated language based directly on commonplace treated obliquely. In this sense the surface of the Concerto is possibly the smoothest of any of Stravinsky's mature works; on the whole it avoids the breaks in style we associate with his music, which may paradoxically be one reason why it lacks the last degree of individuality, even while obviously drawing power from coherence.

A proper analysis of this language would be beyond the scope of the present study; but some attempt ought to be made to exemplify it at least. In general the secret of Stravinsky's integration of classical formulae with his own personal mode of expression, which essentially never changed much, lies in his ability to select those formulae most instantly typical of classical genres, so that a strong image is economically projected which can then survive or even absorb techniques and idioms that might seem alien to it. Such a formula is the E minor arpeggio in the first bar of the work. Together with the two-bar phrase embodying a motivic repeat of the arpeggio, it is so unmistakably a 'standard' idea – like the first subject of Beethoven's C minor Piano Concerto – that the ear automatically assumes a classical tonal context to go with it and probably does not notice that the single most decisive note in establishing a key in tonal music, the leading-note (in E minor, the note D sharp), is studiously avoided for no less than twenty-six bars, to be exact until the eighty-seventh crotchet beat at moderate tempo, while the modal inflection of that note – D natural – is made crucial through both its melodic and harmonic relation to the keynote. This can be seen in bar 2, where the bass D initiates a whole-tone descent that serves to brace the entire ten-bar introduction and to lead it eventually, by way of the *upper* leading-note F natural (and with still no intervention of any D sharp) to a strong downbeat entry of the first subject proper in bar 11 (Ex.40). At the same time the D acts as dominant of the chord of G major, which Stravinsky systematically opposes to that of E minor by alternating the E of the one with the D of the other – a procedure he was to repeat with still more drastic effect in the Symphony in C, where the opposed triads are those of C major and E minor. Incidentally, a comparison

*Ex. 40* Concerto for two pianos

of these two cases rather suggests that the opposition of chords was the embryonic idea. In the Symphony, which is in a major key, the triad on the mediant (E) has the home leading-note (B) as its dominant, whereas in the Concerto, in the minor, the mediant (G) has the *flattened* leading-note as its dominant (Ex.41). This is quite sufficient to account for the strong role played by B and D in the respective works. If so, the chant melody

which forms a kind of hidden device throughout the first movement of the
Concerto, and which covertly links it to the *Symphony of Psalms*, must have
emerged from the modal relation of D to E. However that may be, the
importance of chant melodies within the texture of this music suggests that,
even at its most dense, the underlying principle is that of a single line, slow
moving, enlivened by rapid decorative scales, arpeggios and cimbalom-like
repeated notes such as we observed in the Capriccio and the *Duo concertant*.
On this view the arpeggio theme, despite its apparent pre-eminence, is in
fact an embellishment.

Turning to the variation third movement, together with the finale Prelude
and Fugue based on the same theme (and apparently composed before the
variations), we find the same dependence on what one writer has compared
to the *cantus firmus* technique of Renaissance music.[9] In fact the theme is

*Ex. 41*

less a melody than a series of notes from which Stravinsky derives the middle line of each variation and, in due course, the subject of his fugue. The line is framed by free rhythmic and chordal ostinatos, much as Bach would frame the melody in a chorale prelude. It is neither treated in strict phrase-structure manner, as Haydn or Mozart would have done (or Brahms in his Haydn Variations), nor is it varied motivically. Variety is supplied, instead, by linear and decorative digressions, and by a technique of octave displacement and fragmentation which looks startlingly like a crude version of Schoenberg's serial variation procedure, which Stravinsky almost certainly knew nothing about in 1935. Indeed when Stravinsky started using serial methods consciously in the early 1950s, he at first used a straight-through linear version of the technique which, allowing for the comparative freedom of approach in the Concerto, is in essence the same.

These variations seem to absorb the rather strained, rhapsodic tone of the *Duo concertant* into a kind of music that is altogether tighter and more directed, thanks partly to the binding effect of its ostinatos. These ostinatos are interesting in themselves. Like most of Stravinsky's neo-classical figurations, they combine the dynamic energy of his Russian ostinatos with chords that suggest a tonal context and a regular phrase-structure. They illustrate very simply the art with which he brings a classical suggestion to methods that are really quite personal, even when direct stylistic allusion is lacking. The fourth variation, for example, has a chordal ostinato that obviously harks back to the seventh chords of *The Rite of Spring*. It has several features of the earlier style. It is treated as a cell of variable size, and laid out over a secondary cell (Piano II, left hand) with an independent pattern of stresses, so that, just as Boulez found in the 'Mysterious Circles', the harmonic relation between the two changes within a strictly limited set of possibilities (Ex.42). But when one plays or listens to this variation one is struck by its smoothness and regularity when compared with the erratic patterns of the 'Dance of the Young Girls' or the complex interplay of systems in the 'Dance of the Earth'. The reason is that the secondary, left-hand cell has four (or possibly two-plus-two) beats and fits exactly into a classical four-beat bar; moreover the more irregular chordal cell always has its evolution curtailed by the recurring entries of the theme (Piano I), which itself takes the form of a cell laid independently over the four-beat scheme but which is also invariably curtailed, or perhaps positioned, so that the whole sequence can start again on a strong downbeat. Admittedly the scheme becomes less simple later in the variation, but it never loses its four-beat articulation in the left hand of Piano II until the last six bars, which slow down to a five-beat bar to make a transition into the Lento music of the finale prelude. Incidentally Stravinsky uses the same seventh chords for the dazzling ostinato figuring in the middle section of the first movement (bar 92), and here too a cellular treatment is rigidly contained by a four-beat left hand.

This gift for adopting just as much of the basic syntax of classical conven-

*Ex. 42* Concerto for two pianos

tion as is necessary to establish a symbolism without apparently inhibiting his own native method or invention comes out in all Stravinsky's neo-classical music. But the Concerto for two pianos is perhaps its classic expression. One has only to listen to the subtle way he offsets the innocent-sounding G major opening of the 'Notturno' by a gently percussive bottom-heavy spacing of the accompaniment with B rather than G in the bass, and again with the fifth of the chord conspicuously absent; or notice how quickly the smooth four-quaver beat of this piece is broken up into uneven bars interrupted by caesuras; or, in the first movement, hear how much is made of the embroidery of a single common chord (especially in the long central group after bar 92) – a procedure essentially foreign to the classical way of reserving pedal harmony for moments of structural delay. Here Stravinsky seems less and less to be confronting us with the irreconcilable nature of classicism and modernism and more and more to be synthesising a sort of personal classicism out of precisely their reconciliation. In the fugue of the Concerto, by far the most convincing of his essays in this genre, it is no longer easy to be clear about which elements are classical and which merely appear so; or even to be sure whether the distinction still has any meaning. Neo-classicism dissolves into a classicised modernism, in Valéry's sense.

This achievement might have initiated a distinct phase in Stravinsky's music, as happened in Bartók's of the same period. But later developments suggest that the balance struck in the Concerto was precarious and not able to invigorate further work. In 'Dumbarton Oaks', as we have seen, a measure of disintegration is accompanied by touches of irony. In *Jeu de cartes* actual quotation begins to suggest some conscious alienation from the music's stylistic models. And in the Symphony in C, the last work Stravinsky wrote as a French resident, there is more than a hint of academicism, especially in the first two movements, which Craft places 'among the peaks of refinement in Stravinsky's art', but adds 'they are also a cul-de-sac'.[10]

The Symphony was another American commission, written for the fiftieth anniversary of the Chicago Symphony Orchestra, and of all Stravinsky's 1930s scores it is the one which most obviously fits into a conventional celebration within the institutional life of a conservative culture. What could be more standard than a symphony in C, in four movements, written for an orchestra of double woodwind (with piccolo), brass (with tuba), strings and timpani? The very character of the music, with its orchestral 'bloom', suggests the comfortable glamour of the great symphony concert. Looking at this work with Stravinsky's previous music in mind, it is easy to explain it as an extreme case of *Mavra*-esque synthetism, with popular Beethoven supplying the imagery previously taken from Glinka and Tchaikovsky. But it is doubtful whether the audience at the Chicago première, which Stravinsky himself conducted in November 1940, was 'shocked' by the model or the new work's relation to it, as the Paris audience in 1922 was and was meant to be. While there is much to be said about the symphony's classical 'symphonicness', its posture is no longer polemical, in which respect it merely confirms the development we have traced in the ten years since Stravinsky's previous American symphonic commission, the *Symphony of Psalms*.

However, the Symphony in C is also a work of transition. The first two movements were composed in France (1939), but the other two not until Stravinsky had taken up residence in the USA in March 1940. It is generally agreed that the break in time, if not the change in domicile, is reflected in the music. The well-padded first movement and lyrical second, whose roots are in the slow movement of 'Dumbarton Oaks', contrast sharply, if not damagingly, with the brittle, suite-like scherzo and peremptory finale. These later movements evoke fleetingly the scurry and glitter of celluloid America. The brilliant scherzo, with its flood of ideas and drastically irregular metre, certainly abandons classical models; and though the finale is cyclically related to the first movement, it enjoys closer links with Tchaikovsky than with Beethoven. The slow introduction might be some nightmare evocation of the start of the 'Pathétique' Symphony, with its groaning bassoons, while the treatment of the main theme owes a good deal to the well-tried Russian romantic technique of the changing background. Moreover it is hard to resist a comparison of the whole work with the typical academic Russian symphony of the Rimsky era, written painstakingly according to the best models, though doubtless without any synthetic or ironic intention. The idea that, at a moment of stylistic anxiety, Stravinsky intuitively grafted back on to his roots is by no means contradicted by his music of the mid-1940s, as we shall see in the next chapter. Here, the similarity of the main scherzo theme (especially its diatonic form at fig.99) to the opening music of *Petrushka* is suggestive and goes beyond a mere resemblance of outline. At the end of the whole work Stravinsky conjures up once more the transcendent calm of those slow hieratic codas peculiar to his Russian works from the 'Cantique' and *The Wedding* to the *Symphony of Psalms*. The long chain of wind chords on the final page restores the harmonic context of the first movement and outlines its theme. But in atmosphere they are some way from the plush symphonic world of the opening.

The first movement was the subject of a much-quoted article by the American musicologist Edward T. Cone, who drew attention to its idiosyncratic tonal structure, in which the keys of C major and E minor are fused in such a way that the B that figures so prominently in the Beethoven-like first subject enjoys a pivotal role as leading note of the former key and dominant of the latter.[11] Its leading-note character lends a cadential flavour to page after page of this music, just as the flattened seventh of the Concerto for two pianos studiously avoids that flavour. All the same, this dominant-to-tonic colouring is never more than a suggestion, a melodic device which rarely blossoms into a chord until the very end of the work, where the G major element of the last chord is one aspect of its finality. In the first movement Stravinsky ignores G major, though he makes much of G minor.

His second subject is in F, the subdominant of C. Thus, quite typically, Stravinsky freezes the great dynamic contrast of the classical symphony into one gesture. It is amusing to compare his first subject group with one obvious classical ancestor, the first movement exposition of Beethoven's C major Symphony. The themes are in a sense similar; they concentrate on the same notes, C, B and G, with E thrown in to complete the harmony. Stravinsky even copies Beethoven's typical procedure of repeating the theme one step up, on D. But when it comes to journeying on, via the chord of the dominant, back to the tonic, Stravinsky clouds the issue and, instead of Beethoven's grand cadential peroration, mutters a few figures in G (around fig.10) before returning unrhetorically to C a couple of bars later. The two melodies are also worth comparing for their tonal-rhythmic values (Ex.43). Beethoven makes no bones about his tonic note, which hogs most of the downbeats. Stravinsky, by contrast, prefers to mark his downbeats with the leading-note B, resolving to C often on weak quavers or upbeat crotchets. This is in accordance both with the motivic shape of the theme and with the composer's desire to stress the ambiguous role of the note B. There is no C in the accompanying ostinato, so until the B resolves to C each time (in the melody) we have no C major chord but rather one of E minor (the bass note is always E), and it is a good question in the psychology of musical perception why most listeners nevertheless hear this music as unambiguously in C. The observant will notice at once that, in the D minor repeat of the theme, the tonic chord is by contrast placed normally, with a D in the bass, presumably for the simple reason that there is no issue of tonal architecture dictating otherwise.

One other evident quality of this movement which distinguishes it from Beethoven is its lack of conciseness, in which respect it also diverges from most of the music Stravinsky himself had written since he first arrived in

Ex. 43(i) Beethoven: Symphony no. 1 in C major

(ii) Symphony in C

Paris in 1910. Where Beethoven's music is driven forward by its inherent tensions, Stravinsky's for ever turns back on passages which, in themselves, embody harsher tensions than those of classical music but lack a strongly implied resolution; and this is why the first movement at least, apparently committed to travelling the entire natural course of a symphonic movement, seems to take so long about it. Cone found hidden in these seemingly arbitrary stretches of repetition a cunning arithmetic of symmetries, which proves, what we have already observed, the fundamentally architectural, non-discursive character of Stravinsky's thinking. Yet curiously even this great composer whose music is instinctively motivic rarely composed a movement as rigorously thematic, in the all-pervading sense so much admired by Schoenberg in Brahms. Its motivicism is even at times ostentatious. It guarantees unity, but it perhaps does not guarantee that cogency of argument without which, according to Robert Simpson, a symphony cannot properly be so called.[12]

Craft was right to call this music a cul-de-sac. It carries to the limit that synthetic tendency which had enlivened Stravinsky's music of the 1920s and which had briefly looked like producing a more stable compound in the Concerto of the early mid-1930s. And perhaps there are moments when, in modelling itself well, it does not always see where it should turn for fresh ideas. The refinement praised by Craft is rather to be found in the lovely slow movement, with its purity of melody and incomparable chamber scoring, effortlessly adapted from the repeated-note figures and decorative scales and octave displacements of the Concerto for two pianos and the *Duo concertant*. In the shanty-like horn tune of its middle section it even seems to anticipate the boldness of the American years. Here refinement becomes a matter of voicing rather than embellishment. Notice the cunning discrepancies between the solo horn and the accompanying violins in this tune (Ex.44). In such details Stravinsky is once more completely himself, the master of integrated movement and colour.

*Ex. 44* Symphony in C, 2nd movement

# 9

# A Citizen of America: Tango and Symphony

Stravinsky's first public act in America after his arrival there in September 1939 was not a musical performance but the series of Harvard lectures which were later published under the title *Poétique musicale* (*The Poetics of Music*).[1] The six lectures, ghost-written for the composer by Roland-Manuel and delivered in French, are the culminating statement of the aesthetic ideas which had taken shape during Stravinsky's long residence in France. Here we find the classic expression of his view of art as a construct, and of the artist as a builder, mixed in with attacks on romanticism and romantic concepts such as revolution and nationalism. In place of the traditional artistic battle-cries, we read what Stravinsky calls 'an explanation of my personal experience, faithfully related to concrete values' and dwelling on 'the musical phenomenon in itself, insofar as it emanates from a complete and well-balanced human being endowed with the resources of his senses and armed with his intellect.'[2] Though polemical in content and liberally peopled with Aunt Sallies wheeled on to have sticks thrown at them, the book is studiedly severe, didactic and even pedantic in tone and method. In all these attributes it embodies that very Gallic love of analytical precision spiced with frequent bad-tempered diatribes against the devotees of rival systems, which comes out also, more recently, in the writings of Boulez.

While there is nothing in the *Poetics*, with its account of musical creation as a sort of serendipity subjected to a strict craft discipline and circumstantial constraints, that need have made Stravinsky ashamed of the music he wrote when he settled in the USA, the change in atmosphere is none the less very pronounced. It is natural to feel that the *Poetics* belongs to the world of *Apollo*, the *Symphony of Psalms* and the Concerto for two pianos, with their sense of order imposed on materials of diverse origin with the humble yet lofty object, to quote the first lecture in the *Poetics*, of promoting 'a union of man with his fellow-man and with the Supreme Being'.[3] But in the USA, Stravinsky found himself obliged at once to start composing at the dictates of a commercial market. From this period date a succession of parodies of commercial styles composed, however, not out of a purely artistic interest in demotic music, such as seems to have prompted the easy waltzes and polkas of the First War years, but because a popular style was called for by the commission. Thus the *Circus Polka* (1941–2) was written for a so-called Ballet of Elephants at Barnum and Bailey's Circus in New York, the *Four Norwegian Moods* (1942) for a film of the Norway landings, the *Scherzo à la russe* (1944) also for a war film, set in Russia, the *Scènes de ballet* (1944) for a Broadway revue, the *Ebony Concerto* (1945) for Woody Herman's jazz band. Even the Symphony in Three Movements (1942–45) contains music written for a film, *The Song of Bernadette*, just as the *Ode* (1943) has a movement originally composed for Robert Stevenson's screen version of *Jane Eyre*. Stravinsky had to endure a good deal of opprobrium over some of these works, and it is true that they seem collectively a symptom of stylistic, as well as financial, unease. This is moreover borne out by the diversity of style in the other works of the period, which include the beginnings of the Mass, the revision of the 'Sacrificial Dance' from *The Rite of Spring*, the Sonata for two pianos, with its unexpected evocation of Russian folk tunes, alongside works like the *Danses concertantes* and, just after the war, the Concerto in D for strings, which broadly speaking draw on the vocabulary of the Violin Concerto and the Symphony in C.

Stories cling to the American commercial parodies that might have been specifically concocted to ward off accusations of potboiling. Of the *Circus Polka* we read that Stravinsky only agreed to write the piece if the elephants were young ('music for schools'); of the *Scènes de ballet* that he would not agree to its being reorchestrated in a conventional saccharine idiom (though the *Circus Polka* seems to have been first performed in a commercial arrangement); the *Four Norwegian Moods*, in their original cinematic version, were rejected by the film producer or director apparently because their style was too astringent.[4] These details are of course no more relevant to a response to the music than the question whether Stravinsky did or did not agree to the butchery of *The Rite of Spring* for Disney's film *Fantasia* in 1939. If the music of these years is open to objection, it is on account of its uneven inspiration rather than because of any cheapening of style or technique. These commercial parodies have in general very much the same precision of aim, the same quality of crystallising the essential characteristics of a genre or an entertainment into a few gestures, that one observes in the easy keyboard pieces and dance parodies of nearly thirty years earlier. The little Tango for piano (or piano with voice) which Stravinsky wrote in 1940 before the performance of the Symphony in C is typical of these works at their best. The parody is now much smoother than in the easy pieces, with their splintered rhythmic surface, and coincides at more points with its model. Unlike the tango in *The Soldier's Tale*, it is a piece that could be of use in a ballroom, even if the hint of exaggeration in the free use of added

dissonance and the slightly overdone syncopations might suggest to the
dancers a more choreographic, statuesque routine than would be natural
for a couple dancing *ad hoc*. In this sense the Tango is a period piece, like
an Art Deco silhouette. When it came to commissioned music this gentle
strain of poker-faced mockery stood Stravinsky in excellent stead, since it
enabled him to satisfy a market that, in essence, wanted his name to attach
to a stereotype of its own devising, while he kept just enough distance
from the stereotype to preserve what Suzanne Langer would have called
the 'virtual' or symbolic character of the work.

For example in the *Four Norwegian Moods* (a suite better described by its
French title, 'Quatre pièces à la norvégienne') Stravinsky does little more
than place a series of actual folk tunes into drily appropriate settings in the
manner of Grieg but with every ounce of sentimentality processed out. The
atmosphere and somewhat static charm of these orchestral pieces is quite
close to that of the arrangements in the two suites for small orchestra,
especially the national 'types' such as 'Balalaika' or 'Española'. But the
music is again much more straight-faced, the distortions so marginal that
some familiarity with the composer's style is needed in order to perceive
the curious individuality of its slightly bumpy ostinatos and cyclic phrase-
repetitions.[5] Only rarely did Stravinsky allow what was expected of him to
influence his attitude to his material. In the *Circus Polka*, which is in any
case a flimsy piece of work by his standards, the sudden intrusion of a
crude quotation from Schubert's best-known *Marche militaire* (almost in the
manner of Saint-Saëns's Berlioz parody in *Le Carnaval des animaux*) bursts
the fragilely held illusion of ponderous vulgarity, and descends into actual
ponderous vulgarity.

By contrast, the *Scènes de ballet*, the Stravinsky score most often accused
of vulgarity, is in reality a clever example of a stereotype subjected to
gentle mockery through imitation, like the Tango and *Norwegian Moods*, but
weakened by material slightly below the composer's best. There certainly
seems no reason to doubt the well-known story (corrected, presumably for
the last time, in *SPD*) of Stravinsky's refusal to allow the *pas de deux* to be
rescored with swooning strings for the reprise of the C major trumpet tune,
since it is essential to the artistic 'distance' of the work that it presents the
rhetoric of this highly conventionalised moment without succumbing to its
emotionalism.[6] The most significant thing about the story of course is that
the 'portrait', as Stravinsky himself called it in *Dialogues*, is so accurate that
the only fault the professionals could find with it lay in precisely that
obliquity which turns the piece into a work of art.

*Scènes de ballet* is perhaps best understood in terms of a more lasting
preoccupation of Stravinsky's: with the idea of the abstract, or formula,
ballet, a preoccupation which, in turn, it is easy to associate with the
whole synthetic posture of neo-classicism. Such a work, already, is *Apollo*. I
suggested that in *Apollo* the story, such as it is, is no more than an emanation
of the form, and it is noteworthy that when that ballet was staged in Paris

by Diaghilev in June 1928 (six weeks after the Washington première) the choreographer was a young Russian dancer, Georges Balanchine, whom Stravinsky came to regard as by far the most musically alert and literate of all his dance collaborators. In Balanchine, he found a choreographic mind able to think directly from music to gestures. 'Balanchine's visualisation of the *Movements* [for piano and orchestra]', Stravinsky wrote later, 'exposed relationships of which I had not been aware in the same way. Seeing it, therefore, was like touring a building for which I had drawn the plans but never completely explored the result.'[7] And of Balanchine's choreography to the Violin Concerto (in *Balustrade*), 'the result was a series of dialogues complementary to and co-ordinated with the dialogues of the music'.[8] Of Stravinsky's original ballet scores, Balanchine was responsible for choreographing *Jeu de cartes*, *Orpheus* and *Agon*, as well as the *Circus Polka* and, finally, the television drama *The Flood*, the working notes for which were published in *Dialogues*. Although these works fluctuate between the abstract and the narrative, they reflect as a group the particular attraction, for a composer of Stravinsky's pantomimic tendencies, of collaborating with a choreographer who worked not as a scenarist but as a dance contrapuntist, realising his images directly from the interior relationships of the music.

It would be impertinent for a non-specialist to attempt an analysis of this collaboration as such. The musician will note that Balanchine's article on 'The Dance Element in Stravinsky's Music' is one of the most intelligent short studies on the composer.[9] It not only draws attention to certain specifically balletic elements in Stravinsky's music, and shows how basic they are to his whole style, but it reveals how Balanchine himself was happy to work with these elements unmediated by any implied action. An extreme case was the dance he composed in 1945 to the *Elegy* for solo viola, in which 'I tried to reflect the flow and concentrated variety of the music through the interlaced bodies of two dancers rooted to a central spot of the stage'[10] – the work being a two-part invention for the solo instrument, with a fugue at its centre. Balanchine also refers to the gestural precision of Stravinsky's music. 'Each measure', he writes, 'has its complete, almost personal life, it is a living unit. There are no blind spots anywhere.'[11] From Stravinsky's sketches, we know that this is an accurate analysis of the way he imagined his musical ideas. His organisation of rhythm, on which Balanchine also naturally dwells, is the corollary of the absolute, objective and almost spatial, sculptural quality of these ideas, since it is only through movement that they can assume temporal form. It is easy enough to understand how these two complementary elements – the frozen gesture and the form-giving rhythm – lend Stravinsky's music its uniquely balletic character.

From *Apollo* onwards there is evidence of an increasing interest in this idea of music rendered directly into dance. *Jeu de cartes*, written in 1936 for the newly formed American Ballet, has a plot of sorts but it is a curiously inconsequential affair, like a scenario grafted on to a pre-existent score (though this was not in fact the case, and the idea seems to have been in

Stravinsky's mind from the start). A dramatised game, in which the pieces or, as here, playing-cards, are personified as dramatis personae, inevitably has some feeling of the psychological archetype, with the ebb and flow of the contest serving as a visual symbol for the ritualised tensions in the music. And of course Stravinsky and Balanchine pursued this idea still further in their final theatre collaboration, *Agon* (the Greek word for 'contest'), where it is merely the abstract principle of competition, rather than any particular game, which fills the space between music and gesture.

In the light of the two pseudo-ballets which followed – *Danses concertantes* and *Scènes de ballet* – *Jeu de cartes* is notable more for its character as a symbolic ballet, abstracted from the tradition of the romantic story ballet, than for its narrative or even, one might add, musical content. All three works seem to be formulated as ballet 'kits' – put together, that is, according to a formula, but a formula capable of modification within limits, just as the symphonic and concertante works of the 1920s and 1930s refer variously to classical and baroque prototypes. As regards form they deploy more or less the same elements, and in much the same order. An introduction is followed by a *pas d'action*, a set of variations, a *pas de deux* with or without variations for the leading dancers, another *pas d'action*, and a closing dance of triumph or apotheosis. In *Danses concertantes* this formula is offered not as a theatre piece at all but as a concert work where, it might be said, the action is symbolised exclusively in the music. But the distinction is more apparent than real, since in style and gesture *Danses concertantes* is not noticeably different from *Jeu de cartes*, except that its small orchestra and its adaptation of ballet form to the *concertino-ripieno* principle of the baroque concerto relate its texture rather to a chamber work like 'Dumbarton Oaks', where *Jeu de cartes* has the slightly souped-up Beethoven sound of the Symphony in C. Musically these works are products of the 'lingua franca' phase of Stravinsky's neo-classicism. *Jeu de cartes* alludes to Ravel and Tchaikovsky and famously quotes Rossini, while *Danses concertantes*, a work of tighter and more regular construction as presumably befits its nature as a concert work, draws more directly on Stravinsky himself, particularly the recent symphony, which seems to be the source of the theme of the *pas d'action* (cf. the finale theme in the symphony) and of the shanty-like horn tune in the first variation. However, a comparison between the symphony and the abstract ballet suggests that the reversion from strict symphonic formal model back to a dance model based on prescriptions of formal sequence but not formal procedure has actually encouraged greater refinement and precision in the manoeuvring of superficially conventional elements. On the surface, *Danses concertantes* is one of Stravinsky's smoothest scores. But this fluency conceals a watchmaker's concern for exact balance and placing of minute detail. Balanchine found both this score and *Jeu de cartes* rhythmically more complex than *Apollo*, with its overt metric constructs. In *Danses concertantes* we find both regular barrings fragmented internally, like the horn variation already mentioned, where there seems no constant relation between the melodic metre and the barred metre; and passages where the bar-length itself changes continuously, so that the music has rich patterns of inner mobility. One can hardly resist pointing out that the revision to the 'Sacrifical Dance', which was essentially a metric revision, followed less than two years after the completion of *Danses concertantes*. And to compare the two scores is to see the complete range of Stravinsky's practice up to the 1940s, from an architecture made out of violent rhythmic gestures but with a largely static texture to a design where flexible rhythm is the main agent bringing internal movement to an outwardly flowing discourse. This relation between discourse and a variable construction of small cells is certainly what lends Stravinsky's music of this period its fascination, and is no doubt what gave Balanchine a choreographic hold on the music, without benefit of narrative or the picturesque.

*Scènes de ballet* pursues similar preoccupations, but with more emphasis on heightened textural or colouristic factors which suggest a move back from the abstract theatre of the concert ballet to the symbolic theatre of the cinema screen: that type of fantasy theatre which gave the spectacular cinema of the 1930s and early 1940s one of its main images. In *Scènes de ballet* we 'watch' the dancers on their stage, but included in the spectacle are a screen audience and screen lighting and, implied within the virtual frame, an entire screen theatre with its billboards, its backstage scandals, its not quite believable romance. We are in the world of *The Red Shoes*. Stravinsky makes brilliant use of orchestral effects, including the piano, which he had not used in an orchestral score since *Persephone*,[12] to suggest the exaggerated lighting and colour of that kind of world. The trumpet of the *pas de deux* falls on the tune like a spotlight,[13] and the woodwind in the dance for the *corps de ballet* creates swirls of colour. All this is managed without crudity or vulgarity, though one may well feel that Stravinsky's ideas here lack the freshness of *Danses concertantes*. Perhaps it was never possible to symbolise the world of Billy Rose without entering in some sense into its artistic limitations. Even so *Scènes de ballet* is a much better and more arresting score than its bad reputation and almost complete neglect might have one believe.

But there was little danger of a lasting accommodation between Stravinsky and the celluloid atmosphere of American show business. It simply was not in his nature to compose without irony to a stylistic prescription, and it seems that then, as now, the slightest obliqueness of approach puzzled those for whom *vox populi* (as measured by *vox denarii*) was *vox Dei*. After *Scènes de ballet* he made only one further assault on the palaces of entertainment, in the shape of the *Ebony Concerto* which he wrote for Woody Herman's jazz band the following year, 1945. But jazz was never a popular style in the commercial sense, and the *Ebony Concerto* is less self-consciously a showbiz parody than it is an idiomatic study in the manner of Stravinsky's ragtime pieces. Instead of merely evoking the world which gave birth to such music, it isolates details of style, like the syncopations,

which Stravinsky breaks away from their moorings of a constantly felt
pulse; the blues harmonies; and in particular the actual sound of the jazz
orchestra, which Stravinsky treats as a thing-in-itself, a musical entity with
a personality as distinctive and fertile as the wind ensemble in the
*Symphonies of Wind Instruments* or the strings in *Apollo*. If we compare this
concerto with the Concerto in D for strings which Stravinsky wrote in 1946
for Paul Sacher in Basle, the main differences which emerge lie in this region
of characteristic style. Thematically, in general scale, form and concertante
treatment, the two works overlap at many points. But their gestural differences keep them distinct. The string concerto is a concise and elegant study
in the line of the Symphony in C, a tonal work that plays openly on the
classical instrumental tradition in ways that are perhaps more refined but
are not essentially different from those that underlay the Octet or Piano
Sonata. The *Ebony Concerto* merely uses conventions from that tradition as
a framing device for a study in jazz idioms. So strong is the symbolism in
each case – just as it was strong in distinguishing the Russian songs of
*Pribaoutki* from the easy keyboard pieces – that one can very well overlook
the technical similarities: the fact, for instance, that the Concerto in D is as
much a rhythmic study as the *Ebony Concerto*. Hans Keller's observation
that 'in the *Ebony Concerto* . . . every upbeat serves its own opposition,
serves to be beaten back or beat itself back'[14] could also be applied to the
D flat major second subject of the string concerto (fig.27), where silence
and syncopation have the same effect of duplicating the functions of upbeats
and downbeats (Ex.45). It would be hard to imagine a better demonstration
of the role played by style in Stravinsky's neo-classical music than the
differences and similarities of these two short concertos.

 While he was thus exploring the further possibilities of a synthetic music,
Stravinsky was beginning almost imperceptibly to experiment in ways
which would eventually lead him away from such a music altogether. Taken
as a whole the 1940s are the most confused decade of his career. The picture
of the early American years is of an established synthetic method attaching
itself to a succession of not very promising models, while the later 1940s
show a guarded retrenchment. The Symphony in Three Movements, the
Concerto in D, *Orpheus* and *The Rake's Progress* generally confirm the central
tradition of neo-classicism, at the very moment that works of less intrinsic
merit, like the *Ode*, *Babel*, the Elegy for viola, the Sonata for two pianos, or
works tentatively begun, like the Kyrie and Gloria of the Mass, suggest a
new creative energy in search of new kinds of model. It is almost as if
Stravinsky the perpetual renouncer were at war with Stravinsky the
admired master. If *Orpheus*, at least superficially, is exactly the kind of ballet
Lincoln Kirstein must have imagined he was commissioning for his Ballet
Society in 1946, so *The Rake's Progress* is the kind of opera both Stravinsky's
admirers and his increasingly vocal detractors probably assumed he would
write as news of the collaboration with Auden started to leak out in 1948

*Ex. 45* Concerto in D for strings, 1st movement

or 1949. Robert Craft, who came into Stravinsky's life at the same time as Auden, has written of a creative crisis associated with the opera:

> In September [1951], in Venice, *The Rake's Progress* was regarded by most critics as the work of a master but also a throwback, the last flowering of a genre. After the première, conducting concerts in Italy and Germany, Stravinsky found that he and Schoenberg were everywhere categorised as the reactionary and the progressive. What was worse, Stravinsky was acutely aware that the new generation was not interested in *The Rake*. [Some time later back in California] he asked to go for a drive. . . . On the way home he startled us, saying that he was afraid he could no longer compose and he did not know what to do. For a moment he broke down and actually wept. . . . [15]

In about 1950 most musicians certainly thought they knew where to place Stravinsky in relation to new music. His reactionary status even had its theoretical underpinning, in the shape of Adorno's devastating attack in his book *The Philosophy of New Music* (1948), and when Stravinsky began to adopt serial technique in the 1950s, his followers were so astounded that a whole literature flourished for a time examining the reasons for the change, or, in a few cases, protesting that it was not surprising at all and could, indeed should, have been predicted.

To try to understand this process we should go back to the starting-point of this chapter, the *Poetics* and Stravinsky's emigration to America. Though it presents itself as a general treatise on musical aesthetics, the *Poetics* really belongs to a period in his work which was then coming to an end. While the works written in France suggest, for all their diversity of source and technique, a magisterial certainty and clarity of aim appropriate to a sometime candidate for the Institut de France, the works which follow his arrival in the USA are scattered and opportunistic, aiming this way and that, as unsettledly brilliant as one might expect of a Russian composer, the greatest of his age, but twice exiled by war and arriving in a country of alien language and culture (France was not that to an educated Russian), a country well-known, moreover, for its predatory attitude to famous men. In France Stravinsky had composed a succession of major works, each one (except for the Concerto for two pianos) written through before the next was begun, each firmly under the control of his own ideas and intentions. In America his writing became largely *ad hoc*. Obviously 'major' works, like the Symphony in Three Movements and the Mass, were started but set aside. The symphony, begun in 1942, was not finished until three years later; the Mass, begun in 1944, went into cold storage until 1948. Even the *Danses concertantes* took Stravinsky fifteen months to complete, while the *Scènes de ballet*, of about the same length, was written in three. To some extent, no doubt, this instability was a general symptom of wartime. After 1945 and until the completion of *The Rake's Progress* the old pattern of major projects was resumed. But an undercurrent of change can be detected in the music itself from 1943 at the latest, and this current flows into the post-war masterpieces, only partly concealed by the aura of the established *grand maître* so assiduously cultivated by the American publicity machine and mocked by the historicist Adorno.

The indications of change are somewhat diffuse and hardly amount to a definite direction, even in the light of what happened to Stravinsky's music after 1951. They can be summed up only negatively, as a tendency to abandon the stable framework of neo-classicism, with its synthetic tonal and formal processes and its symbolic frames of reference. The tendency is spasmodic and assumes various forms. For example, we find episodes of chromatic fragmentation in the same work as passages of extreme diatonic plainness and simplicity. The *Ode* for orchestra, written in 1943 in memory of Natalie Koussevitzky, opens with a passage of tentative angular chromaticism that, for a few bars, seems to be groping towards the kind of disrupted motivic lines associated with Webern, before it settles, still a shade hesitantly, into what Werfel called 'a kind of fugue with accompaniment'[16] in an unstable C minor – a flowing, slightly amorphous piece as far as possible from the crisply articulated fugues in the *Symphony of Psalms* or the Concerto for two pianos. On the other hand the second movement, which is the piece Stravinsky had written for the hunting scene in *Jane Eyre*, adopts an almost Sibelian diatonicism and an untypically regular metric scheme. Stravinsky had attempted a similar contrast in one previous work, the *Duo concertant*, whose second movement is also called 'Eclogue' (or to be exact 'Eglogue') and is a plain diatonic movement, in the style of a Russian *kazachok*, following a lyrical movement of uncertain tonal focus. But the *Ode*, a more coherent piece overall than the *Duo*, also anticipates *Orpheus*, whose Attic calm is from time to time disrupted by the same kind of broken chromatic line and harmony, intensifying its feeling of elegy.

While working on the *Ode*, Stravinsky wrote the slow movement of the Symphony in Three Movements, ostensibly in his synthetic tonal style, but then turned again to an experimental music, this time of extreme and practically unbroken diatonicism. On the face of it the Sonata for two pianos is a well-behaved neo-classical piece in three movements with a sonata-form moderato and brisk ABA finale framing a slow variation movement, as in the Octet. But its style and technique are in fact unlike those of the synthetic period. With the apparent exception of the very first theme, its main ideas are all adaptations of Russian folk tunes which Stravinsky found in a nineteenth-century collection in his own library.[17] But these tunes are neither treated with ethnographic respect, as they might have been thirty years before, nor are they projected into a virtual world of neo-romantic picturesqueness, like the little melodies of the *Four Norwegian Moods* or even the *Scherzo à la russe* which Stravinsky composed in 1944 after the model of Rimsky-Korsakov's *Dubinushka*. Instead they are treated as subject-matter for improvisation within a tight framework provided by a regular pulse, regular barring, and a four-part texture which typically confines itself to the notes of the scale of the melody. The Sonata is in fact like a free-wheeling melodic study arranged in sections according to the rough outlines of a traditional sonata. The outer movements are attractive if slightly inconsequential. The variation movement, however, is stricter, and offers a prototype for Stravinsky's early serial experiments, such as 'Tomorrow shall be my dancing day' in the Cantata, or the Septet. The twenty-nine notes of the theme are played in strict order three times through, with a canon by inversion at a bar's distance, supported by a free part made up exclusively of the notes of the chord of G major (Ex.46). This is followed by four variations in which the theme, still treated as a strict note sequence, is

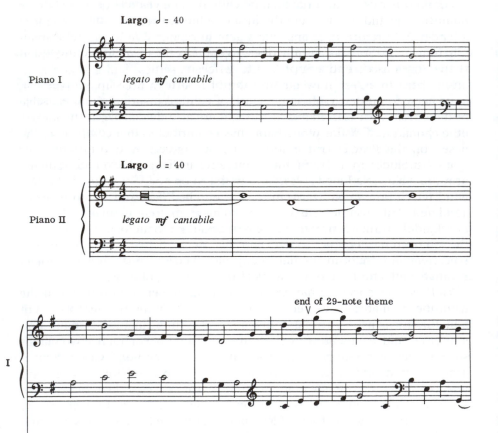

*Ex. 46* Sonata for two pianos

variously a *cantus firmus* (like the variation theme of the Concerto for two pianos), a fugue subject and a chaconne bass. There is little or no chromaticism, and the effect of the theme itself is much closer to that of a round, like 'Frère Jacques' or 'London's Burning', with clean, immobile harmony, than anything esoterically modern. There is not the slightest similarity to the music of Schoenberg and his associates, except for the idea of a note order, which is in any case also found in Purcell's ground basses and the *cantus firmus* music of the late Middle Ages. All the same, strict linear writing of this kind obviously gave Stravinsky a precedent when he turned his mind consciously to serial method eight or nine years later. His starting-point then would be precisely the idea of a limited tonal *cantus firmus* with a tendency to return over and over again to a pivotal note, as the Russian folk tune in the Sonata typically does. Eventually the idea of pivoting would shape Stravinsky's entire approach to serialism.

It is hard to assess how far this abrupt return to Russian sources may have been connected with some sense of cultural disorientation: a protest of the *déraciné*. Russian habits of thought are also detectable in the curious little choral piece, *Babel*, which Stravinsky contributed to a composite work based on the *Book of Genesis* (to which Schoenberg also contributed his *Genesis* prelude) in 1944; in the Symphony in Three Movements; in the beautiful solo viola Elegy (1944); and in the Kyrie and Gloria for chorus and wind which Stravinsky wrote in the autumn of 1944. And it hardly seems accidental that this unobtrusive return to his roots accompanies a new wave of religious enthusiasm, perhaps less dramatic than the one of 1926, but in the long run hardly less influential on his music. *Babel*, as a commissioned piece, was no doubt incidental to any reconversion, though it provided a positive model for later sacred works like *The Flood* and *A Sermon, a Narrative and a Prayer*. Its speaking narrator (a lectern figure very different in function from the dramatically conceived speakers in *The Soldier's Tale*, *Oedipus rex* and *Persephone*); the graphic spiccato string writing in the episode of the scattering and destruction of the tower; the two-part choral incantations, so prescient of passages in the Mass and *Threni* – all these details were to assume importance later on. At the same time *Babel* displays atavistic features. It reverts, for example, to certain chromatic aspects of the octatonic scale not associated with classical tonal usage, exactly as the *Symphony of Psalms*, Stravinsky's last religious work of any size, had done, and as the Symphony in Three Movements, already two-thirds written, was doing. The opening of *Babel*, quite apart from its obvious textural reminiscence of *The Firebird*, is like a voice from the past, quite as much as a voice of the future: the voice of *Fireworks* and the *Scherzo fantastique*, as much as of *Threni* and *The Flood*.

But the Elegy and the Mass movements, written in the autumn, sound a more immediately personal note. Though the Mass is of course the greater work, the case of the Elegy is interesting. Stravinsky provided it at the request of the violist, Germain Prévost, in memory of the founding violinist

of the Pro Arte Quartet, Alphonse Onnou, who had died in 1940. According
to Craft, Stravinsky had known Onnou only slightly; moreover he states
that the music was sketched long before the commission (in November
1941). On internal grounds, however, one prefers the official date, and it
seems that Stravinsky may have sketched the music in a different mood
and tempo from those of the work as we know it, as Craft has indicated
he did on other occasions (for instance at the time of the *Symphonies of Wind
Instruments* and the Octet). The comparison between the *Ebony Concerto* and
the Concerto in D shows how Stravinsky could make similar material and
techniques serve contrasted expressive or symbolic ends.

The Elegy refers briefly to the type of *parlando* folk melody that opens
*The Rite of Spring* and *The Wedding*, but its development is more lyrical and
linear than anything in the Russian period, and the richly expressive two-
part fugue flows quite spontaneously out of this introductory music (which
returns after the fugue). On the whole it is easy to relate this kind of writing
to certain parts of the Mass, where Stravinsky applies the ornamental
devices of Russian folksong to a type of melody derived from plainchant.
The start of the Gloria, written just after the Elegy, is an obvious example.

The Mass itself forms the climax of this atavistic, religious, experimental
phase of Stravinsky's work, and it is probably the key to his stylistic, and
eventually creative, difficulties of the time. He wrote it without commission,
evidently from a deeply felt spiritual need. There is no documented
evidence that the work gave him trouble, and we can assume that he only
did not complete it in 1945 because other work, necessary to his livelihood,
intervened. He completed the Symphony in Three Movements, wrote the
*Ebony Concerto*, the Concerto in D and *Orpheus* (all commissioned scores),
and rewrote *Petrushka*, the *Symphonies of Wind Instruments*, the 1919 *Firebird
suite*, and *Apollo*, before returning to the Mass in the autumn of 1947. But
even the masterpieces in that list look like part of a mopping-up operation
by comparison with the Mass, which not only establishes a number of new
sources for Stravinsky's symbolic language, but also prepares the ground
technically for the works of his final period. Of course this was not its
conscious purpose, nor was it understood or understandable in any such
light for several years. The Mass is an excellent illustration of how genius
pursues its own evolutionary laws, sometimes apparently quite independent of its visible manifestations, which are merely symptoms – though
they may develop an impetus of their own which for a time seems to deny
the hidden laws any significance.

Like *Babel*, the Mass supplies links between the early Russian works and
the late period, and its conception may even have influenced Stravinsky in
his revision of such a work as the *Symphonies of Wind Instruments*, with
which it has points in common. Or the Mass may have come partly out of
Stravinsky's reappraisal of the earlier work – we know too little about the
chronology to be sure.[18] In any case, wind chord-voicing of the type that
is fundamental to the *Symphonies* turns up again in the Mass, albeit often

in a simpler, 'cleaner' style which may reflect the diatonic character of Stravinsky's recent work, or it may come from the fact that the work is vocal and moreover explores traditional vocal techniques. We know that Stravinsky wanted to write a liturgical Mass; that is, he wanted his work to be practicable for church resources, and he wanted it to be significant. He uses only ten instruments and four-part choir, with boy sopranos and altos ('children's voices', the score stipulates), and he completely rejects elaborately evolved musical structures, and especially climaxes, that do not have to do with a straightforward declamation of the words. He hoped, of course, that by setting a Latin rather than Slavonic text he would bring the work within the purview of the Catholic Church, which at least permits instruments in church (the Orthodox does not) even if it rarely gets them there in practice – apart from the ubiquitous Hammond Organ and the occasional electric guitar. In fact the practical aspect of Stravinsky's score is so impressive that one can easily be carried away by it and completely misinterpret the work in consequence.

It should be evident from careful listening that the Mass is something more than a simple liturgical setting. It is an affirmation of faith cast symbolically in a form peculiar to ancient praxis which evolved at a time when Christian faith was instinctive and general, in precisely the sense that it was neither instinctive nor general by 1944. The Mass contains, in both senses of the word, a powerful swell of spiritual emotion. Moreover its expression of faith is unqualified. Stravinsky records his reaction to a set of Mozart Masses, 'these rococo-operatic sweets of sin', which he played through in about 1943 and which it is fairly clear he regarded with distaste for their decorative and euphuistic mannerism.[19] His Mass, by contrast, would be cold, severe and lofty. It would studiously avoid the elaborate symphonic method that Stravinsky, too, had at his disposal, and base itself instead on idioms traditional to the church: plainsong, syllabic word-setting, fauxbourdon homophony (block-chording), interspersed with strict polyphony, antiphony, with alternations between solo voices and the choir, and tropes (which here take the form of melismatic embellishments of introductory words like 'Gloria' and 'Sanctus'). Stravinsky later claimed that he only got to know Machaut, and by implication the other music of the Ars Nova, after he had written the Mass. But the parallel is none the less remarkably close, as was suggested by Craft and shown many years ago in an article by Herbert Murrill.[20] Moreover the sound of the Mass is clearly by intention archaic. In this sense especially its atmosphere spills over into the music Stravinsky began to write after *The Rake's Progress*, where he explored strict polyphonic techniques initially in the context of the antique sound-world to which they properly belonged. As late as *Threni* the explicit link is maintained between serialism and medieval devices like troping, antiphony and the *cantus firmus*. After that the connection goes underground; but it is never entirely lost.

The Mass was therefore a reaction against Stravinsky's immediate musical

environment: his own work and other people's. And not for the first time
in his life the reaction worked by reference to an earlier and unfashionable
music. Perhaps, as with *Mavra*, there was some faint desire to pull the
noses of all those well-heeled art connoisseurs who thought they had got
him taped. But no one who knew his music well need have been surprised
at this particular turn. The *Symphony of Psalms* had shown that the intensely
personal and the intensely religious could coincide for Stravinsky. And as
for its form and hieratic atmosphere the Mass is so close to the *Symphonies
of Wind Instruments* and parts of *The Wedding* that the surprising thing might
be that more than twenty years separate it from them.

What he does, in effect, in the Mass is to adapt types of procedure and
expression that he has used before in other contexts to the liturgy he has
in front of him, using for the purpose certain cognate devices from other
music of that liturgy. In the Gloria, he brilliantly equates the idea of the
trope and antiphon to the form of the invocation and dance which opens
*The Wedding*. In the Credo he goes further and fuses the pure choral chant
of his own earlier Creed setting (which at that time existed only to a Slavonic
text) with the rhythmic-balletic chanting in the finale of the *Symphony of
Psalms* and the cellular forms of *The Wedding*, again making play with the
'normal' word stress to produce a smoothly irregular metric scheme. The
whole movement is an almost unbroken chant, introduced by the priest's
intonation and concluded by a short unaccompanied canonic Amen. In the
Sanctus the antiphon idea embraces a greater variety of Stravinskian types,
including a kind of 'Podblyudnye' chorus to the words 'Hosanna in
excelsis', a rigid little fugato on 'Pleni sunt coeli' and even a suspicion
of Handelian double-dots for the Benedictus. Throughout, a textural and
dynamic terracing of extreme clarity and precision articulates the different
sections, which are invariably short and characterised by distinctive wind-
scorings (or, rarely, unaccompanied). The harmonies push against the
underlying consonance of the fifth or the third like the back of a wooden
pew: apt but not always comfortable. They express a determinedly severe
attitude to a habitual observance. But Stravinsky's ear never lets him down,
and as in the *Symphonies of Wind Instruments* the radiance of these sounds
rings in the mind long after the compact and, as Ansermet observed,
humble masterpiece that engendered them has faded away.

Not many of Stravinsky's neo-classical conventions survive in the Mass,
and those that do – like the oboes in thirds accompanying the imitative
'Christe eleison', or the dotted rhythms in the Benedictus – seem de-conven-
tionalised or perhaps re-conventionalised. This was accepted at the time as
part of the work's religious function, and no great importance seems to
have been attached to it. But the two other major works of the period just
before *The Rake's Progress* – the Symphony in Three Movements and *Orpheus*
– also show some weakening of these conventions, in contexts that might
normally be expected to perpetuate them: a symphonic work for orchestra
and a ballet on a classical subject. The Symphony has usually been discussed

as if it were directly comparable to the Symphony in C or the concertante works of the 1930s. Stravinsky himself drew attention to its cinematic origins,[21] but documentation has remained sketchy, though the episodic character of the music is plain to see. We do not know whether Stravinsky wrote the first movement (in 1942) intending it for a symphony; Tansman reported hearing him play it in that year, and that it was so intended, but he also reported that it already had a concertante part for piano, of which Craft claims there is no sign in the score until a considerably later version, while Stravinsky himself tells us in *Expositions* that he thought of the work as a concerto for orchestra. The second movement was, he adds, taken direct from his aborted score for *The Song of Bernadette*, which 'became' the Andante of the Symphony. But perhaps the least helpful information of all is the composer's barely credible, and apparently spontaneous, 'war-programme' for the outer movements, set out in copious detail in *Dialogues* (pp. 50–52) and then impishly disclaimed: 'in spite of what I have said [that the symphony is programmatic], the Symphony is not programmatic'.

The truth is that, to an unusual extent, the symphony incorporates material taken from earlier works of his, but that it alters or extends their expressive meaning to the point where it seems virtually to sweep away all memory of a previous context. The Concerto for two pianos is laid under particularly heavy contribution. The main motive of the whole symphony, for instance, which Vlad linked rather speciously to the famous motto of Brahms's Third Symphony,[22] comes from the fourth variation of the Concerto, where it supplies an ostinato bass to a pattern of alternating seventh chords, exactly as it does in the exposition of the Symphony. The only crucial difference is that the Concerto groups the ostinato in fours, *with* the barring, whereas the Symphony groups it in threes, *across* the bar. Moreover there is an obvious similarity between the whirlwind texture of this passage in the Symphony and the subsidiary episode in the Concerto's first movement (bar 92), which happens to be based on exactly the same chords as the fourth variation but without the minor-third ostinato (Ex.47, cf. Ex.42). The fugue in the finale of the Symphony is unlike the one in the Concerto, but has a crucial melodic figure in common. However, the slow movements of the two works are so similar in their ideas, and have so much in common texturally, that they look almost like variant treatments of the same melodic and decorative motives. Admittedly some of these devices are found elsewhere in the neo-classical music. The minor third figure, for instance, crops up often; in the Capriccio it is linked to the same unison sweep up a minor ninth that starts and finishes the first movement of the Symphony. This same figure even crops up, apparently quite out of context, in the finale of the Symphony in C (fig.165), where it takes the same Phrygian form as in the Capriccio, but starts on G, like the Symphony in Three Movements (where the scale itself is mixolydian, with the A flat dissonant). And, as if by some hidden reflex, the scale in the Symphony

*Ex. 47(i)* Symphony in Three Movements, 1st movement

in C triggers off exactly the same so-called 'Brahms' motive as it does in the Capriccio and the later Symphony (Ex.48).

What these by no means trivial parallels suggest is that the neo-classical pieces had left some residue of energy in these ideas unused, perhaps because of the constraints of the classical posture itself. In the first movement of the Capriccio there is a distinct sense that the introductory flourish is left hanging in mid-air each time it comes (and it comes four times during the movement). But the comparison with the Concerto for two pianos is the most revealing in this regard. Craft reasonably sees this as the most powerful of Stravinsky's 1930s works, but its power is restrained, deliberately, by the strictness of its form. It has the severity of a forceful but controlled personality. The Symphony, by contrast, unleashes its material without regard to strict formal considerations, and the result is the most physically violent and exciting music even Stravinsky had written for thirty

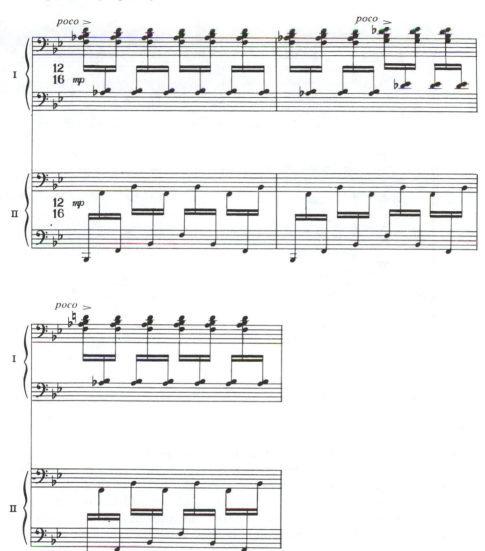

*(ii)* Concerto for two pianos, 1st movement

years. This in turn poses exceptional problems of architecture which have to be solved *ad hoc* in a way that had previously been avoided. The 'development' section in the first movement is based on the same motives as the exposition, but in feeling and mode of continuity it is quite different. Against the mechanistic ferocity of the opening (up to fig.34) it opposes a more hesitant set of ideas laid out as a series of instrumental dialogues, with chamber scoring. In some respects these episodes have the fluid contrapuntal texture of Stravinsky's typical 1930s style; but their character as independent instrumental colloquies often takes them outside the general

*Ex. 48(i)* Symphony in Three Movements, 1st movement (strings only)

flow so that they seem to lead a separate life, like the initial episodes in the
*Symphonies of Wind Instruments*. Such a passage is the series of dialogues
beginning at fig.71, which Craft tells us was the first part of the work to
be drafted.[23] The slow movement, where an obbligato harp replaces the
piano of the first movement, has comparable moments. On the whole
the Symphony performs a miraculous balancing act between the implied
continuities of classical tonality and gesture and the architectural non-conti-
nuities with which Stravinsky had worked in his Russian period, and which,
as the Mass shows, were starting to interest him again. It is no surprise to
learn from the sketches that the symphony, like *The Rite of Spring*, was
composed out of order and in chunks.

    The Russian strain in the Symphony in Three Movements clearly links it
to contemporary works like the Mass and *Babel* (not to mention the *Scherzo
à la russe*) and takes it out of the ambit of neo-classicism. The violence of
the outer movements blows a Polovtsian wind down the streets of
Manhattan, with thrilling percussive writing for piano and strings. And
the harmony of these movements supports their Russianism. As in *The Rite
of Spring* the octatonic scale – a powerful force for the first time since

*Ex. 48*(ii) Symphony in C, 4th movement

*Ex. 49(i)* Symphony in Three Movements, 2nd movement

the *Symphony of Psalms* – generates grinding semitonal dissonance and interferences between competing chords and tonal plateaux, and is less used than in the Concerto in D of 1946 to imply leading-note tonal harmony. Even in the slow movement, the music most like that of the string Concerto, the F sharp of the tune and the F natural of the accompaniment keep their distance, like the north and south poles of a magnetic field, where at the start of the Concerto they are drawn together in a nearly sensual way by melodic attraction (Ex.49). In general the Symphony is a work where melodic continuities are often relinquished in favour of impulse and layered textures, through which Stravinsky is typically able to make a virtue of his somewhat disparate material.

By contrast, Stravinsky saw *Orpheus* as an essay in 'mimed song' which would lead him inevitably towards an opera as his next work.[24] On the face of it this may seem an enigmatic judgement, for *Orpheus* has probably less sustained melody in it than *Apollo*; its song is broken up, just as Orpheus himself, the primal bearer of melody, is torn to pieces by the Bacchantes in the penultimate dance. But the secret of *Orpheus* is that the song is often suppressed. Stravinsky wanted the harp accompaniment to the oboes in the 'Air de danse' to sound 'dry and choked', and indeed this sonority of the harp, played *près de la table*, is from the very first note of the ballet representative of that sense of loss which begets all music. The curtain, rising immediately, reveals Orpheus weeping for Eurydice: 'He stands motionless, with his back to the audience.' From time to time later in the ballet, melody comes to the surface as if coming into earshot, as in the 'Air de danse', where the oboes start their tune in mid-phrase. The one long melodic outpouring, in the 'Pas de deux' where Orpheus leads Eurydice

*Ex. 49(ii)* Concerto in D for strings

out of Hades, is abruptly curtailed and a bar of silence accompanies Orpheus
tearing the bandage from his eyes and Eurydice's second death.

The melodic writing here subscribes to severer models than in *Apollo*,
where the defining technique was above all metric. Certain devices of strict
counterpoint reflect the later ballet's proximity to the Mass. Orpheus is
apotheosised to the strains of a canon for two horns with a *cantus firmus*
for trumpet and solo violin; and in the 'Pas de deux' the writing, though
not strict in the same sense, is authentic counterpoint with a strong guiding
bass that lends it an intensity quite different from the oblique polyphony
of the early neo-classical pieces with their schematic basses. Writing much
later, when serial counterpoint had taken over much of his conscious
musical thinking, Stravinsky praised this movement and the first interlude
'where a developing harmonic movement and an active bass line relieve
the long chain of *ostinati*'.[25] He was obviously less disposed to praise dances
like Orpheus's first 'Air de danse', where a line that evolves melodically is
supported by more mechanical patterns, even though they are remarkably
discreet, with scoring of extreme finesse. Of these movements the most
conventional are the 'Pas d'action', in which Orpheus's eyes are bound
ready for the return journey, and the second part of the 'Pas des furies',
whose ostinato figures come dangerously close to the Stravinskian equi-

valent of an Alberti bass. For the composer of Movements and the Huxley Variations, such passages must have seemed embarrassingly repetitious, just as he claimed to find the sustained ending of the introduction too motionless. But *Orpheus* is by nature a slow-moving work, framing the most statuesque of all Stravinsky's classical dramas, and even its violent episodes are played with restraint. The 'Pas d'action' for the Bacchantes as they dismember Orpheus is sinisterly calm, with such markings as *pizzicato*, *spiccato*, and *leggiero* dominating string music that is only discreetly supported by wind. For a dozen bars towards the end the music explodes in the manner of the Symphony in Three Movements (whose harmonies are closely related to those of the ballet). But for the rest the murder of Orpheus, like his grief, is enacted with his back to the audience.

This unique tone of Stravinsky's last classical ballet reveals it as hybrid, and like other major transitional works of his a masterly balancing out of elements that one might suppose mutually incompatible. As a ritual re-enactment of a violent human sacrifice, it harks back strikingly to *The Rite of Spring*, with its gestures now conveyed through a calmer musical language. But *Orpheus* goes still farther than *The Rite* in presenting a ritual drama with named characters whose exploits are familiar to us, like those of Oedipus, not to mention Jesus in the liturgical Passion re-enactment of the Mass. There is even a true sense in which Orpheus dies that we might live; in terms of that neo-classical aesthetic which Stravinsky borrowed from Nietzsche, the killing and apotheosis of Orpheus stand for the taming and ordering of those orgiastic elements which music took over from the Dionysian rituals of primitive culture – a process without which art as we understand it would cease to exist. 'The present hour', Stravinsky had told a Uruguayan reporter in 1936, 'demands a totally different music [from *The Rite*], in which the decorative element surrenders to the spiritual and intellectual. The composer must renounce colouristic orgies in order to develop healthy and strong concepts.' This is a prophylactic version of the famous remarks about Apollo and Dionysus already quoted in Chapter 6.[26]

Although the narrative element in *Orpheus* is another pointer towards the full-scale opera he was shortly to write, its ordering is almost completely subjected to the abstract principles of his ballets since and including *Apollo*. Once more we have a 'typical' ballet sequence of formal dances culminating in a *pas de deux* (but without variations) and Apotheosis; and it is to this formula that the 'Pas d'action' for the Bacchantes has to submit – it must, that is, avoid breaking the frame by a too graphic specificity, a fact which nicely relates the form of the ballet to its dramatic meaning. On the other hand *Orpheus* infringes Stravinsky's proud claim for *The Rite of Spring* that it includes not a single bar of pantomime. The *pas d'action* movements of the abstract ballets are of course purified by their lack of real action (which means they can only justify themselves in musical and formal terms), while *Orpheus* does contain admittedly brief episodes that lack vividness away from the stage, which is perhaps why it has been little played as a concert work, despite the sublime beauty of its finest pages. Stravinsky's next ballet, *Agon*, would revert to the abstraction of *Apollo*. But meanwhile the narrative stage beckoned in its most highly developed form, the three-act opera.

# 10

# The Rake's Progress

The idea for an opera on *The Rake's Progress* was Stravinsky's own, prompted by a visit to a Hogarth exhibition in Chicago in May 1947. There he presumably saw all eight of Hogarth's famous cycle of pictures (the prints, apparently, rather than the oils), and found in them a suitable starting-point for the opera in English which, he tells us in *Memories* (p.154), he had wanted to compose since arriving in the USA. These eight satirical tableaux, with their intense, symbolic, but narratively somewhat elliptical quality, thus have something of the same status as the 'waking vision' which inspired *The Rite of Spring* or the reading of Kireyevsky that led to *The Wedding*. Brilliant compositions though they are, they inhabit a very flat and purely contemporary world compared to the many-tiered moral, literary and musical universe of the opera which Stravinsky and his librettists W. H. Auden and Chester Kallman erected round them. On the other hand, though it is by far his longest and most dramaturgically complex work, *The Rake's Progress* remains firmly attached to that Hogarthian world, just as *The Rite* never abandons the primitive tribal world of its first vision. As in all Stravinskian theatre, the variety of allusion is in strict relation to a given context.

As usual with Stravinsky, we lack detailed information about how his ideas developed from the first impulse to the finished work. The correspondence with Auden is impoverished by the fact that the two men spent a week together in November 1947 collating their thoughts, as well as by the unhesitating speed and resourcefulness with which the poet responded to the composer's few requests for change or addition. We cannot follow, as we can with Hofmannsthal and Strauss, the route by which a simple conception was transformed into a network of interlocking motifs. Auden does not lecture Stravinsky on the relation between Theocritus and *The Beggar's Opera*, or between Baba the Turk and Jean-Paul Sartre. Instead he works on the principle that 'it is the librettist's job to satisfy the composer, not the other way round'[1] while tactfully impressing on Stravinsky suggestions of his own, as we can safely assume from the consistency of the main ideas in *The Rake* with certain preoccupations of Auden's own early poetry.[2] But precisely because *The Rake* was a true meeting of like minds, we do not have the fruitful discussions and disagreements of tenser or more discordant collaborations.

It looks as if Hogarth's prints at first suggested to Stravinsky a straightforward 'number' opera with spoken dialogue and a stereotyped sequence of arias, ensembles, choruses and finales, rather in the manner of his recent formula ballets. At the same time this idea of a synthetic classical (or baroque) opera will have appeared as the vehicle for a morality more explicit than in any of his stage works since *The Soldier's Tale*. In his first letter to Auden he already lays down formal requirements while drawing attention to the Faustian elements in the story: 'I think that the hero's end in an asylum scratching a fiddle would make a meritorious conclusion to his stormy life.'[3] In Hogarth the violin is a subsidiary motif, played by a music-teacher in the second picture and by one of Rakewell's fellow lunatics in the last. But obviously it reminded Stravinsky of the instrument's archetypal significance, as in *The Soldier's Tale*. And thus the figure of the Devil was implicit in his dramaturgy, though absent from Hogarth, before any discussion with the moralist Auden. Whether we can go further and deduce that the pastoral dimension, so central to the opera, was already in the back of Stravinsky's mind by association with the soldier and his violin is certainly more debatable. Hogarth's morality is about the evils of city life without any hint that rural life might be preferable for a feckless character like Rakewell. But in an earlier series, 'The Harlot's Progress', which Stravinsky may also have seen, the heroine is openly a country girl corrupted by urban ways. One of the evil influences on her is Captain Macheath, the anti-hero of *The Beggar's Opera*, of whose first production in 1728 Hogarth painted a famous picture and which, as the most famous opera of the period, certainly exerted a musical influence on Stravinsky.

There is no mention of Mozart in this first letter of Stravinsky's, but by the time of his meeting with Auden the following month he had written to his publisher, Ralph Hawkes, asking for scores of the four famous Mozart operas, 'the source of inspiration for my future opera'.[4] Mozart is indeed to *The Rake's Progress* what Bach had been to 'Dumbarton Oaks' or Beethoven to the Symphony in C. Hogarth's London was that of Handel and Gay rather than Mozart, though Mozart, aged eight, was in London when Hogarth died in October 1764. But Stravinsky's preference for Mozart as an operatic model was no more a solecism than his intrusion of Delibes into a ballet constructed on the metrics of Boileau. As subject-matter *The Rake's Progress* lends itself to universalisation along the lines of such a moral fable as *Don Giovanni*, which confronts the Age of Reason with the dark menace of rampant sensuality. Stravinsky certainly alludes to that opera in his graveyard scene and in the final quintet, which not only embodies a sententious moral like the sextet in *Don Giovanni* but in doing so wittily avoids stating the real moral of the story we have witnessed, just as Mozart and da Ponte wave away the cataclysm of their Dinner Scene with a bland 'Questo è il fin di chi fa mal' ('that's what happens to naughty boys'). But a more specific source of ideas for the score of *The Rake* was *Così fan tutte*, though whether Stravinsky favoured it for its perfection of form and style, or for its apparent remoteness of narrative from his own work, or simply because it was at that time by far the least well-known of the three da Ponte operas, is a matter for conjecture. *Così* is, like *Don Giovanni*, a work which presents to an ordered society the menace of repressed passion. It moreover stages its passionate drama against a backcloth of the Garden, the eighteenth-century symbol for man's control of his environment. The relevance of such details to *The Rake* will be considered in due course. But so far as Stravinsky's music is concerned, *Così* offered a model of a more general kind, whereby certain types of formalism could channel certain degrees of emotion into certain more fluid but still disciplined structures.

*The Rake* thus became a 'number' opera whose continuity is provided, not by dialogue as in the English ballad opera or the German Singspiel, but by recitative with harpsichord accompaniment. This *secco* recitative often flows, as in Mozart, into that species of accompanied recitative known as arioso, or into free ensembles which permit a much more flexible social interchange than in either ballad or Handelian opera, both of which are dominated by solo song. The developed operatic ensemble was a specifically Mozartian device. Already in *The Marriage of Figaro* it spins off into whole scenes of continuous music that are not merely the prototypes of the symphonic drama of the romantic era but its most perfect examples, since they achieve dramatic growth and continuity without sacrifice of formal articulation. In the later *Così fan tutte*, an opera peculiarly *about* pairings-off manoeuvred and observed by third parties, the ensemble is the main vehicle of the plot, and its ideal formal expression. These ensembles are typically brief, conveying psychological action at something like conversational speed, while preserving the artificiality or 'game' element which is so much a part of this particular work. In *Così*, as in *Figaro* and *Don Giovanni*, the so-called finales are in effect elaborate multiple ensembles in which the abandonment of recitative links conveys the feeling that the action is coming swiftly to a climax.

For Stravinsky one might conjecture that the combination of artifice and socio-psychological verisimilitude was a prime attraction of *Così*. It fitted his Meyerholdian conception of the theatre as a place where purely theatrical conventions served to relay truths about the human condition; it fitted his love of 'frames'. But at the same time it suited a subject located firmly in time and space: 'eighteenth-century England'. Above all it went with a drama about the dangers of unbridled submission to impulse. And finally, it could hardly have been better adapted to a modern interpretation of a theme so much bound up, for the modern mind, with the repressions of the Age of Reason and yet so directly relevant – if we could only bring ourselves to admit it – to those of our own age. There is a sharp significance in Stravinsky's exhortation to Auden, in his first letter, to 'feel absolutely free in your creative work on the chosen theme. Of course there is a sort of limitation as to form in view of Hogarth's style and period. Yet make it as contemporary as I treated Pergolesi in my *Pulcinella*.'

Needless to say, Auden was uniquely equipped to respond to such a specification. His early lyrics show his genius for investing regular metres with an intellectual and colloquial contemporaneity which seems to belie their formal and rhythmic simplicity. And one has only to compare, say, the choral minuet in the final act of *The Rake* – 'Leave all love and hope behind' – with 'Now the leaves are falling fast' or the final section ('Earth, receive an honoured guest') of *In Memory of W. B. Yeats*, to see how brilliantly this gift suited the formal and expressive requirements of the kind of opera Stravinsky had envisaged. Auden's libretto generally is a treasure-trove of such verse, in a dazzling variety of forms and metres and with a verbal content which only occasionally spills over into the verbose or obscure.[5] The pattern follows da Ponte in alternating prose and rhymed verse, which respectively invite setting as recitative and as formal aria or ensemble. Stravinsky sometimes overrides this distinction; he will occasionally set rhyming couplets as recitative or prose as arioso. But in general he adheres to the antique convention of prose recitative and rhymed arias, and this is a crucial element in his re-creation of a 'classical' artifice in modern terms. In setting these various metres, he adopts the same freedom of stress that we have grown accustomed to in his settings of Russian, Latin and French, and it goes without saying that when *The Rake* was first performed in English-speaking countries (the world première had been in Venice in September 1951) Stravinsky came under fire for his insensitivity to the language, which he had set only once before, in *Babel*. But the refutation of this criticism, which incidentally Auden himself explicitly rejected,[6] lies in the apparently deliberate way in which Stravinsky now does, now does not, 'get the stress wrong'.

These oblique accents, as we might call them, have to be seen against the background of the regular accentual schemes mostly favoured by Auden in his search for an accurately eighteenth-century verse rhythm. The sources of this rhythm are themselves various: there is the jogging, vernacular pattern of 'Since it is not by merit', with its 'Jolly Ploughboy' sentiments; there are straightforward ballad songs like 'If boys had wings and girls had stings' or riddling songs like 'Lanterloo'; there are sententious, sermonising songs like Shadow's 'In youth the panting slave pursues'; and there are more fluid, intimate verses in iambic tetrameters, such as 'Vary the song'. But most of these verses have in common a metric regularity which, by virtue of the stylisation involved, defies the composer to ignore it in favour of any 'natural' scheme of accents, while threatening him with monotony if he adheres to it too slavishly. Many of Stravinsky's misaccentuations look like replies to this dilemma. That is, they are deliberate glosses on Auden's metres, and amount to musical variants on them, retaining their general shape while so to speak inclining the plane of accentuation at an angle to that of the simple metre.

As an illustration of this technique it is instructive to study the famous 'Lanterloo' chorus in the brothel (Act I, scene 2), which Stravinsky thought one of the most beautiful gifts ever made by a poet to a composer. Behind the entire setting of this riddle song is the idea of a musette in the time of a courante with its standard hemiola cross-rhythms, which Stravinsky in effect uses to justify irregular displacements of the verbal accent by the odd quaver beat. Similar displacements are a feature of nearly all those pieces where Stravinsky retains the *general* sense of the metre. It seems that there are various ways of understanding such a procedure. In the (usual) absence of specific instructions to the singer, the conventionally trained musician will probably try to bias his accentuation towards correct verbal stress while also noticing the musical accents implied by the barlines. Others may try to make a virtue of the wrong accent. But there is some evidence that Stravinsky intended the variant barrings set up by a correct verbal stress to chime against the regular metre of the music (itself usually a derivative of the regular verbal metre). In the second part of 'Since it is not by merit', the lines:

> Till I die then of fever,
> Or by lightning am struck,

are set so perversely in the sense of the strict iambic metre and against the true verbal accent as to produce an effect of Beckmesserish incompetence unless the tenor swings the line towards the right accents, as shown, after all, by the melodic stress, with the focal word 'lightning' on the highest point of the phrase (Ex.50). There are ample precedents for this way of

Till    I    die then of    fe - ver, or    by light - ning am    struck,

*Ex. 50 The Rake's Progress*

thinking in Stravinsky's music, both vocal and instrumental, as well as in the vocal part-music of the polyphonic age, where barring was not used and each singer naturally accented his part without reference to a common metre.[7] The crude alternative, that Stravinsky simply got the stresses wrong, is too absurd to consider. By 1948 he had at his disposal the young Robert Craft, who went through the text with him and indicated the relative accents and rhythms. Moreover there are many examples in the score of prosody that is both correct and memorable: for example, the duet 'My tale shall be told', or 'Thanks to this excellent device', to say nothing of the incisive and constructive character of most of his 'mistakes'. It may well be that Stravinsky, whose English was never fluent or automatic, miscalculated the precise extent of the discomfort his manipulations might give to the Anglo-

Saxon ear, as he certainly did with his French prosody in *Persephone*, but presumably not with his Russian in *The Wedding* or *Mavra*. But the fact may equally be, as Craft has written, that 'the claims of English stress and accent did not trouble him very deeply. He was far more concerned with singability, with vowel sounds in vocal ranges, with the effect of words on vocal quality and the other way round.'[8]

It seems likely, in any case, that the artificiality of the effect was of some importance to Stravinsky. False accentuations colliding with a musical-metric scheme more consistently regular than in any large-scale work he had written for forty years would obviously make a bold, and often distorted, effect. This is the synthetism of *Mavra*, transported on to a larger stage and into a historical and artistic world much more familiar to any likely audience. But if *The Rake's Progress* is a neo-classical opera – or to be more exact a neo-Mozartian or neo-rococo opera – in the sense that the Symphony in C is a neo-Beethoven symphony or *The Fairy's Kiss* a neo-Tchaikovskian ballet, its apparatus is so much more elaborate than theirs that it challenges us to define in what ways such a work can be at one and the same time both classical and modern. The case with *Mavra* was clearer, because that opera was short and openly polemical in intention. *The Rake's Progress*, a three-act opera as long as Verdi's *Otello*, could hardly expect to hold the stage if its main point, like some modern version of Rousseau's *Le Devin du village*, were to prove the superiority of one convention over another.

All the same there are suggestive similarities between *Mavra*, perhaps Stravinsky's first neo-classical work, and *The Rake's Progress*, perhaps his last. In both operas he evokes a particular period, partly through stage setting and plot, partly through the use of appropriate artistic conventions. And in neither, even after we have allowed for modernisms of style such as dissonance or irregular rhythm, does the result add up remotely to a pastiche, as such. For one thing the musical conventions used are taken from here and there and would never have co-existed on the contemporary stage. In *The Rake* Stravinsky brings together bits and pieces of ballad opera, ensembles from Mozart, choruses from Gluck, dances from the French *ballet de cour*, and even, in the last act, a suspicion of Bach polyphony and expressive embellishment. The ballad style which could be seen as the native genre of Hogarth's picaresque London – the genre of *The Beggar's Opera* – lies behind the choruses of Roaring Boys and Whores in the brothel scene, and is openly the style of the offstage duet 'If boys had wings', which later also lends a sardonic note to the graveyard scene where Shadow demands his wages. But it is also a presence in Anne's lullaby, Tom's 'Since it is not by merit', and elsewhere. These numbers hardly suggest a Mozartian style at all. Instead they conjure up the musical vernacular of the day to express the coarseness, or moral vacuity, or even the simple tenderness of the common life. By contrast 'Vary the song', whose *ennui* brings out that finer side of Tom's nature which will eventually help save him, is not only Mozartian (in a sense) but lifts its obbligato horn melody shamelessly from the quartet 'È nel tuo, nel mio bicchiero' in *Così fan tutte*. There is no question here of dramatic association; the melody is rather in the nature of a stylistic association, just as the Mozartian oboe figures of the opening duet embower Anne and Tom in a kind of spiritual virtue without referring us to any actual Mozartian context. If Stravinsky does sometimes use Mozartian accompaniments that seem to propose a common scenic backcloth – for instance, in the quartet 'I wished but once', or the arioso 'Dear father Truelove', or the duettino 'Farewell for now' with its reminiscences of the opening duet in the first garden scene of *Così* – the association is undermined by choruses like 'How sad a song', where Mother Goose's whores, surprised by compassion, rise to the same idiom (complete with viola countermelody), but in a context closer to that of Gluck's Furies placated by 'Mille pene, ombre sdegnose', an aria which in turn may well have suggested Tom's 'Love too frequently betrayed'. Finally in the second act, when Anne comes looking for Tom in London, her rustic sense of the grandeur of well-to-do urban life is reflected in a courtly French pavane and sarabande, which accompany the arrival of Baba in her sedan-chair and her descent from it and unveiling of her beard to the citizens. This is presumably a surviving remnant of the 'Choreographic Divertissement' Stravinsky had from the start planned for the finale of the first act (of what was to be a two-act opera).[9]

But beyond these considerations of musical style and convention is the major question of subject-matter. Just as *Mavra*, though a possible essay in stylistic allusion for Pushkin, could never have been set as an opera by Glinka or his Russian successors, so *The Rake's Progress* is an impossible operatic subject for an eighteenth-century composer, even in the *buffo* tradition which admitted servants as central characters provided the treatment was comic. In Mozart, servants figure among the main characters in a non-farcical opera such as *Figaro*, but on the appearance of the gardener the plot and music descend temporarily into farce; and picaresque urban characters do not figure in Mozart at all, though the subject-matter of his operas was certainly revolutionary for its time. On the other hand the ballad opera tradition initiated in England by *The Beggar's Opera*, almost sixty years before *Figaro*, set up low-life characters and sordid incidents specifically as a counterblast to the remoteness, artificiality and foreignness of the fashionable Italian opera. By definition they avoid the kind of musical elaboration which appealed to the sophisticated operatic audiences of the day; and for the lofty classical, historical or biblical subjects favoured in the opera-house, they substituted political and social satire, often *ad hominem*, in the manner of contemporary broadsheets.

The only real common ground between the full-blown opera of the late baroque and early classical period on the one hand and the ballad opera on the other seems to lie in the pastoral tradition, which surfaces everywhere in the history of opera between Peri's *Dafne* and Mozart's *Magic Flute*. Eight-

eenth-century pastoral amounted to an allegorical convention with connotations of lost innocence or the Age of Gold; but the popularity of archetypal
subjects like Orpheus suggests that the more primitive symbolism of nature
as that part of our own selves most in need of proper understanding and
proper development was never wholly abandoned. There is a ferocious
Orphic dimension to Mozart, which comes out in the fact that his two most
sexually anarchic characters, Don Giovanni and Almaviva, are shown at
their worst – and eventually worsted – in their fondness for corrupting
country girls. But these were revolutionary dramas. In earlier and more
conventional work the pastoral life is regarded as self-contained: a complete
world in the sense of Theocritus or Virgil, however vapid or prettified. It
might at worst seem like nothing so much as metropolitan life peopled by
courtiers in peasant smocks; and in any case it rarely collided with town
life as such, as it had done so spectacularly in Shakespeare, and continued
to do, more anecdotally, in the theatre of Farquhar, Goldsmith and others.

By combining all these different traditions in one opera, Auden and
Stravinsky were not so much re-creating classical opera in a modern image
as using a variety of historically connected ideas as co-ordinates for plotting
an essentially modern line of thought. In Hogarth, the fate of Rakewell
might argue graphically the evils of a society where easy money reflected
the breakdown of traditional ethics; translated into some imaginary operatic
hero, along the lines of Don Giovanni, he might be turned into an image
of the vengeance taken – and rightly taken – by ordered society on those
who deny the connection between privilege and responsibility; or, in the
hands of a da Ponte and a Mozart, he might rise up like a threat to those
who imagine that society can be run like a machine without taking account
of the needs and nature of individuals. Auden, however, turns out to be
much more interested in the implications of Rakewell's misdemeanours for
the individual than for society. In the opera, 'eighteenth-century London'
is a weird stylisation, a kind of nightmare monster with tentacles all over
the place which shoot out to grab the man who breaks the moral law in
pursuit of wealth, happiness or power. The starting and finishing points
are successive springs, the returning climax of both the pastoral and the
Christian years, and a touchstone of the natural, in every sense: that is, the
life in which man realises his fullest potential according to the ordinary
rhythms of existence. This is not meant to seem an unduly repressive sort
of life, though it has obvious connotations of Protestantism, the work ethic,
bourgeois marital fidelity, and so forth. In both the first and last scenes the
love allegory refers to Venus and Adonis, rather than Hera and Zeus. And
while we may wonder whether the erotic significance of this relationship
is sufficiently emphasised as against its connection with the Fall (Adonis
having died because he disobeyed the goddess's orders), it does successfully
lift the morality out of reach of the high-street sentiments of the quintet
coda, which, it should hardly be necessary to point out, is formal and
ironical rather than explanatory.[10]

The town into which Tom is dragged almost the instant he wishes for money without having to earn it is a kind of hell, where not only are the people corrupt, but their pleasures are uniformly and aimlessly perverse, from the lurid debauchery of the Ugly Duchess, Mother Goose, and her entourage, to the 'curious viands' and 'marriageable girls' of 'Vary the song', and culminating in the repulsive sex-object of the bearded lady, Baba the Turk, who is practically worshipped by the jaded Londoners who long only for a sight of her face. This is the hell of Auden's own *New Year Letter*: 'its fire the pain to which we go if we refuse to suffer'. The *acte gratuit* – or purposeless act – which Tom commits in marrying Baba expresses, no doubt, the emptiness of total freedom, both in itself and as a way of establishing the identity or 'meaning' of the individual who performs such an act. The bread-making machine similarly implies the absurdity of a world without laws; even if the machine were genuine it would not make anyone happy, since the object of life is not simply having enough to eat. Auden's London does admittedly have elements of a social or political satire, like Hogarth's. It conveys an attack on certain fashionable philosophies: on existentialism (of the kind disowned by Camus), and on moral relativism. But it has a sharp moral point of its own as well. Tom has sinned against life and nature by wanting to be free of its laws; he is grabbed by the Devil and shown a world which seems to respond to his desires and to do so, moreover, under the guise of 'Nature', who is continually invoked in the libretto as the patroness of this perverse and futile existence. In the end the Devil takes Tom to a graveyard, demands his wages and tells him to kill himself (the ultimate *acte gratuit* of the committed existentialist). He insists that Tom can no longer save his soul, but this appears to be a lie, and the card-game which the Devil (Shadow) proposes, apparently for no reason, a ruse to trick him into agreeing to his own damnation. Tom does in fact agree, but – helped by chance and the redeeming memories of Anne Truelove – he unexpectedly wins the game. For his sins he is punished by madness, which in moral terms looks like an atoning period in Purgatory, but dramatically is probably a mechanism to avoid the moral nonsense of a romantic redemption by woman's love. The truth is that Tom is obviously not bad enough to stay in Hell; unlike Don Giovanni, who never repents at all, Tom keeps repenting throughout the opera but lacks the moral courage to act on his repentance. Or else he lacks the moral certainty. In either case he makes a good study for modern urban man with his rootless materialism and wishy-washy permissiveness, just as Don Giovanni and Count Almaviva were suitable bogeymen for an age that thought it had its passions under control. It is a nice comment on modern humanity that even in its sins it cannot be whole-hearted enough to merit damnation.

From Stravinsky's point of view, nevertheless, the parallel with the eighteenth-century morality opera – whether of the ballad or Mozartian sort – was of central importance. The reason is that, although the subject and at least the main approach to it came from him, it was apparently not, on the evidence of history, *his* kind of opera. For thirty years he had written dramas where either a lofty, spiritual character came through in the absence of direct narrative, or (as in *Oedipus rex*, *Persephone* and *Orpheus*) the story was so ritualised as to take on almost sacred or eschatological meaning. Of the apparent exceptions – overlooked, incidentally, by Gabriel Josipovici when he makes this same point[11] – *Mavra* uses its narrative form polemically, while *The Fairy's Kiss* treats genre ballet in surrealist fashion as the vehicle for a fable about creativity.

In taking on his Hogarth subject, Stravinsky therefore needed a frame by way of justification of the narrative form, and this he found in the established artifice of the classical *opera buffa*. Just as Auden's modernisms move always against the rigid backcloth of Hogarth's pictures, so Stravinsky's suggest a commentary on Mozart. However, the distancing effect of this posture is very much less marked, in relation to the whole dramatic impulse, than it was in *Oedipus* or *Apollo* or *The Fairy's Kiss*. Josipovici rightly observes this difference when he says, quoting Boucourechiev, that 'these works eschew expressivity, psychology and mimesis: they do not say "I am" or "I wish", but "It is" and "It shall be".' But the difference is more one of emphasis than he suggests. *The Rake's Progress* is also to some extent a ritual work of re-enactment, but it is one that has been swamped by present action. Threading its way through the opera is a theme closely related to the cyclic idea of seasonal renewal which had motivated nearly every major stage work of Stravinsky's from *The Rite of Spring* to *Persephone*. Every time Anne Truelove appears on the scene, the natural order reasserts itself against the perverse and the surreal; her wind scoring stands, at key moments, for the eternal sprouting and falling of leaves.[12] So in the background of *The Rake's Progress* is the myth of the Fall and the origin of seasons. But it is a fairly remote background. As we saw, Auden was more interested in the fate of the individual than in the cyclic rituals in which he was supposed to participate, just as he was more interested in a specific moral teaching than in group affirmations. By an odd twist, his own first surviving idea for the opera is that it should have an address to the audience between the acts, in the manner of the Greek *parabasis*, which suggests that he was already aware of Stravinsky's taste for such devices.[13] But in the finished work *parabasis* plays only a very minor part, and certainly lends little tone to the drama until the final quintet, where it comes not from Aristophanes but from Mozart.

In sacrificing the ritual tone to the light conversational, Stravinsky was taking one of his boldest steps, considering the ambitious scale of the work, since the start of neo-classicism. The precedent was *Mavra*. But that was six times shorter and could be thought of as a *jeu d'esprit*, whereas *The Rake* is a profound and substantial work wearing its erudition lightly. The balance between the conversational style and the underlying solemnity of the proceedings is preserved by the ironical, slightly deprecatory handling of classical artifice, for which Mozart proves such a good model because he was the first composer to see how rigid formulae could be turned to dramatic advantage by the delicate use of irony (as for instance in Dorabella's 'Smanie implacabili', which has its parallel in Baba's comic rage aria, 'Scorned! Abused!'). The dry recitatives, with their quizzical harpsichord accompaniment, have the same kind of force. With their flavour of eithteenth-century politeness and restraint mixed in with a pinch of smart, scholarly modernism, they exactly convey the idea of a prosaic yet artificial context for the offsetting of destructive urges. When Truelove sings that Anne's advice is needed in the kitchen, we may laugh at such a sentiment finding musical expression, but perhaps no more than Mozart's audiences will have done when Despina stirred the drinking chocolate in *recitativo secco*. In this sense the high classical conventions of formal artifice, control, and the containment of every aspect of life within a limited gestural framework – conventions already shattered by the ballad opera and German Singspiels like Mozart's own *Entführung* – take on a universal aspect. Both in themselves and by association they permit overwhelming issues to be examined without heaviness and in a context of what passes for real life. In the case of a twentieth-century drama like the Stravinsky/Auden *Rake*, they provide a distancing formula that is musically, dramaturgically and poetically consistent, and at the same time apt to the resonances of a story that has a meaning, *mutatis mutandis*, for both ages. And the test of this is that, while any incongruity between the various worlds of *The Rake* – the Arcadian, the metropolitan, the eighteenth- or twentieth-century, the prosaic or poetic – is absorbed in the brilliant stylistic ironies of the treatment, it would be hard to imagine a successful staging that took the work out of its eighteenth-century context and put it, say, into modern dress. Such a device would leave the music and the poetry stranded in a sea of gratuitous modernism, and would thus, paradoxically, undermine its genuine, authentic modernity.

For Stravinsky, needless to say, the classical constraints served as a stimulus. *The Rake* is the climax of that neo-classic tendency, which we already noted in *Oedipus rex*, towards regular barring schemes. Yet it is also one of the most rhythmically alive of all his works, a seeming paradox brought about by the subtle interplay of verbal and musical accent of the kind examined earlier, by unexpected patterns of phrase-structure, by cross-rhythms and other procedures designed to cut across our expectations of uniformity set up precisely by the smooth barrings and superficially conventional tonal harmonies. In fact these procedures are by no means new in Stravinsky, and their special interest here – as in the *Danses concertantes* – lies in their extreme refinement in relation to an increasingly simple background style, influenced directly by Mozart but also by the popular melodies and plain harmonies of ballad opera. Certainly the tunes in *The Rake*, perhaps consistently the best in any work by Stravinsky, lose nothing by their adherence to simple models, as Anne's lullaby, with its haunting accompaniment for two flutes, would be enough to prove. But while the opera's opening has charm and the last two scenes a dark poetic intensity uncommon in his music, it is for its irresistible vitality expressed in a succession of vocal scherzos that seem like so many rebounds off Tom Rakewell's ebullient but dangerously unmanaged energies, that the work perhaps most deserves a high place in the Stravinsky canon. The best of these pieces, like the 'Lanterloo' chorus or Sellem's auctioneering song, have a seductive brillance that seems to belie their association with the most corrupt tendencies in the story – significantly enough. By contrast, the scherzos more directly connected with Rakewell, like 'My tale shall be told' or 'Thanks to this excellent device', have a slightly false heartiness which fits his shallow, excitable nature. But they are none the less invigorating for that.

In one major and significant respect Stravinsky made little attempt to imitate Mozart. Although as he himself pointed out *The Rake* contains more continuous music and less recitative as it intensifies emotionally and dramatically, which was exactly the tendency that led Mozart to the continuous, proto-symphonic finale, it never attempts within a single movement or section the formal elaboration which, in Mozart, went with this development. There are no great rondos like 'Per pietà' or concerto movements *manqués* like 'Ach, ich liebte' in *Die Entführung*, though Anne's cabaletta 'I go to him' obviously mimics the range of such arias, especially if heard in conjunction with the preceding lament 'Quietly, night', from which it is physically separated by recitative like the typical nineteenth-century Italian cabaletta.

The characteristic form of *The Rake's Progress*, by contrast, is the verse-and-refrain, which Stravinsky adapts from ballad opera to the more subtle demands of his own work by a variety of ingenious devices and variants. In Sellem's song, for instance, the auctioneer's patter as he offers each lot provides the refrain, while the 'verse' is formed by the main bidding sequence, culminating the third time round in the unveiling of Baba who duly continues the final verse of *her* rage aria at the point where she was interrupted in the previous act. The next scene, in the graveyard, opens with a verse-refrain form built out of variations on the ballad-song heard offstage in the auction scene. There it had twice interrupted the verses of the final ensemble. Here it alternates between sombre ornamental variations in the minor key (Tom pleading with Shadow for more time) and exultant refrains of the tune in its original major key as Shadow reveals to Tom his true identity. This is followed by the card-playing duet, accompanied by solo harpsichord, which falls naturally into refrains as Tom tries three times to guess the card in Shadow's hand (the third time, however, to fresh music); by a short reprise of Anne's cabaletta theme, as Tom guesses the Queen of Hearts correctly; by a rage song for Shadow, in two strophes, written in the full score with repeat signs; and by a closing refrain of the ballad, in its Act II key (B flat), sung by the now demented Tom. So the whole of this crucial scene is built round verse forms, an extraordinarily bold solution to a psychological crisis of such weight. But the forms reflect, for the listener, the ritual solemnity of the moment, in which time literally stands still as Shadow arrests the clock at the ninth stroke of midnight. For Stravinsky they are a perhaps surprising link with the distant past of *Renard* and *The Wedding*, which had adapted the forms of popular lyrics to stylised ritual drama. But more significantly they look forward to later works like the Cantata, where verse forms taken from medieval English lyrics, and accompanied by a small band very like the wind groups of the pastoral scenes in *The Rake*, provide the basis for an experiment with temporal structures that has great importance for Stravinsky's last period.

These and other links with later works are reassuring to those who insist that, through all his apparent changes of style, Stravinsky remained a completely integrated artist. But they do not alter the fact that, in most essentials, *The Rake's Progress* was more of an end than a beginning. In style it adheres to the synthetic principle which had dominated his music since *Mavra*, and it is his last work of which that is true. Moreover it is his last word on the subject of Apollo and Dionysus, those twin patrons of the classical spirit whose reconciliation had been his explicit concern since the *Poetics* and his implicit concern at least since *The Wedding*. For behind the tale of the wayward young man who destroys himself for lack of balance in his nature there lies a parable of that tension between the principle of the individual and the principle of self-abandonment which Nietzsche – who seems to have invented Stravinsky's dichotomy – regarded as the origin of Greek tragedy. Indeed, if *The Rake* had ended up as a tragedy, it might have been a demonstration of Nietzsche's thesis. As a tragi-comedy, it would doubtless merely confirm him in his view that real tragedy came to an end when Euripides and Socrates kicked Dionysus off the Attic stage and out of Athens.

# 11

# *The Final Spring:* Agon *and* Threni

At the time of the Venice première of *The Rake's Progress* on 11 September 1951 Stravinsky was sixty-nine. Two months earlier Arnold Schoenberg had died in Los Angeles at the age of seventy-six. Although the two composers most often cited as the greatest of their time had for some years lived in the same suburb of the same city, they had not met since 1912, when Stravinsky had heard *Pierrot lunaire* in Berlin, following the music in a score handed him by Schoenberg. In recent years their separation had become an issue of musical politics, fomented above all by their respective adherents and merely tacitly sanctioned by the masters themselves, who seem to have had no more than a rudimentary knowledge of each other's music.[1] But it evidently originated in a real divergence of artistic paths, which can be located with some confidence in the years between 1922 and 1925. Stravinsky's music had featured in the programmes of Schoenberg's *Verein für musikalische Privataufführung* (Society for Private Musical Performance) of 1919–21, and had met with the admiring approval of the Viennese circle. But Schoenberg quickly took against the synthetic manner of the Piano Sonata, which he presumably heard Stravinsky play in Venice in September 1925, and which provided the barely disguised object of his scorn in the *Three Satires*, op.28, composed that same autumn. Early in 1925 Stravinsky had referred dismissively, in an interview with *Musical America*, to those who tried to write 'the music of the future', a reference which Schoenberg seems to have taken personally. How far Stravinsky prompted Arthur Lourié's article 'Neogothic and Neoclassic' is at present hard to ascertain, though Craft – always a Stravinsky-and-Schoenberg man – argues that 'Stravinsky's associates . . promoted a sense of rivalry between him and the Schoenberg school.'[2] In any event Lourié's essay is a *locus classicus* of that factious and generalising tendency which is more common among artistic ideologues than among artists as such, and of which Adorno's much later *Philosophy of New Music* is a more brilliant and better-informed example (though both Lourié and Adorno were as it happens composers). Lourié opposes the two 'camps' in terms that were to fix the either-or relationship between Stravinsky and Schoenberg for almost a quarter of a century. Schoenberg ('to put it exactly') stands for 'neoromantic emotionalism', Stravinsky for 'classical intellectualism', and 'these systems [*sic*] . . . are diametrically opposed; one excludes the other.' Schoenberg's is 'always egocentric . . . and ends only in an affirmation of self or the personal principle'. Stravinsky's 'seeks to affirm unity and unalterable substance'. The ignorance this critique displays about the aims and techniques of Schoenberg and his Viennese colleagues overrides any value there might be in its broad aesthetic distinctions. But its survival, as a dialectical idea, depended on that ignorance being maintained. When Craft entered Stravinsky's household in 1948 the composer was 'curious about Schoenberg but hid this fact'. He studiously avoided any display of interest in Schoenberg's serial method, preferring, in Craft's words, not 'to examine his own prejudice . . . that Schoenberg was a slave to a rigid, abstract system.'[3]

It seems plain that by the later 1940s the autocratic Stravinsky, for so many years a leader and renewer, was aware that this 'system' of which he was, so to speak, ignorant-on-principle posed a threat to his standing as the most searching creative intellect in modern music. The 'howling manifestation' against the *Four Norwegian Moods* in Paris in 1945 certainly could not be construed as another moral victory for the progressive spirit, like the attack on *The Rite* or the puzzlement at *Mavra* or *Apollo*, since the *Moods* were, as Stravinsky saw at once, too slight to bear such a weight.[4] Could it be, then, that the attack came *from* the progressive spirit? Paris was now the capital city of a new musical avant-garde which acknowledged Schoenberg, Webern and, on the other hand, Messiaen, as its spiritual leaders. In René Leibowitz's books *Schoenberg et son école* (1946) and *Introduction à la musique de douze sons* (1949) French modernism discovered a new orthodoxy, while to the young Pierre Boulez and his contemporaries, who looked rather to the 'mathematical' Webern than to Schoenberg as the model for structures of surpassing rigour, even Leibowitz was out of date. To all these musicians, who represented the revitalised aggression of French cultural polemic, neo-classicism was as dead as the dodo. And the aggression spread quickly to Germany, Italy and elsewhere. After the première of *The Rake's Progress* 'Stravinsky found that he and Schoenberg were everywhere categorised as the reactionary and the progressive' and that 'the new generation was not interested in *The Rake*'.[5]

What steps Stravinsky would have taken if Schoenberg had still been alive as 1951 faded into 1952 we shall obviously never know. But it looks certain that Schoenberg's death was not the only necessary condition (if it was necessary) for Stravinsky's gradual adoption of the method hitherto associated almost exclusively, in the popular mind at least, with the Viennese master. It was at least as important that, apparently purely by chance, the musician to whom he was closest at the time of *The Rake*, and afterwards, held Schoenberg and Webern in an esteem nearly as high as that in which he held Stravinsky. Unlike most of Stravinsky's circle, Robert Craft knew the work of these composers well. He conducted it often after his arrival in Los Angeles, and was moreover, by his own confession, to some degree innocent of the political objections to talking about it in Stravinsky's presence. It seems obvious that Craft provided an earth for the electrical charge between the two camps. His knowledge and enthusiasm made it possible for Stravinsky to absorb those aspects of serialism that could be of creative value to him without stepping outside his own artistic front door. He could, for example, attend Craft's concerts and rehearsals with the excuse of friendship, while for the time being preserving his opinion of the music from public scrutiny. Moreover Craft felt that 'Stravinsky *wanted* to be influenced' by him.[6] This seems to mean that the composer had become aware of an impulse to change direction across the wind, as he had done after *The Rite of Spring*, and again in *Mavra, Apollo* and perhaps the Mass, but that he lacked the old certainty and courage to do so entirely on the authority of his own instincts. Craft gave him that courage. And Schoenberg's death must certainly have made the step easier, by removing the threat that his 'change of mind' could be interpreted as a confession of error. Sacrifices to the dead are after all simpler to make with dignity than apologies to the living.[7]

One other crucial factor remains to complete the equation between the two sides of this ancient controversy: the factor of Stravinsky's own artistic development. Clearly he did not, and could not, put on this strange new method like a new fur hat. On the contrary its interest for him had to be found in existing similarities of procedure which could bypass the considerable aesthetic and temperamental differences between his music and that of the Viennese School whose property the method was supposed to be. If we look at Stravinsky's first, somewhat tentative experiments with note-ordering procedures, we find that mostly they take the form of ordered versions of note-sets or groups. As it happens, the set – considered as a collection of notes without any principle of order – is a basic element of nearly all Stravinsky's music after *The Firebird*. For instance, the modal cells in *The Rite of Spring* are to all intents and purposes sets: note-collections which provide all the necessary material for both melodies and chords – in which respect they closely resemble the motives in Schoenberg's pre-serial atonal works. In the first of the Three Pieces for string quartet, as we saw, he introduced a numerical cycle into this technique, and in other pieces of the time there is evidence of constructivist planning in the way melodic elements combine to make chordal complexes. But serialism as such rarely goes beyond the mechanical repetition of ostinato patterns, like the four-note bass to the violin tune in *The Soldier's Tale*, and it is never unmistakably linked to any idea of chromatic 'completeness', such as is fundamental to Schoenberg's music both before and after it went serial.[8] In two widely spaced works of the neo-classical period an extended note-order is established and stuck to: in the slow movement of the Octet and in the slow movement of the Sonata for two pianos, both variation movements. The

33-note melody of the Octet is treated partly like a Purcellian ground, partly as a note-sequence for rhythmic variation in march, waltz and chorale characters. In the Sonata the 29-note theme is treated mainly in this second way, though its initial statement as a theme with strict canon by inversion suggests a dawning interest in contrapuntal techniques that happened also to be basic to Viennese serialism. Of course these melodies differ from anything in Schoenberg in that they make no effort to avoid strong tonal focus. The Octet theme is octatonic with a decisive preference for the notes A and C sharp; the Sonata is entirely in the scale of G major. The length of the themes is achieved through the rotation of short melodic cells round a pivot note or notes, exactly like the 38-note melody in the quartet piece, which has only four different notes. And it was through this familiar device of small rotating cells anchored to one or two controlling pitches that Stravinsky was able to enter the realms of serial composition.

In the Cantata of 1951–2, for instance, the long central carol 'Tomorrow shall be my dancing day' (Ricercar II) for tenor solo and the work's tiny ensemble of flutes, oboes and cello is a compendium of the ways in which existing Stravinskian method could accommodate serial technology without for a moment indulging in weak imitations of style or modish modernism. The piece is a series of canons on an eleven-note melody (played in the first bar by first flute and cello) and subsequently sung by the tenor in the four 'serial' forms: prime (P-O), retrograde (R-O), inversion (I-8), and retrograde-inversion (RI-8).[9] The tune has only six different notes, B–F upwards in the scale of C major/minor, with an emphasis on C and E natural; and this same pivot applies to the inversion Stravinsky chooses; the only difference in content between PO and I-8 is a change from E flat to C sharp. The result (Ex.51) is a typical Stravinskian decorated cantilena, such as we find in his music from the *Pastorale* of 1907 to the Gloria of the Mass and the music for the return of spring in the final act of *The Rake's Progress*. The harmony consists only of notes of the six-note set (or, if we take the whole passage including the C sharp of the inversion, seven-note), clashing gently in whole-tone discords through the unblended sounds of oboes and cello. In later canons, however, Stravinsky expands the harmonic vocabulary to the brink of full chromaticism, by combining row-forms at less compatible transpositions. In the second canon ('Then afterwards baptiz'd I was') he makes polyphony out of R-10 (tenor), P-5 (cello) and R-7 (first oboe), where the first two of these forms supply eleven chromatic notes with the twelfth coming, rather pointedly, from the first note of the remaining form, which starts a bar later (Ex.52).

Although such a passage looks as if it might be governed by a chromatic 'completeness' principle like Schoenberg's, there is no such feeling to the music when one hears it. The entire sense of the music is melodic; the tune has first been established purely as a line, at the start of the movement, and it retains that sense, never once passing from one instrument to another in mid-statement and never depositing notes into the harmony. So even

Ex. 51 Cantata

when three versions of the row are combined at different pitches, we remain aware of the separate identity of each six-note set: its identity, that is, as an 'immutable' pattern. There is an evident parallel here with Stravinsky's careful layering of set complexes in his earlier works, and especially highly constructed examples like the first quartet piece. Like those earlier pieces, the canonic writing in the Cantata has a calm, hieratic air. As polyphony it is closer to the attenuated character of Webern than to the saturated

*Ex. 52* Cantata

chromaticism of Schoenberg. But the pivoting of its separate lines ensures a tonal focus – even in mid-chromaticism – that Webern was at pains to avoid. In the second canon, for instance, the tenor winds through three different forms of the row, each one starting with the final note of its predecessor and each one circling round B flat. Such polarisation is completely foreign to Webern.

Another factor working against chromatic 'completeness' is the nature of the harmony. In this case Stravinsky is forced by the canonic technique to take his chords from notes other than merely those used by the top line of melody, as he had done in the initial statement, so that the passage is a genuine twelve-note set. But he manages the harmony in such a way that open, or what might be called semi-consonant, chords abound, and the texture keeps a certain radiance quite unlike the neutral dissonant tone of the Viennese chamber sound. He can do this, it is fair to add, because his canonic writing is confined to the order of pitches and does not apply to the rhythm, as it would in Bach and does in Schoenberg's *Pierrot lunaire*. Moreover the canons are positioned in the texture among free parts, somewhat at random. All the same, when Stravinsky came to write stricter canons, in the *Canticum Sacrum* and *Threni*, he continued to engineer harmony of similar distinctiveness and clarity, partly, as we shall see, by careful planning of the row itself, which is exactly how Schoenberg and his colleagues ensured the harmonic quality they desired.

In his next work, the Septet for clarinet, horn, bassoon, piano and string trio, Stravinsky explored the methods of this Cantata movement to the point where they dominate an entire three-movement work – albeit one of scarcely greater length. Here we find an eight-note set deployed in a variety of different ways, all of them referrable to existing Stravinsky procedures, even where it is obvious – from internal or external evidence – that the example of Schoenberg was acting as a guide and inspiration.[10] The sonata-form first movement hardly even suggests new techniques. The form is similar to that of the parallel movement in the Octet (but without a slow introduction), the tonality, A major/minor, is just as emphatic, and the main themes have a certain mutual resemblance. There is a still closer resemblance to the start of 'Dumbarton Oaks';[11] so it is impressive that this latest piece of neo-Bachian wizardry, one of Stravinsky's most vivacious movements for a decade, is textured with canons and small-scale imitations, including a broad three-part canon by augmentation and inversion in the wind parts from bar 1. Since these operations take place against a background of fixed and limited pitch, they are not in themselves perhaps any more remarkable than the internal manipulations in the revised versions of the *Pastorale*, or the accumulation of repeated melodic cells over a static pedal in the introduction to *The Rite of Spring*; they merely infuse the pitch-set idea with a modicum of linear ordering. What is striking is how readily the old cellular technique marries with the new excitement of integrated counterpoint. It is as if the idea were already latent in every piece Stravinsky had written before, waiting only for the right electric charge to bring its particles into line.

The climax of this process comes in the finale of the Septet, the whole of which is organised through the contrapuntalisation of a fixed eight-note set. The piece is a complicated double fugue of great brilliance. Although its various instrumental lines are always derived, section by section, from one or other transposition of the basic set, the fact that the transpositions are not at any given moment the same for all instruments ensures that the whole polyphony has a kind of mobility, and a potential for extended discourse, which it lacked in the first movement. The music is closer in technique to the overlaid canons in the 'Ricercar II' of the Cantata. But instead of the strict canonic ordering of that piece, we now have the much broader controls of a dynamic fugue in the manner of, say, the finale of the Concerto for two pianos. Thus the formal framework is strict: a three-part string fugue is repeated by the piano solo (fig.32) against another three-part fugue for wind, based on the same subject in free rhythmic augmentation, then the sequence is repeated with the original fugue in inversion and a new augmented counter-fugue also based on the inverted theme. But as in a classical fugue, there are free voices governed only by the general rules of good counterpoint, which in Stravinsky's case are enshrined in the setting principle. The music thus combines the rigid stratifications of his earlier work with the patterned dialogue of classical polyphony. And it strikingly anticipates the serial technique of later works like *Movements* for piano and orchestra, which manipulate hexachords – or six-note sets – in rotations which concentrate attention on their individual tonal qualities at the expense of their chromatic completeness.

The one relevant technique not used in the Gigue of the Septet, however, is serialism; the only ordering of pitches is that of the fugue subject itself, which is copied by the other entries and by the later repeats and inversions, which is no more serialism than what happens in any baroque double fugue. Similarly the Passacaglia second movement is hardly more serial than Bach's great C minor work in that form. The movement is cast in the standard baroque form, with a set of eight variations over a repeating eight-bar ground bass in slow triple time, the theme being the sixteen-note sequence which will later provide the subject of the Gigue. There is certainly something in the scattered presentation of this theme, passed backwards and forwards from instrument to instrument and from register to register, that suggests Webern (for instance, the opening of his Symphony, op.21); and there are what look like proto-serial workings in the variations, which are based on canonic manipulations of the theme and, in one case, a sensationally athletic dovetailing of the prime, inverted and other forms at quick tempo on the piano (upbeat to fig.17). But the real model for all these devices might just as well be a work like Bach's canonic variations on *Vom Himmel hoch*, which Stravinsky actually recomposed soon afterwards, with added counterpoints and re-texturings *à la Pulcinella* but with none of the splintering of line so characteristic of Webern's famous transcription of the six-part Ricercare in the *Musical Offering*.

Not until his next two works, both modest in scale, did Stravinsky experiment with serial technique as distinct from a canonic technique layered in terms of fixed pitch-sets. The difference is shown by the first of the *Three Songs from William Shakespeare*, which Stravinsky wrote in the autumn of 1953 just before the planned meeting with Dylan Thomas that was to have led to their collaboration, and at a time when he must have been having his first thoughts about *Agon*. In the setting of the sonnet 'Musick to heare', for mezzo-soprano, flute, clarinet and viola, the vocal line spins a long thread of melody from a four-note series, in such a way that the melodic identity of the series itself is subsumed in the broader identity of the cantilena, while at the same time guaranteeing it a strong interior consistency and coherence. The series, in other words, is no longer a melody – as in the Octet or duo-Sonata variation themes, or 'Tomorrow shall be my dancing day', or the fugue subject of the Septet – but has declined to the status of a tiny matrix of four different notes, which provide a nucleus for the evolution of melodies as such (Ex.53). The same process takes place, more fragmentedly, in the accompanying instrumental parts. And indeed this is very much how Schoenberg first worked with series, in the piano pieces of opps.23 and 25 and the Petrarch setting in the Serenade, a work Stravinsky heard at about this time. The row is not used to make harmony,

*Ex.* 53 'Musick to heare' (Three Songs from William Shakespeare)

except by the planned coincidence of different row-forms. Nor is it invariably co-extensive with the melodic phrases – phrases can end in mid-series. Like Schoenberg, Stravinsky repeats notes freely but only at the point of occurrence in the row. For instance, the line 'Mark how one string, sweet husband to another', syllabically set, needs only the last three notes of P-O for its eleven syllables. But he practically never brings in repetitions out of order. There is indeed a slightly routine quality about the serial orbiting, and this is certainly the least musically interesting of three songs the other two of which revert to the freer set-principle, with strict serial elements thrown in.

Although the linear rigidity of 'Musick to heare' slightly softens the usual rhythmic and harmonic bite of Stravinsky's style, it still shows many distinguishing marks of his utterly personal attitude to serial method. The four-note row (though its compact, cellular chromaticism may remind one of the mini-series in Webern) is actually a tonally distinct unit, with the major/minor third alternation of the Cantata and the Septet, from whose first movement theme it is in effect lifted. Far from trying to disguise this tonal character, Stravinsky makes the most of it. The song begins and ends in C (clarinet and viola actually play a broken C major scale in the first and last bars), and from the outset the prime form of the row is lent a dominant flavour by this context, while its G-feeling is cemented by the reflex addition of I-9, with its A flat (Neapolitan) colouring which seems to rotate the music back to G ready for P-0 again. Stravinsky then leads the tune away to I-0, which happens to end on C, adding a fifth in the accompaniment through the agency of P-9, which ends on G. Such polarising devices remained standard coin for Stravinsky up to and including *Threni*, can still be traced in *Movements*, and reappear in the *Requiem Canticles*. In particular the cadential open fifth of 'Musick to heare' still survives in the otherwise far more chromatic context of *Movements*, and it irresistibly recalls Stravinsky's claim that 'I compose vertically and that is, in one sense at least, to compose tonally' and 'I hear harmonically, of course, and I compose in the same way I always have'.[12]

The setting of Dylan Thomas's 'Do not go gentle into that good night' which forms the centre-piece of *In Memoriam Dylan Thomas*, written after the poet's death in November 1953, has a good deal in common with 'Musick to heare': free linear composition with a short series (five notes this time, but still within the spread of a major third), syllabic setting, and harmonic rhyming. But the music is much more passionate – because more personal – and more integrated, perhaps because the texture is more thoroughly steeped in the elements of the row itself. From the start the piece delighted Schoenbergian hearts.[13] Not only was the row, within its compass, fully chromatic, but every detail of the music derived from it, and there was even some use of serial harmony, if not chords taken from a single statement of the series, while tonal emphases are much less in evidence. The most striking example of serial harmony is in the string-quartet introduction to the song, which Stravinsky uses as a refrain – a kind of musical equivalent to the line repeats of the poem's villanelle form. The refrain begins and ends with the same chord (altered in register), and elements of the chord are then taken over by the first melodic phrase, leading from I-6 into R-0 so that the whole phrase retrogrades back to its beginning (Ex.54).

Including the 'Dirge-Canon' antiphonies between strings and trombones which frame the song, the *In Memoriam* is a full six minutes of music based entirely on a single five-note row. Its audible unity, together with the expressive intensity which comes in part from its chromaticism, displays the practical virtues of a fully integrated serial method. The piece is one of the most satisfying and most moving of all Stravinsky's shorter compositions. But it would be harder to argue that it is one of his most characteristic. The slightly strained chromatic lyricism, with its Schoenbergian compound semitone leaps and flowing rhythmic patterns snagged by seemingly random unidiomatic stresses, misses the ritual atmosphere of the typical Stravinskian threnody; and it is unusual in his music to find lyrical expression so innocent of tonal colouring and vocal repose. There is more ceremony in the 'Dirge-Canons', whose hierätic trombone note-repetitions suggest a study of Gabrieli, and help bracket the work with the neo-Venetian masterpieces which followed, the *Canticum Sacrum* and *Threni*. But these canons are serially more primitive than the song-setting, and are 'chunked' together like the canons in the Cantata, as Craft pointed out in *Avec Stravinsky*. Though the song is also sectional, like the poem itself, and audibly cyclic – as the row-forms return within the returning lines of the villanelle – the process is smoothed over by the rather neutral character of the serial line. Stravinsky rarely wrote in this manner again. Instead he seems to have gone out of his way to adapt the 'chunking' technique to music based on full chromatic twelve-note rows.

Taking this small group of works after *The Rake's Progress* as a whole, one detects in them a provisional quality unusual for Stravinsky, despite many fine and characteristic passages, like the stormy duet 'Westron Wind' in the Cantata, the Gigue in the Septet, or the beautiful setting of 'Full fadom five' in the Shakespeare songs, where a series based on a cycle of fourths creates an aura unlike anything previously associated with serial technique (possibly excepting the harmonic sets, or 'tropes' in Berg's *Lulu*). His earlier experimental or transitional music had rarely lacked creative precision, even if the actual techniques were subsequently discarded, as was the case with the quartet pieces. Now there is, momentarily, some such lack. This might be some reflection of a real creative block, as reported by Craft, or it might simply be due to the difficulty of adapting a strongly formed and complex method, evolved for quite a different sort of music, to his own style – though, as I have tried to show, it would be a mistake to exaggerate that difficulty, or the degree of adaptation called for, in Stravinsky's case. In any event the *In Memoriam* impressively confirms the technical solidity he soon achieved with the method. And his next work, which indeed he had

*Ex. 54 In Memoriam Dylan Thomas*

already started when he wrote the Dylan Thomas piece, proves in the most dazzling way that the block, if such it was, had been purely temporary.

*Agon* had been brewing in Stravinsky's mind, we may assume, since Lincoln Kirstein had first suggested the addition of a third ballet to the classical pair, *Apollo* and *Orpheus*, which were on the same bill when the latter was first performed by Kirstein's Ballet Society in April 1948. But *The Rake* had by then intervened, and it was not until 1953 that Stravinsky, now in a new creative mood, formally accepted the commission for the new piece. The first musical notations were made in December (before the *In Memoriam*), but work only got under way in earnest in the second part of 1954, to be interrupted once more at the end of the year by the commission to write a choral work for the Venice Biennale of 1956. Not until after the completion of the *Canticum Sacrum* and the *Vom Himmel hoch* transcription (made for the same concert) was Stravinsky able to return to *Agon* and complete it, in April 1957.

This prolonged, disrupted period of gestation had its effect on the character and content of *Agon*, which is one of the richest in allusion of all Stravinsky's great theatrical masterpieces. At the time of Kirstein's original proposal it was certainly assumed by everyone except the composer (whatever he may or may not have assumed) that the new ballet would be on a classical subject like the other two. As early as 1951 Kirstein, Auden and others were tossing ideas at Stravinsky which suggest that there may have been discussion viva voce about a scenario to do with the idea of classical myth as an archetype of modern urban life, or else to do with the death of heroism in the post-war world, as in Eliot's fragmentary dialogue *Sweeney Agonistes*, which was for a time considered (rather oddly, we may now think) as a possible source. Stravinsky's own passing idea of the Odyssean episode of Nausicaa may even have arisen from a reading of Eliot's Sweeney poems, where the Phaeacian princess is transmogrified into the prostitute Doris.[14] This modest suggestion was countered by Balanchine with the idea of

> a competition before the gods; the audience are statues; the gods are tired and old; the dancers reanimate them by a series of historic dances. . . . It is as if time called the tune, and the dances which began quite simply in the sixteenth century took fire in the twentieth and exploded.[15]

Though evidently suspicious of the grandiosity of this scheme, Stravinsky seems to have accepted it in essence as the basis for a 'Concerto for the dance', for which Balanchine could create a 'matching choreographic construction'. Hence there emerged the idea of an abstract dance-contest, in which the music would suggest a sequence of symbolic groupings or 'matches' – a development of the idea behind *Jeu de cartes*, but stripped of its genre or anecdotal content. At the same time Kirstein sent Stravinsky a copy of de Lauze's manual, *Apologie de la danse* (1623), in the new edition which supplemented the text with music examples taken from Mersenne.[16]

The most striking sentence in Kirstein's letter is of course the last, which disposes of the theory that the supposed variations of style in *Agon* were in some way a result of the lapse of time between the two main stages of composition (as was certainly the case with *The Nightingale*). The idea of an interaction between antique musico/choreographic imagery and a modern abstract or constructivist setting was built into the original scheme; and it may well have been this particular aspect of the Kirstein/Balanchine proposal which finally triggered Stravinsky's active enthusiasm and got him going with the music. In several recent and current works, new techniques were associated with an imaginery archaic world: the world of the semi-sacred Elizabethan lyric in the Cantata, of the instrumental *cori spezzati* of Gabrieli in the *In Memoriam Dylan Thomas*, and of a musical liturgy *alla prima prattica* in the *Canticum Sacrum*. Moreover Stravinsky had mooted the idea of a re-created choreographic *divertissement* in the manner of the French *ballet de cour* in *The Rake's Progress*, a work which dramatised the symbolism of an antique ceremony transplanted into the modern world and interpreted in the light of modern thought. Stravinsky may have reserved some musical momentum from that work, which then carried him into *Agon*. Kirstein's *Terpsichore* suggestion came within weeks of the première of *The Rake*, though it may rather have been prompted by the seventeenth-century elements in *Apollo*, with which the new ballet was to be teamed.

In any case the symbolic re-enactment of ancient ceremonial was not exactly a new idea for Stravinsky. Ever since *Petrushka* he had been reinventing old rituals and entertainments as a mirror to modern consciousness, and one of his earliest works in the genre, *Renard*, bears a marked resemblance to *Agon* in certain details of form and musical gesture which might lead one to suppose that recent work on revising and reinstrumenting scores from the Russian period had led him to reabsorb characteristics from that earlier time into his new music.[17] The fact that *Agon*, with its explicit allusion to the central 'contest' of Aristophanic comedy (suggested to Stravinsky perhaps by the title of the second of Eliot's two Sweeney episodes: 'Fragment of an Agon'), seems thereby to refer obliquely to the Aristophanic elements in *Renard* is given sharper focus by musical similarities like the resemblance in function between the march which opens and closes *Renard* and the fanfare which opens and closes *Agon*. Above all, *Agon* suggests a reassessment of the earlier style in its reversion to the idea of metrically unrelated formal cells like the separate blocks of the *Symphonies of Wind Instruments*. The *Symphonies* is indeed almost blatantly evoked by the 'Pas de quatre', with its sequence of interruptions in apparently distinct time-systems (though *Agon* sticks to one single metronome mark). Many of the later dances reinterpret this idea in terms of a regular but discreet background metre, like the castanet ostinato in the 'Bransle gay' or the laboured slow-three of the 'Saraband-Step'; but this is a completely different effect from the motor ostinatos of the neo-classical works, which have periodic classical rhythm as part of their imagery, whereas the dance rhythms in

*Agon* are no more than a foothold for perilous rhythmic and contrapuntal gyrations. This restrained background metre has, however, a precedent in a few of the dances in *Orpheus*, such as the 'Pas d'action' of the Bacchantes or the 'Pas de deux'. At curtain-up in both works the protagonist (to count the four male dancers of *Agon* for the moment as one) stands with his back to the audience, and this is a sign of the restraint and even obliquity of the action that follows. The fact that *Orpheus* has a story hardly weakens the mysterious, almost secretive tone it shares with its successor. The essential difference remains that *Orpheus* projects this tone through veiled sonorities and a dreamlike slowness of pace, where *Agon*, a work as musically brisk and down-to-earth as *Renard*, projects it through scenic abstraction with the help of an altogether more broken and elliptical musical grammar.

Linguistically *Agon* marks the biggest change in Stravinsky's music since *Mavra*. From the start its brittle economy of expression contrasts starkly with the generous embonpoint of *The Rake*. But the contrast with the intervening works is hardly less marked. The broad verse-and-refrain forms of the Cantata and solid linear polyphony of the Septet are as foreign to *Agon* as the painstakingly worked mini-serial designs of 'Musick to heare' or the *In Memoriam*. In their place are an ebullience of gesture and boldness of outline which can, of course, be attributed directly to the fact that *Agon* is a work for dancing – a work, that is, in which movement and articulation are of greater importance than line as such. From the sketches (and from hints in the stage directions of the published score) it appears that Stravinsky composed with choreographic movement and stage positions in mind,[18] despite the absence of a preconceived scenario. Space and difference are paramount ingredients in the music, achieved partly through silence, partly through discriminations in registration as refined as in any work since the *Symphonies of Wind Instruments*, and partly through the contrast and disposition of units of form.

The most significant outside influence on all this was not Schoenberg, whose music breathes quite a different air from Stravinsky's, so much as Webern, whose concept of musical space seems for a time to have fascinated him. In passages like the first 'Coda' (miniature score, p.40) both the use of silence to lend significance to the notes it frames, and the angular octave displacements (ninths instead of seconds, and so forth) with an underlying stepwise movement, suggest the roominess of Webern's best writing, while the precise placing of registration of the various musical components might recall hints of such things in, for example, the exposition of Webern's Symphony or (more than hints) in Stravinsky's own earlier music, especially of the Russian years. The sense of movement, almost of flight, about this piece is however purely Stravinskian. It dances across spaces which, in say Webern's Saxophone Quartet (a piece studied by Stravinsky at this period), threaten the music's forward progress. The silences have, that is, a value as pulse, whereas in Webern their role seems to be mainly to provide articulation and expressive tension. Even in the most disjointed textures of

*Agon* – in the 'Pas de deux' and its coda, where the fragmentation of pitch reaches almost Boulezian dimensions – the centrifugal tendency of the lines is invariably channelled into rhythmic energy, as it would be later in the *Movements* and the works of Stravinsky's final years. On the other hand, in the 'Gaillarde' (misspelt 'Gailliarde' in the score) Stravinsky seems deliberately to freeze the dance into a statuesque pose through a specific use of harmony, register, a broad pulse, and an essentially unbroken tapestry of sound. This is very much the seventeenth-century galliard deciphered through the inadequate notations of de Lauze and Mersenne, while in the 'Coda' which follows, the 'explosion' takes place that was hinted at by Kirstein. The 'Gaillarde' is one of the most brilliant illustrations of Stravinsky's creative sense of texture (Ex.55). The C major harmonies (the key being chosen perhaps to make full use of the overtone resonance of the solo cellos' open C and G strings, and to get the best high harmonics on the double-basses) are simply turned upside-down and inside-out. At the bottom a single viola and the three cellos, filling the octave below the bass-clef C, provide a substratum of close chording such as one might normally expect to find at the *top* of such a chord, while the double-basses and flutes touch in the upper partials of this chord three octaves higher, and the mandolin and harp fill the intervening space with a stately but, in the nature of their sound, restrained canon on the actual dance tune. By giving slight textural and dynamic emphasis to the extremities of the harmony, Stravinsky achieves an effect like an aural tunnel, at the far end of which the dancers revolve in their endless courtly patterns. The 'Coda' then dissolves the image, picking up the C chord (open fifths on trumpets and mandolin) but quickly melting it into the elfish and ultra-modern gigue of the solo violin.

This process of dissolution is in some sense typical of the whole form of the ballet, and brings us to the role of serialism in this first large-scale work which Stravinsky planned that makes any use of the technique. So far as the history of that usage is concerned, it appears that the 'Coda' to the 'Gaillarde', which was the last piece he wrote before shelving *Agon* at the end of 1954, is his first music composed with a chromatic twelve-note row. The *Canticum Sacrum*, written in 1955, is in part but by no means exclusively twelve-note. And of the dances in *Agon* which Stravinsky wrote later, the 'Branle-double' (sometimes called 'Bransle de Poitou'), and the 'Pas de deux' and the duos and trios of the final section are all more or less freely dodecaphonic. *Threni*, completed in March 1958, is dodecaphonic from start to finish.

*Agon*, by contrast, is at no point organically serial in a Schoenbergian, Webernian, or any other sense. Harmonic serialism is largely avoided except at the end of the first 'Coda', whose final chords are made out of serial aggregates, and isolated chords in the 'Bransle double'. As for the sweeping twelve-note melodies which characterise this *bransle*, the 'Coda' to the 'Pas de deux' (which is not as serial as it sounds), and the duos and trios, their

*Ex. 55 Agon, 'Gaillarde'*

whole character springs from the relation between an achieved chromaticism, an achieved sense of order, and a sustained rhythmic impulse. This
emergence of a powerful linear thrust linked to a 'complete' melodic range
is easy to see if one compares the 'Four Trios' with the opening music of
the ballet, where both the movement and the chromatic colouring are

more erratic. So the feeling of evolution towards a particular state is more fundamental than the specific unity of the stages of that evolution. Throughout *Agon* the idea of chromaticism is strongly bound up with the idea of line, but never – as in Schoenberg or Webern – with one particular line. In the fast 'Double' and 'Triple pas de quatre' it comes out, bit by bit, as a function of small melodic cells (in themselves similar to the subsets in a Webern row) which spiral out from firm pedal notes. Even in the 'Coda' to the 'Gaillarde', where the solo violin is serially accompanied, the solo line itself is built up only gradually from proto-serial fragments, whose basis in the straight chromatic scale is audible, but which only complete that scale in the fifty-first bar of the piece, with the violin's pizzicato B flat. In the later stages Stravinsky uses at least three different twelve-note rows, no more than passingly related to each other, as well as short series like the six-note row of the horn-and-piano variation in the 'Pas de deux'. The general impression is of a kaleidoscopic variety of linear possibilities, reflected in the constantly changing instrumental and choreographic groupings. Each possibility is dissolved by the next grouping, and especially by the formal 'regrouping' music of the interludes, which whirr softly like a motor idling in neutral gear.[19]

These 'static' episodes contrast increasingly with the strongly driven later dances. But, in a sense that is soon apparent beneath the purposeful surface of these dances, they share the cyclic 'whirring' character of the interludes, and it is at this point, perhaps more than anywhere else, that the difference between Stravinsky and the Viennese serialists shows up. Where for Schoenberg serialism was a way of sustaining the organic forms of German classicism and the harmonic and structural unity of music that was at the same time intricately varied in detail, it seems to have been the closed system itself that interested Stravinsky. His serial treatments typically make capital out of the fact that twelve-note rows are in essence repetitive, in that the natural next note (after twelve) is the original starting note, and the natural next interval (but one) is either the original starting interval or the finishing one. By nearly always preferring bold linear forms, Stravinsky throws this property of serialism into relief, making us at least subconscious of the fact that the various twelve-note forms are no more than different routes through the whole field, like so many changes in a peal of bells. In *Agon* the sense of climax seems to be associated in some way with the purest expression of this idea towards which the music has worked. In the 'Four Duos' a single line swings backwards and forwards through seven statements of the row, prime or inverted, but always in root position;[20] then the 'Four Trios' treat the prime form, up a fifth (P-7), to a stretto canon at the fifth below (P-0) and above (P-2), ending with P-7 again, forwards and backwards, closing on the C of the first horn which reintroduces the repeated-note motive of the very start of the work. It seems that the intensification of the 'chromatic field' by means of the three-part canon is enough to polarise the music so that the sudden return to a more stable tonal language not only does not jar but actually sounds like the most natural outcome possible. But this is merely an *ad hoc* explanation of a stroke of genius. It would be just as helpful, probably, to speak in terms of a metaphor, such as forms the basis of the drawings of M. C. Escher, which use optical illusions of endless staircases, circular flowing rivers or self-reversing perspectives as images for what Hofstadter calls 'strange loops'.[21] In the Escher sense, *Agon* describes a strange loop, which comes back on itself just when it seems to have travelled farthest from its starting-point. The idea that this might involve an illusion, as such, is purely a matter of convention where music is concerned, since the language has no outside referent against which its behaviour can be tested. Nevertheless, one is inclined to feel that the particular achievement of *Agon* would not have been within reach of any artist who had not already established Stravinsky's linguistic range, and the techniques to go with it.

In the literature on Stravinsky there seems to be some guardedness on the exact stature of *Agon*, as compared with the obviously profound sacred masterpieces which followed it. But I believe it to be one of his greatest and most original works. What astonishing creative vitality to seize hold, at the age of nearly seventy-five, of an established and supposedly alien technique and convert it at a stroke into something that had been beyond the reach of its originators: a work of buzzing energy and richly absorbing entertainment, a masterpiece of freshness, taste and inventive wit, which somehow takes into its nature both the cerebral intensity of the outside works to which it is indebted, and the sense of movement and space and formal balance of Stravinsky's own best works, from *Petrushka* and *The Wedding* to *Orpheus* and *The Rake*. When planning *Agon*, Stravinsky called it a 'dancing symphony';[22] and certainly the co-ordination of contrasted 'movements' justifies that description. But neo-classical, in any earlier Stravinskian sense, *Agon* hardly is at all. Even its synthetism is of a new order; a change has taken place between the *ballet de cour* of *The Rake* and the esoteric saraband and galliard and *bransles* modelled on the technical manuals and iconography of the day. The classicism of *Agon* is that of a new age of scholar composers, who will see in earlier models a kind of authority and technical inspiration only covertly dependent on superficial association – whether picturesque or, as so often in Stravinsky, polemical. *Agon* seems to have been a key work in fixing the idea that modern composition techniques might form a natural alliance with modern scholarship and research, an alliance which comes out in Stravinsky s own much-publicised investigations of old music, his 'edition' of Gesualdo (the *Tres sacrae cantiones*, made in 1957), his study of Bach and Monteverdi, and of still earlier music which apparently did not have, in the mid-1950s, the attraction that it would annoy fashionable modernists to find him interesting himself in it. And not only the boldness of movement in *Agon* but also, and perhaps above all, its sound was to influence a whole generation of younger composers who may have had little taste for the neo-classical stereotypes of *The Rake*, but who equally were reacting guardedly (at best) to the febrile introspection and dogmatic historicism of Schoenberg. Certain sonorities in *Agon* – the twang of mandolin and harp, the textural inversion of the galliard and its startling blend of flute and double-bass harmonics (a *trompe l'oreille* found also in the interludes), the general preference for high, light double-bass, the dry trumpet duets and piano thuds, the machine ostinatos of the opening and closing music and interludes – were to imprint themselves on the minds of composers as different as Berio and Birtwistle, Bennett and Gerhard.[23] The varied and unpredictable ensembles with which Stravinsky represented his changing stage-groupings may well have done as much for the chamber music of the 1960s as did *Pierrot lunaire* or the neo-gamelan of Boulez's *Marteau sans maître*.

Stravinsky himself, however, was far from ready to be typecast. The *Canticum Sacrum*, written in the interstices of *Agon* and completed before it in November 1955, and *Threni*, composed in the year following the completion of *Agon*, are sacred choral works of an essentially monumental cast with Latin texts and a predominantly slow, reverential tone. If *Agon* is the climax of Stravinsky's lifelong preoccupation with the music of dance and spatial movement, these two great devotional scores are the climax – though not the end – of his fascination with synthetic ritual forms and liturgies. Neither work is in itself liturgical. The *Canticum Sacrum ad honorem Sancti Marci nominis*, to give its full title, is a concert work for performance in church, with a text assembled from the Vulgate on the central theme of Faith; and *Threni, id est Lamentationes Jeremiae Prophetae*, though also for concert use, sets a selection of the Lamentation texts in the manner, but not the form, of an extended penitential observance. Just as de Schloezer had predicted a mass after the grandeurs of *Oedipus rex* and the restraints of *Apollo*, it could perhaps have been foreseen that the solemnity of the Mass (when it came) and *Orpheus*, combined with the composer's growing interest in techniques associated with the great church composers of the Renaissance, would in due course lead to a large-scale sacred work in the severest manner. *Threni* is that work. As previously mentioned, it was the first score by Stravinsky entirely composed with twelve-note serialism; and on every page it uses those processes as a kind of devotional act – a genuflection. That is, they belong to the music's imagery almost as much as to its technique.

From the start of the *Canticum Sacrum* there is a feeling that the processes are to be laid out for our inspection. The dedication, set for two male voices in the manner of a two-part motet with trombone accompaniment, is as studiously Venetian as the start of 'Dumbarton Oaks' was candidly Bachian. Later the 'Euntes in mundum' chorus ('Go ye into all the world'), together with its mirror image, the closing 'Ille autem profecti' ('And they went forth'), is punctuated by organ versets as in a seventeenth-century organ mass, while the tripartite central movement, 'Ad tres virtutes hortationes', has what amount to organ plainsong versets but with perceptible twelve-note rows in place of the modal lines of plainchant. If one adds to these the prominence in the 'Virtues' movement of strict serial canons for voices with or without instruments – the canons now tending to be rhythmic as well as melodic, which makes them much easier to hear – and the fact that the mirroring of the first choral movement by the last is as literal as is possible within the limitations of music notation, one has a work as self-consciously put together, perhaps, as any by a major master since Bach, and as painstakingly devised for its purpose, which was that it should belong as completely as possible within the physical and historical atmosphere of St Mark's Cathedral in Venice.

What significance does all this have for Stravinsky's artistic development, and for the general value of this particular work, granted that we cannot always (or perhaps ever) hear it in the context for which it was written any more than we shall ever hear Gabrieli's polychoral music sung from the galleries of St Mark's?

Like *Agon*, the *Canticum Sacrum* is a work which balances a seeming plethora of styles and techniques so skilfully that in performance its unity is never in doubt. And as with *Agon* this is evidently for reasons other than its use of the supposedly unifying serial method. For here too the music is neither completely twelve-note (movements 1, 5 and the Dedication are not), nor are its serial parts all based on the same row. In *Agon* the form had depended on Stravinsky's control of pace and the rate of tonal change, as much as on superficial unity of materials. In the *Canticum Sacrum* it depends a lot on our acceptance of the work's ritual or quasi-liturgical symbolism. For this is a predominantly slow work, with few changes of pace and much repetition of texture. Admittedly one takes away an impression of speed, because the main outer movements are both quick and brilliant, with much brass note-repetition in the manner of the baroque *stile concitato*. But between these strong pillars the music is almost entirely slow, unrhythmic, and episodic even by Stravinsky's standards. It can hardly be understood except as a kind of liturgy, heard preferably in a resonant and not too well-lit basilica. Indeed we know that Stravinsky regarded these conditions as part of the *Canticum*, because he used reverberation as a linking device at the end of the sections of the outer choruses. The long bass notes on the final chords are meant to hold the music up, so to speak, while the more brilliant high sounds die away – an effect hardly reproduceable in a modern concert-hall.

As a pseudo-liturgy, the *Canticum Sacrum* derives its continuity from the verset-alternatim structure which the 'Virtues' section shares with the outer movements. The enigmatic organ interpolations in 'Euntes in mundum' seem to draw us in towards the central mysteries of the faith, and as we venture tentatively forward the coolly enticing tenor aria 'Surge, aquilo' encourages us and prepares us for the greater linguistic complexities of the central exhortations. The formal process is comparable to that of *Agon*. In 'Surge, aquilo' Stravinsky introduces a twelve-note row, treated in thoroughgoing linear fashion, but without the severities of note-order that typified the bold instrumental lines of the ballet. In particular, the tenor adopts the purely vocal device of melisma, in the form not just of embellishments to particular syllables, but of ornamental oscillations between pairs of notes of the row. And this softening device is mimicked by the instruments, so that the chromatic treatment constantly subsides on to points of repose, often madrigalistically enhancing words like 'perfla' ('blow') or 'fluant' ('flow') or 'aromatibus' ('spices'). In the 'Virtues', the same idiom is at once related to the incantatory style of plainchant. After the opening organ verset or intonation ('Caritas'), the bass trombone repeats the series isorhythmically but in retrograde, while other wind instruments embroider its line with melismatic versions of the row. The choir then enters with the first of its several strict canons on the same series.

This central 'Virtues' section, which Craft called a 'cantata within a cantata',[24] seems to have served Stravinsky as a model for the expanded quasi-liturgical design of *Threni*. The entire piece is treated as a mosaic of tightly prescribed formal gestures, like the solemn and often-rehearsed 'actions' of the Mass or the Litany. But although the atmosphere is studiedly austere and inpersonal – even when the gestures are ornate – the music itself never wholly lets go of those characteristic tonal functions and colourings which, apart from a few pages of *Agon*, have typified Stravinsky's serial practice from the start. Just as, in the Cantata and the Septet, he had dealt with limited pitch-sets with a definite tonal focus, so here he devises his melodies to give the impression of 'setting' – of forming small, distinctively coloured pools of notes, some of them brought out of the texture by doubling or accent. Moreover these are features he can emphasise by the way he combines different row-forms. Where Schoenberg had usually preferred a method of combination which specifically avoided bringing out particular notes or note-groups,[25] Stravinsky takes the opposite course of designing and combining his series so as to bring out particular notes or particular harmonies. Two frequent examples of this are the cadential open fifth, which we first traced in the song 'Musick to heare'; and the device of the 'retained note', where one or two notes persist in an otherwise changing texture, either because they happen close together in different row-forms, or because they are purposely sustained by a free part. *Threni* makes use of all these ideas.

The first thing that must strike any newcomer to *Threni* is its unrelenting austerity. Craft suggested that, whereas the *Canticum Sacrum* is a 'concert', with separable parts and a measure of virtuoso display, *Threni* is a work of purely liturgical cast, capable of being grasped only as a whole and with some sense of its inner intention. However, if we allow for the much greater intensity and inwardness of the Lamentations settings, *Threni* still displays a form not unlike that of the *Canticum*. The work is again in five main parts, though that number includes the three sections of the long central part ('De Elegia tertia') which were counted as one in the *Canticum*. The outer parts similarly lead the participant into and out of the central mystery, which here consists of a tripartite ritual of 'Complaint – Hope – Repayment', and which, like the 'Virtues' section of the *Canticum*, amounts to a long sequence of formal acts in the style of a litany or commination. The opening part 'De Elegia prima', is again preceded by a Dedication – 'Incipit Lamentatio Jeremiae Prophetae'. And the progress of this liturgy is likewise reflected in discreet musical schemes. After the dedication, set as in the *Canticum* for two solo voices with instruments, the main first part consists of three quick-moving ensemble sections carried on ostinatos, twice interrupted by slow unaccompanied duets for two solo tenors which fulfil the same structural role as the organ versets in 'Euntes in mundum'. The first part, 'Querimonia', of the long central section is sung completely without accompaniment, matching the abject despair of the prophet's complaint with a sequence of strict canons increasing from a simple monody to a double canon in four voices and punctuated by the choral settings of the Hebrew alphabet which Stravinsky uses throughout *Threni* as an enumerating device but also with some of the cadential qualities of the 'Amen'. When the orchestra enters for the more mobile and less tightly drawn music of the next section, the 'Sensus spei' ('sense of hope') of the title flows back into the music, bringing a subdued feeling of reactivated life which debouches beautifully into the opening of the third section, 'Solacium', whose 'solace' Stravinsky seems to interpret musically in the modern sense of 'comfort' rather than the Old Testament sense of 'repayment'. Finally the short 'De Elegia quinta' is a prayer for renewal which suggests on the one hand the spirit of benediction common to Stravinsky's endings from *The Wedding* to the *Symphony of Psalms* and the Mass, and on the other the idea of recurrence which has also been, in all these works, one of his preoccupations.

In the *Canticum Sacrum* Stravinsky had adopted varying degrees of chromaticism to dramatise a pseudo-liturgy of this type. But in *Threni* he completely abandons the stylistic distinctions of the *Canticum* and for the first time builds his repertory of contrasts entirely from within the possibilities of serialism. Like the *In Memoriam*, *Threni* is audibly unified by the continually recurring melodic shapes of its basic series – with the added quality, of course, that that series is now twelve-note rather than five-note. Much of the writing is in strict canon, and when the canons are not strict, still the common cycle of pitches brings the various lines together into a network of imitative patterns, broken only by the very brief sections where Stravinsky allows the sequence of notes to spill into barely sustained chords, or where (as in the final chorus) he lets the lines criss-cross between the vocal parts so that the identity of each is liquidated in the general harmony. The monotony – the sense of perpetual recurrence – in all this is needless to say a vital aspect of Stravinsky's view of the spirit of lamentation, just as in *The Wedding* it expressed the simple inevitability of the cycle of birth, life and death. Indeed it is one of the most remarkable aspects of *Threni* that, at the moment of his fullest identification with the chromatic twelve-note method, he should suddenly rediscover some of the purest gestures of his first maturity.

It is worth, without embarking on that most facile and unrewarding of musicological operations, a serial note-count, tracing the relation of these gestures to serial method in the pages of *Threni*. Two principles control the structural functions of the series: first, each section of music is precisely defined by the simple statement of a few related set-forms, in free counterpoint with each other but presented complete as melodies; secondly, within each section the row operates in a pivotal way which helps emphasise the integrity and self-sufficiency of each stage in the 'liturgy'. Sometimes this pivoting happens because of inherent properties of the row; sometimes it depends on the way Stravinsky composes with it; sometimes both.

He typically starts with a row which combines 'badly' in Schoenbergian terms: that is, which sets up clear harmonic areas that are echoed by many different row-transpositions, and which thus create regions of consanguinity, like the modal fields of earlier works, when these related forms are combined. A good example is the two-part 'Diphona I' in the 'De Elegia prima' (Ex.56). Here the two voices continually make perfect fifths and fourths, but each line of music begins and ends with a chord of a minor third. Partly this reflects combinational properties of the row-forms in use (on the first line R-0 in the first tenor, I-0 in the second; on the second line RI-6 and P-0 respectively); partly it comes from Stravinsky's manipulations of them. But for whichever reason, the same quality is a consistent feature of the work. Here are a few more examples: the Hebrew letter 'Res(h)' (p.15), where the blatant movement from B minor to the dominant of E comes from the careful combination of four row-forms a minor third away from each other; the E flat minor colouring at 'Scrutemur vias nostras' (p.36) (R-0, I-0, P-0 combined); the similar colouring in E minor at 'Invocavi nomen tuum' (p.48); the densely complicated surge of the final three pages, where the music heaves itself from E flat minor to A minor through a combination of up to eight row-forms and much crossing of parts.

Other pivoting has less to do with tonal fields than with a sense of orbiting lines. The classical example is the refrain section of the 'De Elegia prima', 'Quomodo sedet' (p.7, the first of three identical occurrences), where Stravinsky rotates two row-forms (R-0 and RI-0) several times like ostinatos, supported moreover by actual rhythmic ostinatos in the accompanying strings. The solo tenor and flügelhorn travel through R-0 at different speeds, the tenor twice, the flügelhorn no less than five times, while the women sing RI-0 twice. Not only do these two row-forms set up fields of tonal agreement, but they actually seem to pirouette round each other, especially at the start, where the inversional relation comes out audibly in the sequence C-F sharp followed at once by F sharp-C (Ex.57). The different rate of travel of solo voice and instrument is due to the fact that while the flügelhorn goes straight through note-by-note, the tenor adopts a *reculer pour mieux sauter* approach, advancing through the row a

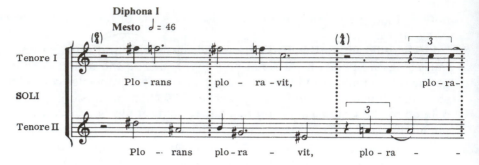

Ex. 56 *Threni*

few notes at a time, then going back to the start, then advancing a bit
further, and so on. A similar pattern can be traced in the chorus part (RI-
0), which is worth outlining numerically: 1-2-3-4-5 – 1-2-3-4-5-6-7 – 4-5-6-7-
8-9-10 – 8-9 – 8-9 – 8-9-10-11-12 – 12-12-12-12-12-12-12-12-12-1-2-3-4 – 5-6-7-
8-9-10-11-12-(12 repeated several times). The effect of spiralling recurrence
is prototypical of Stravinsky's whole approach to serialism, and gives this
music a hypnotic quality wholly different from the fluid, protean character
of serial Schoenberg. Later, in the 'Querimonia', Stravinsky extends the
idea of rotation into the manufacture of new versions of the row by taking
two or three notes from the start and tacking them on to the end. For
instance, the two-part canon on 'Aedificavit in gyro meo' (p.22) is based
on I-0 with the order 3-4-5-6-7-8-9-10-11-12-1-2 followed by P-0 as 4-5-6-7-8-
9-10-11-12-1-2-3 (the canon is at the minor sixth above: I-8/P-8). Perhaps the

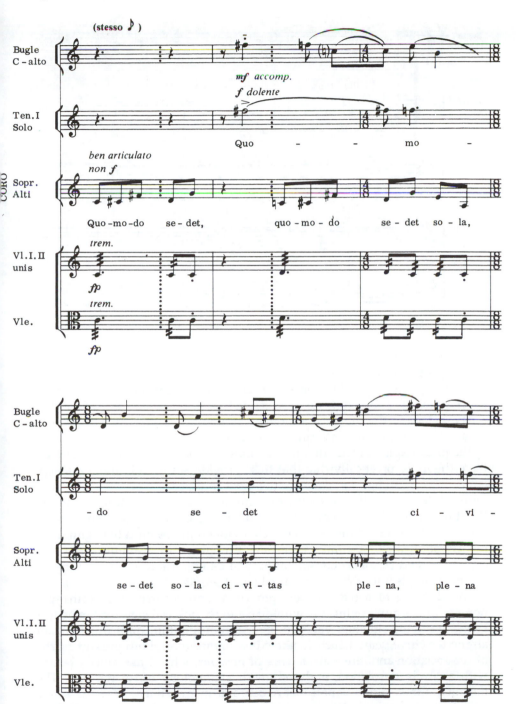

*Ex. 57 Threni*

*Ex. 58 Movements*

rotation was suggested by the words 'gyro' ('in a circle') and 'circumdedit' ('he has surrounded'). He also uses partially reversed orders and, in the 'Solacium', new rows obtained by ordered selection from the original – a procedure (also adopted by Berg) which in this case has the value of lending a new colour to the music at a moment of spiritual transformation. Taken as a whole, these devices can be explained as pure cerebration, in the Pythagorean spirit of the identity of numbers and music, though they do have the more practical virtue that they provide sufficiently fresh material (since the beginnings and ends are the most recognisable parts of a melody) without destroying the repetitive or incantatory aura so vital to the work. Rotation, especially, is a characteristic device of the composer who, as we saw in *Agon* feels his material to be cyclic – not bound by ends or beginnings, but simply providing a musical terrain through which innumerable paths can be marked out. This consideration will be important when we turn, in the next chapter, to Stravinsky's final serial works.

The drawing of a relation between ritual and recurrence is scarcely a novelty in his music, and it is quite feasible to look at *Threni* and, say, *The Wedding* side by side and begin to see common ground, even in detail, for all the forty-five years which separate their conception. Both present rituals of renunciation and renewal (as does *Oedipus rex*, which, like *Threni*, begins with a city in desolation, and ends with a ceremony of repayment). The fact that *Threni* offers a proto-Christian liturgy while *The Wedding* offers pagan rituals (with Christian observance somewhere offstage) and *Oedipus rex* a Greek religious festival, is a difference of subject-matter but not necessarily of approach. Musically, *The Wedding* is marked by the incantation of modal melodic cells, accompanied by or forming ostinato patterns, with sharply defined bell colourings in the orchestra. *Threni* is also a work of incantation, but in place of modal cells it depends on cells temporarily isolated from a twelve-note row, or on melismatic oscillations between pairs of notes, like the 'Invocavi nomen tuum', which irresistibly recalls the lament of the two mothers at the end of the third tableau in *The Wedding*. Certainly *Threni* is not dominated by rhythm as the ballet was. It is not, after all, a ballet. Even so, rhythm plays its part, often precisely in the form of ostinatos made out of rapid repetitions, like tribal chanting. The *parlando* chorus on 'Quomodo sedet' is an obvious parallel in this respect with the first chorus of *The Wedding*, a parallel which sheds as much light on the functions and derivations of the earlier work as on those of the later one. In both, the relevant passage is a refrain running through the whole first section, after which it is summarily dropped. In each case the music is like a rallying-call or shibboleth, like the twig-divining dance at the equivalent point of *The Rite of Spring*.

Like all such comparisons, this one can easily be pushed too far. *Threni* is a very different sounding work from *The Wedding*; its pace is slower, even while the music is denser and more convoluted, and its basis is free chant, rather than dance. Though both start with the Stravinskian harmony of the semitone dissonance with octave spacing, the imagery is starkly different: in *The Wedding*, bells and the brightness of creation; in *Threni*, string tone dulled by the sustained drag on the dissonant semitone, depicting the weariness of captivity. And this difference in weight goes right through. It comes out in the very different scoring of the two works. Even in its early version, *The Wedding* never had the hieratic solemnity of texture of *Threni*, and when Stravinsky tried to enrich or fill out its sound, in the version with harmonium and pianola, he merely robbed it of its life. *Threni*, by contrast, has its moments of brittle vitality, when the large orchestra seems to shatter into those hard gleaming fragments which we shall have cause to remember in *Movements* (piano sound to the fore) and *The Flood*. But its deeper character is felt in the heavy weight of trombones, horns, and tuba, and the darker colouring of clarinets, a type of instrument Stravinsky often excluded from his sacred works. As in the *Canticum Sacrum*, these neo-Venetian sonorities are deployed with fine regard to their special qualities – there are no tuttis, no big orchestral splashes. The more or less common factor is the voices; and beyond them are only the light and shade of instrumental nuance. At the end nothing but the four horns remains as an echo of the double choir and its anxieties.

*Threni* was the culmination of Stravinsky's investigations of the possibilities of serial method. It both sophisticates the various idioms of the Cantata and the works which followed, and it lays down technical resources which Stravinsky was to explore more fully and refinedly in the ensuing scores. In one obvious respect – its scale – *Threni* is not like the later pieces.

In this, *Agon* was to be more prophetic. But as a transitional and synthetic masterpiece *Agon* remained at some distance from the ethereal world of 1960s Stravinsky. The *Canticum Sacrum* and *Threni* are the real key to the eschatology that seems to dominate his creative thinking from now until his death.

# 12

# *Requiem aeternam*

While Stravinsky was composing *Threni*, the conversations took place which were eventually to appear in print as the first of several volumes of dialogues with Robert Craft.[1] The *Conversations*, which probably originated in some feeling that the composer's career was nearing its close, ended by marking a new phase – the last, certainly, yet one far from valedictory in tone. Perhaps half the book is devoted to reminiscences: 'I've known enough great men to make me a professional memorialist if I didn't stop thinking about them,' he growls in *Avec Stravinsky*.[2] The other half, however, revolves round questions of aesthetics, and here Stravinsky reveals the extent to which the neo-modernism of the 1950s had invaded his mind while he was struggling to renew his creative urge. In his discussion of modern music, the overriding assumption is that the current post-serial orthodoxy is the only possible direction for new music – an assumption which all too lamely echoes the violent polemics of Boulez's 'Eventuelle-ment' and the empty historicism of Hodeir's book *Since Debussy*, though Stravinsky was admittedly not yet ready to follow Boulez in rejecting Schoenberg, having only just reached the stage of accepting him in the first place. To see the greatest artistic empiricist of the age deferring in this abject way to the latest party line from France is, in hindsight, not the least painful image in that distressing phase in the intellectual history of music. Stravinsky is even kind to those young lions who (in Craft's formulation) complain of his recent music that 'triadic harmonies and tonic cadences are solecisms in the backward direction of the tonal system'.[3] His reply is a barely disguised apology for the neo-classical works, and an acknowledge-ment of the younger generation's right (at least) to dislike them, a concession Stravinsky had never extended to the world at large.

In recent years Robert Craft has tacitly admitted that the persona of the conversations was to some extent his creation;[4] but we can accept the ideas as authentic, if doubtless influenced by Craft, on the unimpeachable evidence of Stravinsky's music after *Threni*. In its brittle angularity his next work *Movements* for piano and orchestra, might be a conscious translation into sound of the composer's famous drawing of his recent music in *Conver-sations* (p.108) – a diagram which combines the point-to-point functionalism of a printed circuit with the randomness of the chart of a typical week of

English weather. Moreover, Stravinsky's remaining works, without significant exception, show that same reverence for serial system which informs his remarks on the New Music. These works were in due course (but within his lifetime) to spawn a self-contained analytical literature which would conclusively prove the benefits of serial method, if not to art, at least to the research programmes of university lecturers: a literature which finally drove Stravinsky himself to lament, with good reason, that his last works were more analysed than performed. Finally, an unsympathetic listener to *Movements* could well hear it as a musical riposte to Craft's insinuation about tonal references in *Agon* and the *Canticum Sacrum*. The absence of obvious tonal pivots is the most drastic thing about this ten-minute concerto, compared to those earlier works (as well as *Threni*), and the one which most clearly aligns it with the more modish aspects of neo-modernism as displayed by, say, Boulez's *Structures*, Stockhausen's *Kontra-Punkte*, or their scriptural texts, the Concerto and orchestral Variations of Webern and the piano studies of Messiaen.

*Movements* certainly marks the most abrupt stylistic caesura in all Stravinsky's long history of renunciation. A few bars here and there in *Threni* and one or two pages of *Agon* are the only premonitions of this new manner which was to serve him as an integrated and fully developed language for the remaining decade of his creative life. Of the repetitiousness of the neo-classical and proto-serial music there is hardly a trace. Audible ostinatos, though not entirely abandoned, are few and fleeting enough to call for notice when they happen. The same is true of stable harmony, at any rate at first. Stravinsky simply abandons these features of all his previous music in the interests of concentration and speed. *Movements* is well-named: every resonance of the word – both its sense of pace and its sense of change – is in the music. In this respect it has most in common with *Agon* among its predecessors; but the allusiveness of *Agon* is completely discarded, along with its vestiges of tonality and its quality of the statuesque. *Movements* has really no features that the listener can readily relate to his normal experience – or rather, it has such features, but they are distanced almost to vanishing point. The music's one synthetic aspect is precisely its adoption of a kind of aggressive modernism which effectively removes it from the experiential world of even sophisticated devotees, to whom *Agon* and the *Canticum Sacrum* had presented few difficulties.

Since conscious mannerism had never previously stopped him writing music of genius (*Oedipus rex* and *The Soldier's Tale* are in this sense mannered works), there is obviously no case for arguing that, where mannerism is in the direction of the awkward or the abstruse, it is *ipso facto* invalid. Only those who reject all Stravinsky's music since *The Wedding* can afford to believe that.[5] *Movements* is no more modish than the Octet, only the mode it adopts is problematical. Yet the more one listens to it, the more its style, as such, starts to melt away. For instance, although the influence of Webern on its scattered lines seems obvious, and is amply borne out by the extrava-

gant compliments Stravinsky pays Webern in the various conversation
books, the Webernism is in practice transformed to the same extent as the
Bachism in the Piano Sonata or the Verdi-ism in *Oedipus rex*. For Webern,
the tiny three- or four-note serial units which supply the working material
for all his late works seem to be microcosms, to the point where the
extended work itself implies a contradiction that needs to be resolved, either
by audibly systematic patterning, as in the first movement of the Concerto
op.24, or by building silence into an attenuated structure, as in the Variations op.30. In *Movements*, by contrast, the material has rather the character
of a medium through which the energy of the musical idea passes. The
serial process now acts as a guide, directing the sound rapidly along a route
marked out by a succession of choices. But the energy itself seems to exist
outside – to pre-exist – the crude selection of notes, which is not indeed
random (it reveals noticeable patterns and tendencies) but neither is it
governed by rules which would enable even the most attentive and intelligent listener to predict, with more than a remote likelihood of being right,
what the next notes or rhythms will be. Randomness within strictly defined
limits would be a fair working description of the effect of *Movements* in
performance.

It may seem odd to talk of serial music being random, since the attraction
of such music to the analyst is the attraction of precise determination – the
possibility of explaining logically the choice of one note rather than another
at every stage. But serial analysis as a precise science is almost exclusively
concerned with derivations. Given a sequence of notes, it will tell us the
connection between those notes and some original sequence or shape, but
it will seldom give us compelling (that is, logical) reasons why that particular
derivative occurred rather than one of a large number of possible alterna-
tives. Partly this may be because the history of serial music is bound up
with the German classical tradition of organic tonal and thematic structures.
In serial Schoenberg, the combination of a strictly limited repertoire of row-
forms with a largely conventional rhythmic and gestural language will often
allow a note-count to elucidate purely local 'tonal' materials in a large form
that is implicitly traditional in its play of contrasts, its discursive flow, and
its dialectic of tension and release. But in most later serial music (including
a few works of Schoenberg himself) this kind of assumption can no longer
be made. When one has explained the entire serial apparatus of *Kontra-
Punkte* or *Kreuzspiel*, one has explained precisely nothing about the music
unless one can proceed from there to some account of what this apparatus
delivers to the ear. The analytical tradition is to take such matters on trust.
To the suggestion that Stockhausen's serial technique is merely an arbitrary
mechanism for the selection of musical dimensions which, after all, do have
to be decided, the note-counter has apparently little to say.

In the case of Stravinsky's later serial music starting with *Movements*, all
the same, a general description of the processes involved will to some
extent support that very conclusion. *Movements*, like *Threni*, is composed

entirely with material yielded by a single twelve-note row. But though it
begins and ends with complete statements of this row, most of the music
in between is based on half-rows, or hexachords, which are subjected to a
variety of rotations and internal surgery by no means all of which is easy
to understand in terms of significant motives or pitch centres. In any case
the technique seems to follow no particular system until the last two of the
five movements. Here Stravinsky's working notes show that he found a
way of making chords by writing out the four basic row-forms in what
amounts to four-part harmony, and then treating the twelve chords which
result as independent groups or sets.[6] The start of the fifth movement has
these twelve groups played successively by the solo piano as accompaniment to a solo trumpet playing the straight retrograde of the row, and Spies
gives an example of their occurrence later in the movement. At the start of
the fourth movement there is a sustained chord – much more of a harmony
than the Spies examples – which is an embryonic form of a related way of
deriving chords which Stravinsky was to use more systematically in later
works. Take the first hexachord of the prime form of the row, and write
out underneath it five more versions of this hexachord such that the first
note is always the same (E flat in this case) but the sequence of intervals is
rotated one place to the left each time (coming back in at the right-hand
end, like the lost portion of a TV picture where the horizontal hold has
slipped). You get a square grid six notes long and six notes deep (Ex.58),
which in effect concentrates particular attributes of the six-note original –

Ex. 58

same intervals, same starting note – and which you can use to make melodies or chords that to some extent reflect those attributes. The first held chord in this fourth movement is the second 'six-note' chord of the grid in question (it actually has only four notes because there are two duplications; as for the first chord in the grid, that is of course by definition a unison E flat). Its occurrence here could well be a serial 'accident', since the notes can just as well be explained by linear analysis, and since the next sustained chord in the movement (bar 110) cannot be analysed as a grid chord, a serious inconsistency. In fact the most striking, not to say drastic, succession of chords in this fourth movement is at the end, where Stravinsky puts together no fewer than eight *un*rotated hexachords in block harmony, with counterpoints supplied by two further hexachords in the strings. This is a very good example of music which can be explained serially, but not (at least not obviously) heard as such.

It may be apparent from all this that the serial technique in *Movements* is hybrid. Spies shows us, with understandable satisfaction, how Stravinsky worked out the chords in the fifth movement; but he does not show the musical purpose of the method. One can point out certain similarities between the four-note chords in this sequence. One can, for instance, observe that a chord of four linked whole-tones occurs four times (nos. 3, 6, 8, and 12), and that four of the other chords, including the two two-note ones and the one three-note one, are also whole-tone. But Stravinsky does not usually compose them as chords; they come as networked sets, more or less correctly grouped, but with irregular overlappings and rhythmic irrelevancies which effectively obscure the underlying pattern, even supposing it to be potentially audible. For instance, a grace-note (of the kind which abounds in the piano writing of *Movements*) may not belong to the same chord as the note it graces. On the other hand the most systematic aspect of these chord sequences (at bars 141 and 167 respectively) is a pure arithmetical abstraction. If we divide the twelve chords as if they were a note-row into two hexachords – 1-6 and 7-12 – we find that each hexachord keeps its correct order both times, though they are shuffled into each other. If we give the chords their order numbers (1-12) we find that the sum of the pairs increases always by two, giving a curious relation between the opening sequence and the reversed form of the later sequence, such that the sum of the two corresponding serial numbers is in every case but two 13 (the exceptions, which are adjacent, simply change places):

bar 141 (chord no.)   1 – 7 – 8/2  –  9 – 3 – 10 – 4 – 5 – 11 – 12 – 6
bar 167               12 – 6 – 5/11 – 10 – 4 –  3 – 9 – 8 –  2 –  1 – 7

The rotations on the other hand are related to audible patterns, though often in what sounds like an arbitrary way. It may be that, as Stravinsky tells us in *Memories* (p.106), 'every aspect of the composition was guided by serial forms', but the evidence is rather that he used serial forms to generate notes to fit broad compositional needs. It also looks as if he may have hit on the grid rotational scheme while writing *Movements*, which uses it only spasmodically compared with later works like *Abraham and Isaac* or the Variations. Both these works have extended passages composed by tracking backwards and forwards through the grid (*Abraham and Isaac* is substantially composed in that way). This particular technique is not used in *Movements*, though tracking would suit its rushing monodies as much as it suits the vocal cantilena of *Abraham and Isaac*. In fact many of the rotations in *Movements* are not even found on a grid constructed in the way outlined above. They occur on an 'old-fashioned' serial lay-out based on the twelve-note row. Stravinsky takes hexachords from here and there, freely rotating one or more notes, and often reassembling pairs of hexachords from different places in the system back into twelve-note rows – a device which is made possible by the special character of the row itself. This principle of complementation is a consistent, though not systematic, backcloth to the composition of *Movements*, and one which, incidentally, goes against one of the ideas of the grid technique – that of pitch limitation. Since focal pitches are nevertheless very much a feature of the music, it may even be that the grid idea emerged during work on *Movements* but was only incorporated in it piecemeal.

Stravinsky described *Movements* as 'anti-tonal', a coinage which perhaps says something useful about the music's fiercely energetic temper (composers as a race dislike the term 'atonal', which makes their music sound as if something has been left out by mistake), but is misleading as regards its tonal qualities. Highly chromatic it certainly is. In *Threni* the row had obvious tonal attributes which were emphasised in the composition. But *Movements* has a purely chromatic row based, in Webern fashion, on three-note groups separated by minor thirds and tritones. The model for this may be Webern's Concerto, op.24, where a basic three-note row is built up into a twelve-note row by adding an inversion, a retrograde and a retrograde-inversion, at suitable transpositions. Stravinsky typically unbalances his scheme by moving a note (D) from the first set of three to the end of the first hexachord – a kind of primordial rotation which sets up, in theory at least, the dynamic tension of the music (Ex.59). But this does not alter the symmetrical fit of the two hexachords, seen as mobile or rotating units of six notes, and it is this fit which guarantees the flow of twelve-note pairings mentioned in the last paragraph.[7] At this level Stravinsky's row is actually more chromatic than anything in Webern, since the three-note groups are all tones and semitones, where Webern (perhaps remembering his Viennese ancestry) tends to frame his sub-groups by thirds, as in op.24. The clash of the semitone or tone, almost invariably spaced out by an octave or more,

Ex. 59

had been a Stravinskian fingerprint at least since *Petrushka*, so in adopting it as his bread-and-butter in *Movements* he was truly taking back his own.

But while these intervals are everywhere in *Movements* – treated as melodies, ornaments, interference notes and occasionally motives – they represent only one side of the music. They are, perhaps, its dynamic or exuberant aspect. The rocketing minor ninth of the very first gesture (flute, trumpet, then at once piano and violins) – a gesture which has its equivalent at the start of each of the five movements – seems to precipitate a cascade of melodic fragments and irrational rhythms. But after seven rapid bars the music reaches a point of repose, and here a new interval asserts itself, the open fifth played as a held piano chord (A flat-E flat). The fifth, with its inversion the fourth, is another 'possession' of Stravinsky's, again harking back to *Petrushka* and the other works of the Russian period. In the proto-serial works, as we saw, the fifth was a standard cadential sound usually not serially derived. In the row of *Movements*, as it happens, there are two fifths (or fourths: the inversional equivalence of serialism destroys their theoretical, though happily not their actual, difference): one between the two three-note groups of the second half (between notes 9 and 10), and the other at the end of the first half, manufactured by the rotation of the D. Fifths therefore crop up as a matter of course, even in the brittle semiquaver passages such as the first seven bars, but they tend to be cancelled out by the quickfire rattle of semitones. The held fifth in bar 8 is probably the first of which the listener will be conscious, though he will have felt the openness of texture to which earlier fifths have contributed, and he may even be vaguely aware that the A flat is not new but has provided a kind of discreet pedal to the previous four bars. Later in the work fifths often group themselves round sustained notes. The start of the fourth movement is only the most obvious example. In the first-time bar of the first movement, which has a formal repeat of its first section, the held C acquires both a G and an F (and there are other fifths in this relatively stable passage). The C-G-F grouping, a segment of the universal cycle of fifths, highlights an aspect of the *Movements* row which constantly works against its chromaticism. Each hexachord contains two of these cycles: for instance, in P-0, hexachord 1, A flat-E flat-B flat and D-A-E; hexachord 2, F-C-G and B-F sharp-C sharp; and though the notes are only serially adjacent in the last case, a glance at the score on almost any page will show that Stravinsky tends to work with such cycles as a specific colour (Ex.60).

Whether this can sensibly be described as a 'tonal' colour is a moot point. The handling is invariably discreet: trumpets play flutter-tongued G flat/D flat *con sordino* (page 1); the cello C in the *prima volta* is a soft harmonic 'doubled' by piano, with middle pedal sostenuto; a viola solo plays soft melodic fifths (start of the second movement) but blurred by interfering tones and semitones; the long fourths and fifths of movement 4 are high string harmonics with restricted resonance – all these effects perhaps show the influence of Webern on Stravinsky's orchestration, where the bolder

*Ex.* 60 *Movements* for piano and orchestra

writing of the Allegro passages has an American zip to it, with a hint of Copland or Carter. In these passages the 'tonal' intervals may do no more than glimmer faintly as the music passes through them. But throughout the work there is a noticeable pull between the dynamic chromaticism and the stable fifths. And this is as much an expression of the form as of the harmony. The association between chromaticism and instability of rhythm and texture is established at the very start, and quickly counteracted by sustained fifths in mid-register, where they are most easily perceived. The second part of the movement is *meno mosso*, and leads naturally, via the first of the four interludes Stravinsky added as metric transitions, to the second movement, where the melodic fifths dominate a brief attempt at lyricism. After this the music never regains its opening tempo; the finale is nominally almost as quick but lacks the mercurial vehemence of the first movement. Here the chromatic writing (Spies's chords) is at its most relaxed and the trumpet solo has a positive radiance. But the close is enigmatic; the music's ebullience dies away in a succession of Webernian sighs, and a piano/harp chord of B-C sharp-F sharp which seems to clinch the fifth-cycle harmony but is wiped out by the dry thud of G and F, the last two notes of the row.

*Movements* is often thought of as a difficult work because of its brittle and supposedly dissonant harmonic language. But the real problem with this for-the-last-time-new Stravinsky is its sheer brevity and speed. The sound, certainly, is dry and skeletal. The piano darts around as if it were taking random samples from a repertory of pitches and rhythms, while the orchestral melody instruments (there is no percussion) contribute only fragments of expressive line, some discreet sostenuto chords, and prismatic flickers of colour. This is very much the language of the 1950s, the age of the Darmstadt summer school and the composer-as-technician. But Stravinsky renewed this language as he renewed all the others he borrowed; and the fact is that *Movements* is not hard to listen to, in the way that the piano sonatas of Boulez or Barraqué are hard because they grate on the ear. Its sounds are as finely judged as in any work by Stravinsky; its textures are, for the most part, spare and transparent. A characteristic buoyancy of movement lifts the music far out of the avant-garde rut, and lends it a vitality and formal precision which one can only – at this stage of a book on the composer – describe as Stravinskian.

The rate of change remains, all the same, a genuine difficulty. Not only are the ideas themselves – the melodic figures and rhythmic cells – hard to catch hold of, however much they may colour the music in an individual, and overall unmistakable, way; but the swift flow of formal elements, as marked out simply by changes of texture and scoring, continually leaves the ear behind. This is above all true of the odd-numbered movements, where the instrumental repartee (with the piano as the one more or less constant factor) to some extent echoes the decomposition of melody and rhythm. Stravinsky himself acknowledged this unusual density in his serial works. We may see it as a typical old-man's music. But Stravinsky regarded it also as a property of non-tonal music; 'We are located in time constantly in a tonal-system work, but we can only "go through" a polyphonic work, whether Josquin's *Duke Hercules Mass* or a serially composed non-tonal-system work'.[8] Memory may act differently, as there are no long-term formal requirements we recognise built into the initial terms of a serial work. Serial patterning may therefore provide *ad hoc* connections, but not necessarily criteria of structure. Nevertheless *Movements* strikes one as a work that is concise not because its technique would not tolerate length but because its technique was well-adapted to conciseness. The brevity and pace of this miniature piano concerto are the essence of its meaning; its pitch system is perhaps no more than a vehicle.

A specific interest in the very concentrated comes out in the designedly brief, semi-occasional works which typify this last decade of Stravinsky's creative life. The tiny *Epitaphium* for flute, clarinet and harp, written in the summer of 1959 at the request of Heinrich Strobel in memory of the patron of the Donaueschingen Festival, Prince Max Egon zu Fürstenburg, plays for only a minute and a quarter but manages seven balanced sections of what Stravinsky called 'funeral responses', between the bass register of the harp on the one hand and the treble wind instruments on the other. The very different Double Canon for string quartet, in memory of Raoul Dufy, also written in 1959 (though Dufy, whom Stravinsky never met, had died in 1953), likewise plays just over a minute but gets through six complete canons in that time.

The *Epitaphium*, which was to be played in a concert containing music by Webern (Stravinsky changed his scoring to go with Webern's songs, op.15), is the most Webernish work he ever wrote. It is untypical both in its reserve and in specific qualities like its harmony, where Stravinsky's admitted interest in the sound of clashing seconds led him to cramp his natural style of chording – a problem which arose, perhaps, through treating the interval as a polyphonic event in a slow, restrained texture, rather than as a rhetorical gesture, as at the start of *Threni*. All the same this slightly lifeless piece was important as a stage in the evolution of a particular kind of harp sound which was to play a crucial part in one of Stravinsky's most individual late works, the *Introitus*.

If the Double Canon has nevertheless a stronger profile, it may be because the canonic technique ensures (or encourages) a linear impulse which flows from start to finish. But this is certainly not one of those serial canons where the technique is more or less automatic and one feels after hearing it that any scheme of entries would have made much the same grey, semi-organised effect. Stravinsky starts with a theme that is beautiful in itself. Its mixture of chromatics and the implication of wide diminished intervals suggests Bach, but also, perhaps curiously, Liszt. The theme, which is also the row, rises to its centre then falls back, making an expressive arch which is echoed by the retrograde forms, and which moreover has the effect that, when the double canon strikes up in bar 5 with the retrograde, the four instruments set up a kind of wave pattern surging up to a restrained climax of harmony and texture then dying down slowly towards the end, where once again only the violins are left. At half-way Stravinsky introduces his favourite IR form (the inversion of the retrograde), which, because it starts on the final note of the prime, gives exactly the effect of continuing the arch downwards without a noticeable break. All this sounds supremely natural; and yet the canons are rigorously strict, and the retrograde forms also reverse the rhythms of the original, a device which, for once, can be heard and is important for the work's expressive effect.

The Double Canon turned out to be Stravinsky's last purely instrumental work (apart from the Gesualdo arrangements in the *Monumentum*) until the orchestral variations of four or five years later. For a time he turned his attention to setting Biblical texts in English. He wrote *A Sermon, a Narrative and a Prayer*, an annotated account of the martyrdom of St Stephen, for Paul Sacher in Basle (a commission dating back to 1956), and a version of the medieval play on *The Flood* for, of all things, American TV. He made a dry and unsatisfactory setting of Eliot's 'The Dove Descending' (from *Little Gidding*), a piece which founders on the twin intractabilities of, on the one hand, that curious Anglo-Saxon combination of hymnic plainness and visionary fervour which Eliot inherited from the metaphysical poets, and on the other hand the difficulty most choirs experience in singing lyrical atonal music in tune without instruments. And two years later he set, much more beautifully, a short poem by Auden written specifically for him to compose into his *Elegy for JFK*. In between, and heralding the revived austerities of his very last works, he composed the strange and idiosyncratic *Abraham and Isaac*, on the Hebrew Biblical text.

Both the large-scale English-language narratives have enjoyed a chequered career since first seeing the light of day in the early 1960s. The *Sermon . . .* remains perhaps the least performed of any of the works post-*Threni*; *The Flood* was reportedly a disaster in its original TV production, and semi-staged concert performances since then have not entirely vindicated its untidy mixture of media effects, though like Stravinsky's other most grossly neglected mixed-media score, *Persephone*, it contains music of great brilliance and flair. One genuine difficulty with these works (as well as with their little ancestor *Babel*, aptly enough) is a new form of the language barrier – the barrier of hearing too much and in unsuitable contexts. Stravinsky seems to have been sensitive to this kind of problem in languages other than English. In a conversation with Craft which took place not more than four years before the completion of the *Sermon . . .*, he condemned his own use of 'music as accompaniment to recitation' in *Persephone*,[9] possibly because he was aware of a false rhetoric in the speech which at the same time subordinated the music to the role of pantomime. Yet this very technique is a crucial part of both the *Sermon . . .* and *The Flood*, and it vitiates both works at their most vulnerable point, that of the narrative itself.

Stravinsky's own recordings (the only ones so far made), with their beefy American accents, arouse in English listeners uncomfortable memories of what might be called the Cecil B de Mille Bible; but this is not only a problem of accent, for the Narrator in *The Flood* is Laurence Harvey, and he is hardly more successful with the familiar words than the American narrator in the *Sermon . . .*, John Horton. The truth seems to be that these wordy attempts to get rapidly yet artistically through a somewhat compli- cated story are an embarrassment, treating the audience like children and the composer like a silent-cinema pianist. More especially, they go directly against Stravinsky's proven genius for ritual word-setting and purely statu- esque drama. Where *The Wedding* could manage without speech, and *Oedipus rex* could at least exclude it from its musical continuity, the depen- dence of a work like *The Flood* on straight-faced narration looks like a rare (for Stravinsky) case of artistic indecisiveness. There is an exception which may prove the rule. Stravinsky uses a square-dance caller to announce the entry of each pair of animals into the Ark, a beautiful and witty idea which shows what might have been done with the rest of the narration if it could somehow have been incorporated elegantly into the drama rather than left chattering on its fringes.

The overall hybrid nature of *A Sermon, a Narrative and a Prayer*, which Stravinsky completed in January 1961, looks novel and unclassifiable (and its cumbersome title certainly suggests that the composer thought it so). But it has in fact an honourable history, being the formula on which Bach's Passions are based. At the heart of the work is a story, told from the Bible, and this is framed by an expression of faith and a prayer that we might all find the grace to merit salvation, as Stephen did. The setting of Thomas Dekker's words in this third part is the most beautiful and moving part of the work perhaps because here, for the first time, the concentration of feeling implicit in the central idea of the whole score is matched by a corresponding integration of texture and technique. Essentially Stravinsky takes the prayer and sets it in straightforward solo and choral polyphony, in much the manner he was to adopt a year later with the Eliot *Anthem*. But by discreetly supporting the voices, at first with strings, later with a remarkable and haunting tocsin sound made by three gongs, piano, harp and a double-bass, he transforms a potentially morose expression into a profoundly solemn moment of devotion – one of those unpredictable strokes which separate the genius from ordinary mortals even when he is not altogether on top form. Moreover this movement is also serially inte- grated. It uses largely inverted forms of the row taken from the hexachordal rotation grid, which has the audible effect of focusing the harmony round a kind of centre – the note E flat – an effect Stravinsky enhances, however, not by the orthodox procedure of matching the strict rotations to the phrase- lengths, but by locating E flat at the start and finish of the phrases whatever its place in the rotated form.

In this music the *Sermon . . .* abandons the brittle polyphony of the more fragmented parts of *Movements* without rejecting at all its underlying technique. But in the long central section, the biblical 'Narrative' itself, vestiges of the actual sound of the piano play a not always helpful part in dramatising the context of Stephen's martyrdom while oddly enough keeping silent at the one moment – his stoning – when most graphically minded composers would have had piano sixteenths flying around like lumps of rock. Perhaps Stravinsky was not yet quite ready to make fun of the clichés of neo-modernism (in *The Flood* he was to do so, and 'The Building of the Ark' is a masterpiece of *Klangfarbenmalerei*). The 'Narrative' itself is also afflicted by mannerism. For instance, the much-remarked device of switching from speech (narrator) to singing (contralto soloist) at exalted or significant moments, and especially each time the name 'Stephen' is mentioned, is too self-conscious to work in any but the superficial sense that anyone can hear it happening; and while the use of two-part canon to suggest economically (or perhaps pessimistically) 'the word of God increasing', and of purposely dry counterpoint for the disputation between Stephen and the Pharisees, is certainly authentic and effective madrigalism, the music rarely seems to acquire density through these means but remains at the level of anecdote. The trouble with all these procedures, as well as with the choric speech in the 'Sermon' (St Paul's 'We are saved by hope') and the occasional rhythmic declamation of the narrator, is that they imply an artificial world of ritual which is consistently denied by the matter-of-fact Sunday-school atmosphere of the work as a whole. It is from this atmosphere that the 'Prayer' at last manages to escape.

The same conflict survives in parts of *The Flood*, but is greatly relieved by those elements of pantomime, or peasant comedy, which Craft's compilation took over from the Chester and York mysteries. The mixture was admittedly already familiar from Britten's *Noyes Fludde*. But that was openly a work for children, written in that style of homely modernity which Britten somehow managed to command without either condescension or complication. Stravinsky's is a work for adults, both to perform and to enjoy. It is half as long as *Noyes Fludde* but has much more plot, including the Creation and Fall, and an Epilogue implying (through musical reprise) an allegorical link between these events, the Flood itself, and Christian redemption. Individual incidents are treated much more perfunctorily. If the comedy of Noah's wife refusing to board the Ark goes on too long in Britten, it is succinct to a fault in Stravinsky; Lucifer's fall is in every sense a throw-away; the episode of the raven and the dove is omitted altogether. But in place of these events to which Stravinsky would surely have given more weight if he had been writing for the stage, there is much opportunity for what might be called visual entertainment. The dance element is important, in for instance 'The Building of the Ark' which is one of several orchestral interludes. Moreover the choreographer Balanchine concerned himself with every aspect of the screen picture, as is apparent from the 'working notes' printed in *Dialogues*. He and Stravinsky were full of ideas for presenting *The Flood* as a visual fantasy which made play with television's theoretical versatility in the matters of spatial and temporal transition. Yet their ideas remain rooted in the practical considerations of the travelling or local theatre which was the nature of the miracle play, just as it presumably was of the *skomorokhi* plays that lay behind *Renard* and *The Soldier's Tale*. For example, while God's voice is to be identified 'with abstract patterns of light' (the Deity not being actually visible), the dancers should be on a platform, at audience eye-level, and at the end 'the rainbow could be formed by the dancers . . . their costumes can help to form an arc or a bridge'. The waters of the flood itself might be 'a deliquescent black surface bubbling like an oil-field. Underneath this black tent the male dancers bob up and down from their knees . . . the female dancers move among the mounting and bursting blobs of black. The men are the waves and the women the people drowning in them'. This looks like a screened version of a perfectly stageable idea.

The fantasy-comedy side of the TV show is nicely matched by the music, as one would expect from the composer of *Renard* and the *Pribaoutki*. Indeed the return to the pure musical fun of Stravinsky's early 'peasant' works, after the lofty abstraction of *Apollo*, *Orpheus* and *Agon*, is the most refreshing aspect of *The Flood*. The score starts both amusingly and impressively with a representation of chaos by tremolo chords containing all twelve chromatic notes, and we then proceed to a balletic 'Te Deum' in the best tradition of *The Wedding* and *Threni*, quasi-ecclesiastical in a manner dubbed by Stravinsky 'Igorian chant'. The music comes back at the end for the final 'Sanctus'. The characterisation of God as two basses singing in heterophony to an ostinato rhythm on the bass-drum and low chords on cellos and double-basses, and Lucifer/Satan as a light, fickle tenor (a kind of cross between Schoenberg's Aaron and Stravinsky's own Rakewell) whose music dances gaily against the expected accent, like the music of the Devil in *The Soldier's Tale* or the Shepherd and Messenger in *Oedipus rex*, both show Stravinsky's instinct for the combination of humour and solemnity. Later the purely orchestral episodes of 'The Building of the Ark' and 'The Flood', with its palindromic form like the 'Euntes in mundum' and 'Illi autem profecti' of the *Canticum Sacrum* (apparently meant to suggest the timelessness or universality of world-catastrophe), show the master turning his technical intricacies to simple graphic uses. In 'The Flood' the serial apparatus of the rotation grid is fully deployed in the circling melodies of the violins and flutes, the lightning flashes through a complete statement of P–0, and the ostinato harmony is a verticalised form (not a grid vertical) of one of the inversion second hexachords (Ib2). Actual grid chords have already been used, *all'ostinato*, in God's first conversation with Noah (in the string tremoli), an episode Balanchine saw, perhaps more prosaically, as a kind of tennis-game, 'back and forth from the earth-level view of Noah to the light of the iconostasis, which is the visual anchor throughout *The Flood*.'

Yet the virtues of all these passages are the virtues of a largely episodic, anecdotal kind of music. There are good ideas at every level: visual, aural, technical. Stravinsky was perhaps the first serial composer to take the twelve notes as an image of totality – ordered or disordered as the case might be – while sub-sets illustrate the various stages of terrestrial imperfection. But in the end the music does not command the piece, it illustrates it. And sometimes, inevitably, it falls into the mannerism of an illustrative style that is asked to do more than depict. For instance, if the hammer-and-nails style of post-Boulez serialism is meant to portray the building of the Ark, what is it doing at other times – in the account of the Creation, or the catalogue of animals, or indeed as a latent idiom throughout the work? The answer is, of course, that it is indeed a *lingua franca*, at least for instruments and solo voices (Stravinsky knew from past experience that such writing would not do for chorus voices – hence the reversion to Igorian chant). But whereas in *Movements* the sheer sustained energy of the writing, together with the clarity and economy of the form, with its skilfully contrived scheme of discreet tonal focuses, could override, even make a virtue of, a certain randomness in the melodic and harmonic language, in the *Sermon . . .* and *The Flood* the illustrative function of much of the music constantly raises the questions: why this sort of line, why this texture, why this chord rather than that? The serial analyst is at no loss to give us what he regards as an adequate answer. But, lacking his faith in the archetypal status of the twelve notes, the God-given truth of octave equivalence, and the perceptibility of polyrhythm, we remain unconvinced and end up finding the music shallow, bitty and at times almost (what one might have thought impossible for Stravinsky) empty.

*The Flood* was completed in March 1962, and screened (by CBS) three months later. In August Stravinsky embarked on what was to be the first of his final group of five works leading up to the greatest (with *Agon*) of all those composed with the serial method or under its influence, the *Requiem Canticles*. In general the harvest of these last years is astonishing, if we bear in mind not only that Stravinsky had his eightieth birthday in June 1962, but that he was throughout these years in indifferent health, had suffered his first stroke as long ago as 1956, continued to tour and conduct until 1967, and even embarked in 1962 on an emotionally and physically exhausting visit to Russia – his first since the outbreak of the First World War. In addition to all this he carried out revisions to earlier works: *The Nightingale* was revised as late as 1962, and Stravinsky went on tinkering with *The Rite of Spring*. And he made a number of significant arrangements, of his own music and the music of others. After the reworkings of the late 1940s and early 1950s – made partly for copyright purposes but very much more extensive than would have been called for by that motive alone – he made the orchestration of Bach's canonic variations on *Vom Himmel hoch* to go with the Venice performance of the *Canticum Sacrum*, and proceeded from there to a series of realisations of motets by Gesualdo, which he also hoped would be performed with the *Canticum Sacrum*.[10] The three motets (*Tres Sacrae Cantiones*) all involved composing missing parts, and therefore inevitably some Stravinskification, which is however less striking in these vocal arrangements cast in the same medium as the originals, than it is in the piece which followed, the *Monumentum pro Gesualdo*, which is a transcription for small orchestra (wind prominent) of three of Gesualdo's madrigals. Here the radical change of medium, and the introduction of an element of Venetian *spezzato*, draws attention sharply to that aspect of Gesualdo's style which was precisely what attracted Stravinsky to the music in the first place: its harmonic obliquity.[11]

Both sets of realisations were published in 1960, the four hundredth anniversary of Gesualdo's birth.[12] Two years later, at the time when he was completing *The Flood*, Stravinsky made an elaborate transcription of the exiguous piano pieces of *The Five Fingers* (1921) for an ensemble of fifteen instruments: double woodwind, a horn and string sextet. The arrangement, which was published as *Eight Instrumental Miniatures*, is of interest for its remarkably delicate recomposition of the simple piano textures of the original. Stravinsky not only changed the proportions of some of the pieces, as well as their order and in two cases their keys, but he amplified their textures by the addition of counterpoints and inner parts, in a way which recalls the successive stages of the early *Pastorale*. On the whole this is a more sympathetic reconstruction than the twelve-instrument arrangement of the Concertino which Stravinsky had made at Craft's suggestion ten years earlier to help lift him out of his compositional depression, but which spoils the even textures of its quartet original by a too heavy emphasis on the brass.

It might have been tempting at the time to see all this arranging and revising as some kind of therapeutic work for a composer no longer able to envisage major creative projects. But in truth it was no more than a by-product. The underlying vitality of the *Eight Miniatures*, with their restrained and subtle additions, turns out to be a mere residue of a creative impulse that, in the end – and to judge by the assurance of the *Requiem Canticles* – would only be staunched by the sheer physical frailty which overtook him at the age of eighty-five.

The five original works of this Indian summer are notable for the intensity and directness with which they project their images. Stravinsky's Russian works had had this quality almost of reification, but it was less apparent in the works of the middle period, perhaps because of their increasing use of conventional mannerisms that turn up in a succession of scores. If *Pribaoutki* or *Renard* have in the end a stronger presence than, say, *Jeu de cartes* or 'Dumbarton Oaks', it could be because practically everything in them has had to be invented from scratch. *Abraham and Isaac*, the next new work after *The Flood*, has something of this same quality. Considering that both these works are Old Testament narratives, their dissimilarity is astonishing. *The Flood* is like a picture-book – a patchwork of colourful images and routine story-telling, with a unity, such as it is, based on a *lingua franca* rather than a compelling or consistent artistic thread. *Abraham and Isaac* has neither colourful imagery nor routine. On the face of it it represents an impossible musical concept. A setting in Hebrew, a language Stravinsky did not know, of an essentially dramatic narrative but for a single baritone voice declaiming with almost no interruption, few changes of pace and not much else in the way of superficial contrast. The fact that the work was commissioned by the Israel Festival (in 1962) and is dedicated to 'the people of the State of Israel' hardly encourages one to expect much more than dignity and respectful courtesy in the result.

*Abraham and Isaac* certainly does not go in for striking effects, and many admirers of the composer have found it dull. Stravinsky seems to have envisaged a quasi-liturgical context for his 'sacred ballad' – a context which as usual assumes that the story is known and that its meaning is understood and shared. The story of Abraham is of course the story of the origin of the Jewish nation. The voice of the Rabbi or preacher rarely becomes excited during the twelve-minute narrative, but it does so noticeably at the words 'Ki vareykh avarekkekha . . .' ('That in blessing I will bless thee, and in multiplying I will multiply thy seed as the stars of the heaven, and as the sand which is upon the sea shore'). Otherwise the tone is lofty but even; the story is told swiftly and for the most part syllabically, apparently using the Hebrew syllables to provide the necessary variety within the musical line, as Stravinsky always had done with Russian, and only now and then, briefly, breaking into melisma where the emotion is, so to speak, imposed on the words from 'beyond', rather than simply expressed through them.

The work's ritual character is obvious enough, but it emerges in a form somewhat different from any of Stravinsky's previous 'enactments', or pseudo-liturgies. The absence of incantatory rhythm, and of the sectioning which had always gone with it from *The Rite of Spring* to *Threni*, is a move towards the esoteric which seems to be bound up with Hebrew, a language which for most listeners (though admittedly not the work's original audience) is even more 'secret' than Latin, and which Stravinsky is said to have set respectfully, with attention to its natural accents, as speech rather than dance. The composer tells us that he set the poem of his next work, the *Elegy for JFK*, straight through in the voice before composing the accompaniment, and though he never said anything like that about *Abraham and Isaac* it could almost be true. After the opening bars and before the final page, the only significant passage without voice is the crabbed little processional (and preceding flute cadenza) which accompanies the last stage of the journey to the place of sacrifice. The baritone, on the other hand, is several times unaccompanied, or accompanied only by one or two instruments. These groupings are in a constant state of flux, and in fact provide the main articulation of the form – one which, though discreet, is on the whole more noticeable than the broader textural and metronomic subdivisions insisted on by programme-note descriptions, including Stravinsky's own.[13] Over these fidgety variations of density and colour the voice draws a nearly unbroken line, so that to some extent the piece is like a decorated monody, a journey without pause through a sparsely peopled landscape. This makes it quite unlike Stravinsky's earlier narrative works in feeling or pace. Its relentless vocal line might recall that of the tenor 'Ricercar' in the Cantata, a piece of about the same length. But even there the structure was overtly sectional, and the music wore its technique on its sleeve. In *Abraham and Isaac* the technique is, as it were, alive to the cabbalistic nature behind the whole concept of the work, and it seems to be partly this sense of a hidden coherence bracing a design which, by all accounts, ought to be amorphous, that gives the piece its subtle and lasting fascination.

So far as its serialism is concerned, the work offers a marvellous study of the way the technique can even-handedly provide functional (that is, audible) syntax and arcane structures clearly generated by the system but not obviously detectable as such even by the attentive ear. Once the rotation grid is set up it has a life of its own, and one of its attractions to a mind like Stravinsky's – forever poised between cerebration and superstition – may well have been this blend of the vigorous and systematic with the free and magical. Both factors play a lively role in *Abraham and Isaac*. The serial grid, both in general and in the particular nature of the row in this work, tends to establish networks of potential motives. For instance, the sequence of intervals is repeated in many hexachords; the device of starting every member of a rotation 'family' on the same note provides a built-in method of swivelling from one rotation to another; the fact that rotating gives a high degree of invariance (sameness) from row to row throughout the grid – these are aspects of the system which produce comparatively traditional functions. They help ensure some measure of identity in the material. But the grid also lends itself to what could be called note-generating programmes, which can be set to run mechanically for a time (or in theory indefinitely, but Stravinsky limits himself to a kind of sampling process). The most striking of these is the so-called serial ladder. Here the music pursues a melodic course backwards and forwards, or in one direction only, along adjacent rotations, perhaps completing a full cycle of one part of the grid. Among several examples in *Abraham and Isaac*, the most striking is the angel's speech to Abraham, just before the 'seed of Israel' passage quoted above, where the trigger word 'Vayomer' ('And he said') sets off a complete cycle of Ra forms, starting at the bottom and working upwards (Ex.61). Notice how this mechanism involves a certain consistency of pattern. The common starting-point (F) acts as a reference point along the way, the general sequence of intervals is thematic, and in particular the first interval of each new hexachord automatically repeats the last intervals of the old one, so that we get a pivotal interval as well as a pivotal pitch. It remains nevertheless a mechanism – a system for generating notes. The same can be said of the rotation chords, or serial verticals, whose principle of derivation was described earlier (see *Movements*). The passage describing the ram caught in the thicket is framed by a complete cycle of the chords

Ex. 61(i) Abraham and Isaac

provided by a vertical reading of the IR grid (bars 182–196), starting on the unison F (Ex.62). Spies calls bars 195–6 (the postlude) a 'nonliteral retrograde' of bars 182–3, without pointing out that the audibility of this fact (on which he also comments) is due to the rhythm and scoring.[14] The chords themselves are simply a play-through of the verticals, and indeed such harmonic retrograding as there is is contained *within* each group, because the chord cycle in each hexachord happens with this row to be a palindrome. In any case the exact relation between these verticals and the row itself is a moot point. That the former can be inferred from the latter is a fact *ex hypothesi*, and yet the musical relation remains obscure.

Although mechanisms of this and other kinds are to be found in the *Sermon . . .* and *The Flood*, *Abraham and Isaac* is the first score whose musical density seems commensurate with, and to profit from, the somewhat elaborate technical apparatus that went into its making. And it does seem that, in spite of what Spies tries to tell us about Stravinsky's supposed distaste for 'obscurantism', it is as much the symbolic or magical significance of this apparatus as its lucid rationality which fired the composer's enthusiasm. The characterisation of the Angel of the Lord by a melodic cycle that symbolically but certainly not audibly indicates his perfection; or of the miracle of the Ram by a similarly esoteric chord-cycle; or, above all, the formal association of this same chord structure with the historicist idea of the connection between Abraham's obedience and the role of the Jews as God's chosen people[15] – these suggest a Neoplatonic attitude to number,

*Ex. 61(ii)*

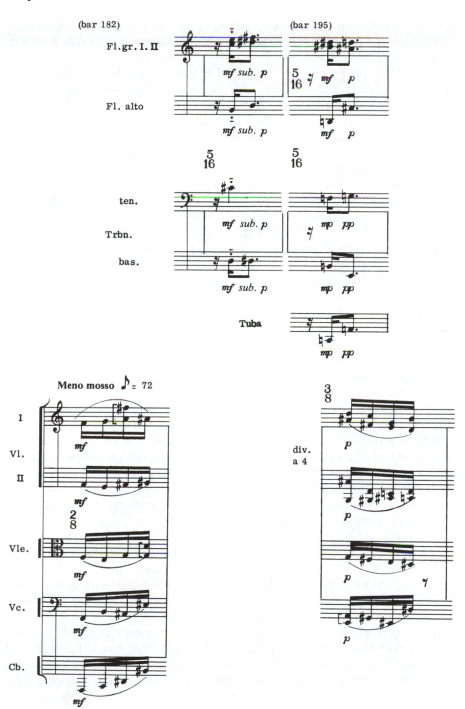

*Ex. 62 Abraham and Isaac*

and they surely link Stravinsky's known belief in the miraculous and the immanence of God with the biblical fundamentalism of orthodox Judaism. At the same time Stravinsky is at pains to endow his symbols with a meaning that can be perceived, even if it is not the whole meaning. The 'obedience' chords are, after all, structural, not only because they recur at obviously important moments, but because chords of any kind are not a general feature of the work's texture, so that when they come they automatically assume a special – perhaps even numinous – significance. This sense of an abstract formalism pervades the whole ballad. Since the normal mode is a light two-part texture, voice and accompanying line (even when the accompaniment is 'hocketed', or split between two or more instruments), any additional line tends to create a sense of 'gesture'. If that line happens to be audibly in canon with the other instrument, that sense will be enhanced. And yet something may remain hidden. When the Angel first speaks to Abraham, tuba and flute accompany the voice in an elaborate canonic trio, with tuba and voice in direct rhythmic canon by augmentation while the flute follows in inversion (unaugmented), and we can hear, as it were, that this is God speaking, from above and below, through the perfection of numerical order (Ex.63). But it seems unlikely that we could hear, without studying the score or being told, that the flute is also in melodic retrograde canon with the voice, or that the complicated rhythms continued by the tuba after the flute has finished are a rationalised multiple of the baritone's triplets in bar 165, which the tuba is still following in rhythmic canon. The whole point of such writing is that consciousness it gives the listener of a significant but transparent surface through which he can perceive, more and more darkly, the shadows, currents, and profound depths of an ocean which he may explore but will never thoroughly and definitively chart. Or, if that seems a rather grandiose metaphor for a comparatively unassuming if masterly work of art, one might refer to that quality in any liturgy which lies beyond the obvious meaning and structure of what is being said and done. What is obscure or esoteric is not necessarily lost for not being directly grasped.

This holds even more true of the work Stravinsky embarked on in the August after finishing *Abraham and Isaac*, the orchestral Variations eventually subtitled 'Aldous Huxley in Memoriam' after Huxley's death in November 1963.[16] He seems to have decided to write an orchestral work simply from preference; the 'in memoriam' element is an inscription, and has no bearing on the work's content, which is exuberant and self-confident. Moreover the abandonment of all text plainly suggests a desire to explore certain abstract formal possibilities within the kind of serial usage that had supported, and in part symbolised, the narrative element in his most recent works. But far from compromising, under these circumstances, with any conventionally thematic design, Stravinsky writes a set of variations *without* theme, leaving the listener to pick up such connections as he can from a few formal and textural hints, from any serial patterns he may be lucky or clever enough

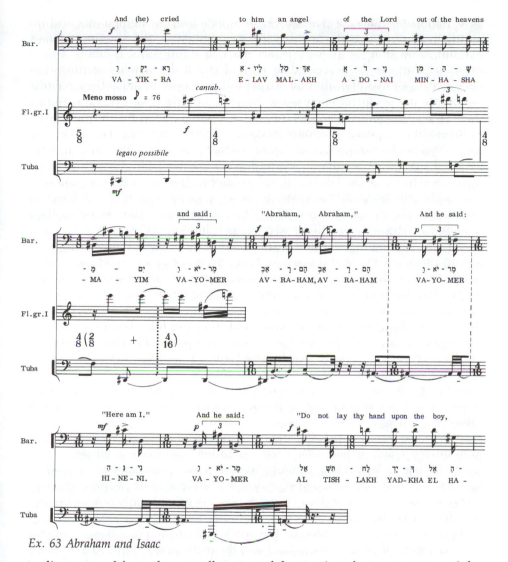

*Ex. 63 Abraham and Isaac*

to discern, and from the overall sweep of the music, whose assurance might
well convince the ear of its coherence even with no other help.

Like *Movements*, with which it obviously invites comparison, the Variations is not altogether a hard work to take in; it is short (no more than
half as long as *Movements*), direct and, in both outline and texture, clear.
In one sense it is like a hollow sculpture which you can easily hold in your
hand, turn round, examine all over, but which somehow resists description
as to its materials or what it might be meant to contain. The work is hard,
bright, and enigmatic. On the other hand it is easy enough to 'analyse'
chemically, once one knows the code.[17] There are twelve variations, of
which the first five form an exposition (stabilised by a repeat of variation 2

as variation 5), the next five are more mobile and developmental, culminating in a fugue, and the last two are recapitulatory. The repeated second variation comes again as no.11, and the three together suggest a refrain form, with the refrains effectively halting the forward rush of the other variations and converting their energy into interior polyphony, while outwardly the music becomes inert. There is an intriguing parallel between this refrain idea and the fourth section of *Movements*, and from there back to Stravinsky's earliest rhythmic designs, like the 'Sacrifical Dance' or the first of the string quartet pieces, where he had first discovered the powerful effect of containing a violent or unstable movement by patterned or cyclic repetition. In *Movements* the music is arrested by a passage which combines harmonic stability with literal rhythmic recurrence. The outer sections of the ternary fourth movement are broadly isometric and include an element of strict isorhythm in the central piano solo, which is rhythmically the same each time. The refrains in the Variations are in the same way both isometric and isorhythmic. But the association between this fact and the formal 'stillness' of these sections is one which exists only in the composer's mind, since the isorhythm as such is certainly not audible. The refrains are written in twelve real parts: the first (variation 2) for solo violins, the second (no.5) for ten violas and two double-basses, and the third (no.11) for woodwind, including a horn. And in each part the quaver pulse is not only variously subdivided but in such a way as to produce minimal synchronisation between instruments. Moreover each repeat has a different distribution of parts, which makes the underlying uniformity of rhythm that much harder to perceive. What *is* noticeable is the evenness of quaver pulse; and, on the other hand, a purely internal animation which strikes the ear as no more than a tremor passing across a fluid but immobile surface. And yet, taken individually, each of these lines has the rhythmic character of the whole work, which is an essentially dynamic character generated by a conflict between rational and irrational elements: between, that is, rhythms that are multiples or factors of the pulse unit, and rhythms that are not. In the opening variation, where the initial chords give way to a bold unison melody sweeping across the whole string range, the entire energy is expressed as a difference between halves, thirds, quarters and fifths of a crotchet unit, and the variation ends with a systematic slowing down from fifths up to whole units. But in the fugal climax the subdivisions are simple and for the most part rational, and this seems to be linked to the idea of a comparatively extended but formally limited kind of contrapuntal movement. Here Stravinsky demands that we should perceive the rhythmic relation between the (no more than four) lines, and he makes it possible for us to do so.

But if the rhythmic design, and with it the form, of the Variations is easy enough to discern (at least in general terms), the same can hardly be said of its serial apparatus. Despite its brevity the work does not, like *Abraham and Isaac*, confine itself to operations on half-rows, but also uses systems based on the complete twelve-note row. It starts off with a series of eleven chords derived from a rotation of the entire retrograded row but only through six of the twelve possible turns, so that the 'verticals' are still six-note chords, as they would be on a complete hexachordal grid. It then proceeds to the unison string passage already discussed, which tracks rapidly through the prime grid melodically, from bottom to top.[18] And this is followed by the first twelve-part refrain, which starts off with twelve different set-forms playing simultaneously but at various speeds. It is again hard to avoid the impression from all this that the pitch structures are a deliberately arbitrary 'programme' for note-generation. Because of the way the row is designed, the prime grid yields no fewer than nine different chords out of eleven; and because of the way it is rotated, the retrograde grid yields another ten. And even if the theoretical organic connection between all this material might in due course become apparent, the work itself is so concise and epigrammatic that it has in practice no chance of doing so. To all intents and purposes the pitches in this cunningly titled work are random.

Harrison Birtwistle has said that he subjects his composition students to a game designed to test their creative resourcefulness. It

> involves picking from a hat bits of paper which have a pitch and a duration written on them. He insists that the order in which they appear should be preserved; the task is to make music from them. This can only be done by the use of dynamics and phrasing, but that, he maintains, is all the leeway the composer needs to create something of interest.[19]

In Stravinsky's Variations the rhythms certainly are not random (not even in the twelve-part sections, where the pulse is highly uniform). And with this additional dimension of choice he can compose an orchestral work of real brilliance. The Variations are demonstrably articulated, athematically, through contrast and uniformities of texture and movement. The refrains make their point as textures of a certain type; the chords at the end clinch the work, even more than the ones in *Abraham and Isaac*, because they are chords in a largely non-chordal work, rather than because of the chords they are. The fugue is articulated through rhythm; and so on. How far the note-generation depends, for the effect required, on the exact configuration of the row used and the method to which it is subjected is an open question. Serial analysts like Spies would claim that it is important, since the alternative is to discount their analyses as irrelevant. Others may have their doubts. The curious fact is that we do not quite know what is inside this fascinating, shiny, hollow sculpture.

The Variations were to be Stravinsky's final experiment along these lines. He made serial sketches for another orchestral work.[20] But the remaining works he actually composed were vocal, and they show definite signs of a wish to restore both melodic and harmonic cohesion within the limitations imposed by words and voices.[21] We can look at the *Introitus* and *Requiem Canticles* and say intelligibly that their slower pacing and, in the latter case, greater length are achieved by reintroducing some measure of redundancy into their language, though this hardly makes them anything but epigrammatic, all the same. As for the two songs, the setting of Auden's 'When a just man dies' (*Elegy for JFK*) for medium voice and three clarinets, and *The Owl and the Pussy Cat* for voice and piano – Stravinsky's final musical 'sigh of relief' – these are deliberately simplified because of the occasion or the text, which is not quite the same thing. Auden's masterly poem for the *Elegy* was written specifically for Stravinsky to compose, and he set it with due concern for its innate properties. He not only observed the seventeen-syllable haiku shape of each verse – setting the words syllabically – but he enhanced the poem's emblematic quality by fitting each verse to a single statement of the row, and by confining himself to row-forms at original pitch. Since the twelve notes have therefore to be drawn out over seventeen syllables we get melodic repetitions, and from verse to verse a certain concentration of pitch: for instance, the rising minor seventh is usually either from D to C or from D sharp to C sharp; the attraction of fifths or fourths between simultaneous row-forms is also once again very marked. The whole setting has a quality of lyrical repose which had been missing from Stravinsky's music since *Threni*, and an intimacy it had not had since the *In Memoriam Dylan Thomas*.[22]

The linearity of the *Elegy* survives to some extent in the *Introitus* which Stravinsky wrote specifically as a tribute to T. S. Eliot after the poet's death in early January 1965.[23] But the context is so different that one is hardly aware of the common ground musically. When all is said and done, the *Elegy* is a secular tribute in a manner that might be characterised as homely oratory; Auden may even have been gently parodying this quality of American speech. The *Introitus*, a setting of the 'Requiem aeternam' from the Burial Service, is an atavistic lament that was surely prompted by something deeper than grief at the death of a fellow artist who had been, however, no more than an acquaintance of the composer's. In a letter to Rufina Ampenoff of Boosey and Hawkes, he calls the work, in Russian, 'Zaupokoynyi' – that is, mourning of the dead.[24] The dark scoring, for male voices, harp, low piano, gongs, timpani, and solo viola and double-bass, and the hieratic solemnity of the harp/piano chords and the calm rhythmic chanting of the tenors and basses – all this has the flavour of some antique ceremony of Old Believers. Its tone, though certainly not its style, is indeed close to that of the chorale in the *Symphonies of Wind Instruments*, written in memory of Debussy. On the other hand the 'muffled drums' are a specifically late obsession. They crop up in the Dekker 'Prayer' of the *Sermon . . .* and again in the Interlude of the *Requiem Canticles*, which Stravinsky tells us was the first part of that work to be composed. They may be only the latest example of a lifelong preoccupation with processions, which goes back at least to the vanished *Chant funèbre* of nearly sixty years before. But while the idea of a 'virtual' liturgy may not be particularly new with Stravinsky, the *Introitus* seems to mark a fresh stage in that history, and one with a completely novel stamp. Unlike the Variations, the *Introitus* is an intensely thematic work, and a richly suggestive one emotionally and atmospherically, without shedding an iota of its modernity.

Formally the piece could hardly be simpler. Like the *Elegy* it is strophic, three verses, each verse consisting of a solemn melody made up of a row-form and its retrograde, followed by a short 'doxology' of *parlando* rhythmic chanting (replaced in the final verse by an instrumental coda). The texts are introduced and interspersed by versets for harp and piano, in the manner of the organ interludes in the *Canticum Sacrum*. Or one could think of them as intonations: three chords each time, with a common rhythm, and a top line like the precentor's initial inflection. The voices are accompanied evenly by timpani, viola and double-bass, the strings being mainly used to bring out the pitches of the kettledrums. The drums themselves play slow sextuplet rolls related to the rhythm of the choral *parlando*.

The most striking aspect of this musically, after the Variations, is the slowness and the very large measure of repetition. Stravinsky continually draws attention to formal recurrences, as well as to the serial design. The strophic scheme is purposely predictable, and each section of text coincides neatly with a row statement, accompanied by another row statement, as in the *Elegy*. Admittedly the intonational chords are more obscure, and perhaps supply an impression of harmony rather than harmony as such. But this is scarcely surprising when one looks at the way Stravinsky derives these chords. In *SPD* (plates 21–2) Craft reproduces the composer's rotation charts for the *Introitus*. They show that Stravinsky laid the row out in groups of four and derived his chords diagonally rather than vertically. But not only did he not do this on consistent geometrical lines, but the charts actually contain errors which allowed Stravinsky to derive chords he could not otherwise have done. The fact is that what creates a sense of consistent harmony in these chords is their common morphology: consistency of scoring, register and spacing, a repeated rhythm, and certain prominent intervals – the tritone, the semitone displaced by an octave. This is the kind of pragmatic chording one associates with an earlier Stravinsky – justified, to be sure, by an appeal to authority equally in keeping with his Thomist mentality. It seems very far from the actual authoritarianism of the note-streams in the Variations, which hardly appear to have undergone his hawk-eyed scrutiny at all.

It seems appropriate that the culminating and most powerful score of this last period should both resolve the apparent conflict in two such important works, and should do so in a manner which aligns it unmistakably with the great ritual works of Stravinsky's heyday. The *Requiem Canticles* may not be Stravinsky's finest score; it would be asking a lot of a composer in his eighty-fifth year (it was composed between March 1965 and August 1966) that he should approach, let alone surpass, the achievement of works like *The Rite of Spring*, *The Wedding*, *Oedipus rex* or the *Symphony of Psalms*. But in its own context the *Requiem Canticles* is not unworthy of standing beside those masterpieces. Not the least of its virtues is that it recognises the limitations of the octogenarian mind, and turns them to account. A work of brief segments, that judiciously sets only select portions of the Proper of the Requiem Mass, it balances them, paces them, and in the end ritualises them. It has that quality of succinctness and reserve one associates with the late periods of great artists; but it is not *merely* concise – as if brevity were a virtue in itself, without consideration of what is being briefly said.

According to a letter from Stravinsky to Nicolas Nabokov,[25] the *Requiem Canticles* started life as a 'symphony' for the orchestra of Princeton University. The orchestral interlude was its first idea. But at this stage, perhaps more than at any previous time, Stravinsky's ideas seem to have been forming as sealed units, and it may well have been the intractability of these units that decided him against a purely orchestral work and in favour of what he called 'a *retablo* of small panels', with a formal or, so to speak, inert text.[26] One can observe how, in the orchestral prelude, the music seems willing to expand only through intensified restatement – by enrichments of the ostinato, or by the accumulation of lines round the solo violin melody, which is itself repeated literally (Ex.64). The music is completely airtight; it does not, like the otherwise comparable units in *The Rite* or *The Wedding*, 'leak' into anything new. Under these circumstances a lapidary text was called for, or one which could be abbreviated without loss of weight, and for this the Latin text of the Requiem was ideal. Stravinsky took only fragments of the Proper and omitted the Ordinary, which he had of course already set in his Mass; he set only the 'Exaudi' from the Introit, overlapping to this extent with the text of his own *Introitus*; of the 'Dies irae' he set only six verses in all, divided as 'Dies irae' (verses 1 and 2), 'Tuba mirum', 'Rex tremendae', and 'Lacrimosa' (the last two verses); and he set the 'Libera me' complete. Each section is compressed, or purified, essence: a distillation, rather than a shortened liturgy for practical use. For instance, the 'Dies irae' merely touches on the instinctive rhetoric of the romantic response to this text, but the gesture is dismissed almost as soon as formulated, though a faint echo of it sounds in the stifled trochees of the Interlude, with its veiled scoring for four flutes, horns and timpani. Only the 'Lacrimosa' is composed out, using for the purpose the automatic serial device of the rotation cycle (the contralto solo tracks all the way round the IR grid). In the 'Libera me' Stravinsky completes the text by having the choir speak it 'congregationally' against a shortened form sung by four soloists – a dramatic effect obviously indebted to Verdi's setting of this prayer, though again avoiding the slight hint of theatre in his work. Even the 'Dies irae' is largely eked out textually by rhythmic *parlando*, like the spoken passages in the *Introitus*; the only essentially choral part of the music is the actual repeated cry of 'Dies irae, dies illa'.

It must be the way in which the *Requiem Canticles* is controlled by strong,

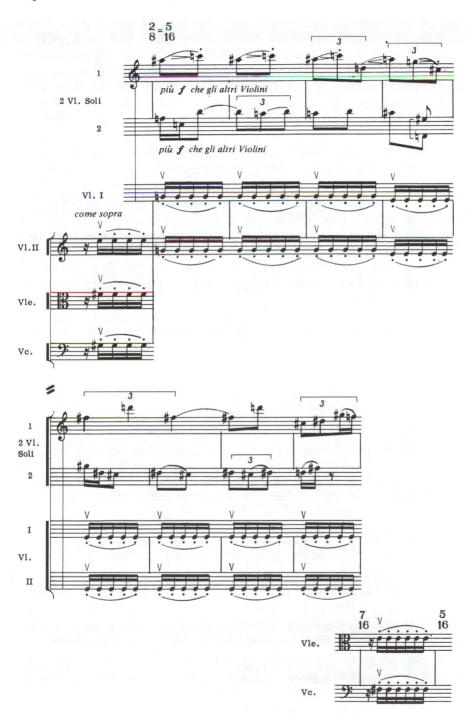

*Ex. 64 Requiem Canticles, 'Prelude'*

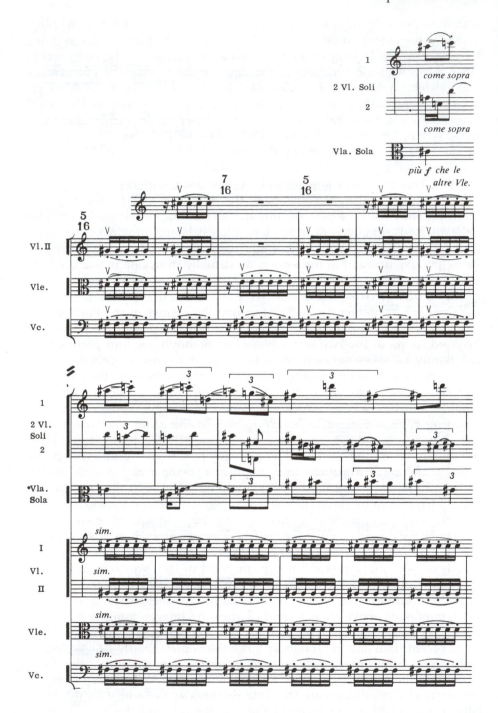

instantaneous musical images of this kind that gives the work a vividness
and to some extent an immediacy which had also begun to emerge in the
*Introitus* but was lacking or only intermittently present in the other works
since *Agon*. It also contributes to the unity of the score. When Stravinsky
was catching hold of musical ideas like this, in a single frame of mind, he
seemed able to match them instinctively, as Forte's analysis of *The Rite of
Spring* shows. One wonders whether he returned to the piano more often
while writing the *Requiem Canticles* than when writing, say, the Variations
or *The Flood*. At any rate, the underlying chordal ostinato of the Prelude,
the 'Dies irae' cry, the chords in the Interlude, the 'Lacrimosa' and above
all the 'Libera me', have both a family resemblance, with their many perfect
fifths (as against the typical tritone of the *Introitus* chords), and suggest –
knowing Stravinsky – a pianistic origin. The fact that the similarity can also
be 'explained' serially is of much less interest, since Stravinsky used two
complete series for this fifteen-minute score and thereby gave himself so
many possibilities within the system as virtually to negate it as a unifying
force. As in the Variations, serial method may help justify any aspect of the
music which otherwise resists analysis, but it seems that the real function of
the rows is to generate notes. The fact that the chimes in the Postlude, so
redolent of the ending of *The Wedding*, are constructed from the prime and
inverted forms of the two series played as homophonic four-part chords,
can hardly be taken seriously as a factor in any sense of culmination or
summation this beautiful ending may have, not least because the four parts
criss-cross, just as the eight parts at the end of *Threni* had done. The serial
bonding must be left as an esoteric aspect of these sonorities: a private
concern of the composer in his workshop. In the same way, the intense
lyrical outpouring of the 'Lacrimosa' may make its effect partly through the
binding force of the sustained accompanying chords, and even partly
through the recurring intervals and pitches of the rotation cycle in the
melody itself; but it can hardly have anything to do with the fact that the
chords happen to be serial verticals of the same grid as the melody.

In the end *Requiem Canticles* makes a moving and satisfying conclusion
to Stravinsky's long creative life, not because it shows him at eighty-four
still as modern-minded as he was at thirty, and certainly not because it
parades a systematic method which, in point of fact, was out of date ten
years before it was written, but precisely because it absorbs these things
into a revived personal vision. With all its hidden technical resources, the
work impresses above all as a fund of arresting images, unified by factors
which are partly thematic, partly tonal (the notes F and C are a tonic axis
more potent than any in Stravinsky since the Septet), partly balletic, partly
associative. If the Interlude dances in much the same way that the 'Gaillarde' had danced in *Agon*, the 'Rex tremendae' harks back as far as the
*Symphony of Psalms* (compare the flute rhythms at the end with the three
bars before fig.20 in the finale of the symphony), and the very opening
suggests a mannerism of neo-classical orchestral works like the Symphony

in C. In a word, the music moves and breathes like Stravinsky. In doing so it avoids any false affectation of heaviness or monumentality. As a Requiem the work has perhaps an unexpected radiance. Spies refers, rightly, to its serenity. As the master turns, with a sigh of relief, to the nonsense verse of Edward Lear, we should not expect him to draw a thick black line under his life's work. On the contrary we find with delight that he can survey it in the same calm, detached yet joyous spirit with which he greeted the death of his first *alter ego*, the puppet Petrushka, and the symbolic death and rebirth of the eternal peasant couple, Nastasya Timofey-evna and Fetis Pamfilyevich.

# Notes

## Chapter 2 A Russian in St Petersburg: **The Firebird**

1 Vera Stravinsky and Robert Craft, *Stravinsky in Pictures and Documents* (Simon & Schuster, New York, 1978), p. 22 (hereafter referred to as *SPD*). The text of this book is apparently entirely by Craft.

2 Igor Stravinsky and Robert Craft, *Memories and Commentaries* (Faber, London, 1960), p. 22 (hereafter *Mem.*).

3 Igor Stravinsky, *Chroniques de ma vie* (Denoël & Steele, Paris, 1935, 1936), translated into English as *An Autobiography* (Gollancz, London, and Simon & Schuster, New York, 1936), p. 15 (hereafter *Chron.*). Page references are to the American edition.

4 Stravinsky himself attributed this omission to Rimsky's wish to avoid favouritism. *Mem.*, p. 58.

5 Kashperova is described in *Mem.*, pp. 25–6; for the others, see Stravinsky and Craft, *Expositions and Developments* (Faber, London, 1962), pp. 42–3 (hereafter *Expo.*).

6 The authority for this is *Chron.*, p. 23. One hesitates to place faith in so unreliable a source, though Stravinsky describes the event not in passing but as a clear and decisive memory. According to Craft, in *Stravinsky: Selected Correspondence II* (Faber, London, 1984; hereafter *SSCII*), p. 432, the music was only begun in November 1908, five months after Rimsky's death. In early April 1908 (NS) Stravinsky was still working on drafts of the libretto. It does not follow, however, that no musical sketches were made at that time.

7 See also Richard Taruskin, *Opera and Drama in Russia* (UMI Research Press, Ann Arbor, Michigan, 1981), pp. 79–140, for a detailed account of a similar hybridisation in Serov's opera, *Rogneda*.

8 *Chron.*, p. 20.

9 *SPD*, p. 22. The letter to G. N. Timofeyev (13.III.1908' OS), is complete in *I. F. Stravinsky: Articles and Materials*, ed. L. S. Dyachkova (Moscow, 1973; hereafter *SAM*), pp. 444–5.

10 Not, as Craft states (*SPD*, p. 608, n. 83), the 'autograph score'.

11 Rimsky himself considered Gorodyetsky's folk language false. Craft, however, describes the poem of 'Song of the Dew' as an 'adaptation' from (presumably authentic) Russian sectarian verse. *SSCI* (1982), p. 421.

12 One later ballet, *The Fairy's Kiss*, refers to this tradition, but can hardly be said to belong to it.

13 *SAM*, pp. 441–42. A translation appears in *SPD*, pp. 49–50.

14 R. Vlad, *Stravinsky* (2nd ed., Oxford University Press, London, 1967), p. 46.

15 *SPD*, p. 39.

16 *Stravinsky, the Composer and his Works* (2nd ed., Faber, London, 1979), p. 188.

## Chapter 3 A Russian in Paris: **Petrushka** and **The Rite of Spring**

1 Stravinsky, letter to Andrei Rimsky-Korsakov, 20 January 1911, *SAM*, p. 453, quoted in *SPD*, p. 67.
2 *Chron.*, p. 31.
3 The main fig. no., here and below, refers to the revised score of 1947, the bracketed number to the original score of 1911.
4 The notes all come from one octatonic scale, but that might well be merely the result of mixing triads a tritone apart.
5 Letter of 16 December 1910, *SAM*, pp. 451–52; also in *SPD*, p. 54.
6 Identified in *SPD*, pp. 608–9, as 'the cries of the vendors of coal, marinated apples and herring'. Craft's information is from Irina Vershinina, *Stravinsky's Early Ballets* (Moscow, 1967).
7 Debussy had also experimented with montage. There are examples in the *Sérénade interrompue* and the orchestral *Ibéria*, which had been played in Paris in 1910. But the formal innovation is not combined with polymetrics, as it is in Stravinsky.
8 Letter of 10 April 1913, in Igor Stravinsky and Robert Craft, *Conversations with Igor Stravinsky* (Faber, London, 1959; hereafter *Conv.*), pp. 48–9.
9 *Expo.*, p. 137.
10 *SAM*, pp. 466–7; quoted in *SPD*, p. 84.
11 *The Two Poems of Verlaine* and *Two Poems of Balmont*, published in 1911 and 1912 respectively, were composed for voice and piano, while the *Three Japanese Lyrics* were from the first accompanied by a mixed ensemble. The ensemble arrangements of the Verlaine and Balmont sets (of scattered date but published in 1953 and 1955 respectively) incorporate changes of musical detail which were then put back into the new versions with piano published at about the same time by Boosey and Hawkes. This illustrates a complication of editions unhappily all too typical of Stravinsky. Richard Taruskin has recently proved that Stravinsky originally set the Verlaine poems in Stepan Mitussov's Russian translation. See 'Stravinsky's "*Rejoicing Discovery*" ', in E. Haimo and P. Johnson eds., *Stravinsky Retrospectives* (University of Nebraska Press, Lincoln and London, 1987), pp. 162–199.
12 See Morton, 'Footnotes to Stravinsky Studies: Le Sacre du printemps', *Tempo* 128 (March, 1979), pp. 9–16. But see also Simon Karlinsky, 'Stravinsky and Russian Pre-Literate Theater', *19th Century Music*, vi (1983), pp. 232–40, especially p. 235, for several alternative possible sources. Karlinsky's article should in any case be read for its fascinating information on the cultural background of all Stravinsky's main works of this period – information which is generally not otherwise available in English. The photograph referred to is reproduced in Theodore Strawinsky, *Catherine and Igor Stravinsky: A Family Album* (Boosey & Hawkes, London, 1973).
13 Morton refers to Yarila as 'the god of spring and fecundity'. Russell Zguta, however, describes a pre-Lenten ceremony still observed by the Eastern Slavs, in which Iarilo is one of the names given to the god of winter, whose effigy is ritually burnt in the form of a straw or wooden puppet. Zguta, *Russian Minstrels* (Oxford University Press, London, 1978), p. 115.
14 *Mem.*, p. 83.
15 Postcard to Florent Schmitt, 21 July 1911. The card is quoted in *SPD*, pp. 61 and 63, but is missing from the Stravinsky/Schmitt correspondence in *SSCII*.
16 *Avec Stravinsky* (Editions du Rocher, Monaco, 1958), p. 105.
17 *Conv.*, p. 51.

18 See *SSCI*, pp. 50 and 51 and Taruskin, *op. cit.* (1987), pp. 170–1. Taruskin's interpretation is similar to mine, but nore detailed and complete.
19 *Chron.*, p. 45.
20 *Chron.*, p. 43. Debussy's letter (14 October 1915) is quoted in *SPD*, p. 66.
21 *Mem.*, p. 30.
22 *Chron.*, p. 31.
23 *The Sketches for* The Rite of Spring (Boosey & Hawkes, London, 1969).
24 Taruskin, 'Russian Folk Melodies in *The Rite of Spring*', *Journal of the American Musicological Society*, xxxiii (Fall, 1980), pp. 501–43. See also Lawrence Morton (1979), pp. 12–16.
25 *SAM*, pp. 470–71; quoted in *SPD*, p. 92. (See chapter 4, n. 35.)
26 'Stravinsky demeure', in Boulez, *Relevés d'apprenti* (Éditions du Seuil, Paris, 1966), pp. 75–145.
27 Allen Forte, *The Harmonic Organization of* The Rite of Spring (Yale University Press, New Haven and London, 1978).
28 Pieter van den Toorn, *The Music of Igor Stravinsky* (Yale University Press, New Haven, 1983). The actual term used there is 'interpenetration', which is a fair sample of the author's prose.

## Chapter 4 Willing Exile: **The Wedding**

1 Stravinsky to Benois, letter of 13 July 1911, *SAM*, pp. 457–9; quoted in *SPD*, pp. 113–14.
2 The correspondence with Sanine, as well as with Stravinsky's publisher Nicholas Struve and the conductor Alexander Ziloti, on the subject of *The Nightingale* is printed in the form of substantial excerpts in *SSCII*, pp. 197–218. In the same volume, Appendix C, pp. 432–47, is an early draft of the libretto, and a series of letters to Stravinsky from his co-librettist Stepan Mitussov. Benois's letters to Stravinsky are in *Mem.*, pp. 134–43, and Stravinsky's to Benois in *SPD*, pp. 113–19, but also, more fully, in Russian in *SAM*.
3 *Expo.*, p. 62n; *Mem.*, p. 131n.
4 *SPD*, p. 132.
5 According to Craft. See *SSCI*, p. 421.
6 *Expo.*, p. 114.
7 In the *Four Studies* of 1928. According to Stravinsky's own programme note on the studies, the orchestrations of the quartet pieces were 'completed in 1917' (Igor Stravinsky, *Themes and Conclusions* [Faber, London, 1972: henceforth *T& C*], pp. 42–3). The fourth orchestration, of the *Study for pianola* of 1917, was added eleven years later.
8 The same is obviously true of passages like the episode at fig.94 in *The Rite of Spring*, where the clarinets' doubling at the seventh creates a complex mixture effect rather than a sense of polyphony.
9 Prokofiev was the first of many to express delight at the way Stravinsky imitates the emptying of the bottle in the oboe/clarinet cadenza. See his letter of 9 December 1919 to Stravinsky, quoted in *SPD*, p. 132.
10 Igor Stravinsky and Robert Craft, *Dialogues and a Diary* (Faber, London, 1968), p. 41. Henceforth *Dial*. This later appeared (1982) in an edition without the 'diary', which had meanwhile been incorporated in Craft's *Stravinsky: the Chronicle of a Friendship* (Gollancz, London, 1972). Page references for the two editions of *Dialogues* are the same.
11 Boulez (1966).

12 Read, *A Concise History of Modern Painting* (Thames & Hudson, London, 1959), p. 106.
13 *Le Coq et l'arlequin* (Paris, 1918), pp. 60, 69.
14 *SPD*, p. 151.
15 Boris Asafyev, *A Book about Stravinsky*, trans. Richard French (UMI Research Press, Ann Arbor, Michigan, 1982).
16 *SPD.*, p. 137.
17 See Karlinsky (1983).
18 The issue is raised and summarily discussed by Mikhail Druskin, in *Igor Stravinsky: his personality, works and views*, trans. Martin Cooper (Cambridge University Press, Cambridge, 1983), pp. 54–7.
19 Among his designers was Sergei Sudeikin, the future second husband of Stravinsky's even more future second wife Vera.
20 Edward Braun, *The Director and the Stage* (Methuen, London, 1982), p. 124.
21 'The Fairground Booth' (1911–12), in *Meyerhold on Theatre*, ed. Braun (Methuen, London, 1969), pp. 119–28 (italics his). The title of the article and some of its ideas originated in Blok's play of that name, which Meyerhold had staged in December 1906.
22 Braun (1982), p. 122.
23 Zguta (1978).
24 *Expo.*, p. 119.
25 *Expo.*, p. 120.
26 Stravinsky, 'Some Ideas about my Octuor', *The Arts* (Brooklyn, January 1924), reprinted in White (1979), pp. 574–7.
27 Karlinsky (1983), p. 240, note 23. Karlinsky is quoting Propp, *Russian Agrarian Festivals* (Leningrad, 1963).
28 *SSCI*, pp. 41–9.
29 On the sound-track of Tony Palmer's Stravinsky film (1982). The first mention of the work in Stravinsky's published correspondence is in Sanine's letter to him of 17 February 1913 (presumably OS). 'You mentioned something to me about your *Svadba* . . . Evidently you have given thought to that work for a long time now.' (*SSCII*, p. 198; the elision is apparently editorial). This seems to confirm that the idea for the ballet originated some time in 1912.
30 *SPD*, p. 151.
31 Though there are striking exceptions, such as the initial sketching for strings of ideas which eventually turned into the *Symphonies of Wind Instruments*.
32 Karlinsky (1983), p. 236.
33 *Expo.*, p. 116.
34 See Craft's foreword to Asafyev (1982), pp. xiii–xiv.
35 In December 1912 Stravinsky wrote to Findeizen about *The Rite*: 'I wanted the whole of the composition to give the feeling of closeness between men and earth . . . and I sought to do this in lapidary rhythms. The whole thing must be put on in dance from beginning to end. I give not one measure for pantomime.' See *SAM*, pp. 470–71, and *SPD*, p. 92.
36 Valentina Kholopova ('Cholopova'), 'Russische Quellen der Rhythmik Strawinskys', *Musikforschung*, xxvii (1974), pp. 435–46.

## Chapter 5 Enforced Exile: **The Soldier's Tale**

1 It seems misleading to say, as Roman Vlad and others do, that after a three-year absence he is not recognised (Vlad [1967], p. 61). The point is that he is regarded as a 'dead' man. According to Frazer: 'in Ancient Greece any man who had been supposed erroneously to be dead, and for whom in his absence funeral rites had been performed, was treated as dead to society till he had gone through the form of being born again' (*The Golden Bough*, St Martin's Library edition, p. 19). This form is presumably not available to Stravinsky's Soldier, because he has sold his soul, in the shape of his violin, to the Devil.

2 See *SSCII*, Appendix E, p. 452 *et seq*.

3 *Mem.*, p. 92.

4 Stravinsky's remark, in *Dial.*, p. 54, that 'I began the *Ragtime* for eleven instruments in October 1918 and finished it on the morning of the Armistice' is typical of his habit of remembering facts as anecdotes, a habit which helped perpetuate (notably in White) the myth of an irrational genius leaping from one isolated masterpiece to another like a giant in seven-league boots. Admittedly the composer did sometimes try to mend the worst effects of this habit, as in the remark about *Pulcinella* quoted above.

5 *Chron.*, p. 78.

6 Asafyev (1982), p. 227.

7 *SPD*, p. 169.

8 *SPD*, p. 623, n. 280.

9 The work was originally to have been called 'The Soldier, the Violin, and the Devil' (*SPD*, p. 168). The second theme of the 'Little Concert' is the tune which Stravinsky says he dreamt (*Conv.*, p. 17), though the originally notated version of this melody, which Craft quotes on the same page of *SPD*, is different in form from the final version which Stravinsky gives as the melody of his dream.

10 *SPD*, p. 631, nn. 47 and 48.

11 Stravinsky took his material from two of Pergolesi's *opere buffe*, *Il Flaminio* and *Lo frate 'nnamorato*, together with a cantata and various instrumental sonatas. These instrumental pieces are no longer considered to be by Pergolesi, but that is of course neither here nor there as regards *Pulcinella*.

12 Picasso's first sketch of the composer was made in Rome that year. See *Conv.*, p. 104.

13 According to *Chron.*, p. 93, he first saw *Parade* at the end of 1920. He had, however, 'played the music on the piano, seen photographs of the scenery and costumes, and was intimately acquainted with the scenario'.

14 Interview in *Le vingtième siècle* of 27 May 1930, quoted in *SPD*, p. 256.

15 It was at this very time that he returned to the Concertino and rescored it for a mixed ensemble of twelve instruments, though he revised and rescored so many early works in the late 1940s and early 1950s that one should perhaps not attach too much significance to such parallels. White (1979) maintains that 'the success of this new version confirms one's feeling that the string quartet was not the ideal medium for the original composition' (p. 291). For what it is worth, my own feeling is the exact opposite. The integrity of the original scoring enhances the music's precision. But see David Drew, 'Stravinsky's Revisions', *The Score*, xx (1957), pp. 55–8, for an illuminating and suggestive discussion of the changes of harmony in the revision, which, in his view, clarify ideas that were merely latent in the first version.

16 Van den Toorn (1983), pp. 342–3.

17 Programme note, reproduced in *SSCI*, p. 339.

18  Apart from simple decorative triplets, Stravinsky does not use irrational *gruppetti* in this work. He seems to prefer simple pulse relations, and to allow such oblique changes of motion as result.

19  1924, pp. 5–6; reprinted in White (1979), pp. 574–7.

20  In 1917 he even arranged the *Song of the Volga Boatmen* for wind and percussion, after Diaghilev decided that the abdication of the Tsar meant that he could no longer use the Russian national anthem.

21  This is not the place to embark on a critical report on the textual problems surrounding the *Symphonies*, nor is all the necessary material yet to hand. But a brief textual history may help the reader to understand what is at issue. Apart from sketches, the primary MS source is the particell, or short-score draft, now in the Paul Sacher Stiftung in Basle. This is dated, at the end, 20 June 1920, and, just before the final chorale, 2 July 1920, the break in sequence being apparently due to the need to finish the chorale for the *Revue musicale* of December. Next comes the MS full score, also in Basle, dated 30 November 1920. This and the orchestral material (apparently one set only) were kept on hire, first by Chester, then, after 1923, by Editions Russes de Musique, and were used by Koussevitzky for the first performance (London, June 1921), and subsequently by Ansermet, Goossens and Stravinsky himself. But although other copies must have been made (for Stokowski in the USA and for Prévost in Antwerp), nothing seems to have been printed apart from Lourié's piano reduction, which ERM published in 1926. The first certain printed material is the set of proofs which Ansermet corrected on Stravinsky's behalf in June/ July 1933. These proofs, also now in Basle, probably led directly to a printed (possibly page-proof) full score which to this day is the version held by Boosey and Hawkes as performing material for the 1920 version. However, a third set of proofs survives (in Basle) which cannot be reconciled with the above sets, but which incorporates a few changes made also straight on to the MS full score (for example a change from horns to bassoons on the first page). So far I have not been able to date this set. In any case ERM almost certainly never brought the work out. When Robert Craft approached the composer about performance material in 1947, Stravinsky not only claimed that it was unobtainable, but seemed not to know whether it had or had not ever been published (see *SSCI*, p. 330; also his letter to Ralph Hawkes of 7 October 1947, in *SSCIII*, p. 318). Soon afterwards he carried out the revision which formed the basis of the work's first full publication.
    In view of Stravinsky's later uncertainty about the publication of the original version, it is by no means easy to establish why the score did not, in fact, come out. There is plenty of evidence that the composer was unhappy with the work, but one cannot claim that the revision settles the point since he published just as comprehensive revisions of other early works which had not previously been withheld: the Concertino for one, *Petrushka* for another. It may be that the work was the victim of its own severity of style and unusual instrumentation and of the fact that, by the time it should have been published, it was completely out of step with Stravinsky's latest work. *The Rite of Spring*, admittedly, was first published in score in 1921, when its style was no longer current. But that was the most notorious score of one of the most famous living composers; it was in the repertory of the Ballets Russes; and it was for a more or less standard symphony orchestra. In any case it would no doubt have appeared sooner but for the war. Not one of Stravinsky's pre-war publishers – neither Chester, nor Hansen, nor ERM, who all had the chance – ever showed any real interest in putting money into the *Symphonies*.

22  Amateur psychologists can amuse themselves speculating why, in a letter to Ansermet of 26 January 1948 (in *SSCI*, p. 230), the composer assured the

conductor: 'you are wrong; there was never an F on the first quaver of the third bar of 45'. There is in fact an F here in every version I have seen of the score before 1947. Since Ansermet had pressed Stravinsky to allow him to conduct the 1920 version, it looks as if the composer was particularly aware of a weakness in the original score at that point and preferred in effect to deny its existence.

## Chapter 6 Synthesis: **Mavra** and the New Classicism

1 Stravinsky met Valéry in 1921 or 1922 (see *Mem.*, p. 73), and Maritain in 1926. But he must have known Maritain's writings before that, in particular *Art et scolastique* (1920), which derives many ideas now associated with neo-classicism from the calm, contemplative spirit of neo-Thomism.
2 See Stravinsky (1924), reprinted in White (1979), pp. 574–7.
3 'Schoenberg, Stravinsky, and Neo-Classicism: The Issues Reexamined', *Musical Quarterly*, lxviii (1982), pp. 527–42.
4 *The Times*, 18 October 1921, reprinted in White (1979), pp. 573–4; also 4 November 1921, in *SPD*, p. 231; and *Le Figaro*, May 1922, in *SPD*, p. 231.
5 *The Times*, 18 October 1921. Cocteau's remark (his italics) is in Cocteau (1979), p. 61.
6 *Le Figaro*, May 1922, quoted in English in *SPD*, p. 231.
7 Asafyev (1982), p. 198 and p. 221 n. 2.
8 *Expo.*, p. 82.
9 *Ibid.*, p. 83. Where Tchaikovsky's *Mazeppa* would have fitted into this picture is unclear but perhaps not crucial.
10 For instance, *Expo.*, p. 82.
11 I am ignoring here the current avant-garde use of the term 'process-music', which involves mechanical, self-propelling systems rather in the manner of Stravinsky's first piece for string quartet.
12 *Comoedia illustré*, 11 December 1920, reprinted as 'Interpretation by Massine', in Minna Lederman ed., *Stravinsky in the Theatre* (Pellegrini and Cudahy, New York, 1949), pp. 24–6.
13 The other was in 1951, after *The Rake's Progress*. Then, too, Stravinsky would go through a period of talking about his music as if it had no past, 'as if,' to quote van den Toorn, 'serialism, construed as some grievously overlooked Final Solution, could in some ultimate sense threaten the legitimacy of all other processes of musical invention.' Van den Toorn (1983), p. 413.
14 Interview in *Le vingtième siècle* (Brussels), 27 May 1930, quoted in *SPD*, p. 217.
15 See for instance Lourié's article 'La sonate pour piano de Strawinsky' in *La revue musicale*, vi (1925), pp. 100–4.
16 The relevant sketches and drafts are in the Paul Sacher Stiftung in Basle. See also Craft's Appendixes E and F of *SSCII*, pp. 452–67. Stravinsky's own remarks on the evolution of the *Piano Concerto* are quoted from an unpublished MS of December 1928 in *SPD*, p. 197.
17 *Petrushka* was also plundered for the Three Movements for solo piano, written for Rubinstein in the late summer of 1921.
18 Asafyev (1982), p. 8.
19 But see *Chron.*, pp. 123–4, where Stravinsky implies, without quite stating, that the four movements were planned so as to fit on two 78 rpm records.
20 Leonard B. Meyer has drawn attention to the characteristic baroque phrase structure of this theme in *Explaining Music* (University of California Press, Berkeley, 1973), p. 209.

21 As Craft points out, the passage after fig.35 rather than the start of this section. The sketch books in the Sacher Stiftung call in question, if inconclusively, Stravinsky's assertion (*Dial.*, p. 39) that 'the first movement came first and was followed immediately by the waltz'. But Stravinsky may have been thinking simply of the sequence of events after the dream which, he claims, gave him his ensemble. In *Chron.*, p. 103, he tells us that he started writing the music 'without knowing what its sound medium would be'. As so often with Stravinsky's self-contradictions it is fairly easy, by fusing the different stories and adding a pinch of salt, to work out a probable sequence of events.

22 Prokofiev's letter is quoted in *SPD*, p. 259. For Samuel's remark, see his *Prokofiev*, trans. Miriam John (Calder, London, 1971), p. 96.

23 White (1979), p. 315.

24 The movement was not Stravinsky's first conception, nor, according to his own view, very much like it. The MS of the original was somehow lost during composition, and Stravinsky was unable to reconstruct the music. *Expo.*, p. 46.

25 This incident, after the premiere of *Mavra*, is touched on in *Conv.*, p. 89, but more picturesquely elaborated by G. D. Painter, in *Marcel Proust*, vol 2 (Chatto & Windus, London, 1965), pp. 340–1.

26 William E. Benjamin, 'Tonality without 5ths: Remarks on the First Movement of Stravinsky's Concerto for Piano and Wind Instruments', *In Theory Only*, ii (November–December 1977), pp. 53–70.

## Chapter 7 The Christian Rites of Spring: **Oedipus** and **Persephone**

1 Letter to Diaghilev, 6 April 1926, *SSCII*, pp. 40–1.

2 *Expo.*, p. 76.

3 Maritain (1935), p. 3 (italics his).

4 Lourié, 'A propos de l'Apollon d'Igor Strawinsky', *Musique*, i (1928), pp. 117–9. See also 'La sonate pour piano de Strawinsky', *Revue musicale*, vi (1925), pp. 100–4; 'Oedipus-Rex', *Revue musicale*, viii (1927), pp. 240–53; 'Neo-Gothic and Neo-Classic', *Modern Music*, v (1928), pp. 3–8. Despite his admiration for and long friendship with Stravinsky, Maritain seems to have taken more interest, in theory at least, in the music of Lourié.

5 *SPD*, p. 211.

6 No doubt the Frenchness of the *Poetics* owes something to the ghost-authorship of Roland-Manuel, who, however, was no Thomist himself (see Craft's Appendix, 'Roland-Manuel and "La Poétique musicale"', in *SSCII*, pp. 503–17).

7 Lourié (1927), p. 240.

8 *Dial.*, p. 21.

9 *SSCI*, p. 94.

10 See for instance *SPD*, p. 270.

11 But at the Kroll production of *Oedipus* in Berlin in February 1928 he wore a black pierrot costume. As a skirmish in Stravinsky's lifelong war with monocled Prussians the reason for this is worth repeating: 'Herr Professor Strawinsky,' the theatre director is said to have pointed out, 'in our country only the *Kapellmeister* is allowed to wear a *Frack*' (*Dial.*, p. 25). Which calls to mind Antheil's story of why Stravinsky refused a well-known maestro permission to conduct *The Firebird*: 'It is too difficult for a German conductor': *Bad Boy of Music* (National Book Association, London, 1949), p. 35.

12 Lourié (1927), p. 252.

13 For details, see the correspondence with Cocteau in *SSCI*, pp. 94–113.

14 Lourié (1927), p. 243.

15 He himself conducted a series of performances of *Petrushka* and *The Nightingale* at La Scala that month. *SPD*, p. 265.

16 This traffic was by no means one-way. Puccini, who was one of the great listeners of his day and a broad-minded musician with latent modernist sympathies, borrowed several ideas from Stravinsky in his later operas, *Il trittico* and *Turandot*. The layered harmonies at the start of *Turandot* are directly indebted to *The Rite of Spring*. For other examples, see Mosco Carner's chapter 'The Score' in the English National Opera guide *Turandot* (Calder, London, 1984), pp. 19–34.

17 The minor third seems, however, to have been the starting-point for many Stravinsky works, from *The Rite of Spring* to the *Capriccio*, *The Rake's Progress*, the Symphony in Three Movements and on to proto-serial works like 'Musick to heare' and *In Memoriam Dylan Thomas*. The equivocation with the major third is also nearly always important.

18 *Poetics of Music*, trans. Arthur Knodel and Ingolf Dahl (Harvard University Press, Cambridge, Mass., 1947), pp. 80–1.

19 See David Bancroft, 'Stravinsky and the "NRF" (1920–29)', *Music and Letters*, lv (1974), pp. 261–71.

20 Apocryphal *Acts of John*, 95, trans. M. R. James (London, 1924).

21 *Dial.*, p. 33.

22 No doubt Maritain did not quite mean this kind of borrowing when he wrote: 'La *conception* de l'oeuvre est tout autre chose que le simple choix du sujet (le sujet n'est que la *matière* de cette conception, et il y a même pour l'artiste ou le poète certains avantages . . . à recevoir d'autrui cette matière)' (1935, p. 237, n. 95). All the same his remarks about the difference between conception and materials can be plausibly extended to such procedures.

23 'Stravinsky and Tchaikovsky: *Le Baiser de la fée*', *Musical Quarterly*, xlviii (1962), pp. 313–26.

24 Vlad (1967), p. 92.

25 The composer told a Belgian interviewer that the symphony was 'inspired by a biblical text of Saint Jerome'. See *SPD*, p. 294.

26 This was, however, the Sunday after Easter. The reference must be to the Resurrection, especially since – though it does not always do so – Russian Easter fell on the same day in that year.

27 *SPD*, pp. 294–5.

28 Maritain (1935). The internal quotations are from Aquinas.

29 Both the Mass and the *Canticum sacrum* are wind-based scores. But curiously enough neither in these works, nor in the *Symphony of Psalms*, nor in Stravinsky's very last sacred work, the *Requiem Canticles*, is a place found for clarinets, whose tone seems to have taken on a profane association for him after the *Symphonies*. In the revised version of that work, clarinet tone is noticeably less to the fore than in the original.

30 Druskin (1983), p. 6.

31 See Arthur Berger, 'Problems of Pitch Organisation in Stravinsky', reprinted in B. Boretz and E. T. Cone, eds., *Perspectives on Schoenberg and Stravinsky* (Princeton University Press, Princeton, 1968), pp. 123–54. Also, in the same volume, Milton Babbitt, 'Remarks on the Recent Stravinsky', pp. 165–85, especially p. 168.

32 A plagal cadence prepares the tonic chord with the subdominant, rather than the dominant (with E flat rather than F in the key of B flat). This is the standard cadence of the Anglican 'Amen'. Its calmer, less dynamic quality is apparently due to the fact that both chords contain the tonic note, which is not the case with the perfect cadence preferred by baroque and classical music.

33 *The Writings of Elliott Carter* (Indiana University Press, Bloomington, 1977),
   p. 301.
34 Certainly it was a synthesis which meant a lot to Gide. The closing stanza of
   the poem:

> Il faut pour qu'un printemps renaisse
> Que le grain consente à mourir sous terre
> Afin qu'il reparaisse
> En moisson d'or pour l'avenir.

   is a paraphrase of the title quotation of Gide's later partial autobiography, *Si
   le grain ne meurt:* 'si le grain de blé ne tombe en terre et ne meurt, il reste
   seul; s'il meurt, il porte beaucoup de fruit', from the *Gospel according to St. John*
   (XII, 24). But the whole subject was fraught with nuances for the homosexual
   author.
35 *Dial.*, p. 37.
36 In Homer Demophoön and Triptolemus are two different sons of Celeus, whom
   Demeter visits in her quest for Persephone. Demophoön she inadvertently
   kills while trying to give him immortality in the flames of Celeus's fire.
   Triptolemus she endows with knowledge of the art of agriculture in return
   for the information that Persephone has been abducted by Hades. Eumolpus,
   the priestly narrator of the *mélodrame*, was also a son of Celeus, but appears here
   presumably because another Eumolpus was priest of Demeter's sacred rites at
   Eleusis. Gide's fusion of these characters makes sense in itself, but does not
   explain Persephone's abrupt rescue from Hades.
37 *Conv.*, p. 24; *Dial.*, p. 37.
38 First pointed out by Craft in Lederman (1949). See his chapter 'Music and
   Words', p. 97.
39 Lucy Beckett, *Parsifal* (Cambridge University Press, Cambridge, 1981), p. 141.
   Stravinsky would not have been amused by any comparison of his work with
   Wagner's, and needless to say there is little common musical ground between
   the two works.
40 This is another example of the same idea yielding different characters. The
   derivation is from 'Reppereram in monte pueram' in *Oedipus Rex*.

## Chapter 8 A Citizen of France: Concerto and Symphony

1 Respectively: *Le journal*, 4 June 1934, quoted in *SSCI*, p. 389; and *Excelsior*, 16
  June 1934, quoted in *SSCI*, p. 390.
2 Nicolas Nabokov, *Old Friends and New Music* (Little, Brown, Boston, 1951),
  quoted in White (1979), p. 115.
3 *SPD*, p. 326.
4 Dushkin's own account of the genesis of the concerto, 'Working with
  Stravinsky', is in *Stravinsky*, ed. E. Corle (Duell, Sloane & Pearce, New York,
  1949).
5 See *SSCII*, pp. 466–7.
6 *Chron.*, p. 171.
7 Stravinsky later gave a copy of this sketch to Craft, who included a facsimile
  of it in *SSCI*, pp. 371–8. On internal grounds, the dating to 1933 seems
  incontrovertible, and Craft has confirmed that 'Stravinsky's marked copy of
  [Cingria's] *Pétrarque* makes clear that the *Dialogue* was composed at the
  beginning of January 1933' (private communication, October 1985).
8 *Dial.*, p. 43.

9 Robert U. Nelson, 'Stravinsky's Concept of Variations', *Musical Quarterly*, xlviii (1962), pp. 327–39.
10 *SPD*, p. 357.
11 'The Uses of Convention: Stravinsky and his Models', *Musical Quarterly*, xlviii (1962), pp. 287–99.
12 See, for instance, his Introduction to *The Symphony* (Penguin, Harmondsworth, 1966).

## Chapter 9 *A Citizen of America: Tango and Symphony*

1 (Harvard University Press, Cambridge, Mass., 1942); English version, trans. Knodel and Dahl (Harvard University Press, Cambridge, Mass., 1947). Page references are to the English version.
2 *Poetics*, p. 16.
3 *Poetics*, p. 18.
4 See respectively: White (1979), p. 412; *Dial.*, p. 50; *Dial.*, p. 53; White, p. 415.
5 One interesting question about this music is what exactly would have been its relation to the subject, as opposed to the setting, of the film for which it was supposedly written. Was there some connection between projected background music to the Nazi landings and the first version of the first movement of the Symphony in Three Movements, which was drafted in June 1942, just before the Norwegian suite was put together? According to Craft, every movement of the symphony had cinematic connections, and Stravinsky himself most untypically described its music in terms of a programme, inspired by sequences from war news-film (see below, p.195).
6 Compare *SPD*, p. 375, with *Dial.*, p. 50. Since writing this chapter I have read the correspondence with Rose and Anton Dolin. The story as commonly told confuses Dolin's request for more effective scoring with Rose's later demand for a reduced version on economic grounds. Stravinsky rebuffed Dolin, but made minor concessions to Rose while refusing to agree to a rescoring by another hand (Robert Russell Bennett).
7 *T&C*, p. 34.
8 *Dial.*, p. 48.
9 See Lederman (1949), pp. 75–84.
10 Ibid., p. 77. But it reminded Stravinsky of 'a pair of lobsters in a restaurant window' (*T&C*, p. 53).
11 Ibid., p. 76.
12 Apart from the as yet unfinished Symphony in Three Movements. But it returns also in the *Scherzo à la russe* of this same summer, 1944.
13 White (1979), p. 423.
14 'Rhythm: Gershwin and Stravinsky', *Score*, xx (1957), p. 29.
15 'Assisting Stravinsky', *The Atlantic Monthly* (December 1982), pp. 70–71.
16 *Expo.*, pp. 77–8.
17 The tunes are identified by Charles Joseph, in *Stravinsky and the Piano* (UMI Research Press, Ann Arbor, Michigan, 1983), pp. 220–7, assembling material provided by Lawrence Morton and Richard Taruskin.
18 The first public sign of any revision to the Symphonies was a version Stravinsky made of the final chorale to fill up a recording of the *Symphony of Psalms* in December 1945. But Craft's evidence has always been that the composer's revisions were the result of long experience and many annotations. Moreover the Kyrie and Gloria of 1944 were not in their exact final form.
19 *Expo.*, p. 77.

20 Lederman (1949), p. 101. Murrill, 'Aspects of Stravinsky', *Music and Letters*, xxxii (1951), pp. 118–24.
21 *Dial.*, pp. 50–2; *Expo.*, p. 77.
22 Vlad (1967), p. 148.
23 *SPD*, p. 370.
24 *T&C*, p. 53.
25 *T&C*, p. 53.
26 *Poetics*, pp. 80–81.

## Chapter 10 *The Rake's Progress*

1 Letter of 12 October 1947, *SSCI*, pp. 299–300.
2 For example, the well-known lullaby 'Lay your sleeping head, my love' (1937), and the *New Year Letter* (1940).
3 6 October 1947, *SSCI*, p. 299.
4 Letter of 9 November 1947. The letter is cited in *SPD*, p. 397, but the cited remark is excluded, without comment, from the letter as published in *SSCIII*, pp. 319–20. The next (published) letter to Hawkes, 25 November 1947, asks for the Busch recordings of the Mozart/da Ponte operas and 'the Mozart opera scores'.
5 All such remarks are limited, of course, by the joint authorship of the libretto. The authors' contributions are itemised in a letter from Auden to Craft (10 February 1959), which Craft published in *SPD*, p. 650, n. 90, and which confirms that Auden wrote the minuet. Griffiths repeats this information but with a confusion between the second and third scenes of Act 1, which makes Kallman the author of the 'Lanterloo' chorus so highly praised by Stravinsky. In fact it is by Auden. See Paul Griffiths, *The Rake's Progress* (Cambridge University Press, Cambridge, 1982), p. 14.
6 In his obituary article, 'Craftsman, Artist, Genius', *The Observer*, 11 April 1971; quoted in *SPD*, p. 406.
7 Among the music requested from Hawkes late in 1947 was an edition of Byrd (Letter of 4 November, *SSCIII*, p. 319). Oddly enough, Stravinsky asked for it 'as a sample of music in Hogarth's time'.
8 'A Personal Preface', *The Score*, xx (1957), pp. 11–13.
9 Letter to Auden, 6 October 1947, *SSCI*, p. 299.
10 As already suggested, Mozart's finales also make deliberately ironic play with shallow moralising.
11 See 'Some thoughts on the libretto', reprinted in *Griffiths* (1982), pp. 60–74.
12 According to Robert Graves, Adonis was a Greek version of the Syrian spirit of vegetation. Aphrodite (Venus) and Persephone quarrelled over him, and were eventually given half shares in his time: the season of growth and the season of dormancy, respectively. *The Greek Myths*, vol. I (rev. ed. Penguin, Harmondsworth, 1960), pp. 69–72.
13 See his letter to Stravinsky of 12 October 1947, *SSCI*, pp. 299–300.

## Chapter 11 *The Final Spring:* **Agon** *and* **Threni**

1 Craft (1982) makes it clear that Stravinsky was almost wholly ignorant of Schoenberg's music in 1951. Schoenberg presumably had heard at least the main Stravinsky works, which were far more often performed than his own.

Craft, however, attributes to Schoenberg the view that Stravinsky's music 'depended on formulas and a bag of tricks' (p. 70). What seems likely is that Schoenberg resented Stravinsky's greater public success and apparently greater musical influence, and was at the same time antipathetic to his neo-classical works in principle. It should be added that Stuckenschmidt, in his biography of Schoenberg, reports Stravinsky as having referred to occasional meetings between the two composers 'in a third place' and as attributing 'the difficulties between them' to the influence of 'the ladies'. But these were no doubt convenient evasions for the benefit of a Schoenberg devotee. See H. H. Stuckenschmidt, *Arnold Schoenberg: His Life, World and Work*, trans. Humphrey Searle (Calder, London, 1977), p. 500.

2 *SPD*, p. 633, note 61.

3 Craft (1982), pp. 68 and 70.

4 See his letter to Manuel Rosenthal, 12 January 1946, quoted in *SSCII*, p. 347.

5 Craft (1982), p. 70.

6 Ibid., p. 73 (italics his).

7 That such considerations carried weight with Stravinsky is also suggested by his later tendency to speak and write as if serialism were and always had been the only compositional method of any importance. The same tone of reconstructing history can be detected in his early neo-classical manifestos. Clearly Stravinsky was no more able than Schoenberg to relax in an atmosphere of lively disagreement, and no doubt his dogmatic cast of mind was yet another reason why it would have been hard for him to take down the fences while the equally dogmatic Schoenberg was still alive.

8 Roman Vlad has argued that there is a sequential build-up of twelve-note and other patterns in *The Rite of Spring*, but his reasoning seems to me tendentious, and the title of his study, 'Row Structures in *The Rite of Spring*', carries an implication by no means borne out by the study itself. 'Reihenstrukturen im "Sacre du printemps"', in *Musik-Konzepte 34/35: Igor Strawinsky* (Munich, 1984), pp. 4–64.

9 The prime form is the original, or main, form of the row, selected arbitrarily on the evidence of the music. The numbers after the code letter refer respectively to the row-form at base pitch (the figure '0'), and at successive upward transpositions by a semitone (the figures '1', '2' etc. up to '11'.

10 In 1952 Stravinsky had sat in on rehearsals for a concert of music by Schoenberg, conducted by Craft, and including the Suite, op.29, which is also a septet (with clarinets rather than Stravinsky's wind trio), and which also ends with a gigue. Stravinsky started his Septet the day after finishing the Cantata (in July 1952), which implies an urgent impulse.

11 This was first pointed out by Craft in *Avec Stravinsky* (1958), pp. 143–4. The Septet was commissioned by the Dumbarton Oaks Research Library and Collection, and first played there in January 1954.

12 *Conv.*, pp. 24–5.

13 See, for instance, Hans Keller's analysis reprinted in his introduction to *Stravinsky Seen and Heard* (Dobson, London, 1982).

14 But Nausicaa had also recently been proposed to Stravinsky by Michael Powell as the subject for a film collaboration. Powell's letter of 5 January 1953 (now in the Paul Sacher Stiftung) reports on a meeting between the two and gives many details. But Powell seems to have lost interest when Stravinsky mentioned his fee. A year earlier the composer had been offered a film script, also on the *Odyssey*, by Simon Harcourt-Smith.

15 The description is Kirstein's (see his letter to Stravinsky of 31 August 1953, in *SSCI*, p. 287). A similar draft scenario, under the title *Terpsichore*, had actually been proposed by Kirstein nearly two years earlier (ibid., pp. 284–5).

16 In parallel French and English, translated with an introduction and notes by Joan Wildeblood (Frederic Muller, London, 1952).

17 He had made chamber instrumental versions of the accompaniments to the Verlaine and Balmont songs, and in 1952 a substantial recomposition of the *Concertino* of 1920 for a mixed ensemble of twelve instruments, in addition to the post-war revisions of *Petrushka* and the *Symphonies of Wind Instruments*.

18 See *SPD*, p. 429.

19 Stravinsky seems not to have borrowed material openly from the Mersenne music examples in the 1952 edition of de Lauze. But many fragments and suggestions are to be found, embedded in his own melodies. For example, the characteristic major-minor third ambiguity in the 'Bransle Simple' occurs, suggestively, in both the 'Bransle gay' and the 'Bransle de Montirande' of Mersenne. The underlying melody of Stravinsky's 'Gaillarde' is a kind of dream-distortion of the 'Gaillarde' in Mersenne, and one of the same figures also yields the trumpet flourish in bar 4 of the whole work.

20 Allowing that Stravinsky uses the inversion of the retrograde (IR-0), as a root form rather than the retrograde of the inversion (RI-0). The forms are the same but at different pitch.

21 See Douglas R. Hofstadter, *Gödel, Escher, Bach: an Eternal Golden Braid* (Penguin, Harmondsworth, 1980).

22 *Times-Picayune* (New Orleans), 30 January 1954, quoted in *SPD*, p. 203.

23 Gerhard's early article on Stravinsky's serialism is still well worth reading. 'Twelve-note Technique in Stravinsky', *The Score*, xx (1957), pp. 38–43.

24 See Craft, 'A Concert for Saint Mark', *The Score*, xviii (1956), p. 41.

25 The ugly term 'combinatoriality', lifted like so much modern musical jargon from set-theory, is commonly applied to this method. Combinatorial row-forms are forms whose corresponding hexachords have exactly opposite pitch-content, and so can be readily combined without doublings or close repetitions.

## Chapter 12 Requiem aeternam

1 Some of the text of *Conv.* had appeared, in German, as 'Antworten auf 35 Fragen' ('Answers to 35 Questions'), in *Leben und Werk* (Atlantis, Zürich, and Schott, Mainz, 1957) – a reprint of the German editions of *Chron.* and *Poetics*. And there is a substantial, though by no means complete, version in the French volume *Avec Stravinsky*. Versions of this early text appeared in English in *Atlantic Monthly* (June 1957), *Encounter* (July 1957), and, slightly expanded, *Saturday Review* (9 November 1957). Among the questions new to the book *Conv.* are some on *Threni*. According to Craft, the original text (which he refers to as 'Answers to 36 Questions') was commissioned for the French edition, which, however, contains many more than that number of questions and answers. In *SSCII*, p. 351 (note 10), he says that they were 'largely written during Pierre Boulez's visit to Los Angeles in March 1957'. But in *SPD*, p. 439, he records that 'much of "conversations with Igor Stravinsky" was written in Venice'. Both statements could well be accurate, the Venetian material being the additional questions beyond the first 35 (or 36).

2 P. 46. The remark is not in the English edition.

3 *Conv.*, p. 125.

4 See his publication of Stravinsky's letter to Deborah Ishlon of 15 March 1958, in *SPD*, pp. 438–9, together with Craft's following comment; and his

suggestive remark in Craft (1982), p. 74, that 'I no longer remember my exact contributions, [but] certainly there were *some* . . . .' (italics his).

5 Pierre Boulez is still today one such, though he conducts neo-classical Stravinsky, defending the inconsistency with the supremely unconvincing argument that detachment is a greater virtue in a conductor than passionate involvement. His masterly performances to my mind prove his sympathy with the music, while intellectually he cannot bring himself to side with it. In this he may simply be a victim of his own past polemics.

6 See Claudio Spies, 'Impressions after an Exhibition', *Tempo* 102 (1972), pp. 2–9, for an account of this procedure, which Spies was the first to decipher.

7 The ninety-six available hexachords boil down to only six *different* ones (considering their content, not their order). So for any given hexachord there are no fewer than sixteen possible complements in the system, all giving different orders.

8 *Conv.*, p. 25.

9 *Conv.*, p. 24.

10 According to White, the Gesualdo item had to be dropped, not because its composer was a murderer, but because the Venetians would not allow the music of a Neapolitan to be played in St. Mark's. White (1979), p. 549.

11 Though Craft's own interest in Gesualdo, and his knowledge of Italian baroque music in general, cannot have been a negligible factor.

12 As was then thought; it is now accepted that Gesualdo was born in 1561.

13 See *T&C*, pp. 58–9.

14 'Notes on Stravinsky's *Abraham and Isaac*', in Boretz/Cone (1968), pp. 186–209.

15 Oddly enough Spies connects Abraham's obedience to 'the angel's timely countermand', but fails to note that the cycle is completed by the chords accompanying God's final blessing of his seed. See Boretz/Cone (1968), p. 193 and n. 12.

16 Before starting the Variations he made an arrangement for eight instruments of Sibelius's string Canzonetta, by way of acknowledgement of the Wihuri-Sibelius Prize which he received that year. It says something for Stravinsky's vitality in his eighties that one still views gaps in his schedule with suspicion, as if the dates might be wrong. He completed *Abraham and Isaac* in March 1963, and made the Sibelius transcription in July. What happened in between? The inevitable answer: a European tour.

17 Spies has done the ground-work here as well. See his 'Notes on Stravinsky's Variations', in Boretz/Cone (1968), pp. 210–22.

18 But not quite systematically. The lowest three rotations are read forwards, the next two backwards, and then the second of these is repeated forwards with a forward statement of the top line to finish with.

19 Michael Hall, *Harrison Birtwistle* (Robson, London, 1984), pp. 43–4.

20 See *SPD*, pp. 484–5, where four excerpts from these sketches are reproduced. Charles Joseph argues that the original intention was a work for solo piano, but that Stravinsky changed his mind. Joseph (1983), pp. 236–7. The sketches have many indications of scoring, and Charles Wuorinen used them as the basis for his own *Reliquary for Igor Stravinsky*.

21 The *Fanfare for a New Theatre*, written for the opening of the Lincoln Square Dance Theatre in April 1964, is the insignificant exception.

22 Spotting errors in serial scores can be a vain form of pedantry, but I should nevertheless like to enter a plea for the E flat clarinet's F sharp (in place of the written sounding F natural) in bar 34. In every other respect this last verse is a *come sopra* repeat of its setting as verse 1, and the F natural is not only serially but also modally wrong in the repeat (though the misprint is already in the composer's fair copy and remains in his recording). This verse,

incidentally, was marked as a refrain by Auden, but it was Stravinsky's decision to start the setting with it. Auden's text begins with verse 2 ('Why then? Why there?'). See *SSCI*, p. 324.

23 Both were, according to Craft, set textually before any accompaniment was added. See *T&C*, p. 61, and *SPD*, p. 474. The initial setting of the *Introitus* was also without rhythm.

24 *SSCIII* (1985), p. 452.

25 21 March 1965, in *SSCII*, p. 417. The letter is not entirely explicit, and the gloss is Craft's (see his note 84).

26 *Dial.*, p. 70. The alternative is that the orchestral work, which he expected to start in July, was simply squeezed out by the *Requiem Canticles*, which he had started by March. Perhaps there is some connection between this symphony and the abortive sketches in *SPD*.

27 Forte (1978).

# Bibliography

## Source works (in chronological order of publication)

*Chron.* – *Chroniques de ma vie*, by Igor Stravinsky (Denoël Steele, Paris, 1935–6, 2 vols) (English edition in one volume: Gollancz, London; and Simon & Schuster, New York, 1936)

*Poetics* – *Poétique musicale*, by Igor Stravinsky (Harvard University Press, Cambridge, Mass., 1942) (English edition, Harvard University Press, Cambridge, 1947).

*Leben und Werk* – von ihm selbst (Atlantis Verlag, Zurich, 1957).

*Avec Stravinsky* – (Éditions du Rocher, Monaco, 1958).

*Conv.* – *Conversations with Igor Stravinsky*, by Igor Stravinsky and Robert Craft (Faber, London; Doubleday, New York, 1959).

*Mem.* – *Memories and Commentaries*, by Igor Stravinsky and Robert Craft (Faber, London; Doubleday, New York, 1960).

*Expo.* – *Expositions and Developments*, by Igor Stravinsky and Robert Craft (Faber, London; Doubleday, New York, 1962).

*Dial.* – *Dialogues and a Diary*, by Igor Stravinsky and Robert Craft (Doubleday, New York, 1963; Faber, London, 1968; reissued by Faber in 1982, without the Diary section, as *Dialogues*).

*Sketches for The Rite of Spring* – (Boosey & Hawkes, London, 1969).

*T&C* – *Themes and Conclusions*, by Igor Stravinsky (Faber, 1972) (this is a revised compilation from two American volumes: *Themes and Episodes* [Knopf, New York, 1966] and *Retrospectives and Conclusions* [Knopf, New York, 1969], omitting diary sections by Robert Craft some of which reappeared in *Chronicle of a Friendship*).

*Stravinsky: the Chronicle of a Friendship 1948–1971*, by Robert Craft (Knopf, New York; Gollancz, London, 1972).

*Catherine & Igor Strawinsky: a family album*, by Theodore Strawinsky (Boosey & Hawkes, London, 1973).

*SAM* – *I. F. Stravinsky: Articles and Materials* (ed. L. S. Dyachkova) (Soviet Composers, Moscow, 1973).

*SPD* – *Stravinsky in Pictures and Documents*, by Vera Stravinsky and Robert Craft (Simon & Schuster, New York, 1978; Hutchinson, London, 1979).

*SSC* – *Stravinsky: Selected Correspondence*, ed. and with commentaries by Robert Craft (in three volumes) (Faber, London, 1982, 1984, 1985).

*Igor and Vera Stravinsky: a photograph album*, captions by Robert Craft (Thames and Hudson, London, 1982).

*A Stravinsky Scrapbook 1940–1971*, by Robert Craft (Thames & Hudson, London, 1983).

*Strawinsky. Sein Nachlass. Sein Bild.* Catalogue of the exhibition of that name in the

Kunstmuseum, Basel, June–September 1984. (Kunstmuseum Basel in association with the Paul Sacher Stiftung, Basel, 1984).
*Dearest Bubushkin: selected letters and diaries of Vera and Igor Stravinsky*, ed. by Robert Craft (Thames & Hudson, London, 1985).


## Other books and articles

Adorno, T. W. (1973), *Philosophy of Modern Music* (trans. A. G. Mitchell and W. V. Bloomster), Sheed & Ward, London.
Albright, D. (1989), *The Music Box and the Nightingale*, Gordon & Breach, New York.
Andriessen, L., and Schönberger, E. (1989), *The Apollonian Clockwork* (trans. J. Hamburg), Oxford University Press, Oxford.
Antheil, G. (1949), *Bad Boy of Music*, National Book Association, London.
Armitage, M. (ed.) (1936), *Igor Stravinsky*, Schirmer, New York.
Asafyev, B. (1982), *A Book about Stravinsky* (trans. R. French), UMI Research Press, Ann Arbor, Michigan.
Babbitt, M. (1968), 'Remarks on the Recent Stravinsky', in Boretz and Cone (1968), pp. 165–85.
Bancroft, D. (1972), 'Stravinsky and the "NRF" (1910–1920)', in *Music and Letters*, liii, pp. 274–83.
Bancroft, D. (1974), 'Stravinsky and the "NRF" (1920–1929)', in *Music and Letters*, lv, pp. 261–71.
Beckett, L. (1981), *Parsifal*, Cambridge University Press, Cambridge.
Benjamin, W. E. (1977), 'Tonality without 5ths: Remarks on the First Movement of Stravinsky's Concerto for Piano and Wind Instruments', in *In Theory Only*, ii, pp. 53–70.
Berger, A. (1968), 'Problems of Pitch Organization in Stravinsky', in Boretz and Cone (1968), pp. 123–54.
Boretz, B. and Cone, E. (eds) (1968), *Perspectives on Schoenberg and Stravinsky*, Princeton University Press, Princeton.
Boucourechliev, A. (1987), *Stravinsky* (trans. M. Cooper), Gollancz, London.
Boulez, P. (1966), 'Stravinsky Demeure', in *Relevés d'apprenti*, Éditions du Seuil, Paris, pp. 75–145.
Braun, E. (ed.) (1969), *Meyerhold on Theatre*, Methuen, London.
Braun, E. (1982), *The Director and the Stage*, Methuen, London.
Buckle, R. (1979), *Diaghilev*, Weidenfeld & Nicholson, London.
Carner, M. (1984), 'The Score', in *Turandot* (ENO Guide), Calder, London.
Cocteau, J. (1979), *Le Coq et l'arlequin*, Stock (originally 1918, Editions de la Sirène, Paris), Paris.
Cocteau, J. (1926), *Rappel à l'ordre*, Stock, Paris.
Cone, E. T. (1962), 'The Uses of Convention: Stravinsky and his Models', in *Musical Quarterly*, xlviii, pp. 287–99.
Corle, E. (ed.) (1949), *Stravinsky*, Duell, Sloan & Pearce, New York.
Craft, R. (1956), 'A Concert for Saint Mark', in *The Score*, xviii, pp. 35–51.
Craft, R. (1957), 'A Personal Preface', in *The Score*, xx, pp. 11–13.
Craft, R. (1982/I), 'My Life with Stravinsky', in *The New York Review of Books*, (10 June 1982), pp. 6–10.
Craft, R. (1982/II), 'Assisting Stravinsky', in *The Atlantic Monthly*, pp. 68–74.
Craft, R. (1992), *Stravinsky: Glimpses of a Life*, Lime Tree, London.
Cyr, L. (1982), 'Le Sacre du printemps: Petite histoire d'une grande partition', in *Stravinsky: Études et Témoignages* (ed. F. Lesure), J. C. Lattès, Paris, pp. 89–147.
Drew, D. (1957), 'Stravinsky's Revisions', in *The Score*, xx, pp. 47–58.

Druskin, M. (1983), *Igor Stravinsky: his personality, works and views* (trans. M. Cooper), Cambridge University Press, Cambridge.

Forte, A. (1978), *The Harmonic Organization of 'The Rite of Spring'*, Yale University Press, New Haven and London.

Gerhard, R. (1957), 'Twelve-note Technique in Stravinsky', in *The Score*, xx, pp. 38–43.

Graves, R. (1960), *The Greek Myths* (vol. I), Penguin, Harmondsworth.

Griffiths, P. (and others) (1982). *The Rake's Progress*, Cambridge University Press, Cambridge.

Haimo, E., and Johnson, P. (eds.) (1987), *Stravinsky Retrospectives*, University of Nebraska Press, Lincoln (Nebraska) and London.

Hall, M. (1984), *Harrison Birtwistle*, Robson, London.

Hofstadter, D. R. (1980), *Gödel, Escher, Bach: an Eternal Golden Braid*, Penguin, Harmondsworth.

Joseph, C. (1983), *Stravinsky and the Piano*, UMI Research Press, Ann Arbor, Michigan.

Karlinsky, S. (1983), 'Stravinsky and Russian Pre-Literate Theater', in *19th Century Music*, vi, pp. 232–40.

Keller, H. (1957), 'Rhythm: Gershwin and Stravinsky', in *The Score*, xx, pp. 19–31.

Keller, H. (and Cosman, M.) (1982), *Stravinsky Seen and Heard*, Dobson, London.

Kholopova, V. (1974), 'Russische Quellen der Rhythmik Strawinskys', in *Musikforschung*, xxvii, pp. 435–46.

Lang, P. H. (ed.) (1963), *Stravinsky: A New Appraisal of His Work*, Norton, New York.

Lederman, M. (ed.) (1949), *Stravinsky in the Theatre*, Pellegrini & Cudahy, New York.

Lessem, A. (1982), 'Schoenberg, Stravinsky and Neo-Classicism: the Issues Reexamined', in *Musical Quarterly*, lxviii, pp. 527–42.

Lourié, A. (1925), 'La sonate pour piano de Strawinsky', in *La revue musicale*, vi, pp. 100–14.

Lourié, A. (1927), 'Oedipus Rex', in *La revue musicale*, viii, pp. 240–53.

Lourié, A. (1928/I), 'A propos de l'*Apollon* d'Igor Strawinsky', in *Musique*, i, pp. 117–19.

Lourié, A. (1928/II), 'Neo-Gothic and Neo-Classic', in *Modern Music*, v, pp. 3–8.

Maritain, J. (1935), *Art et scolastique*, Louis Rouart, Paris (3rd ed.).

Mellers, W. (1963), 'Stravinsky's Oedipus as 20th-Century Hero', in Lang, P. H. (ed.) (1963).

Meyer, L. B. (1973), *Explaining Music*, University of California Press, Berkeley.

Messing, S. (1988), *Neoclassicism in Music: From the Genesis of the Concept through the Schoenberg/Stravinsky Polemic*, UMI Research Press, Ann Arbor and London.

Morton, L. (1962), 'Stravinsky and Tchaikovsky: *Le Baiser de la Fee*', in *Musical Quarterly*, xlviii, pp. 313–26.

Morton, L. (1979), 'Footnotes to Stravinsky Studies: *Le Sacre du Printemps*', in *Tempo*, 128, pp. 9–16.

Murrill, H. (1951), 'Aspects of Stravinsky', in *Music and Letters*, xxxii, pp. 118–24.

Nelson, R. U. (1962), 'Stravinsky's Concept of Variations', in *Musical Quarterly*, xlviii, pp. 327–39.

Painter, G. D. (1965), *Marcel Proust* (vol. 2), Chatto & Windus, London.

Pasler, J. (ed.) (1986), *Confronting Stravinsky*, University of California Press, Berkeley, Los Angeles and London.

Pople, A. (1989), *Skryabin and Stravinsky, 1908–1914: Studies in Theory and Analysis*, Garland, New York and London.

Ramuz, C. F. (1929), *Souvenirs sur Igor Stravinsky*, Mermod, Lausanne.

Read, H. (1959), *A Concise History of Modern Painting*, Thames & Hudson, London.

Samuel, C. (1971), *Prokofiev*, Calder, London.

Schaeffner, A. (1931), *Strawinsky*, Paris.

Schloezer, B. de (1929), *Igor Stravinsky*, Claude Aveline, Paris.

Simpson, R. (ed.) (1966), *The Symphony*, Penguin, Harmondsworth.

Spies, C. (1968), 'Notes on Stravinsky's Abraham and Isaac', 'Notes on Stravinsky's *Variations*', 'Some Notes on Stravinsky's Requiem Settings', all in Boretz & Cone (1968), pp. 186–249.

Spies, C. (1972), 'Impressions after an Exhibition', in *Tempo*, 102, pp. 2–9.

Stravinsky, I. (1924), 'Some Ideas about my Octuor', in *The Arts* (Brooklyn), pp. 4–6; reprinted in White (1979), pp. 574–7.

Strawinsky, T. (1953), *The Message of Igor Strawinsky* (trans. R. Craft and A. Marion), Boosey & Hawkes, London.

Stuart, P. (1991), *Igor Stravinsky—The Composer in the Recording Studio*, Greenwood Press, New York, Westport and London.

Stuckenschmidt, H. H. (1977), *Arnold Schoenberg: His Life, World and Work* (trans. H. Searle), Calder, London.

Tansman, A. (1949), *Igor Stravinsky: the Man and his Music* (trans. T. and C. Bleefield), Putnam, New York.

Tappolet, C. (ed.) (1990, 1991), *Correspondance Ansermet–Strawinsky (1914–67)*, vols 1 & 2 (of 3), Georg, Geneva.

Taruskin, R. (1980), 'Russian Folk Melodies in *The Rite of Spring*', in *Journal of the American Musicological Society*, xxxiii, pp. 501–43.

Taruskin, R. (1981), *Opera and Drama in Russia*, UMI Research Press, Ann Arbor, Michigan.

van den Toorn, P. (1983), *The Music of Igor Stravinsky*, Yale University Press, New Haven.

van den Toorn, P. (1987), *Stravinsky and The Rite of Spring*, Oxford University Press, Oxford.

Vershinina, I. (1967), *Stravinsky's Early Ballets*, Science ('Nauka') Publications, Moscow.

Vlad, R. (1967), *Stravinsky*, Oxford University Press, London (2nd ed.).

Vlad, R. (1984), Reihenstrukturen im "Sacre du printemps", in *Musik-Konzepte 34/35: Igor Stravinsky*, Munich.

White, E. W. (1979), *Stravinsky: the Composer and his Works*, Faber, London (2nd ed.).

Zguta, R. (1978), *Russian Minstrels*, Oxford University Press, London.

# List of Works

The following catalogue is comprehensive only in the sense that it lists all the works Stravinsky completed, together with all the arrangements of other people's music which he published or is known to have completed. It also includes, within square brackets, the four works he is known to have written but which are currently lost (other lost works, known about only vaguely, are omitted). As regards rearrangements of Stravinsky's own works, it includes only his own transcriptions, except where the transcribed version enjoys some primary status (as with the first version of the *Suite italienne* or the *Scherzo à la russe*). But I have not attempted to include all authentic arrangements of individual movements from larger works. And I have excluded unfinished works, whether they survive as significant drafts (like the original string version of the *Symphonies of Wind Instruments*), or as more or less complete versions of music that eventually appeared in another form (like the orchestral original, discussed by Craft, of the first movement of the Sonata for two pianos), or as mere sketches (like the *Dialogue between Joy and Reason*). There is certainly room for a listing of works which, at various times, Stravinsky projected or even thought about writing. But material for such a listing is at present too haphazard; and in any case it would have no place in a 'List of Works' as such.

*Revised versions*
In general I have noted these only where they show substantial changes from the originals. Many of Stravinsky's so-called revisions were little more than corrected versions. Moreover the subject lends itself to a certain kind of over-precision, which has in fact bedevilled the Stravinsky literature for many years. To take an example: *The Rite of Spring* was heavily revised by Stravinsky over the years, but because almost every reprint shows changes from its predecessors, nobody has ever thought of nominating a specific 'revised version' (except for the 1943 'Danse sacrale', which Stravinsky himself had published as such); on the other hand *The Nightingale* is often listed as 'revised 1962', simply because that was the first time, apparently, that the composer got round to tidying up the old ERM/BH text. But he made no really substantial changes (moreover such changes as he did make were made by early 1961, while other corrections and clarifications were made later by the editorial staff of Boosey & Hawkes). The revision of Act I which he made in 1913 or 1914 is much more important, but is usually not even mentioned.

*Titles*
The list follows the practice of the book. Normally I give the title in English, except in cases (again like the *Suite italienne* or the *Scherzo à la russe*) where a 'foreign' title belongs to the stylisation of the piece itself. The Russian title is added for those (earlier) works which Stravinsky himself titled in that language.

*Dates*
The simple bracketed dates show the span of composition, so far as precision is possible in such matters (often there are still earlier sketches and, nearly always, later modifications). This bald information is usually qualified by what follows. For instance, the remark 'dated July 1920' means that Stravinsky himself put that date on a finished version of the score. It may be (as with his later works) on the fair copy, or it may be (as with the Tango) on a complete short score. Consistency in such details is hard to achieve without a much fuller text which would be confusing to consult. I have corrected many accepted datings and where my corrections are controversial or surprising I have tried to give reasons. In general I take the line of 'best-guess' in those numerous cases where certainty is impossible; having had access to more documentary sources than White I can usually adjust his datings with reasonable confidence. But there are plenty of available sources that I have not yet consulted, so any corrections are provisional. In any case I have used White as a launching-pad, and even now, twenty years after his gazetteer was first published, it remains indispensable. It gives me pleasure to acknowledge this debt.

Explanation of abbreviations, and identification of publishers (locations are those at the time of publication)

AMP – Associated Music Publishers, (New York)
arr. – arranged
Bessel – W. Bessel & Co., St. Petersburg
BH – Boosey & Hawkes., London/New York
Byelayev – M. P. Byelayev, Leipzig
Chappell – Chappell & Co., New York
comp. – composed
compl. – completed
ERM – Edition Russe de Musique (Russische Musik Verlag), Paris/Berlin
Faber – Faber & Faber. (Faber Music), London
Forberg – Robert Forberg, Leipzig
fs – full score
Hansen – W. Hansen, Copenhagen
Henn – Adolphe Henn, Geneva
Jurgenson – P. Jurgenson, Moscow
JWC – J & W Chester, London
Mercury – Mercury Music Corporation, New York
nd – no date
orch. – orchestrated (orchestration)
OS – Old Style
perf. – performed
rev. – revised (revision)
Schott – B. Schotts Söhne, Mainz
(un)pub. – (un)published
vs – vocal score

1 **Tarantella** for piano (1898), dated 14.X.1898 (OS). Unpub.
2 **Storm Cloud** ('Tucha') for voice and piano (words, Pushkin) (1902), dated 25.I.1902 (OS). Pub.1982 (Soviet Composers, Moscow: *Stravinsky's Vocal Music*, vol. I; also with Faber).
3 **Scherzo** for piano (1902). Pub.1970 (facsimile, in V. Smirnov, *Creative Formative Years of I. F. Stravinsky*, Leningrad) and 1973 (Faber).
4 **Sonata in F sharp minor** for piano (1903–4), dated Summer 1904. 1st (private) perf., 9.II.1905 (OS), St. Petersburg. Pub. 1973 (USSR), 1974 (Faber).

[5 Cantata for the sixtieth birthday of Rimsky-Korsakov, for mixed choir and piano (1904). 1st perf., 6.III.1904, St. Petersburg. Unpub. Lost.]

6 **How the Mushrooms Prepared for War** ('Kak greebi na voinoo sobbirleece'), for bass and piano (words, Russian folk verse) (1904). Pub. 1982 (USSR; also with BH).

[7 Conductor and Tarantula, for (voice and) piano (1906) (words, *Kozma Prutkov*). Unpub. Lost.]

8 **Symphony in E flat major**, op.1, for orchestra (1905–7). 1st (private) perf. (2nd & 3rd movements only), 14.IV.1907 (OS), St. Petersburg. 1st complete perf., 22.I.1908 (OS), St. Petersburg. Pub. 1914 (Jurgenson; now Forberg).

9 **The Faun and the Shepherdess** ('Favn i Pastushka'), op.2, suite for mezzo-soprano and orchestra (words, Pushkin) (1906–7). 1st perf., 22.I.1908 (OS), St. Petersburg. Pub. 1908 (vs), 1913 (fs) (Byelayev; later BH).

10 **Two Songs**, op.6, for mezzo-soprano and piano (words, S. Gorodyetsky) (1907–8); (1) Spring ('Vyessna'), compl. by July 1907; (2) Song of the Dew ('Rossyanka'), dated 'Ustilug 1908', comp. by 19.VIII.08 (OS). Pub. 1912 or 1913 (Jurgenson; later BH).

11 **Pastorale**, vocalise for soprano and piano (1907). 1st (private) perf., 31.X.1907 (OS), St. Petersburg. Pub. 1910 (Jurgenson; later Schott).
Arrangements: (a) for soprano and wind quartet (Dec. 1923), 1st perf., 7.I.1924, Antwerp. Pub. n.d. (Forberg; later Schott); (b) (extended version) for violin with piano or with wind quartet (1933). Pub. 1934 (Schott).

12 **Scherzo fantastique**, op.3, for large orchestra (1907–8), compl. 30.III.1908. 1st perf., 6.II.1909, St. Petersburg. Pub. c.1909 (Jurgenson; later Schott).

13 **Fireworks**, op.4, for large orchestra (1908). 1st perf., 6.II.1909. Pub. 1910 (Schott).

[14 Chant funèbre for wind, in memory of Rimsky-Korsakov (1908), compl. by August. 1st perf., 13.II.1909. St Petersburg. Unpub. Lost.]

15 **Four Studies**, op.7, for piano (1908). Pub. 1910 (Jurgenson; later A. J. Benjamin, Hamburg/London).

16 'Song of the Flea' (words, Goethe's *Faust*): (1) by Beethoven, arr. for bass and chamber orchestra; (2) by Mussorgsky, arr. for baritone or bass and full orchestra; (1909). 1st perf., 28.XI.1909 (OS), St. Petersburg. Pub. c.1913 (Bessel; later BH).

17 **The Nightingale** ('Solovyei'), lyric tale in three acts (libretto, Stravinsky and S. Mitussov, after Hans Andersen) (1908–9 and 1913–14): Act I, 1908–summer 1909, rev. 1913; Acts II and III, July 1913–March 1914. 1st perf., 26.V.1914, Paris. Pub. 1923 (ERM; later BH).
Arrangement: **The Song of the Nightingale** ('Pyesnya Solovya'), symphonic poem for orchestra (1916–17), compl. 4.IV.1917. 1st perf., 6.XII.1919, Geneva. Pub.1921 (ERM; later BH). Mainly from Acts II and III of the lyric tale.

18 Chopin's Nocturne in A flat and Valse brillante in E flat, orch. Stravinsky (1909), between February and June; for the ballet *Les Sylphides*, in the repertory of the Ballets Russes. 1st perf., 2.VI.1909, Paris. Unpub.

19 **The Firebird** ('Zhar-Pteetsa'), ballet in two scenes for large orchestra (1909–10), compl. 18.V.1910. 1st perf., 25.VI.1910, Paris. Pub. 1910 (Jurgenson; later Schott).
Suites: (a) 1911, from the complete score (ends with the 'Infernal Dance'), pub.1913 (Jurgenson); (b) 1919, for reduced orchestra (ends with ballet Finale), pub. 1920 (JWC); (c) 1945, as 1919 but with extra linking music from the ballet; pub. 1946 (Leeds Music Corp., New York; later Schott)

20 Grieg's *Kobold*, orch. Stravinsky (1910); for the ballet *Les Orientales*,[1] in the repertory of the Ballets Russes. 1st perf., (?25).VI.1910, Paris. Unpub.

21 **Two Poems of Verlaine**, op.9, for baritone and piano (July 1910): (1) Un grand sommeil noir; (2) La lune blanche. Pub. 1911 (Jurgenson).
Arrangements: (a) for baritone and [small] orchestra. Pub. 1953 (BH). The two songs appear in reverse order, and the music is revised. (b) for baritone and piano, pub. 1954 (BH). This is a direct reduction (by Erwin Stein) from (a).

22 **Petrushka**, ballet ('burlesque') in four scenes for large orchestra (1910–11), dated 26.V.1911. 1st perf., 13.VI.1911, Paris. Pub. 1912 (ERM).
Revised version: for reduced orchestra (1946), pub. 1947 (BH).
Arrangement: **Three Movements from Petrushka** for piano (1921). Pub. 1922 (ERM; later BH).

23 **Two Poems of Balmont** for high voice and piano (words, K. Balmont) (1911), July or August: (1) The Forget-me-not ('Nyezabudochka tsvyetochek'); (2) The Dove ('Golub'). Pub. 1912 (ERM; later BH).
Arrangements: (a) for soprano and chamber orchestra, pub. 1955 (BH). The music is revised. (b) for soprano and piano, pub. 1956 (BH), a direct reduction (by ?Leopold Spinner) from (a).

24 **Zvyezdoleeki** ('Starface'), for male chorus and large orchestra (words, K. Balmont) (1911), July or August. 1st perf., 19.IV.1939, Brussels. Pub. 1911 (vs: Forberg), 1913 (fs: Jurgenson).

25 **The Rite of Spring** ('Vyessna Svyashchennaya'), ballet ('scenes of pagan Russia') in two parts (1911–13). 1st perf., 29.V.1913, Paris. Pub. 1913 (piano, 4 hands), 1921 (fs): (ERM; later BH).
Revised version: 'Sacrificial Dance' (1943), pub. 1945 (AMP; now with BH). The complete work underwent repeated revision, as reflected in its many reprints, but was never published in a definitive, corrected revised text.

26 **Three Japanese Lyrics** for soprano with piano or with chamber orchestra (1912–13): (1) Akahito, 19.X.1912 (orch. 29.XII.1912); (2) Mazatsumi, 18.XII.1912 (orch. 21.XII.1912); (3) Tsaraiuki, 22.I.1913 (orch. 22.I.1913). 1st perf. (chamber version), 14.I.1914, Paris. Pub. 1913 (ERM; later BH).

27 Mussorgsky's *Khovanshchina*: orch. of Shaklovity's Aria and realisation of final scene (April 1913). 1st perf., 16.VI.1913. Pub. 1914 (vs of final scene only) (Bessel).

28 **Three Little Songs** ('Recollections of Childhood') ('Tree Pyesyenki – eez vospominani yunosheskikh godov') for voice and piano (1913), Oct–Nov:
(1) The Magpie ('Sorochenka'), dated 19.X.1913; (2) The Crow ('Vorona'); (3) The Jackdaw ('Cheecher-Yacher'), dated Oct–Nov 1913. Pub. 1914 (ERM, later BH).
Arrangement: for voice and small orchestra (Dec 1929–Jan 1930); all three songs appreciably lengthened. Pub. 1934 (ERM, later BH).

29 **Three Pieces for string quartet** (1914): (1) 26.IV.1914; (2) 2.VII.1914; (3) 25/6.VII.1914. 1st perf., 19.V.1915, Paris. Pub. 1922 (ERM; later BH).
Arrangement: for orchestra (1914–18) as nos. 1–3 of **Four Studies**; no. 4 is a transcription (1928) of the Study for pianola (see no. 43). The studies are now named: (1) Dance; (2) Eccentric; (3) Canticle; (4) Madrid. 1st perf. 7.XI.1930, Berlin. Pub. 1930 (ERM; later BH).

30 **Pribaoutki** for medium voice and eight instruments (words, from Afanassyev) (Aug–Sept 1914): (1) Korneelo, 18.VIII.1914; (2) Natashka, 13.VIII.1914; (3) The Colonel ('Polkovnik'), 29.VIII.1914; (4) The Old Man and the Hare ('Staryets ee zayats'), 29.IX.1914. 1st perf., with piano, May 1919, Paris; with ensemble, 6.VI.1919, Vienna. Pub. 1917 (Henn; later JWC).

31 **Valse des fleurs**, for piano duet 'left hand easy'[2] (1914), dated 12.XI.1914. Pub. 1983 (facsimile, in R.Craft, *A Stravinsky Scrapbook 1940–1971*,Thames and Hudson, pl. 290–1).

32 **Three Easy Pieces** for piano duet 'left hand easy' (1914–15): (1) March, 19.XII.1914; (2) Waltz, 6.III.1915; (3) Polka, 15.XI.1914. 1st perf., 22.IV.1918,

Lausanne. Pub. 1917 (Henn; later JWC). According to Craft (*SSCI*, p. 412) the Polka was first published separately 'probably in 1915 – in an unidentified French-language periodical, p. 137'.

Arrangement: for small orchestra as nos. 1–3 of **Suite no.2** (1921). 1st perf. 25.XI.1925, Frankfurt. Pub. 1925 (JWC). See no. 38, **Five Easy Pieces**.

33 **Souvenir d'une marche boche** for piano (1915), dated 1.IX.1915. Pub. 1916 (facsimile, in Edith Wharton [ed], *The Book of the Homeless*, Macmillan).

34 **Cat's Cradle Songs** for contralto and three clarinets (words, from Kireyevsky) (1915): (1) Go to sleep, cat ('Spee kot'), dated 29.VIII–11.IX.1915; (2) Cat on the stove ('Kot na pyechee'), dated 18.V.1915; (3) Lullaby ('Bye-bye'), dated summer 1915; (4) What has the cat the cat ('Oo kota kota'), dated 2.XI.1915. 1st perf. with ensemble, 6.VI.1919, Vienna. Pub. 1917 (Henn; later JWC).

35 **Renard** ('Baika'), a merry play with singing and music, for four male voices and fifteen players (words, Stravinsky, after Afanassyev) (1916), completed in August. 1st perf., 18.V.1922, Paris. Pub. 1917 (Henn; later JWC).

36 **Four Russian Peasant Songs** ('Podblyudnya') for female chorus unaccompanied (words, from I. Sakharov) (1914–17): (1) In Our Saviour's Parish of Chigisy ('Oo Spassa v Chigissakh'), 22.XII.1916; (2) Ovsyen, 14.I.1917; (3) The Pike ('Shchooka'), 16.XII.1914; (4) Mr. Paunch ('Puzischche'), 16.I.1915. 1st perf. 1917, Geneva. Pub. 1930 (Schott), 1932 (JWC).

Arrangement: for female chorus and four horns (1954), with some revision and expansion. 1st perf., 11.X.1954. Pub.1957 (Schott), 1958 (JWC).

37 **Valse pour les enfants** for piano (1916–17), by Jan 1917. Pub. 21.V.1922 in *Le Figaro*, Paris (and in White, p. 248).

38 **Five Easy Pieces** for piano duet 'right hand easy' (1917): (1) Andante, 4.I.1917; (2) Española, 3.IV.1917; (3) Balalaika, 6.II.1917; (4) Napolitana, 28.II.1917; (5) Galop, 21.II.1917. 1st perf., 22.IV.1918, Lausanne. Pub. 1917 (Henn; later JWC).

Arrangement: for small orchestra: nos. 1–4 became **Suite no.1** (1925), in the order 1-4-2-3. 1st perf., 2.III.1926, Haarlem (see *SSCI*, p. 413). Pub. 1926 (JWC). No. 5 became the finale of Suite no.2 (see no. 32, **Three Easy Pieces**).

39 Song of the Volga Boatmen: arr. for wind and percussion (1917), dated 8.IV.1917. 1st perf., ?9.IV.1917, Rome. Pub. 1920 (JWC).

40 **Three Tales for Children** for voice and piano (words, Afanassyev and others) (1916–17): (1) Tilim-bom, 22.V.1917; (2) Geese, Swans . . . ('Goossee, lyebyedee . . .'), 21.VI.1917; (3) The Bear ('Midvyed'), dated 30.XII.1915 (OS: i.e. 12.I.1916). Pub. 1920 (JWC).

Arrangements: no. 1, for voice and orchestra (Dec. 1923), appreciably lengthened. 1st perf. 7.I.1924, Antwerp. Pub. JWC. Nos. 1 and 2, for voice, flute, harp and guitar, as nos. 4 and 3 of **Four Songs** (1953–4). 1st perf., 21.II.1955, Los Angeles. Pub. 1955 (JWC). See no. 50, Four Russian Songs, for the other two items in this arrangement.

[41 Canons for two horns (1917). Unpub. Lost.]

42 **The Wedding** ('Svadyebka'), Russian choreographic scenes (words, Stravinsky after Kireyevsky) (1914–17: final instrumentation 1923): first version, for soloists, chorus and large chamber orchestra, completed in draft 11.X.1917; second version (tableaux 1 and 2 only), for soloists, chorus, harmonium, 2 cimbaloms, pianola and percussion, spring 1919; final version, for soloists, chorus, four pianos and percussion, compl. 5.V.1923 (several other previous orchestrations abandoned or lost). 1st perf., 13.VI.1923, Paris. Pub., final version only, 1922 (vs), 1923 (fs) (JWC).

43 **Study for pianola** (1917), composed in November. 1st perf., 13.X.1921. Pub. Aeolian Co., London (pianola roll T967B).

Arrangement: for orchestra (1928) as no. 4 of Four Studies (see no. 29, *Three Pieces for string quartet*).

44 **Berceuse** for voice and piano (words, Stravinsky) (1917), comp. on 10.XII.1917. Pub. 1962, in *Expositions and Developments* (Faber), with French text only (by C. F. Ramuz).

45 **Lied ohne Namen** for two bassoons (1917 or 1918), comp. before Oct 1918. Pub. 1982 (facsimile, in *SSCI*, Faber, p. 410).

46 **The Soldier's Tale**, 'to be read, played and danced', for three actors, a dancer and seven players (libretto, C. F. Ramuz) (1918). 1st perf., 28.IX.1918, Lausanne. The work was substantially revised after the premiere but before publication. Pub. 1924 (JWC).
   Suites: (a) 1920 (from complete score). 1st perf., 20.VII.1920, London. Pub. 1922 (JWC). (b) 1919, for violin, clarinet and piano. 1st perf., 8.XI.1919, Lausanne. Pub. 1920 (JWC).

47 **Ragtime** for eleven instruments (1917–18), compl. 11.XI.1918. 1st perf., 8.XI.1919, piano reduction, Lausanne; 27.IV.1920, inst. version, London. Pub. 1919 (Editions de la Sirène, Paris; later JWC).

48 **Three Pieces for Clarinet Solo** (1918), comp. respectively 19.X.1918, 24.X.1918, and 15.XI.1918. 1st perf., 8.XI.1919, Lausanne. Pub. 1920 (JWC).

49 Mussorgsky's *Boris Godunov*: First Chorus from the Prologue, ('Na kovo ti nas pokidayesh'), arr. for piano (1918). Unpub. (with BH).

50 **Four Russian Songs** for voice and piano (words, Russian folk verse) (1918–19): (1) The Drake ('Syelyezen'), 28.XII.1918; (2) Counting Song ('Zapyevnaya'), 16.I.1919; (3) Dish-Divination Song ('Podblyudnaya'), 23.I.1919; (4) Sectarian Song ('Syektantskaya'), with obbligato flute, compl. Feb 1919. 1st perf., 7.II.1920, Paris. Pub. 1923 (JWC).
   Arrangement: nos. 1 and 4, for voice, flute, harp and guitar, as nos. 1 and 2 of Four Songs (1953–4). See no. 40, *Three Tales for Children*.

51 La Marseillaise: arr. for solo violin (1919), New Year's Day. 1st perf., 13.XI.1979, London. Unpub. (with BH)

52 **Piano-Rag-Music** for piano (1919), compl. 28.VI.1919. 1st perf., 8.XI.1919, Lausanne. Pub. 1920 (JWC).

53 **Pulcinella**, ballet with song in one act (music and words after Pergolesi) (1919–20), compl. 20.IV.1920. 1st perf., 15.V.1920, Paris. Pub. 1920, piano reduction (JWC); 1924, fs (ERM; later BH).
   Suites: (a) 1920 (from complete score but without voices). 1st perf., 22.XII.1922. Pub. 1924 (ERM; later BH). (b) 1925, for violin and piano, 'd'après des thèmes, fragments et morceaux de Giambattista Pergolesi'. Pub. 1926 (ERM; later BH). (c) 1932, *Suite italienne*, for cello and piano (arr. with Gregor Piatigorsky). Pub. 1934 (ERM; later BH). (d) 1933(?), *Suite italienne*, for violin and piano (arr. with Samuel Dushkin). Pub. 1934 (ERM; later BH).

54 **Symphonies of Wind Instruments** (1920), dated 30.XI.1920, but short score dated 2.VII.1920. 1st perf., 10.VI.1921, London. Pub. 1920, piano reduction of chorale only (in *La Revue musicale*, Paris, December); 1926, piano reduction (by Arthur Lourié) (ERM; now held by BH).
   Revision: 1947 (Oct–Nov) for slightly altered band but with major changes of texture. 1st perf., 31.I.1948, New York. Pub. 1952, (BH).

55 **Concertino** for string quartet (1920), compl. 24.IX.1920. 1st perf., 3.XI.1920, New York. Pub. 1923 (Hansen).
   Arrangement: for twelve instruments (1952). 1st perf., 11.XI.1952, Los Angeles. Pub. 1953 (Hansen).

56 **The Five Fingers** for piano (1921), dated 18.II.1921. 1st perf., 15.XII.1927, Paris. Pub. 1922 (JWC).
   Arrangement: **Eight Instrumental Miniatures** for fifteen players (1962), with

changed order, key scheme etc. 1st complete perf., 29.IV.1962, Toronto. Pub. 1962, facsimile (JWC).

57 Tchaikovsky's *Sleeping Beauty*: 'Variation d'Aurore' and 'Entr'acte (Act 2)', orch. (Oct 1921). 1st perf., 2.XI.1921, London. Unpub (with BH).

58 **Mavra**, opera buffa in one act (libretto, B. Kochno, after Pushkin's verse story 'Domeek v Kolomnye') (1921–2), compl. March 1922. 1st perf., 29.V.1922, Paris (private concert); 1st stage perf., 3.VI.1922, Paris. Pub. 1925 (ERM; later BH).

59 **Octet** for wind instruments (1922–3), compl. 20.V.1923. 1st perf., 18.X.1923, Paris. Pub. 1924 (ERM; later BH).

60 **Concerto for piano and wind instruments** (1923–4), compl. April 1924. 1st perf., 22.V.1924, Paris. Pub. 1924, piano four-hand reduction; 1936, fs (ERM; later BH).

61 **Sonata** for piano (1924), compl. by 22.X.1924. 1st perf., 16.VII.1925, Donaueschingen.³ Pub. 1925 (ERM; later BH).

62 **Serenade in A** for piano (1925), compl. 9.X.1925, 1st perf., 25.XI.1925, Frankfurt. Pub. 1926 (ERM; later BH).

63 **Pater noster** for chorus unaccompanied (1926), comp. before 17 October. Pub. 1932, with Slavonic text (ERM); 1949, with Latin text (BH).

64 **Oedipus Rex**, opera-oratorio in two acts (libretto, J. Cocteau, with Latin by J. Daniélou, after Sophocles's *Oedipus Tyrannus*) (1926–7), compl. in May 1927. 1st perf., 30.V.1927, Paris (concert); 1st stage perf., 23.II.1928, Vienna. Pub. 1928 (ERM; later BH).

65 **Apollo** [Musagetes], ballet in two scenes for string orchestra (1927–8), compl. in January 1928. 1st perf., 27.IV.1928, Washington D.C. Pub. 1928 (ERM; later BH).

66 **The Fairy's Kiss**, allegorical ballet in four scenes (music after Tchaikovsky) (1928), compl. 30.X.1928. 1st perf., 27.XI.1928, Paris. Pub. 1928 (ERM; later BH).
Suite: **Divertimento** (from complete score) (1934). Pub. 1938 (ERM; later BH)
Arrangement: Divertimento for violin and piano (arr. with S. Dushkin) (1932). Pub. 1934 (ERM; later BH).

67 **Capriccio** for piano and orchestra (1928–9), compl. 9.XI.1929. 1st perf., 6.XII.1929, Paris. Pub. 1930 (ERM; later BH).

68 **Symphony of Psalms** for chorus and orchestra (words from Psalms 38, 39, and 150, Vulgate) (1930), compl. 15.VIII.1930. 1st perf., 13.XII.1930, Brussels. Pub. 1931 (ERM; later BH).

69 **Concerto in D** for violin and orchestra (1931), dated 25.IX.1931. 1st perf., 23.X.1931, Berlin. Pub. 1931 (Schott).

70 **Duo concertant** for violin and piano (1932), compl. 15.VII.1932. 1st perf., 28.X.1932, Berlin. Pub. 1933 (ERM; later BH).

71 **Credo** for chorus unaccompanied (1932). Pub. 1933, Slavonic text (ERM); 1957, Latin text (BH).

72 **Persephone**, melodrama in three scenes, for speaker, tenor, chorus and orchestra (words, A. Gide) (1933–34), dated 24.I.1934. 1st perf., 30.IV.1934, Paris. Pub. 1934 (ERM; later BH).

73 **Ave Maria** for chorus unaccompanied (1934). Pub. 1934, Slavonic text (ERM); 1949, Latin text (BH).

74 **Concerto for two solo pianos** (1932–5). 1st movement partly comp. in November 1932, the rest 1934–5, compl. 9.XI.1935. 1st perf., 21.XI.1935, Paris. Pub. 1936 (Schott).

75 **Jeu de cartes**, ballet in three deals (1935–6), compl. on 6.XII.1936. 1st perf., 27.IV.1937, New York. Pub. 1937 (Schott).

76 **Praeludium** for jazz ensemble (1936–7), compl. 6.II.1937. 1st perf., 18.X.1953, Los Angeles. Pub. 1968 (BH).⁴

77 **Petit ramusianum harmonique** for speaking and singing voice unaccompanied (words, C.-A. Cingria) (1937), dated 11.X.1937. Pub. 1938 (in *Hommage à C.-F. Ramuz*, Porchet, Lausanne); 1962, facsimile of MS (in *Feuilles musicales et courrier suisse du disque*, Lausanne); also 1982 (Soviet composers, Moscow: Stravinsky Vocal Music, vol. I).

78 **Dumbarton Oaks** – Concerto in E flat for chamber orchestra (1937–8), compl. 29.III.1938. 1st perf., 8.V.1938, Washington D.C. Pub. 1938 (Schott).

79 **Symphony in C** for orchestra (1938–40), dated 19.VIII.1940. 1st perf., 7.XI.1940, Chicago. Pub. 1948 (Schott).

80 **Tango** for piano⁵ (1940), compl. 14.X.1940. Pub. 1941 (Mercury). Arrangement: for instrumental ensemble (1953). 1st perf., 18.X.1953, Los Angeles. Pub. 1954 (Mercury).

81 Tchaikovsky's *Sleeping Beauty*: 'Bluebird' *pas de deux*, arr. for small orchestra (1941), probably January. Pub. 1953 (Schott).

82 *The Star-Spangled Banner* (J. S. Smith), orch. (1941), by 28.VII.1941. 1st perf., 14.X.1941, Los Angeles. Pub. 1941 (Mercury).

83 **Danses concertantes** for chamber orchestra (1940–2), compl. 13.I.1942. 1st perf., 8.II.1942, Los Angeles. Pub. 1943 (AMP/Schott).

84 **Circus Polka** (1941–2): (1) for piano, compl. 12.II.1942. Pub. 1942 (AMP); [(2) for circus band, arr. D. Raksin. 1st perf., 9.IV.1942. Pub. 1948 (AMP)]; (3) for orchestra, compl. 5.X.1942. 1st perf., 14.I.1944, Cambridge, Mass. Pub. 1944 (AMP/Schott).

85 **Four Norwegian Moods** for orchestra (1942), compl. 18.VIII.1942. 1st perf., 14.I.1944, Cambridge, Mass. Pub. 1944 (AMP/Schott).

86 **Ode**, elegiacal chant in three parts for orchestra (1943), compl. 25.VI.1943. 1st perf., 8.X.1943, Boston. Pub. 1947 (AMP/Schott).

87 **Sonata for two pianos** (1943–4), compl. 11.II.1944. 1st perf., 2.VIII.1944, Madison, Wisconsin. Pub. 1945 (AMP/Chappell).

88 **Babel**, cantata for narrator, male chorus and orchestra (words, Genesis) (1944), compl. 12.IV.1944.⁶ 1st perf., 18.XI.1945, Los Angeles (as part of collaborative *Genesis Suite*). Pub. 1953 (Schott).

89 **Scherzo à la russe** (1943–4): (1) for jazz band (1944) compl. June or July 1944. 1st perf., 5.IX.1944, Blue Network radio. Pub. 1949 (Chappell); (2) for orchestra (1945). 1st perf., 22.III.1946, San Francisco. Pub. 1945 (AMP/Chappell).

90 **Scènes de ballet** for orchestra (1944), compl. by 31.VIII.1944. 1st perf., 24.XI.1944, Philadelphia. Pub. 1945 (Chappell/BH).

91 **Elegy** for solo viola (or violin) (1944), compl. by 5.XI. 1st perf., 26.I.1945, Washington D.C. Pub. 1945 (AMP/Chappell).

92 **Symphony in Three Movements** for orchestra (1942–5): 1st movement compl. 15.X.1942; 2nd movement compl. 17.III.1943; 3rd movement (and rev. of first two) compl. by 20.VIII.1945. 1st perf., 24.I.1946, New York. Pub. 1946 (AMP/Schott).

93 **Ebony Concerto** for clarinet and jazz ensemble (1945), compl. 1.XII.1945. 1st perf., 25.III.1946, New York. Pub. 1946 (Charling Music Corporation, New York; later Edwin H. Morris, London).

94 **Concerto in D** for string orchestra ('Basle' Concerto) (1946), dated 8.VIII.1946. 1st perf., 27.I.1947, Basle. Pub. 1947 (BH).

95 **Orpheus**, ballet in three scenes (1946–7), dated 23.IX.1947. 1st perf., 28.IV.1948, New York. Pub. 1948 (BH).

96 **Hommage à Nadia Boulanger** ('Petit Canon pour la fête de Nadia Boulanger', for two tenors (words, Jean de Meung) (1947), dated 16.IX.1947 (Nadia

Boulanger's 60th birthday). Pub. 1982, facsimile (in Clifford Caesar, *Igor Stravinsky: A Complete Catalogue*, Boosey & Hawkes/San Francisco Press).

97 **Mass** for chorus and double wind quintet (1944–8): Kyrie and Gloria compl. in Dec 1944; remainder comp. 1947–8, compl. 15.III.1948. 1st perf., 27.X.1948, Milan. Pub. 1948 (BH).

98 **The Rake's Progress**, opera in three acts (libretto, W. H. Auden and C. Kallman) (1947–51), compl. 7.IV.1951. 1st perf., 11.IX.1951, Venice. Pub. 1951 (BH).

99 **Cantata**, for soprano, tenor, female chorus and five instruments (words, anon 15th–16th century English) (1951–2), compl. by August 1952. 1st perf., 11.XI.1952, Los Angeles. Pub. 1953 (BH).

100 **Septet** for clarinet, horn, bassoon and piano quartet (1952–3), compl. 21.I.1953. 1st perf., 23.I.1954, Washington D.C. Pub. 1953 (BH).

101 **Three Songs from William Shakespeare** for mezzo-soprano, flute, clarinet and viola (1953), dated 6.X.1953: (1) Musick to heare (Sonnet VIII); (2) Full Fadom Five (The Tempest); (3) When Dasies Pied (Love's Labour's Lost). 1st perf., 8.III.1954, Los Angeles. Pub. 1954 (BH).

102 **In Memoriam Dylan Thomas** for tenor, string quartet and four trombones (words, D. Thomas) (1954), mainly compl. by 21.III.1954, but the Postludium added in June. 1st perf., 20.IX.1954, Los Angeles. Pub. 1954 (BH).

103 **Greeting Prelude** for orchestra (1955), comp. early Feb. 1st perf., 4.IV.1955, Boston. Pub. 1956 (BH).

104 **Canticum sacrum** ad honorem Sancti Marci Nominis, for tenor and baritone, chorus and orchestra (words, Deuteronomy, Psalms, Song of Solomon, St. Mark's Gospel, and first Epistle of St. John, Vulgate texts) (1955), compl. 21.XI.1955. 1st perf., 13.IX.1956, Venice. Pub. 1956 (BH).

195 Bach's Chorale-Variations on *Vom Himmel hoch*, arr. and orch. (1955–6), compl. 27.III.1956. 1st perf., 27.V.1956, Ojai (California). Pub. 1956 (BH).

106 **Agon**, ballet for twelve dancers (1953–57): compl. to the end of the 'Coda' (bar 253) by Dec 1954, the rest comp. 1956–7, compl. 27.IV.1957. 1st perf. (concert), 17.VI.1957, Los Angeles; (stage) 1.XII.1957, New York. Pub. 1957 (BH).

107 Gesualdo: *Tres Sacrae Cantiones*, compl. for six or seven voices (1957–9): (1) 'Da pacem Domine', Sept 1959; (2) 'Assumpta est Maria', Sept 1959; (3) 'Illumina nos', 5.V.1957. 1st perf., 10.I.1960, New York. Pub. 1957 (BH: 'Illumina nos' only); 1960 (BH: complete).

108 **Threni:** id est Lamentationes Jeremiae Prophetae, for six soloists, chorus and orchestra (words, Lamentations, Vulgate text) (1957–8), dated 21.III.1958. 1st perf., 23.IX.1958, Venice. Pub. 1958 (BH).

109 **Movements** for piano and orchestra (1958–9), compl. by 20.VIII.1959. 1st perf., 10.I.1960, New York. Pub. 1960 (BH).

110 **Epitaphium** for flute, clarinet and harp (1959), comp. in May. 1st perf., 17.X.1959, Donaueschingen. Pub. 1959 (BH).

111 **Double Canon** for string quartet (1959), comp. in September. 1st perf., 20.XII.1959, New York. Pub. 1960 (BH).

112 **Monumentum pro Gesualdo di Venosa (ad CD Annum)**: three Gesualdo madrigals recomposed for instruments (March 1960). 1st perf., 27.IX.1960, Venice. Pub. 1960 (BH).

113 **A Sermon, a Narrative, and a Prayer**, cantata for alto and tenor, speaker, chorus and orchestra (words, St. Paul, the Acts of the Apostles [AV], and Thomas Dekker) (1960–1), dated 31.I.1961. 1st perf., 23.II.1962, Basle. Pub. 1961 (BH).

114 **The Flood**, musical play for solo speakers and singers, chorus (without basses) and orchestra (words, Robert Craft, from Genesis and the York and Chester

miracle plays) (1961–2), dated 14.III.1962. 1st perf., 14.VI.1962, CBS TV, USA. Pub. 1963 (BH).

115 **Anthem** ('The dove descending breaks the air'), for chorus unaccompanied (words, T. S. Eliot, from 'Little Gidding', *Four Quartets*) (1961–2), compl. 2.I.62. 1st perf., 19.II.1962, Los Angeles. Pub. 1962 (in *Expositions and Developments*, Faber; later by BH).

116 **Abraham and Isaac**, sacred ballad for baritone and chamber orchestra (words, Genesis, Hebrew text) (1962–3), dated 3.III.1963. 1st perf., 23.VIII.1964, Jerusalem. Pub. 1965 (BH).

117 Sibelius's *Canzonetta* for strings, op. 62a, arr. for eight instruments (1963), compl. 10.VII.1963. 1st perf., 22.III.1964, Helsinki. Pub. 1964 (Breitkopf & Härtel, Wiesbaden).

118 **Elegy for J.F.K.** for medium voice and three clarinets (words, W. H. Auden) (1964), comp. in March, compl. 1.IV.1964. 1st perf., 6.IV.1964, Los Angeles. Pub. 1964 (BH).

119 **Fanfare for a New Theatre** for two trumpets (1964), comp. in March. 1st perf., 19.IV.1964, New York. Pub. 1968 (BH).

120 **Variations Aldous Huxley in Memoriam** for orchestra (1963–4), dated 28.X.1964. 1st perf., 17.IV.1965, Chicago. Pub. 1965 (BH).

121 **Introitus T. S. Eliot in Memoriam** for male chorus and chamber ensemble (words, from the 'Requiem aeternam') (1965), dated 17.II.1965. 1st perf., 17.IV.1965, Chicago. Pub. 1965 (BH).

122 **Canon** for orchestra on the finale theme of *The Firebird* (1965). 1st perf., 16.XII.1965, Toronto. Pub. 1973 (BH).

123 **Requiem Canticles** for contralto and bass, chorus and orchestra (words, from the Proper of the Requiem Mass) (1965–6), dated 13.VIII.1966. 1st perf., 8.X.1966, Princeton University. Pub. 1967 (BH).

124 **The Owl and the Pussy-Cat** for soprano and piano (words, E. Lear) (1966). 1st perf., 31.X.1966, Los Angeles. Pub. 1967 (BH).

125 *Two Sacred Songs* from Wolf's *Spanisches Liederbuch*: (1) 'Herr, was trägt der Boden hier'; (2) 'Wunden trägst du', arr. for mezzo-soprano and ten instruments (15.V.1968). 1st perf., 6.IX.1968, Los Angeles. Pub. 1969 (BH).

## Notes

1 Apparently not *Le Festin*, a ballet in the company's 1909 Paris repertory. *Les Orientales* was on the same bill as *The Firebird*. See R. Buckle, *Diaghilev* (Weidenfeld, London, 1979).

2 Not, of course, for two pianos as stated in most previous listings.

3 White (p. 320) says Donaueschingen, July 1925, but gives no other details. A telegram survives inviting Stravinsky to play the Sonata there on the 25th July, but he was in Nice that day (letter to Werner Reinhart, *SSCIII*, p. 154), and apparently still in Paris on the 20th. The Sonata was in fact played on the 16th by Felix Petyrek. I am grateful to Horst Koegler for this correction to my note in the hardback edition of this book.

4 The note in the published score stating that 'the string parts were added in June 1953' is misleading. The 1937 MS, now in the Paul Sacher Stiftung, Basel, already has parts for strings, and is in fact in essence the same as the published version.

5 Or for piano with voice. A complete autograph of this version is in the Paul Sacher Stiftung, and is contemporary with the piano version. It was intended to publish the piece as a song with 'popular' words by a commercial lyricist, but Mercury were unable to agree terms with him. See Stravinsky's correspondence with Leonard Feist in the Sacher Stiftung.

6 This date, though standard, seems contradicted by an entry in Vera Stravinsky's diary for 18.IV.1944: 'Nathaniel Shilkret at 5 to ask Igor to compose Babel for the Genesis Suite'. See R. Craft ed., *Dearest Bubushkin* (London, 1985), p. 130. The agreement with Shilkret was drawn up on 5.V.1944.

# Index